FAIRY TAIL

59

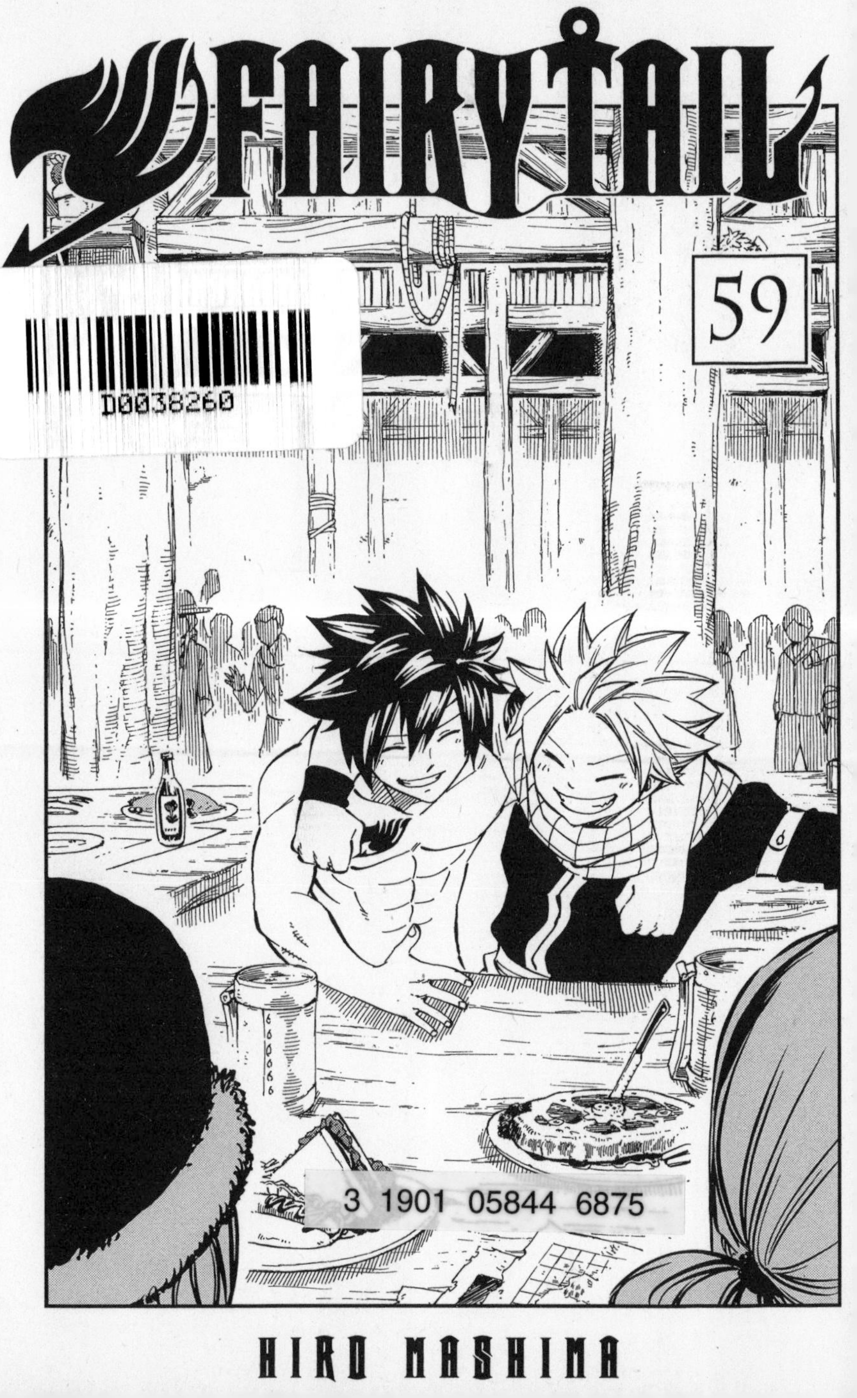

HIRO MASHIMA

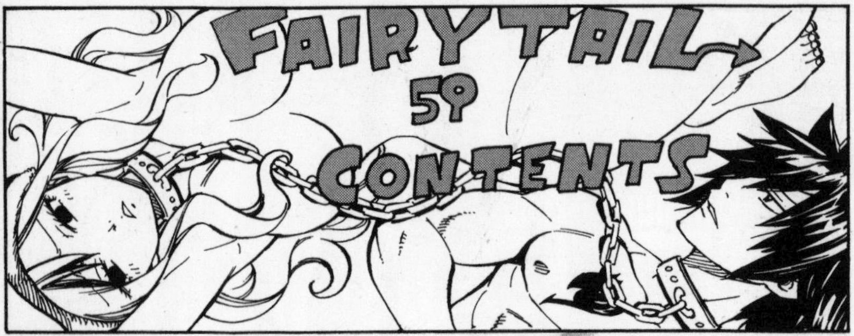
FAIRY TAIL
59
CONTENTS

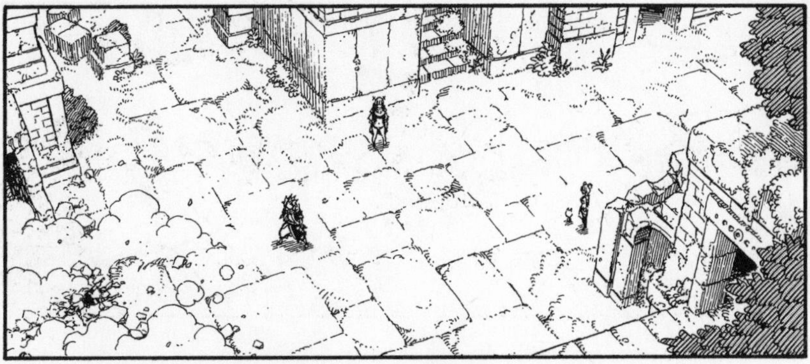

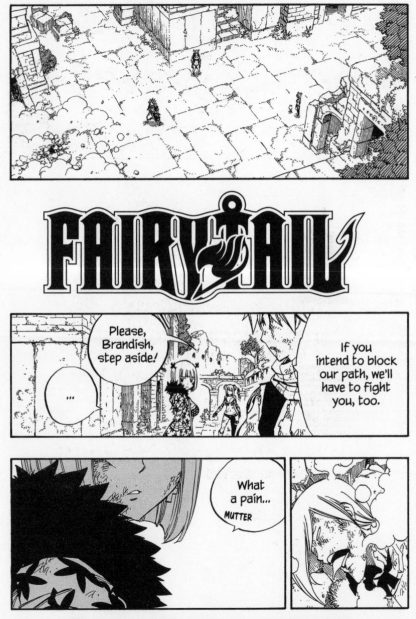

FAIRY TAIL

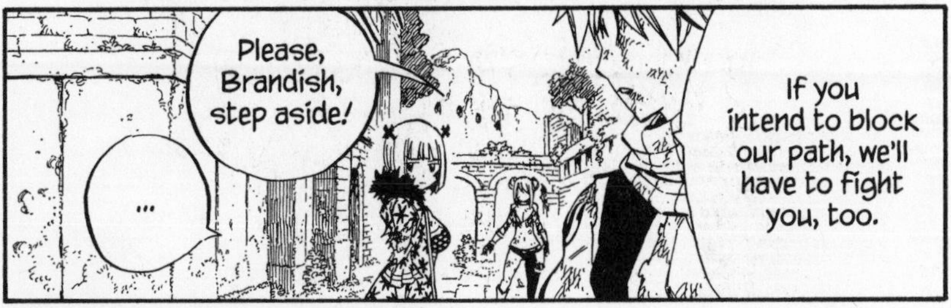
If you intend to block our path, we'll have to fight you, too.
Please, Brandish, step aside!
...

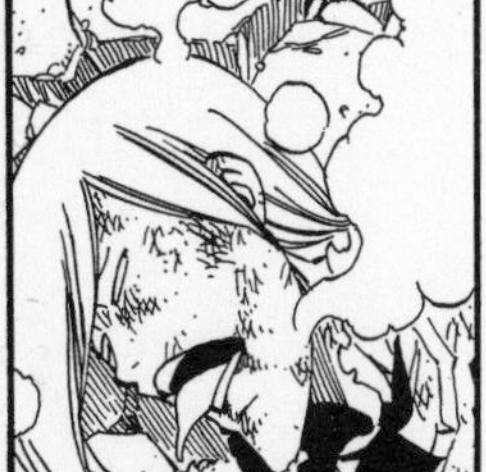

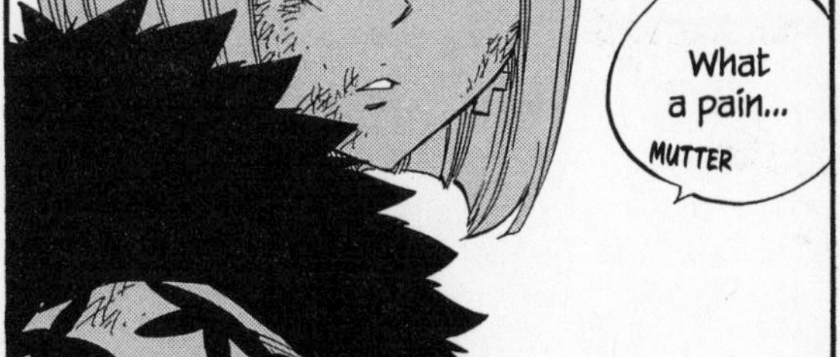
What a pain...
MUTTER

Chapter 501: Mari and Randi

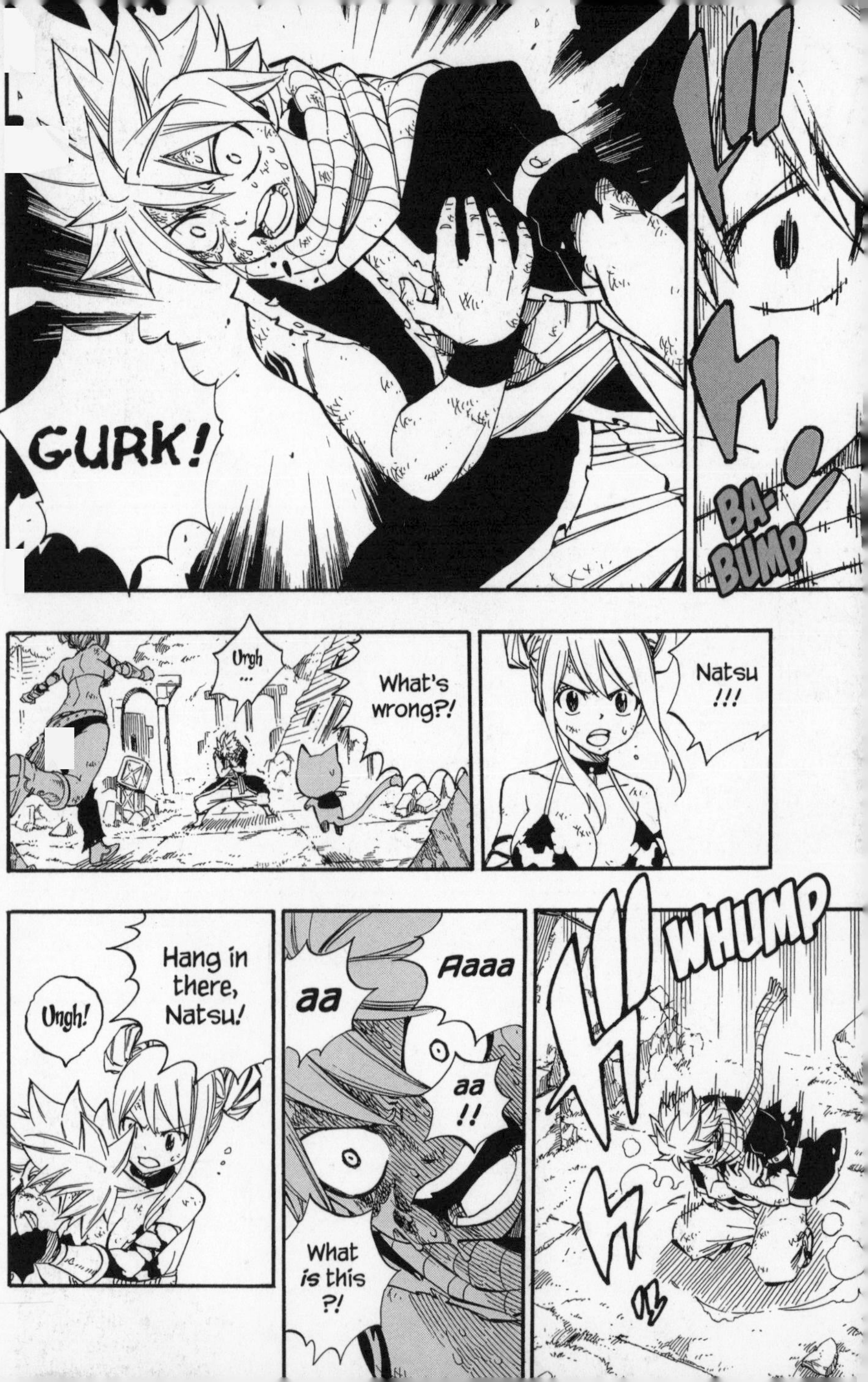
BA-BUMP
GURK!
Natsu!!!
What's wrong?!
Urgh ...
WHUMP
Aaaa
aa
aa!!
What *is* this?!
Hang in there, Natsu!
Ungh!

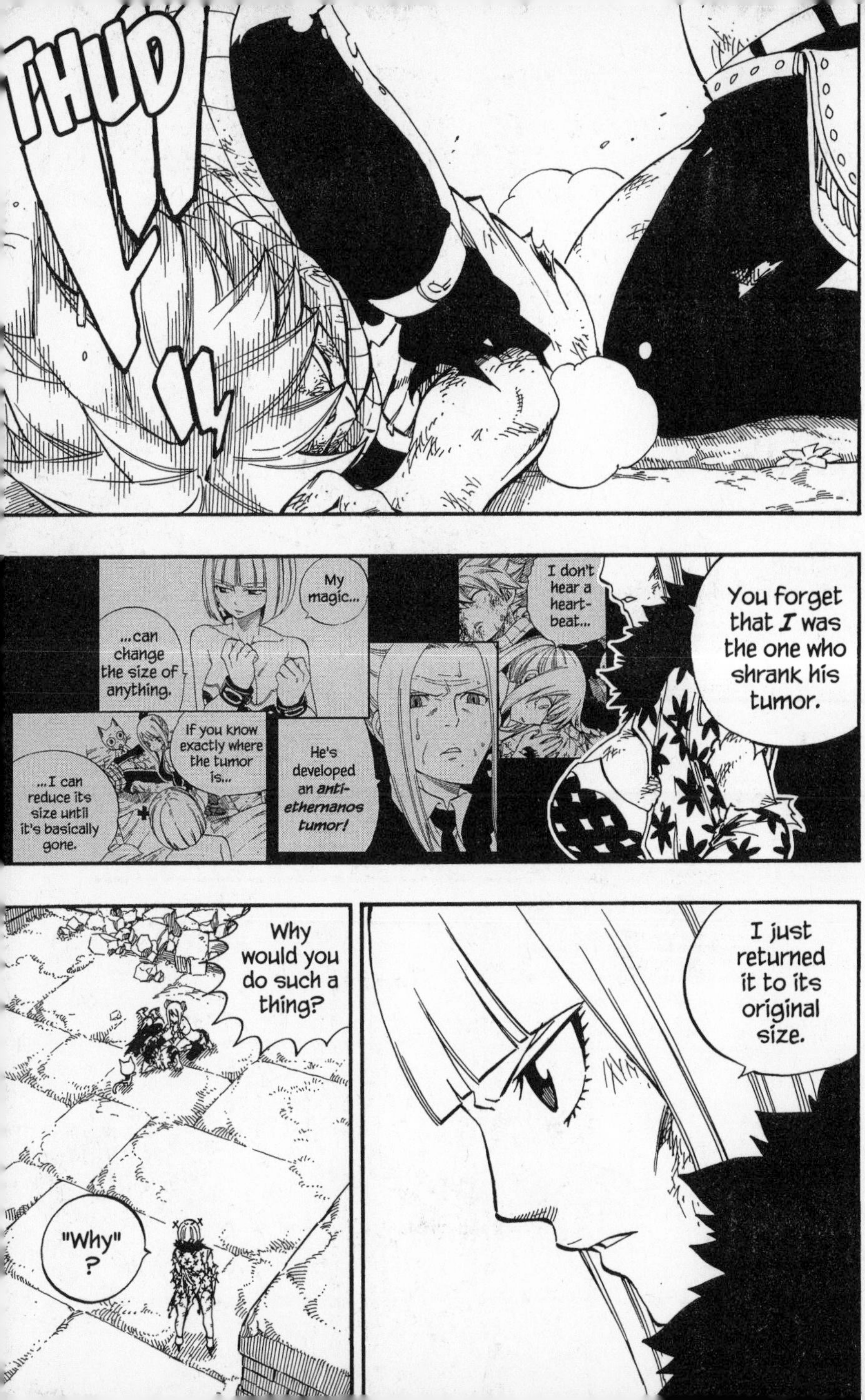
THUD
You forget that *I* was the one who shrank his tumor.
I don't hear a heart-beat...
He's developed an *anti-ethernanos tumor!*
My magic...
...can change the size of anything.
If you know exactly where the tumor is...
...I can reduce its size until it's basically gone.
I just returned it to its original size.
Why would you do such a thing?
"Why"?

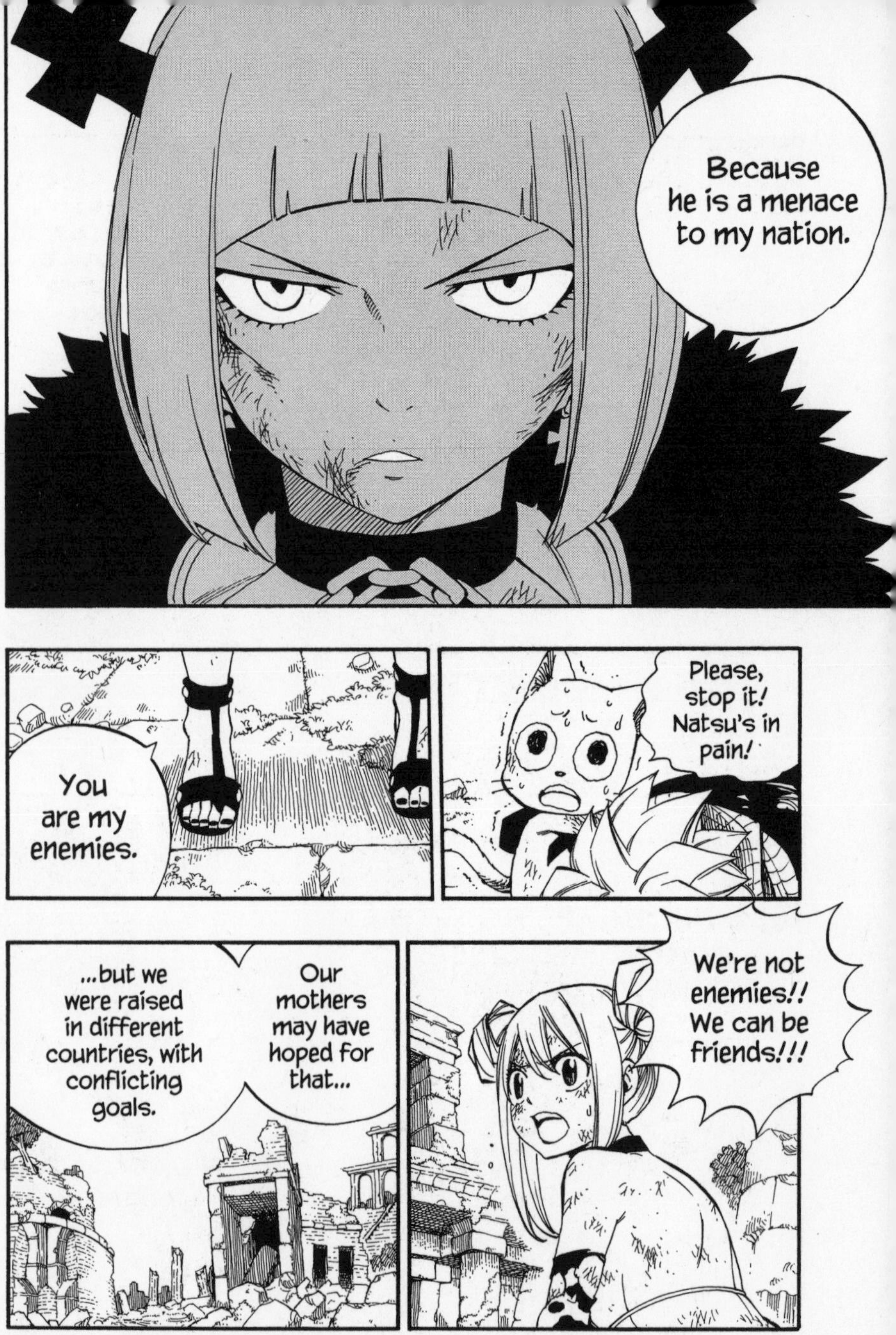
Because he is a menace to my nation.
Please, stop it! Natsu's in pain!
You are my enemies.
We're not enemies!! We can be friends!!!
Our mothers may have hoped for that...
...but we were raised in different countries, with conflicting goals.

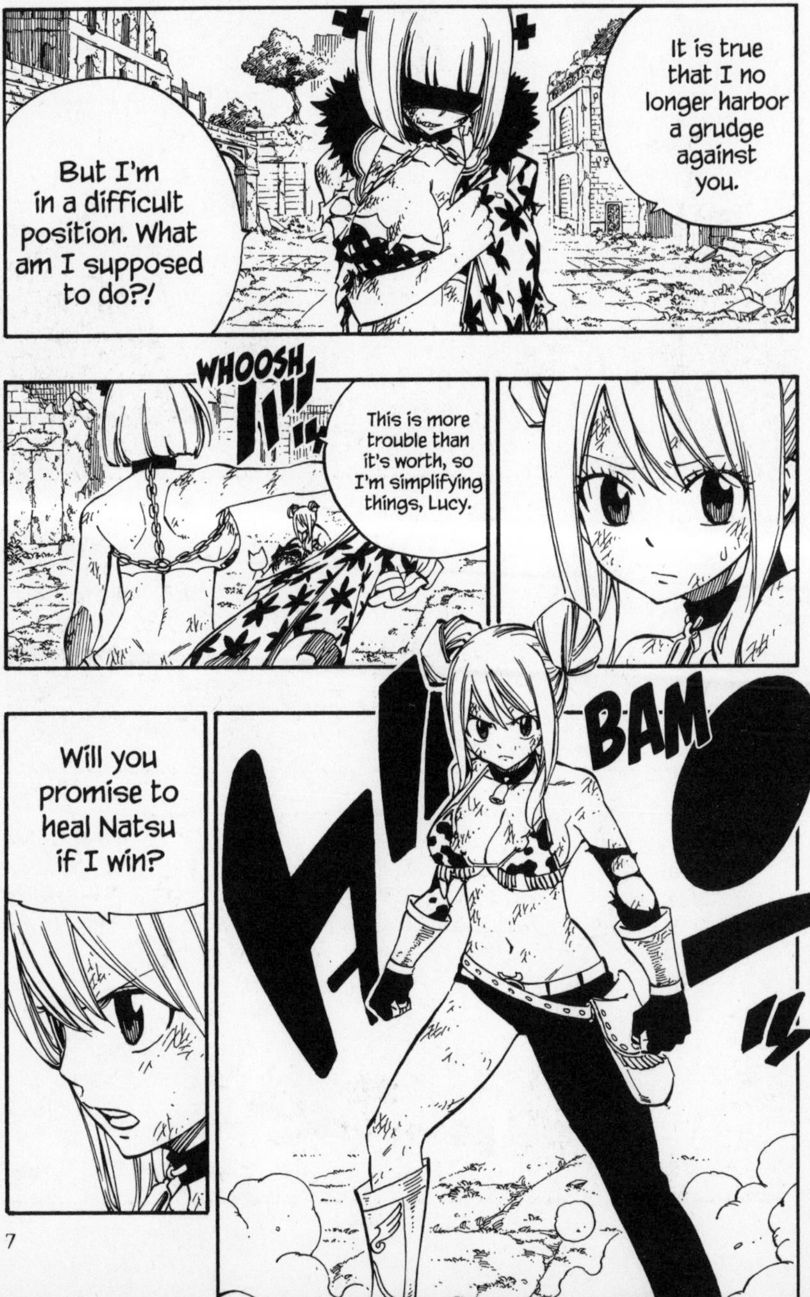
It is true that I no longer harbor a grudge against you.
But I'm in a difficult position. What am I supposed to do?!
WHOOSH
This is more trouble than it's worth, so I'm simplifying things, Lucy.
BAM
Will you promise to heal Natsu if I win?

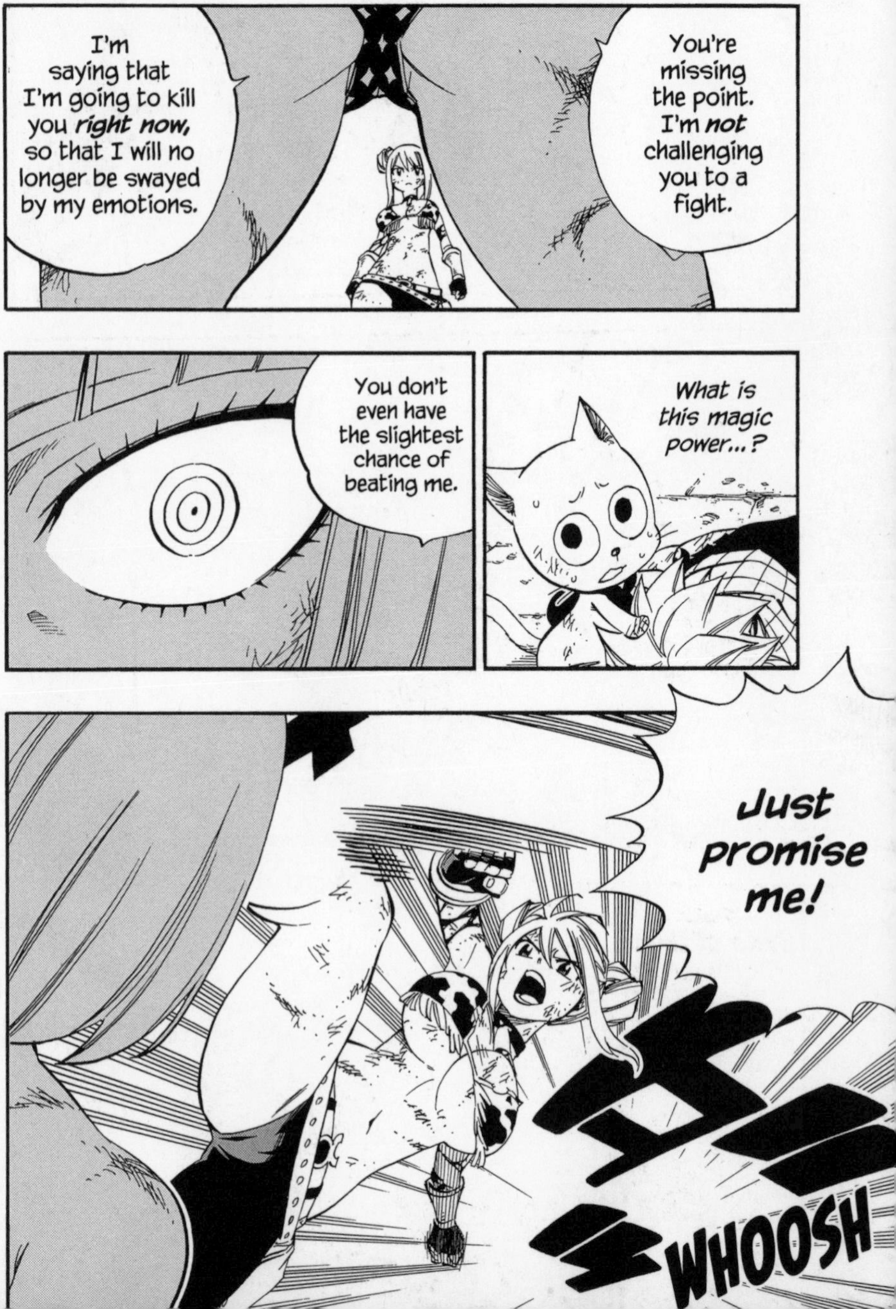
You're missing the point. I'm *not* challenging you to a fight.
I'm saying that I'm going to kill you ***right now,*** so that I will no longer be swayed by my emotions.
What is this magic power...?
You don't even have the slightest chance of beating me.
Just promise me!
WHOOSH

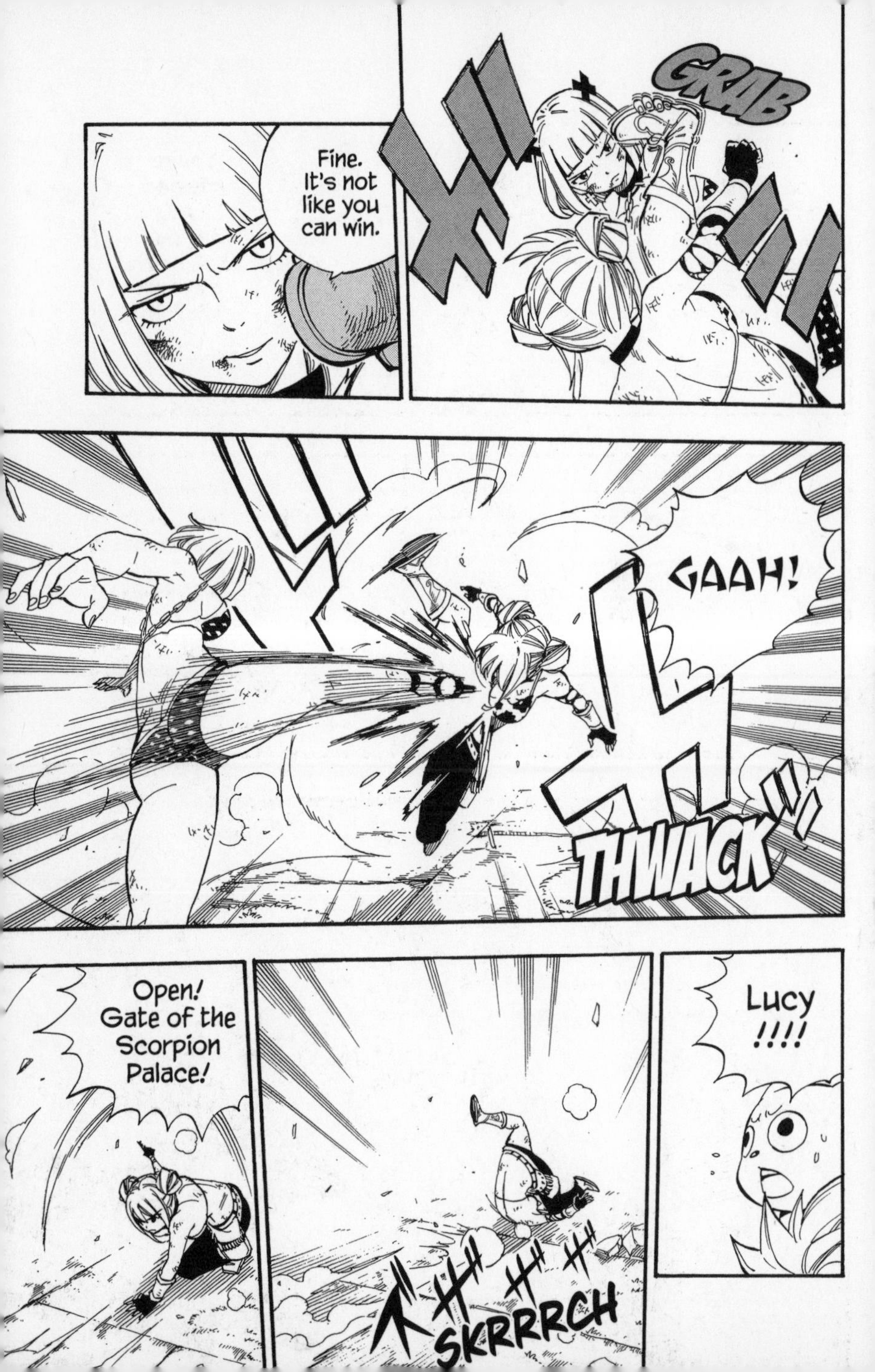
GRAB
Fine. It's not like you can win.
GAAH!
THWACK
Lucy !!!!
SKRRRCH
Open! Gate of the Scorpion Palace!

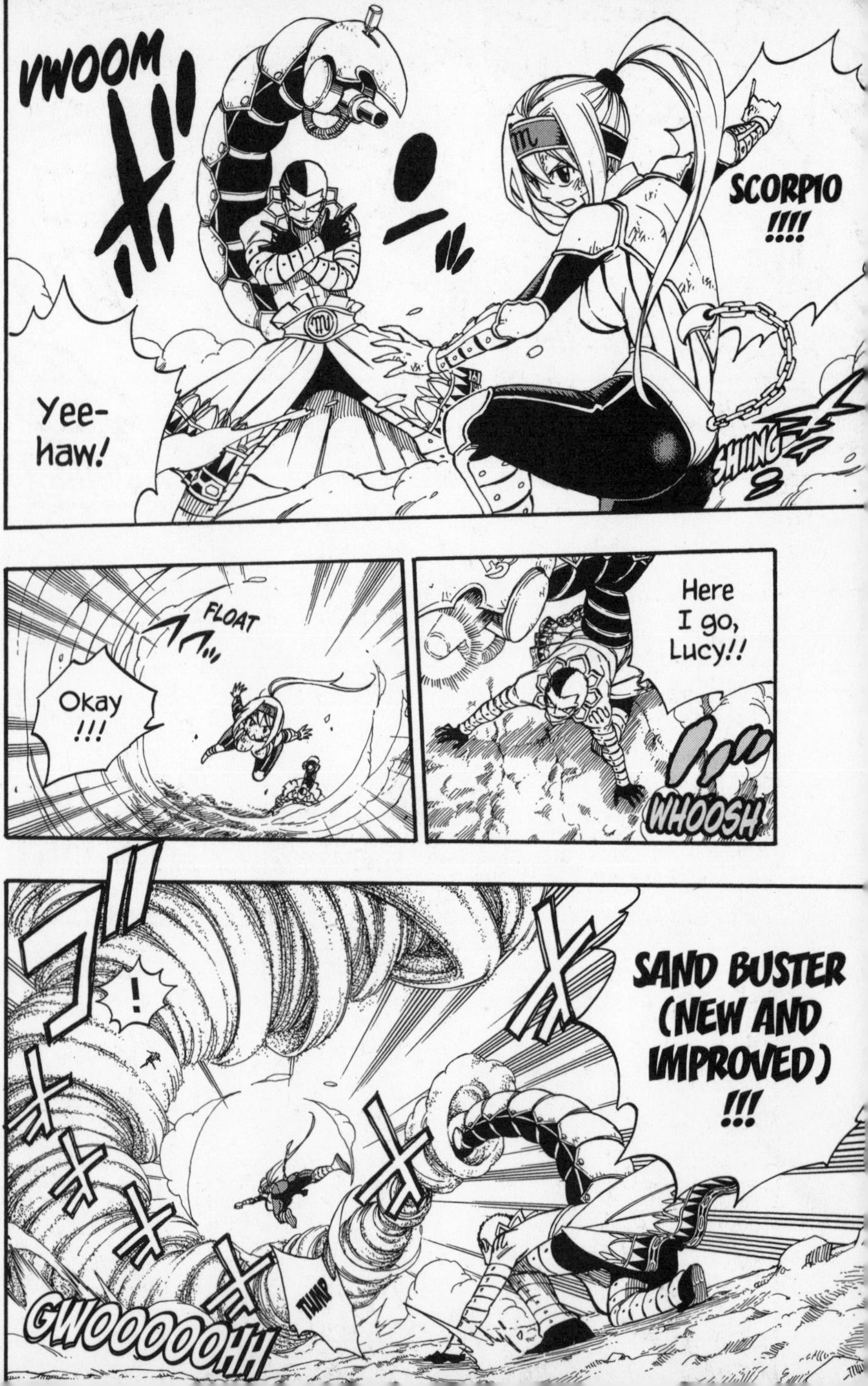
SCORPIO !!!!
VWOOM
SHIING
Yee-haw!
Here I go, Lucy!!
WHOOSH
FLOAT
Okay !!!
SAND BUSTER (NEW AND IMPROVED) !!!
!
TUMP
GWOOOOOHH

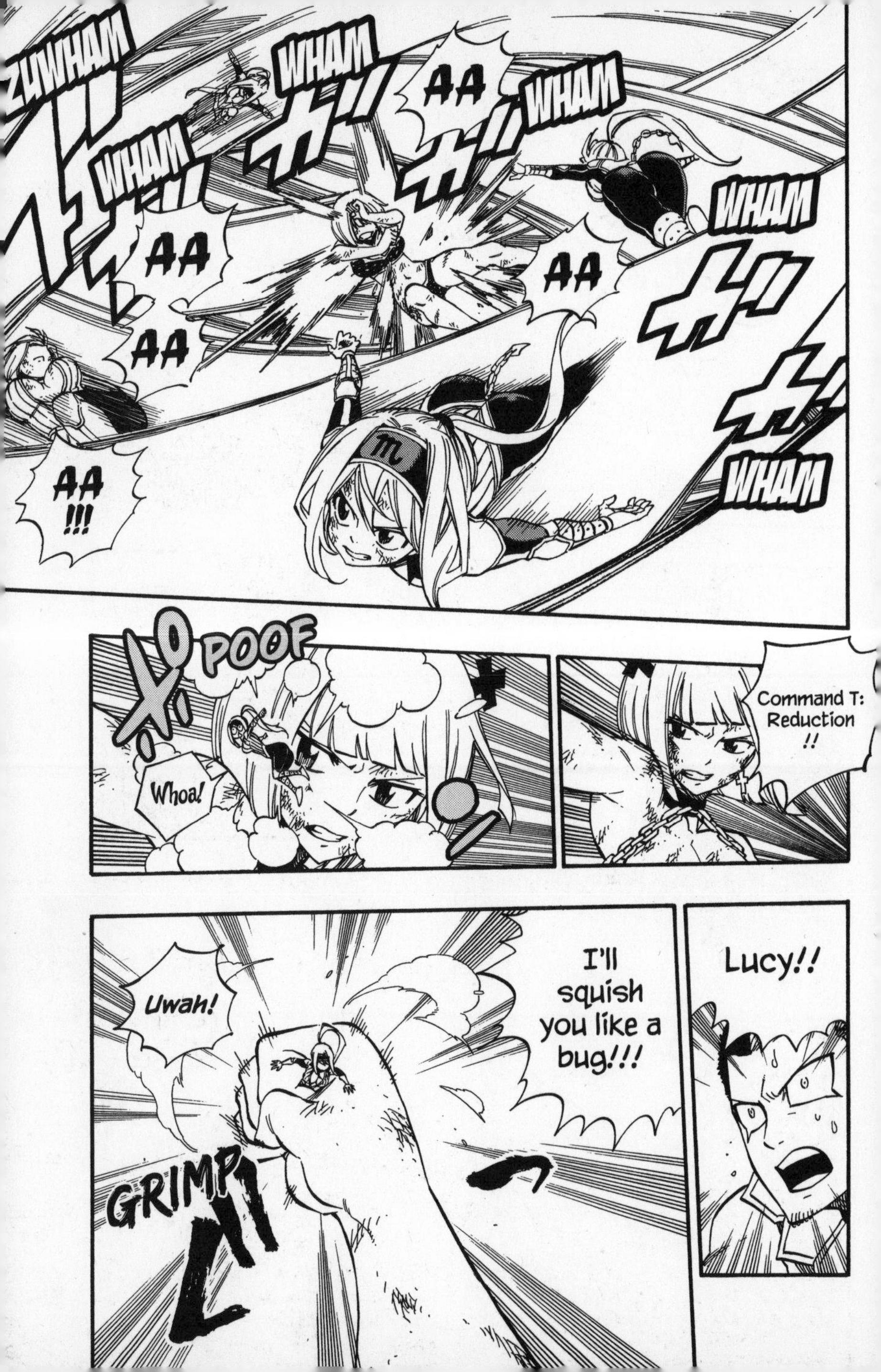
WHAM
AA
WHAM
ZUWHAM
WHAM
AA
WHAM
AA
WHAM
AA
AA!!!
Command T: Reduction !!
POOF
Whoa!
Lucy!!
I'll squish you like a bug!!!
Uwah!
GRIMP

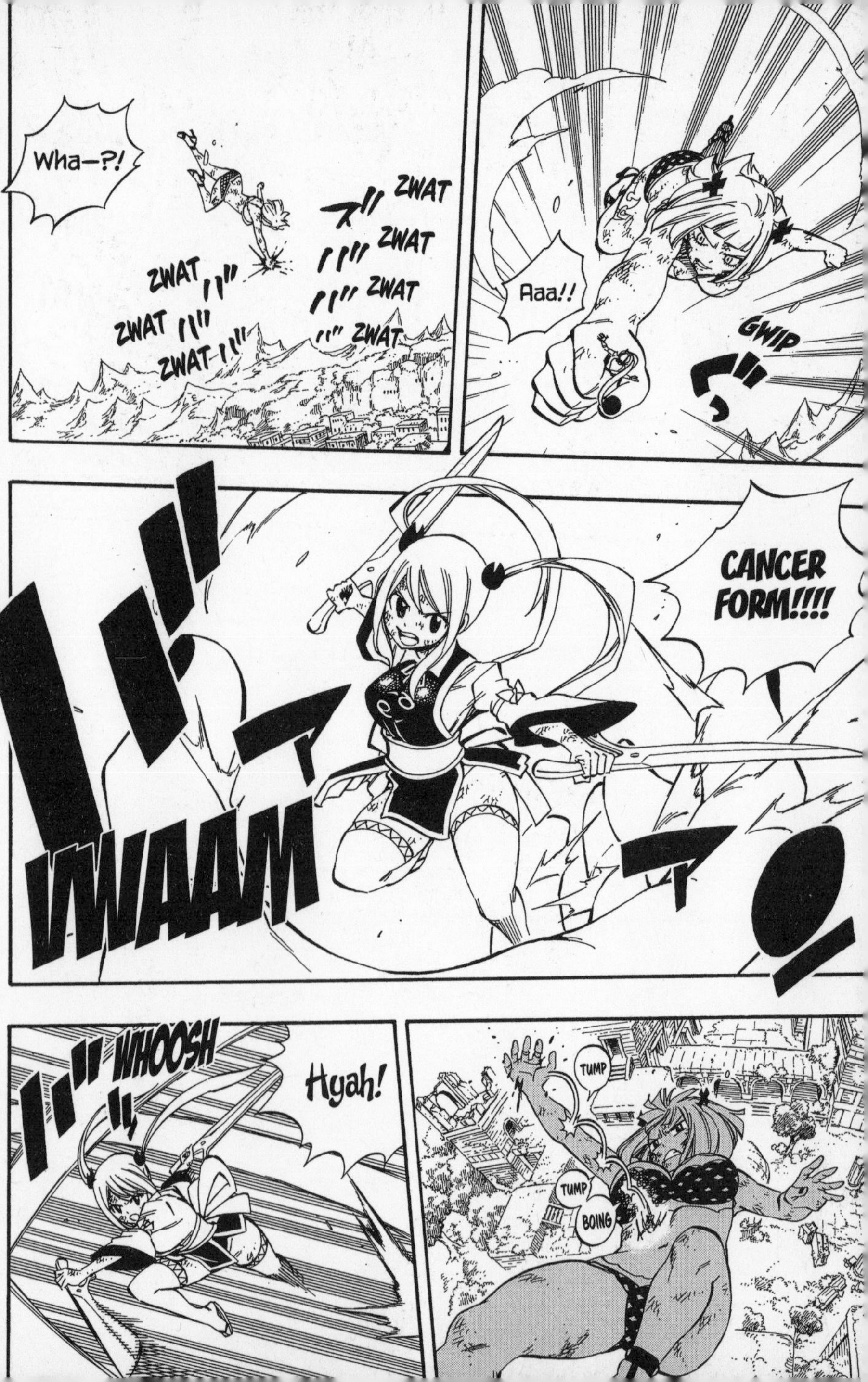
Aaa!!
GWIP
Wha–?!
ZWAT
ZWAT
ZWAT
ZWAT
ZWAT
ZWAT
ZWAT
CANCER FORM!!!!
VWAAM
TUMP
TUMP
BOING
WHOOSH
Hyah!

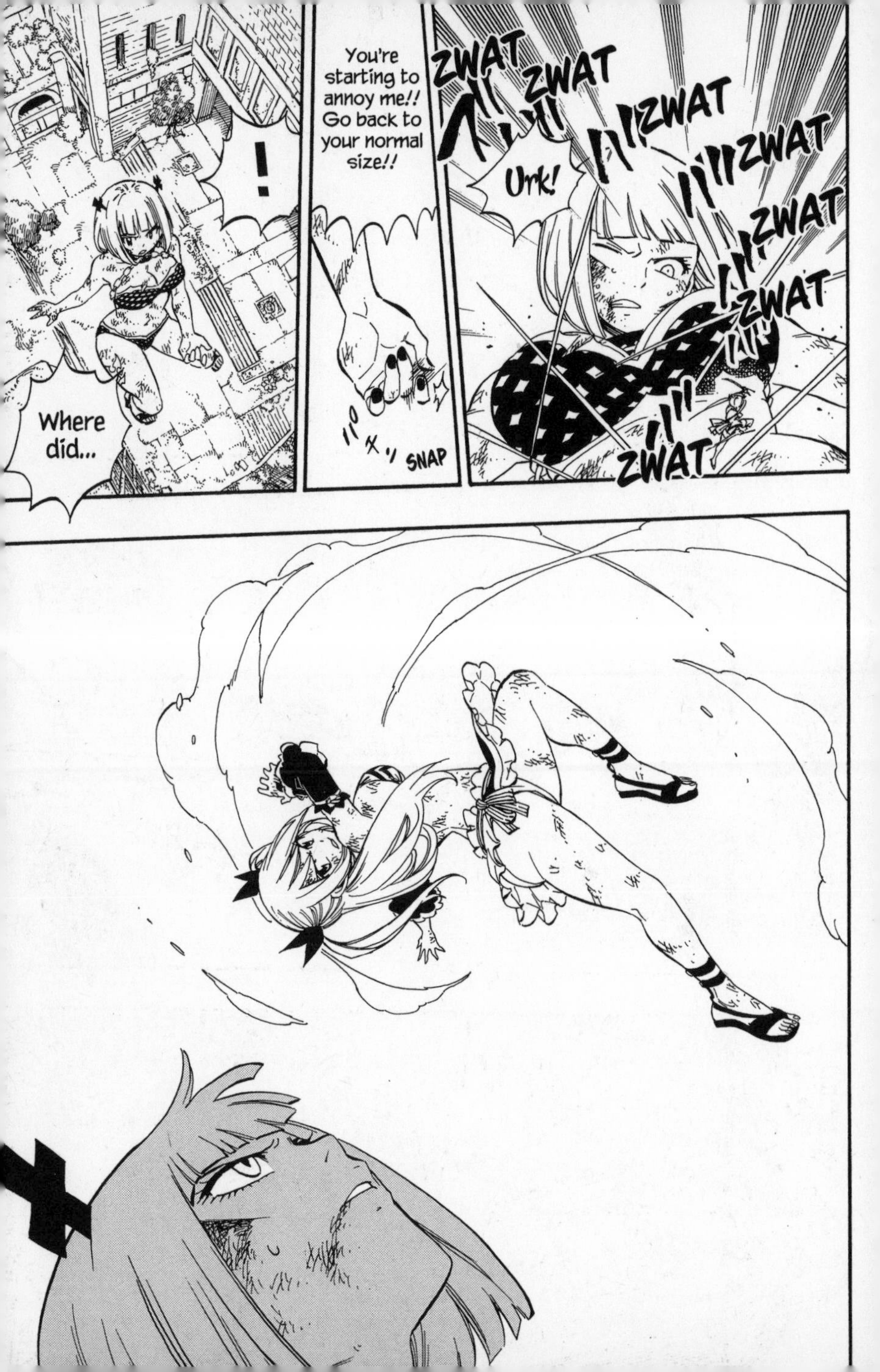
ZWAT ZWAT ZWAT ZWAT ZWAT ZWAT ZWAT
Urk!
You're starting to annoy me!! Go back to your normal size!!
SNAP
!
Where did...

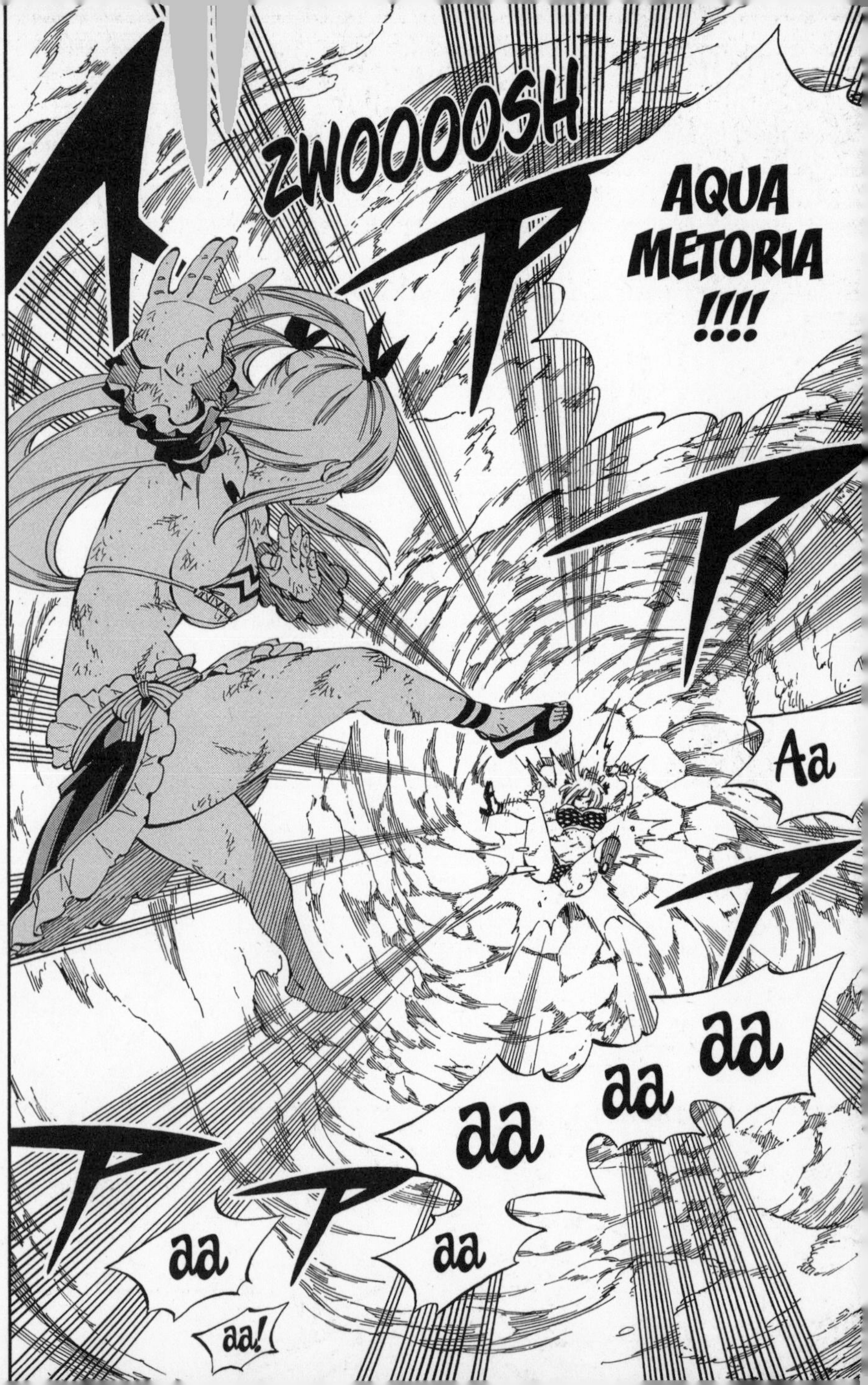
ZWOOOOSH
AQUA METORIA !!!!
Aa
aa
aa
aa
aa
aa
aa!

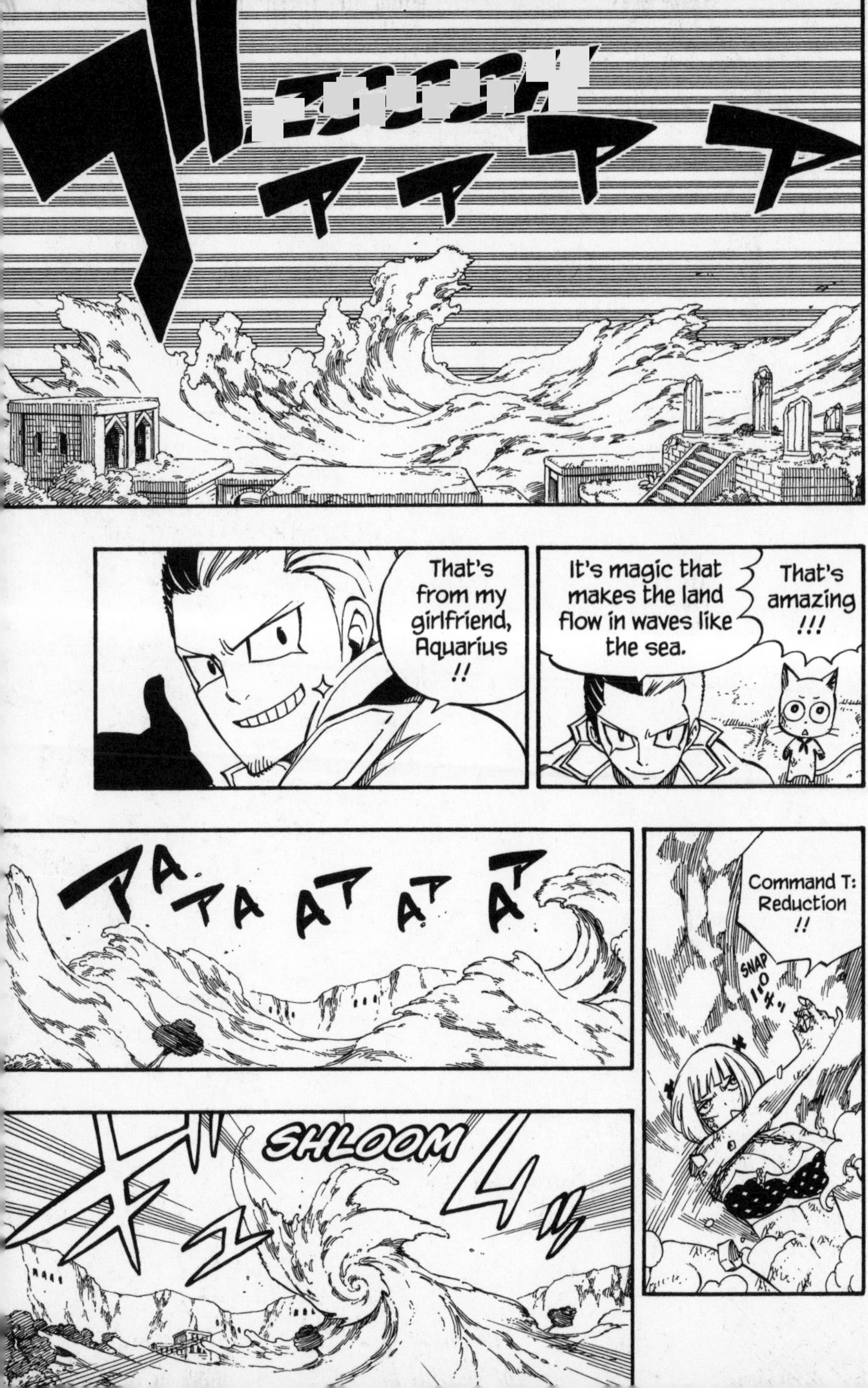
That's amazing!!!
It's magic that makes the land flow in waves like the sea.
That's from my girlfriend, Aquarius!!
Command T: Reduction!!
SNAP
SHLOOM

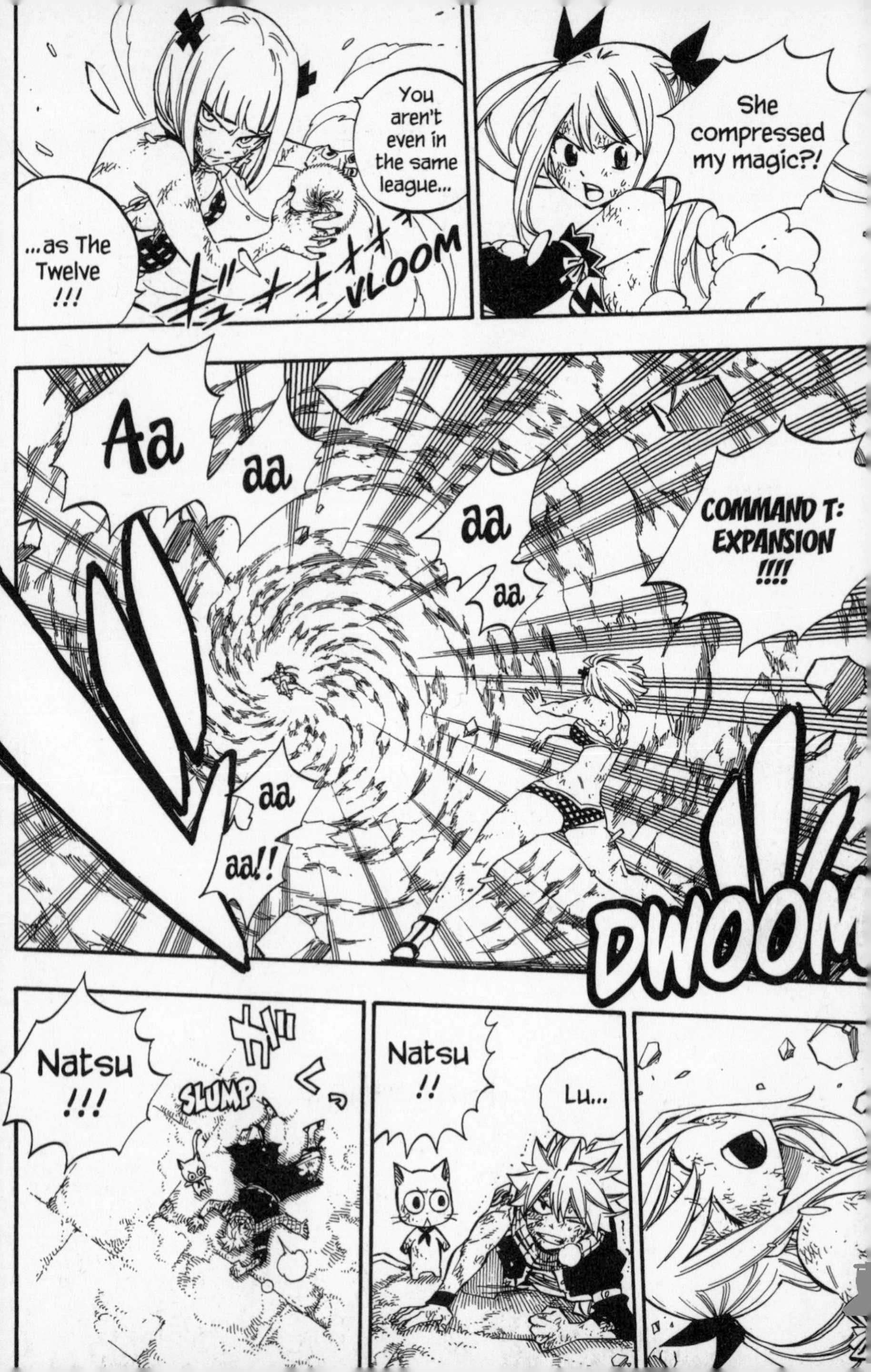
She compressed my magic?!
You aren't even in the same league...
...as The Twelve!!!
VLOOM
COMMAND T: EXPANSION!!!!
Aa aa aa aa aa aa!!
DWOOM
Lu...
Natsu!!
Natsu!!!
SLUMP

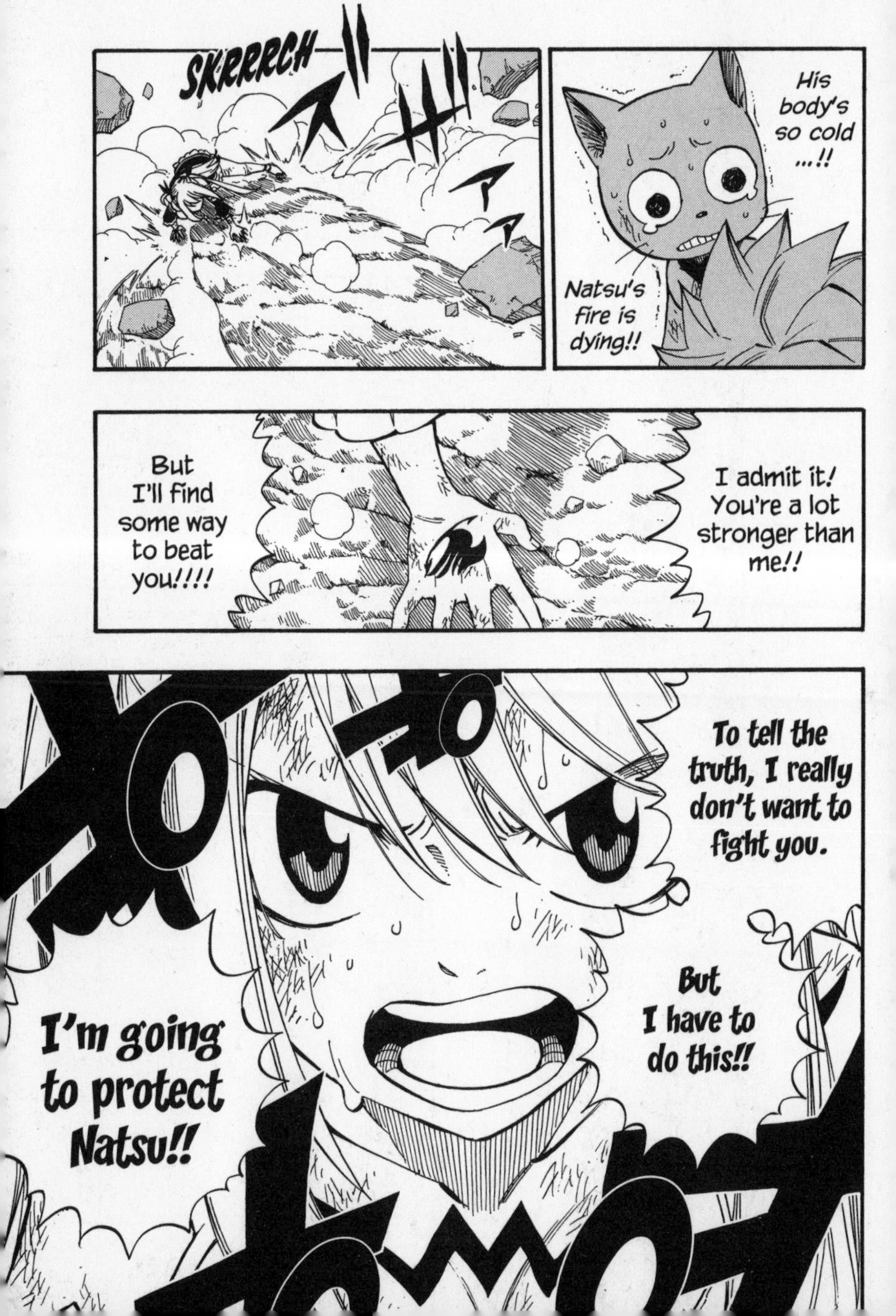
His body's so cold ...!!
Natsu's fire is dying!!
SKRRRCH
I admit it! You're a lot stronger than me!!
But I'll find some way to beat you!!!!
To tell the truth, I really don't want to fight you.
But I have to do this!!
I'm going to protect Natsu!!

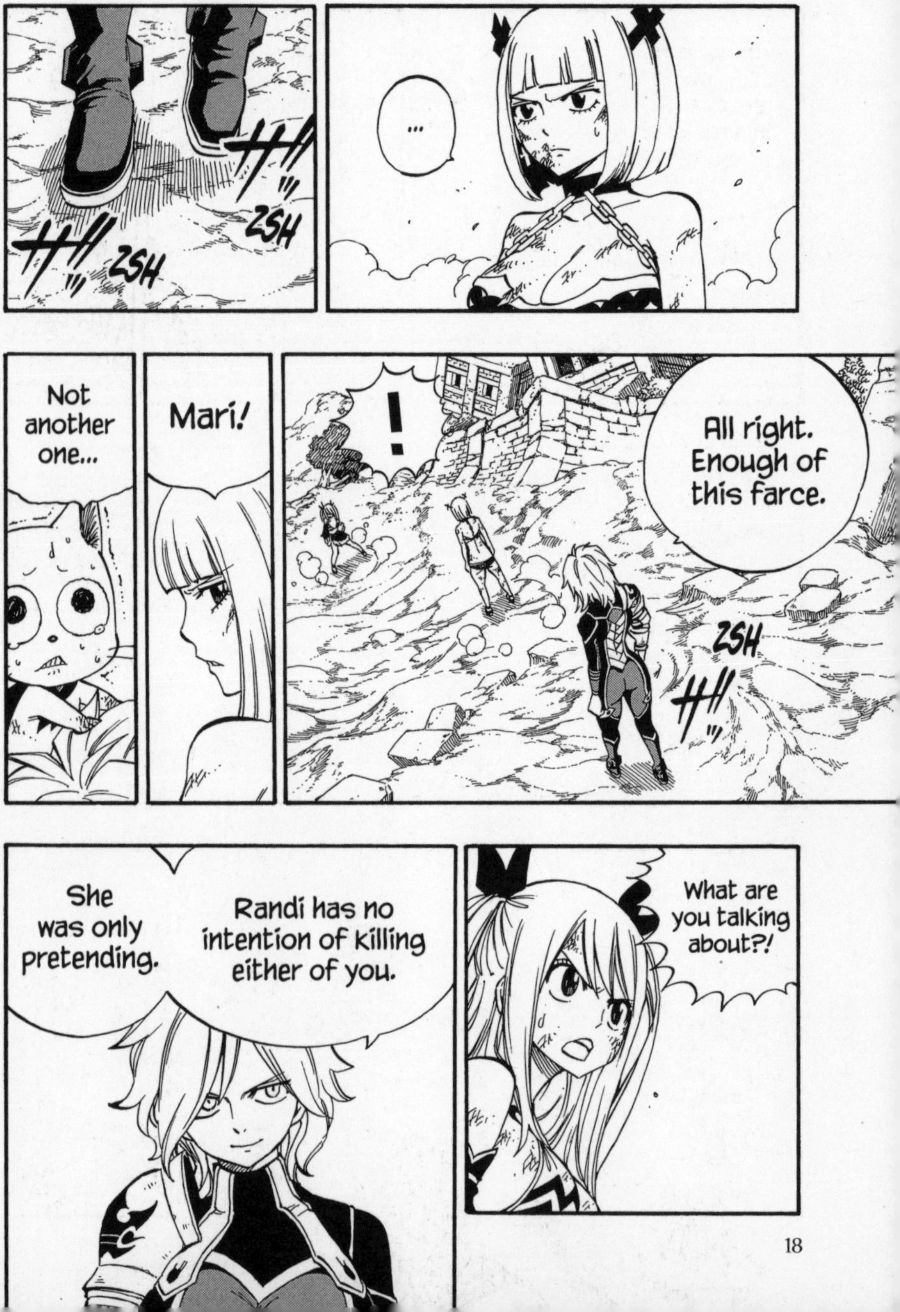
...
ZSH
ZSH
!
All right. Enough of this farce.
ZSH
Mari!
Not another one...
What are you talking about?!
Randi has no intention of killing either of you.
She was only pretending.

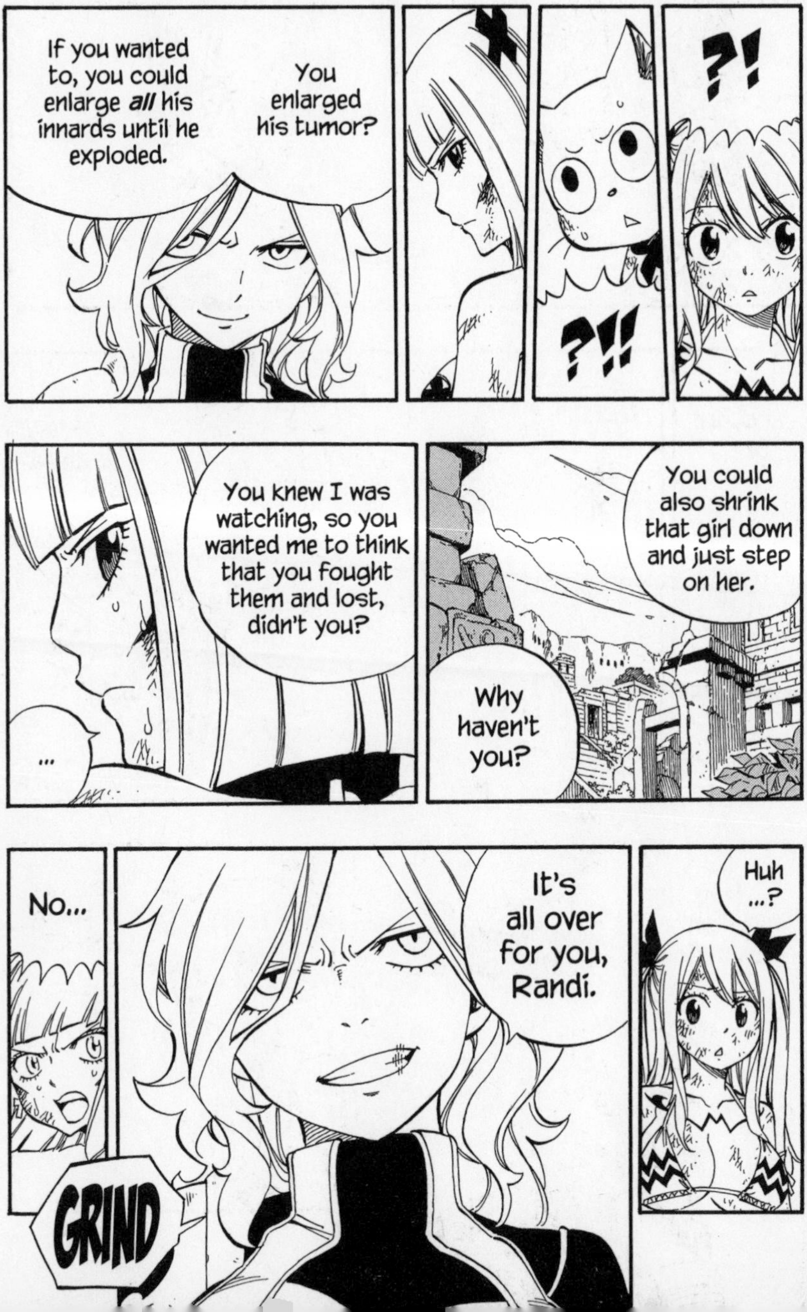

?!
?!!
You enlarged his tumor?
If you wanted to, you could enlarge *all* his innards until he exploded.
You could also shrink that girl down and just step on her.
Why haven't you?
You knew I was watching, so you wanted me to think that you fought them and lost, didn't you?
...
Huh ...?
It's all over for you, Randi.
GRIND
No...

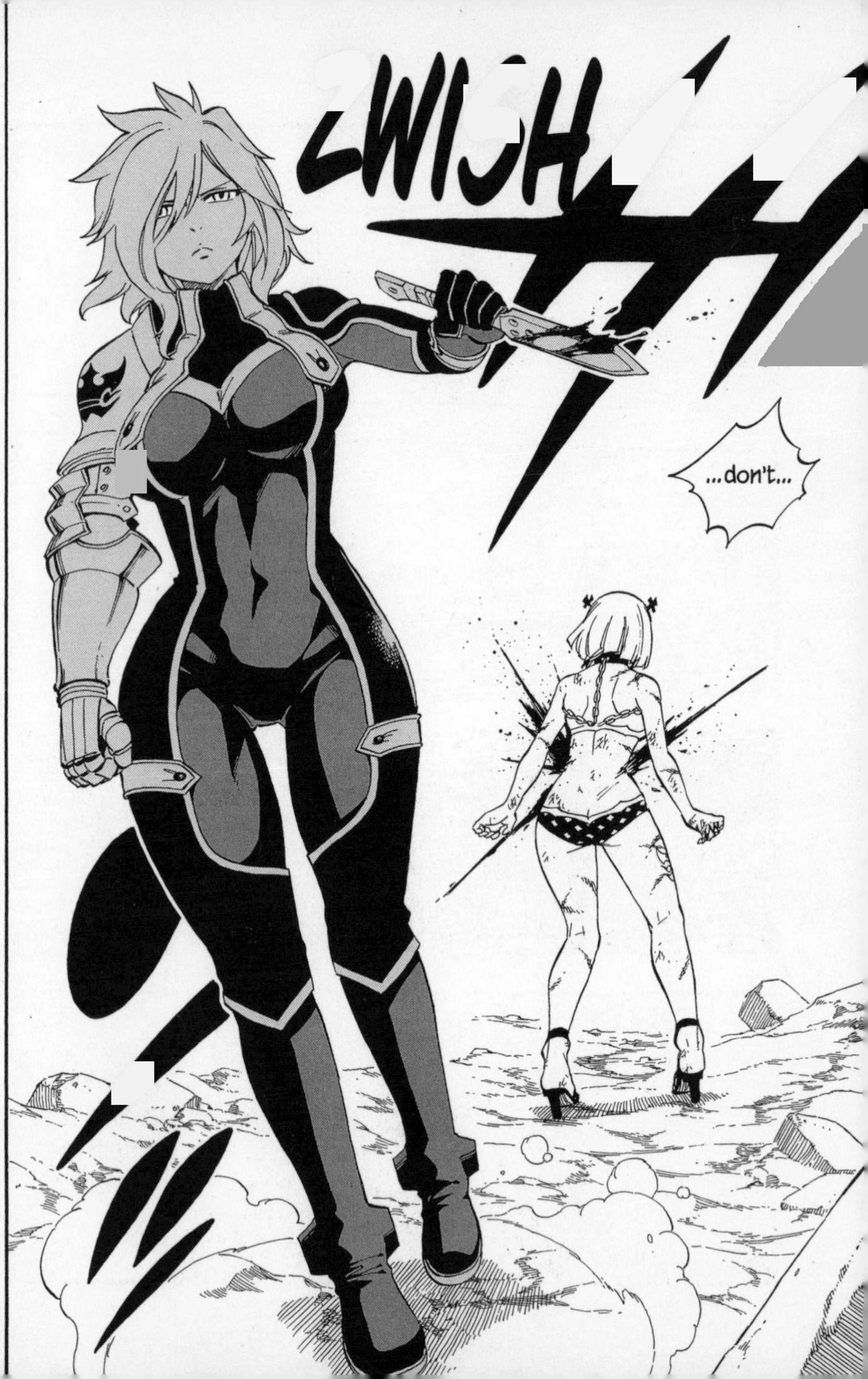
ZWISH
...don't...

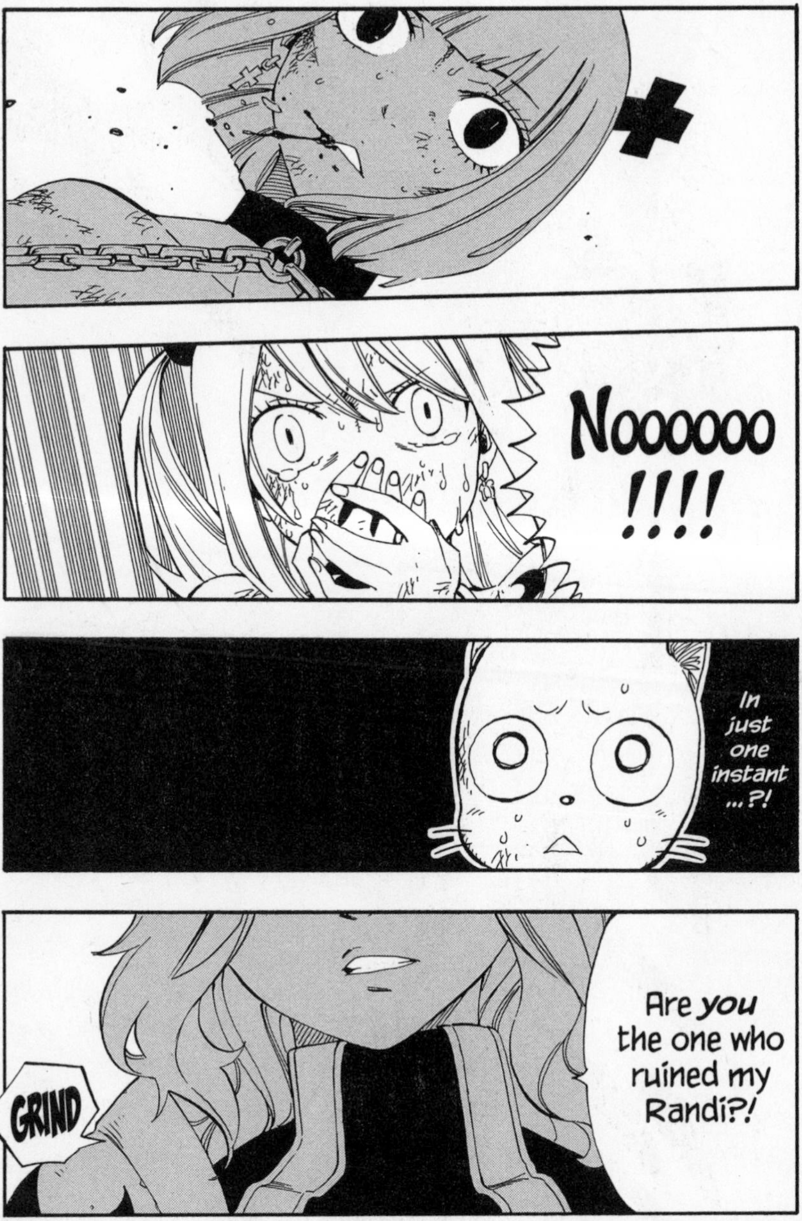
Nooooooo
!!!!
In just one instant ...?!
Are *you* the one who ruined my Randi?!
GRIND

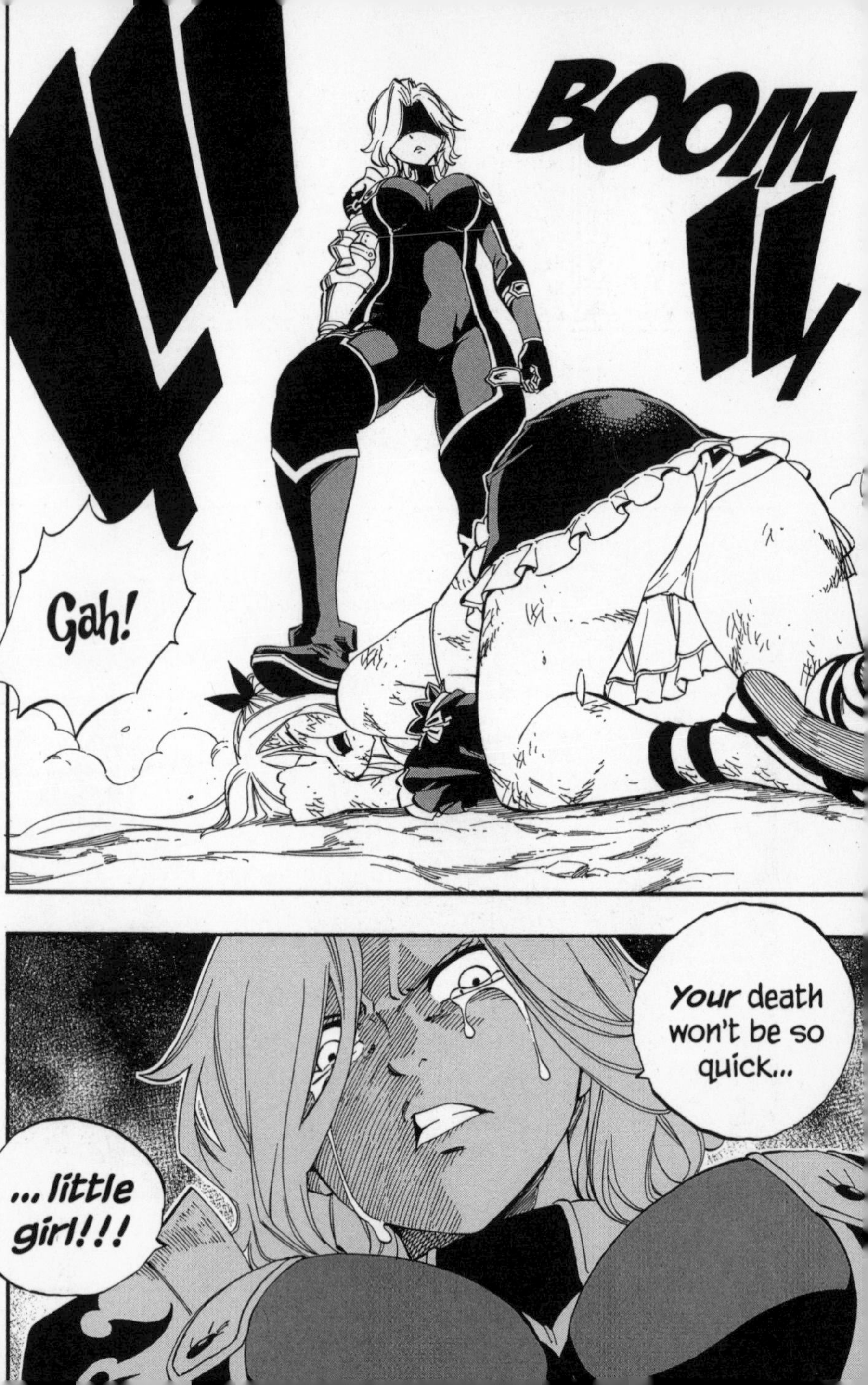
BOOM
Gah!
Your death won't be so quick...
... little girl!!!

FAIRY TAIL

フェアリーテイル

Chapter 502: Mavis and Zera

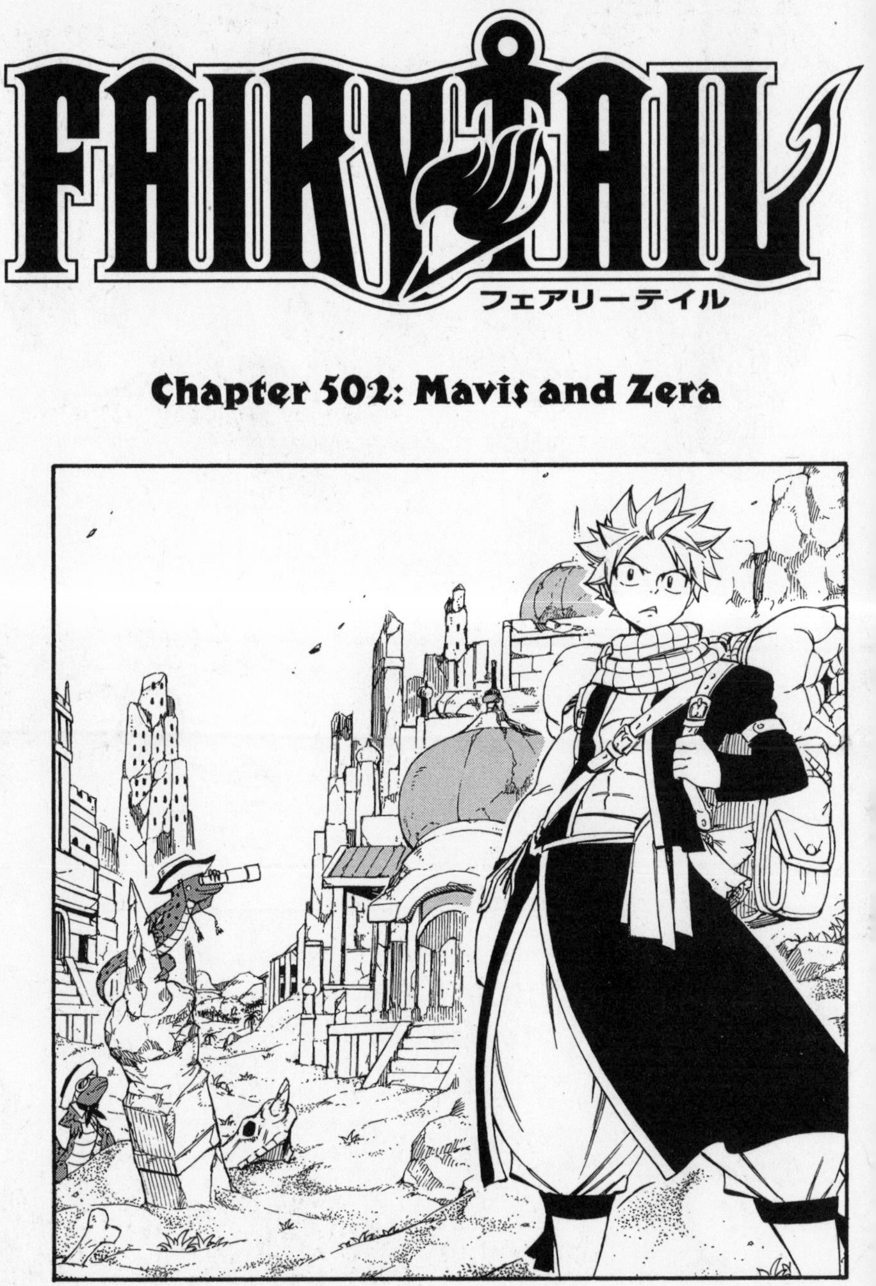

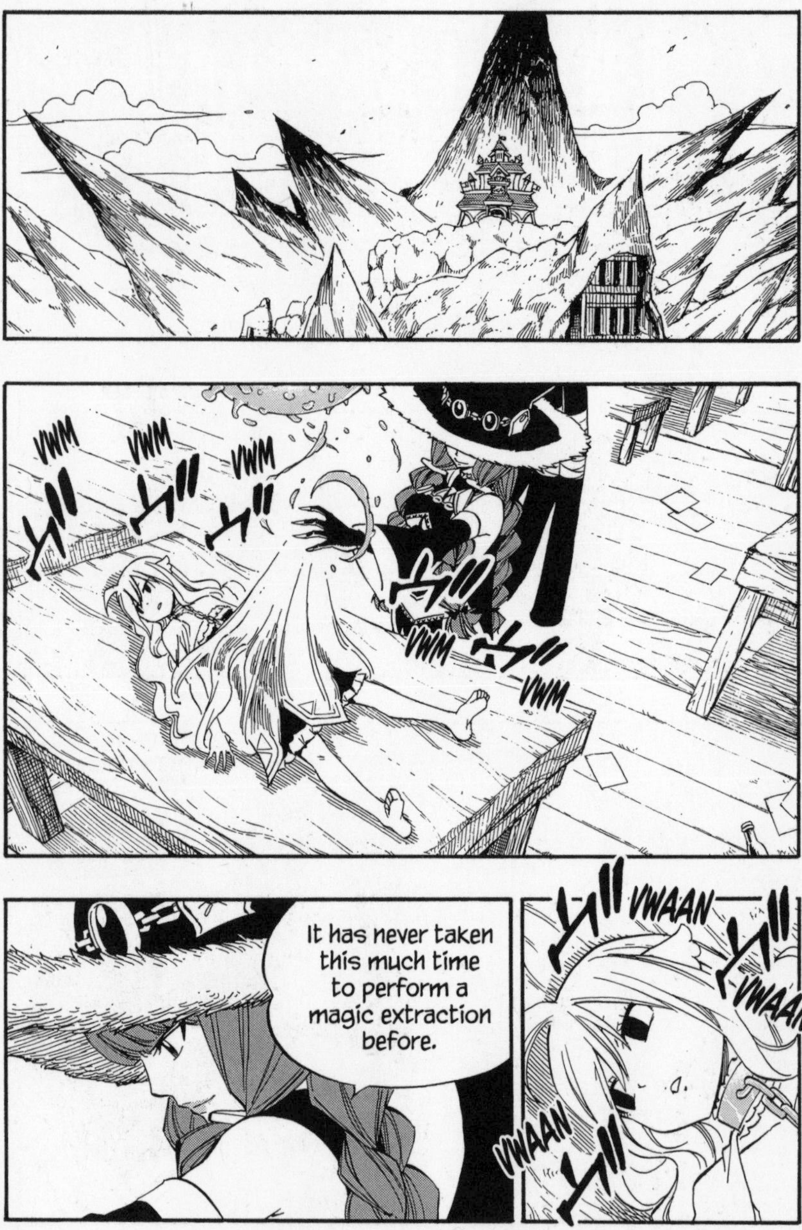
VWM
VWM
VWM
VWM
VWM
VWAAN
VWAAN
VWAAN
It has never taken this much time to perform a magic extraction before.

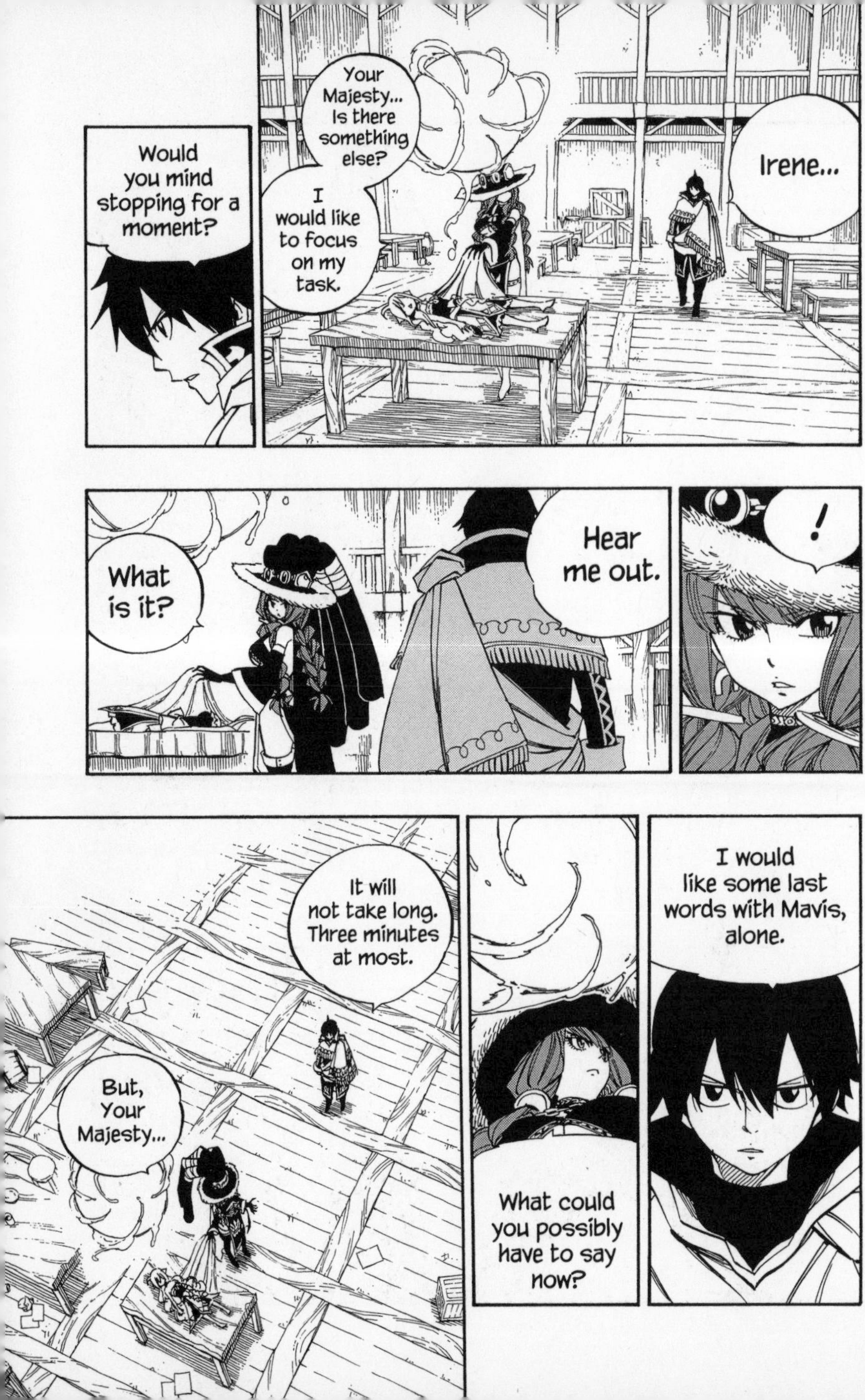
Irene...
Your Majesty... Is there something else?
I would like to focus on my task.
Would you mind stopping for a moment?
!
Hear me out.
What is it?
I would like some last words with Mavis, alone.
What could you possibly have to say now?
It will not take long. Three minutes at most.
But, Your Majesty...

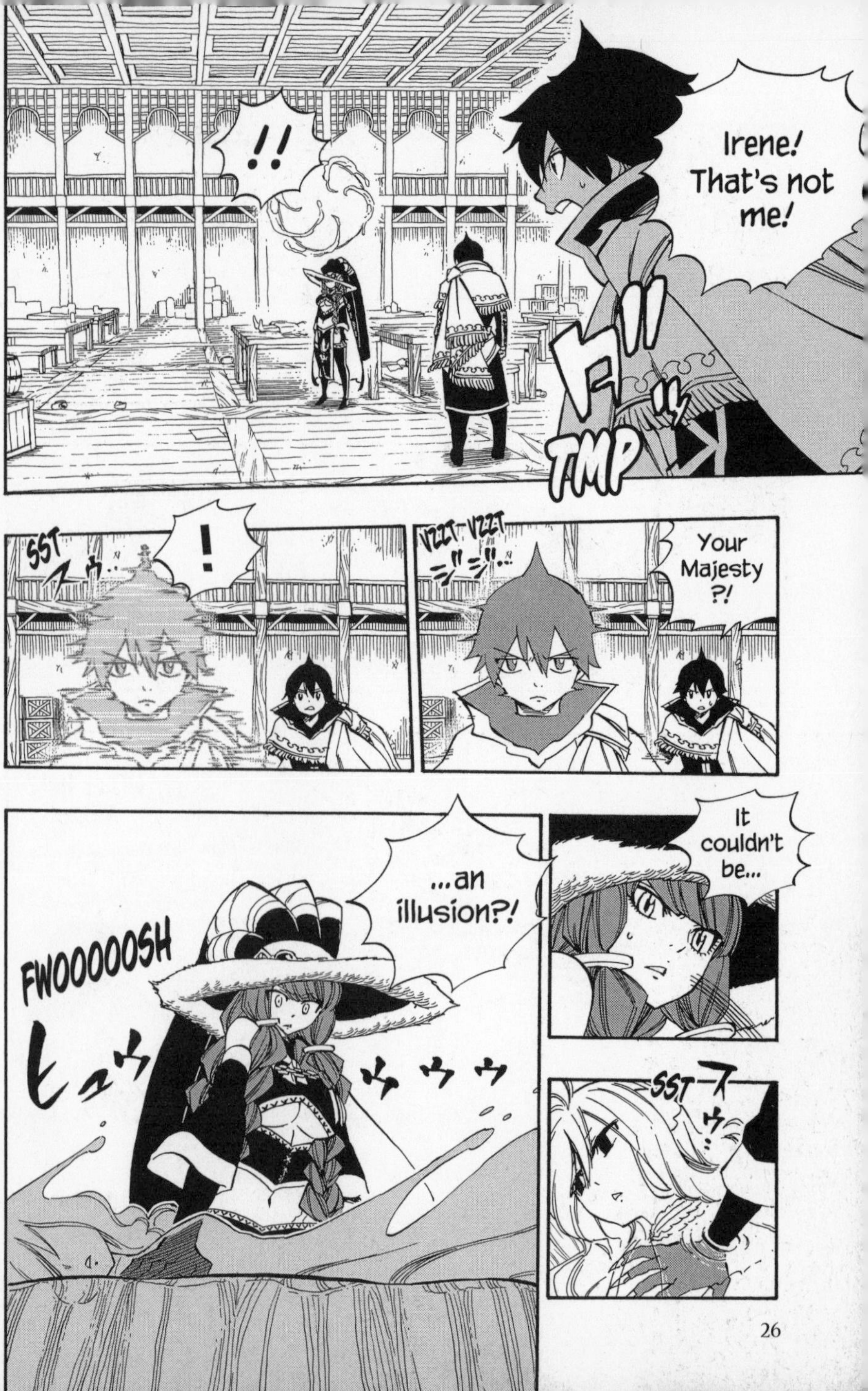

Irene! That's not me!
TMP
!!
VZZT-VZZT
Your Majesty?!
SST
!
It couldn't be...
SST
...an illusion?!
FWOOOOOSH

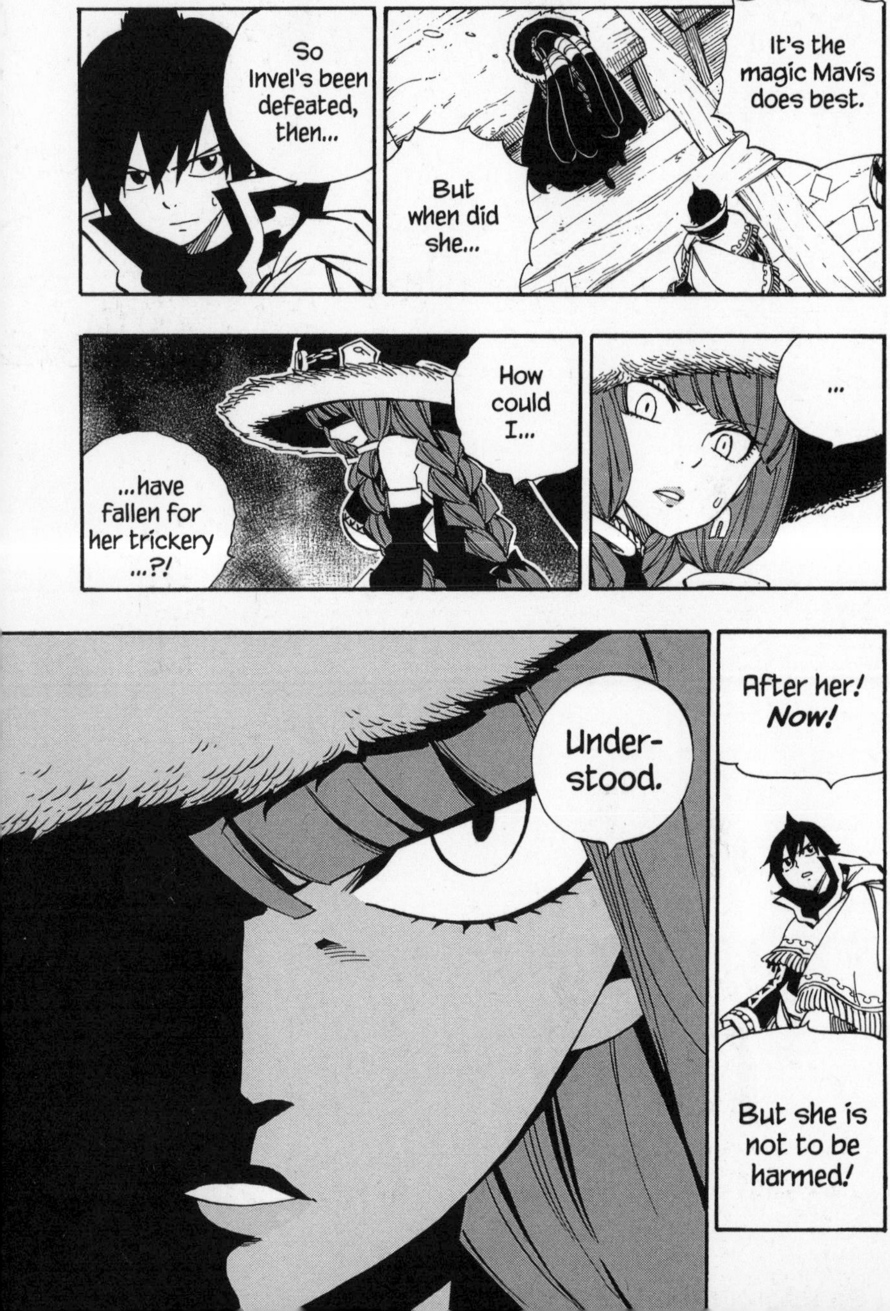
It's the magic Mavis does best.
But when did she...
So Invel's been defeated, then...
...
How could I...
...have fallen for her trickery ...?!
After her! *Now!*
But she is not to be harmed!
Under-stood.

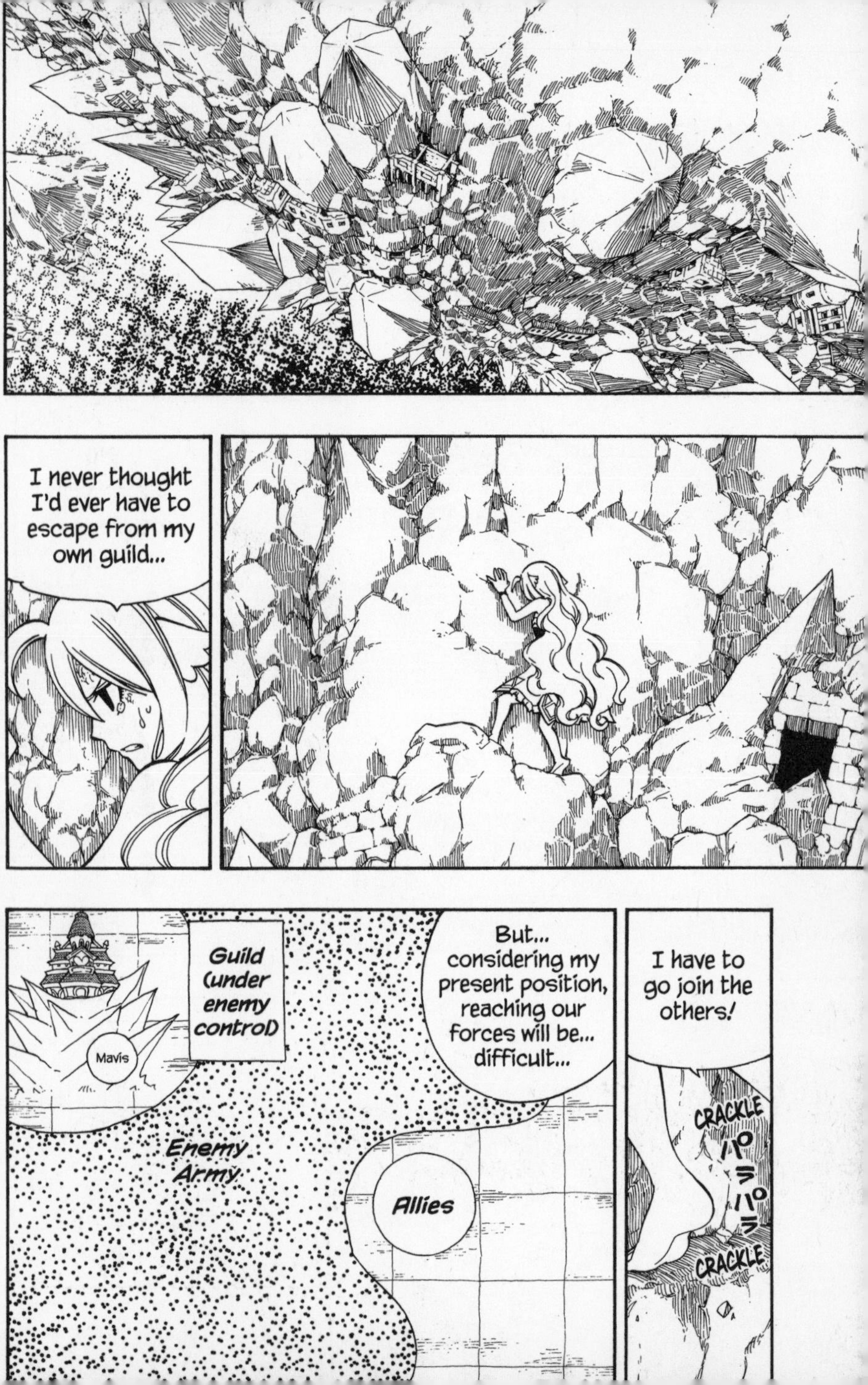
I never thought I'd ever have to escape from my own guild...
I have to go join the others!
CRACKLE
パラパラ
CRACKLE
But... considering my present position, reaching our forces will be... difficult...
Guild (under enemy control)
Mavis
Enemy Army
Allies

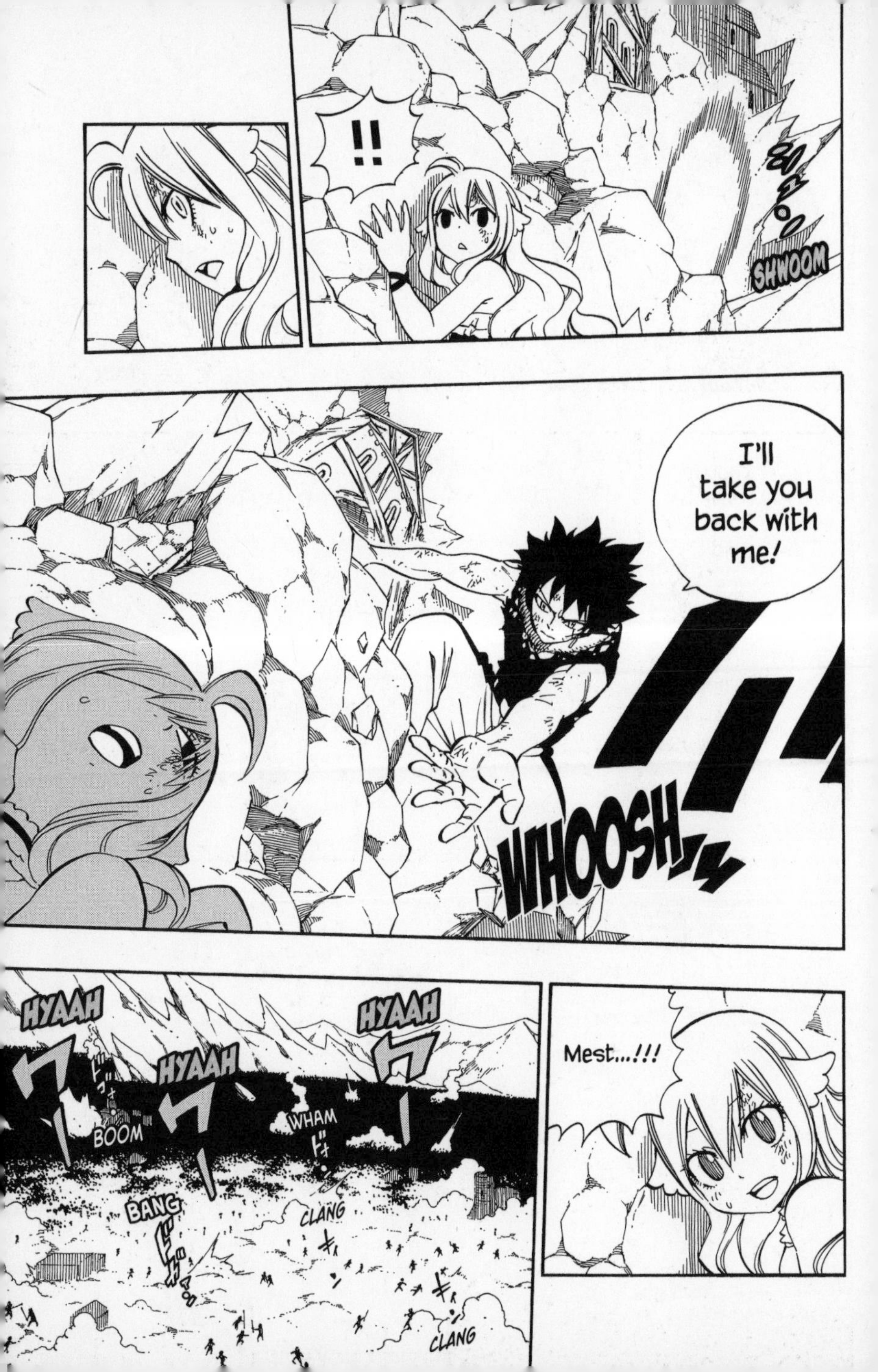
!!
SHWOOM
I'll take you back with me!
WHOOSH
Mest...!!!
HYAAH
HYAAH
HYAAH
WHAM
BOOM
CLANG
BANG
CLANG

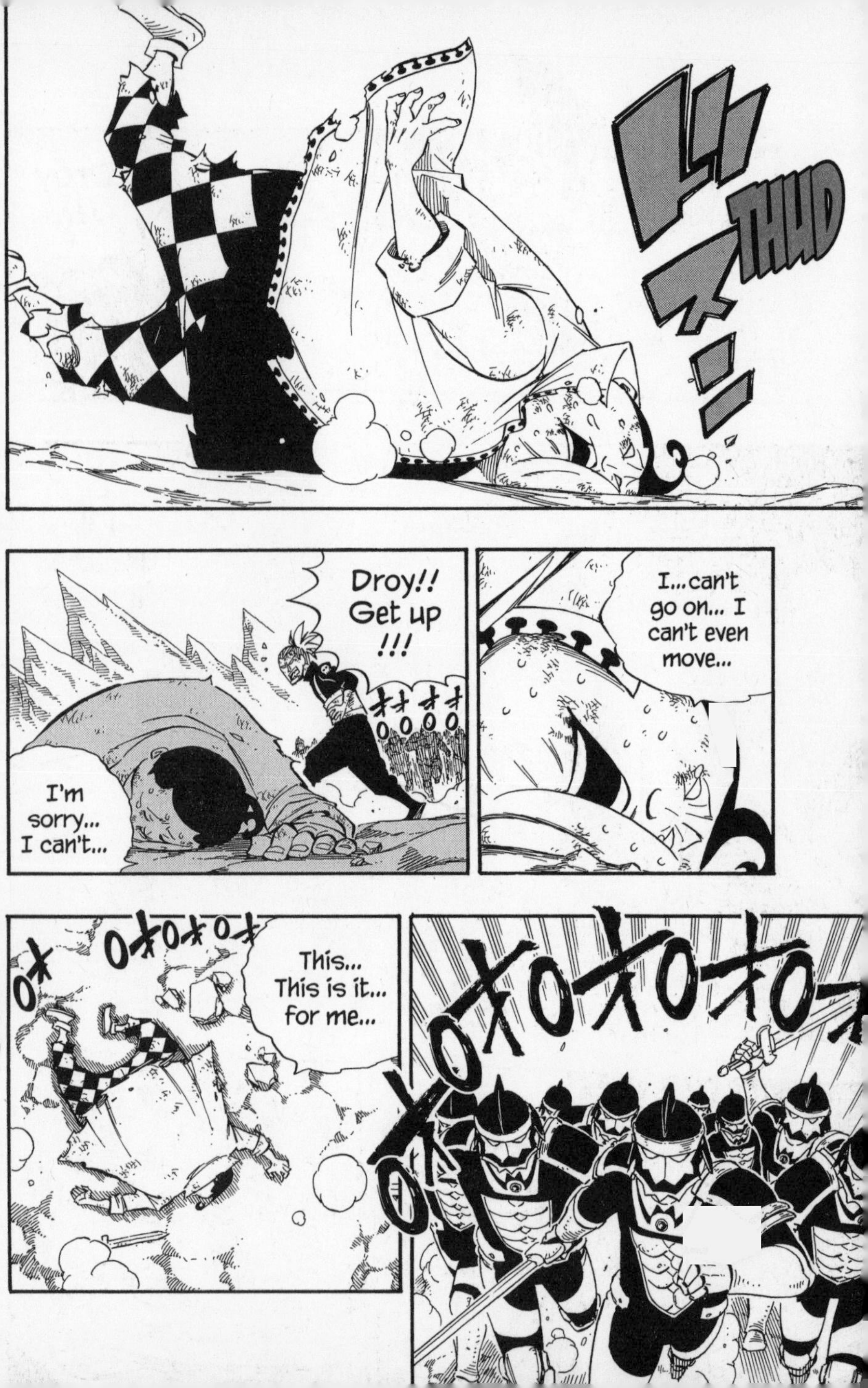
THUD
I...can't go on... I can't even move...
Droy!! Get up !!!
I'm sorry... I can't...
This... This is it... for me...

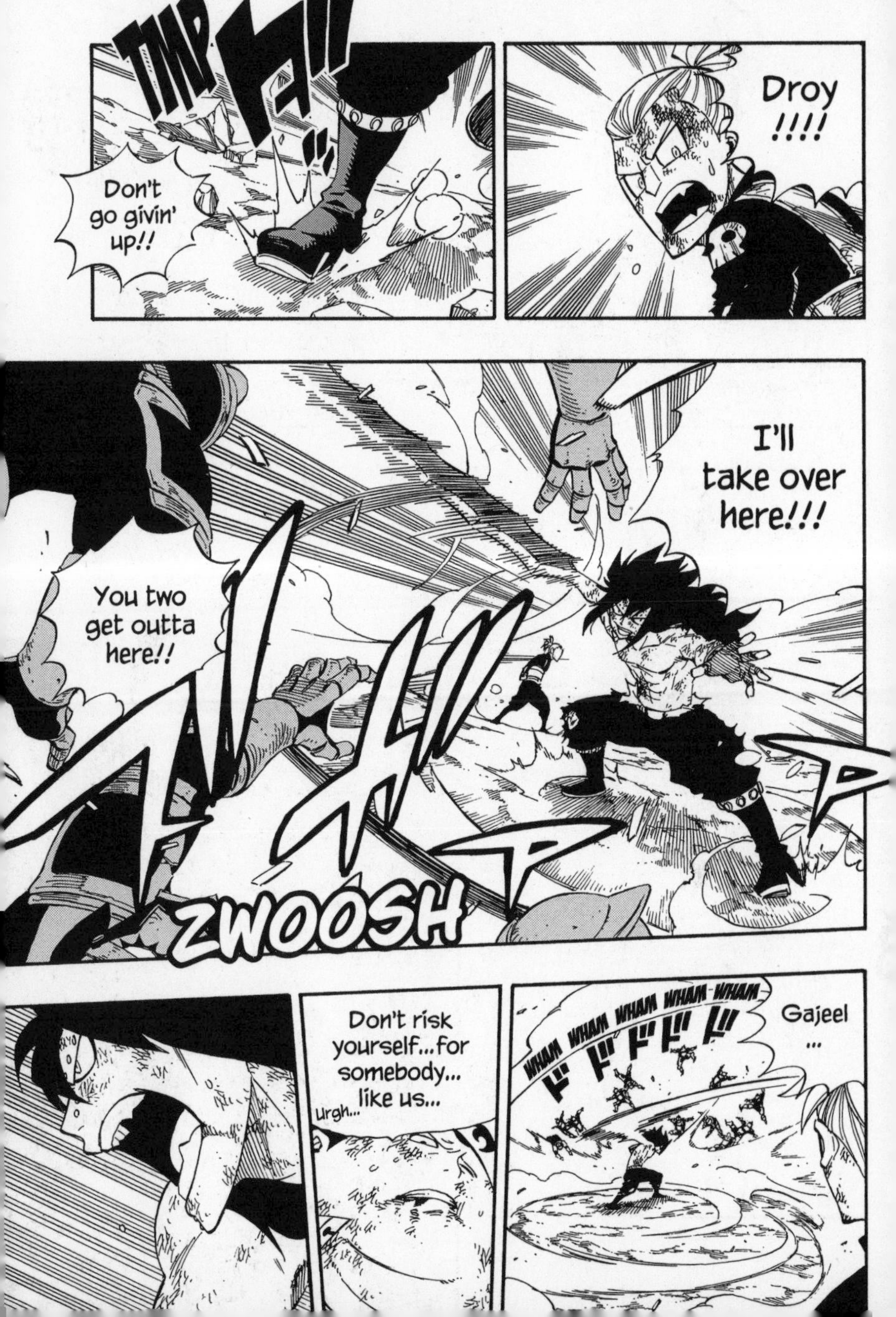
Droy !!!!
TMP!!
Don't go givin' up!!
I'll take over here!!!
You two get outta here!!
ZWOOSH
Gajeel ...
WHAM WHAM WHAM WHAM-WHAM
Don't risk yourself...for somebody... like us...
Urgh...

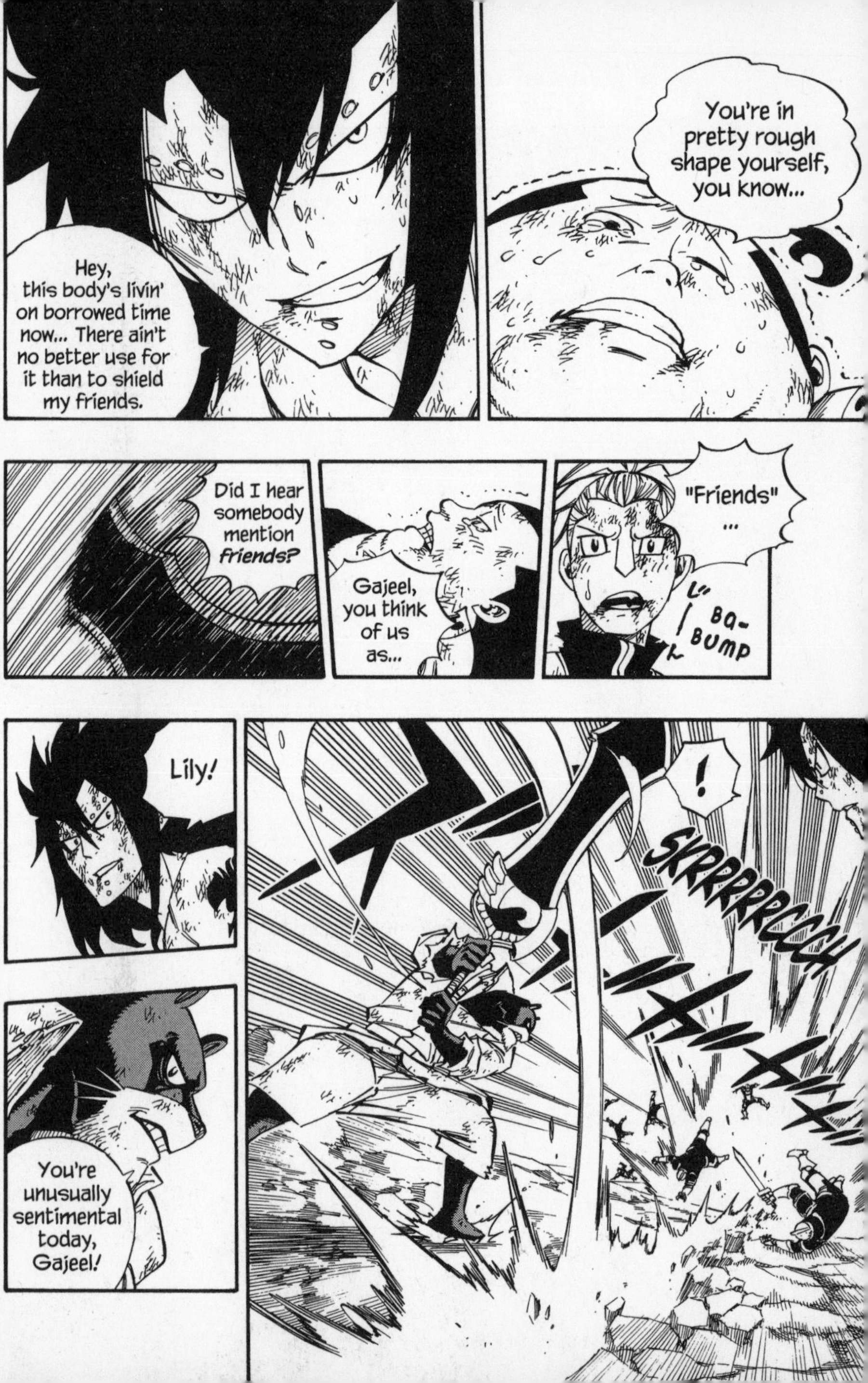
You're in pretty rough shape yourself, you know...
Hey, this body's livin' on borrowed time now... There ain't no better use for it than to shield my friends.
"Friends" ...
BA-BUMP
Gajeel, you think of us as...
Did I hear somebody mention friends?
!
SKRRRRRCCH
Lily!
You're unusually sentimental today, Gajeel!

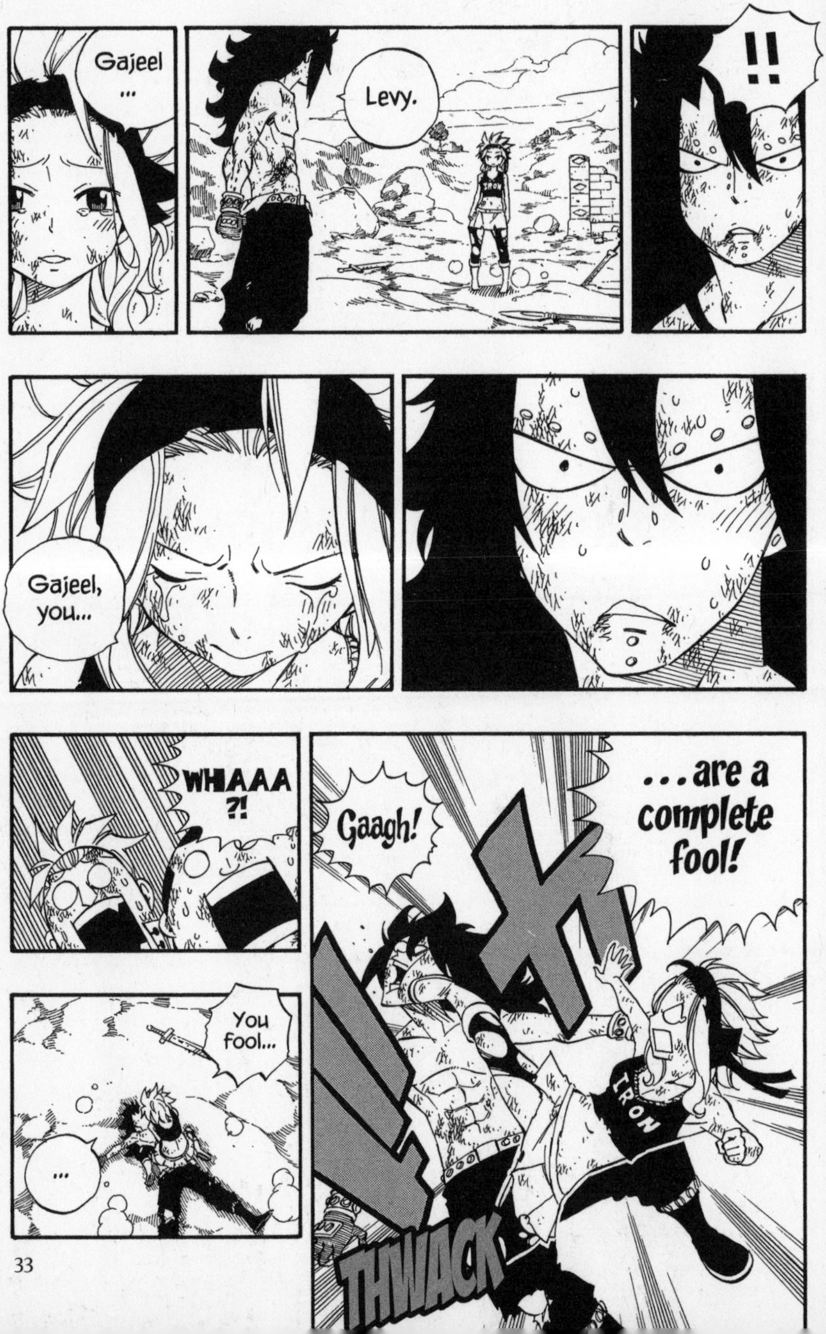
!!
Levy.
Gajeel ...
Gajeel, you...
...are a complete fool!
Gaagh!
THWACK
WHAAA ?!
You fool...
...

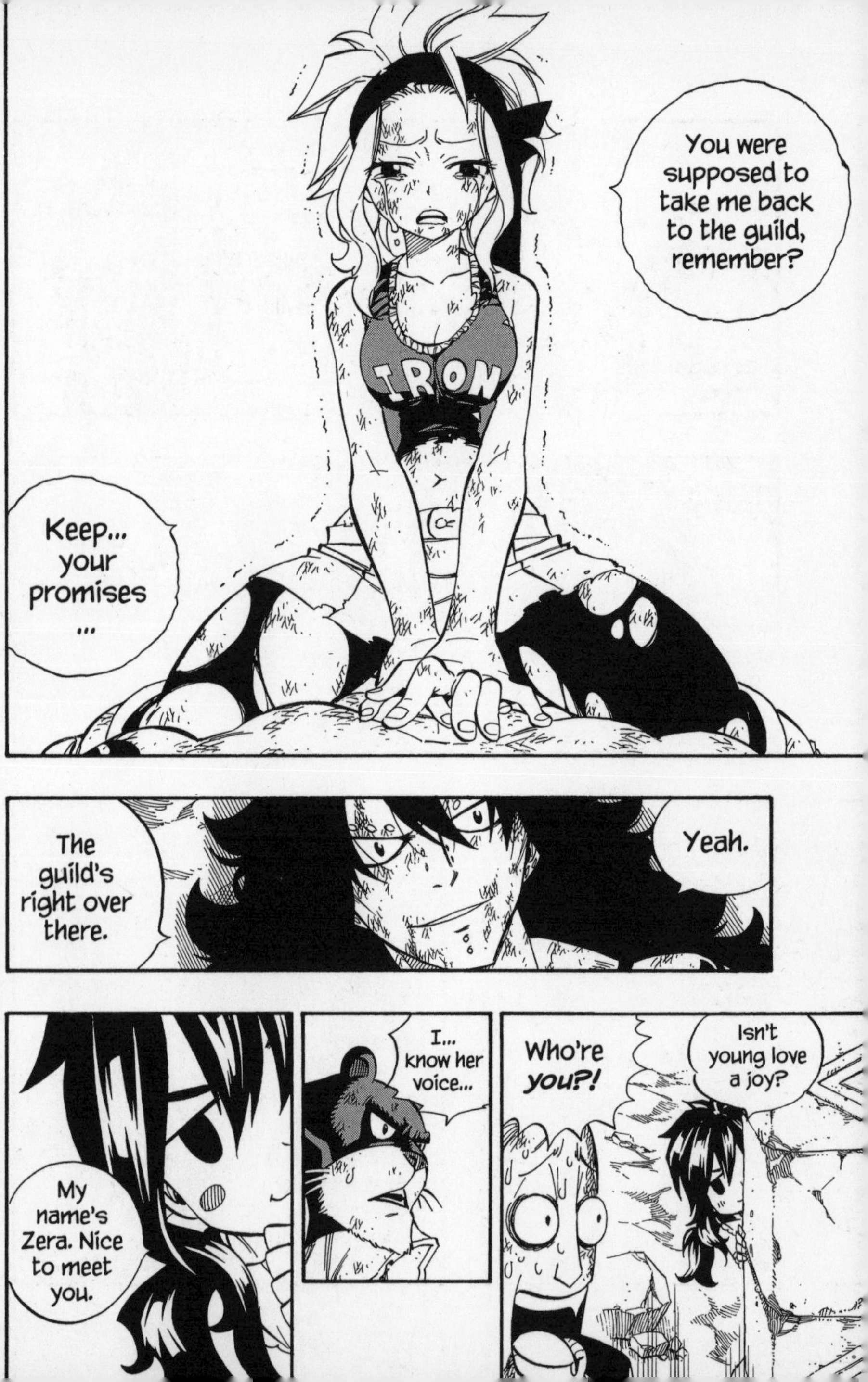
You were supposed to take me back to the guild, remember?
Keep... your promises ...
Yeah.
The guild's right over there.
Isn't young love a joy?
Who're *you?!*
I... know her voice...
My name's Zera. Nice to meet you.

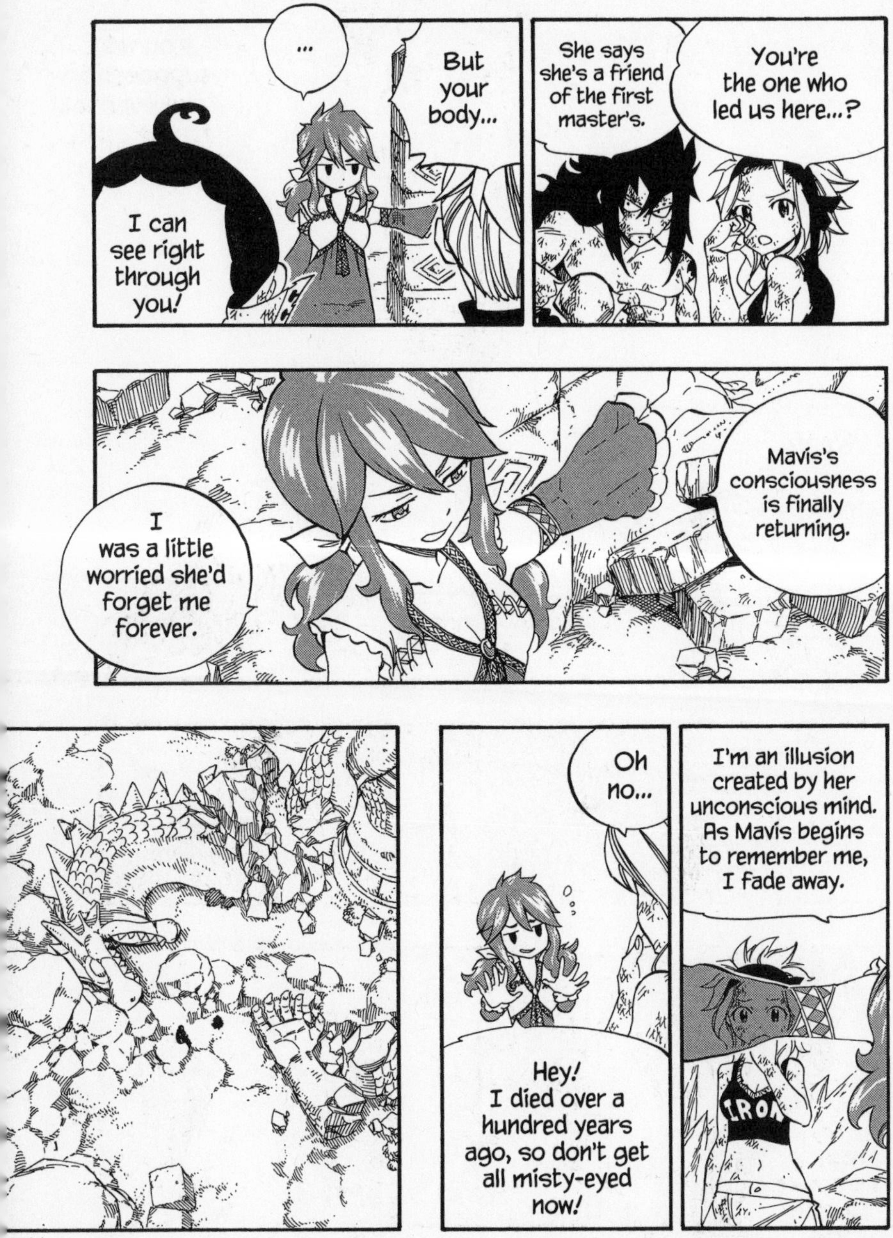
You're the one who led us here...?
She says she's a friend of the first master's.
But your body...
...
I can see right through you!
Mavis's consciousness is finally returning.
I was a little worried she'd forget me forever.
I'm an illusion created by her unconscious mind. As Mavis begins to remember me, I fade away.
Oh no...
Hey! I died over a hundred years ago, so don't get all misty-eyed now!

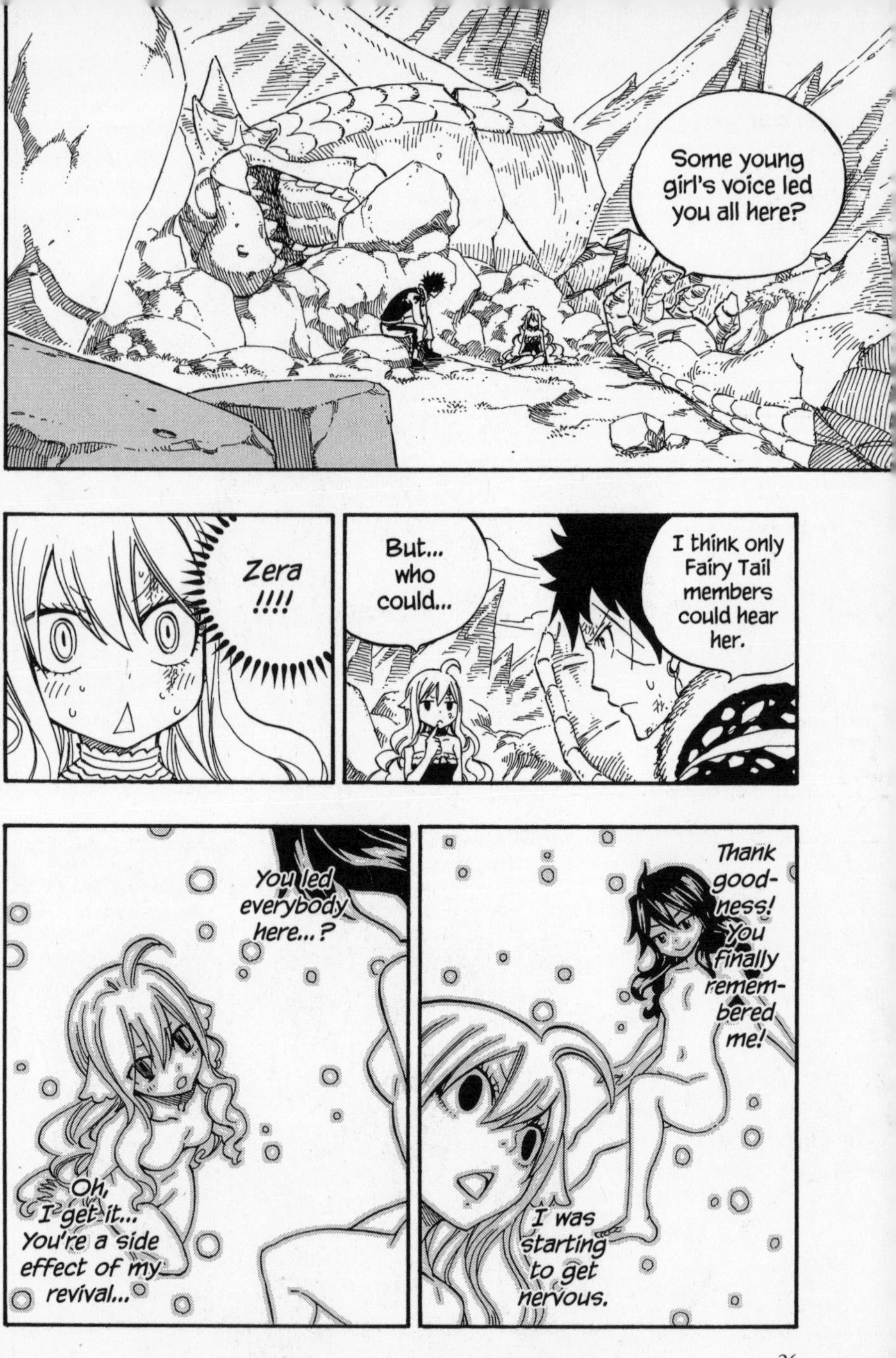
Some young girl's voice led you all here?
I think only Fairy Tail members could hear her.
But... who could...
Zera !!!!
Thank goodness! You finally remembered me!
I was starting to get nervous.
You led everybody here...?
Oh, I get it... You're a side effect of my revival...

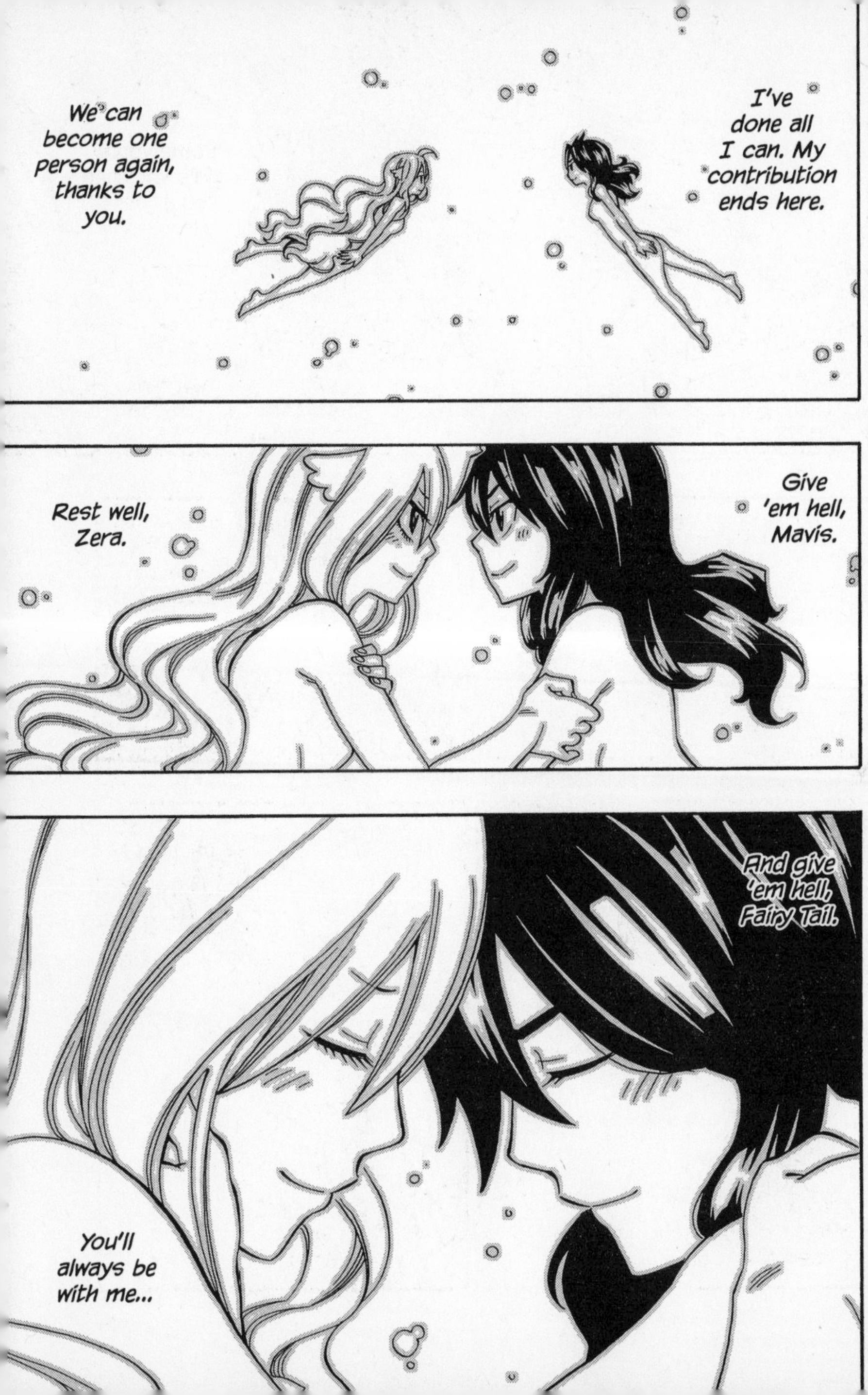
I've done all I can. My contribution ends here.
We can become one person again, thanks to you.
Give 'em hell, Mavis.
Rest well, Zera.
And give 'em hell, Fairy Tail.
You'll always be with me...

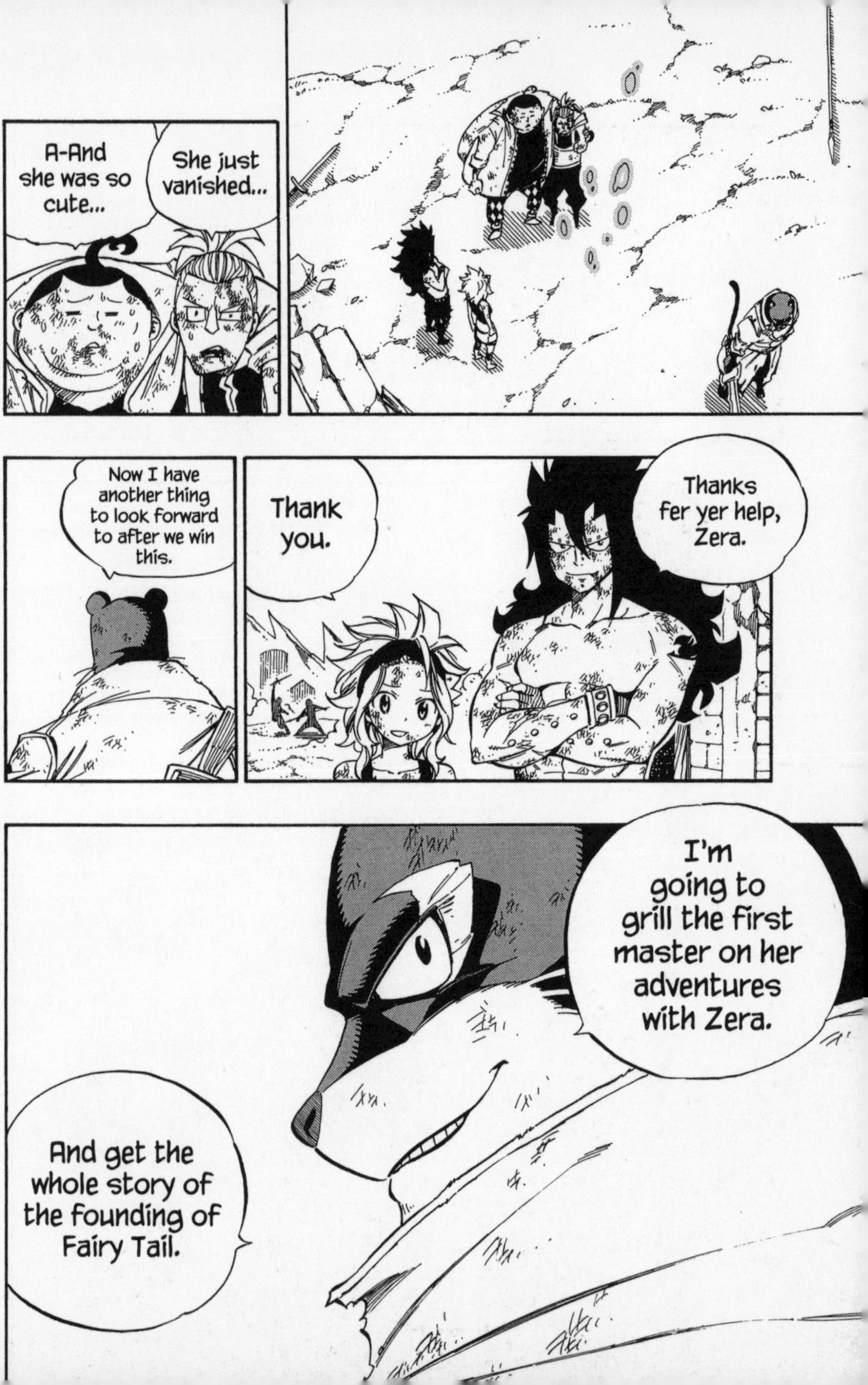
She just vanished...
A-And she was so cute...
Thanks fer yer help, Zera.
Thank you.
Now I have another thing to look forward to after we win this.
I'm going to grill the first master on her adventures with Zera.
And get the whole story of the founding of Fairy Tail.

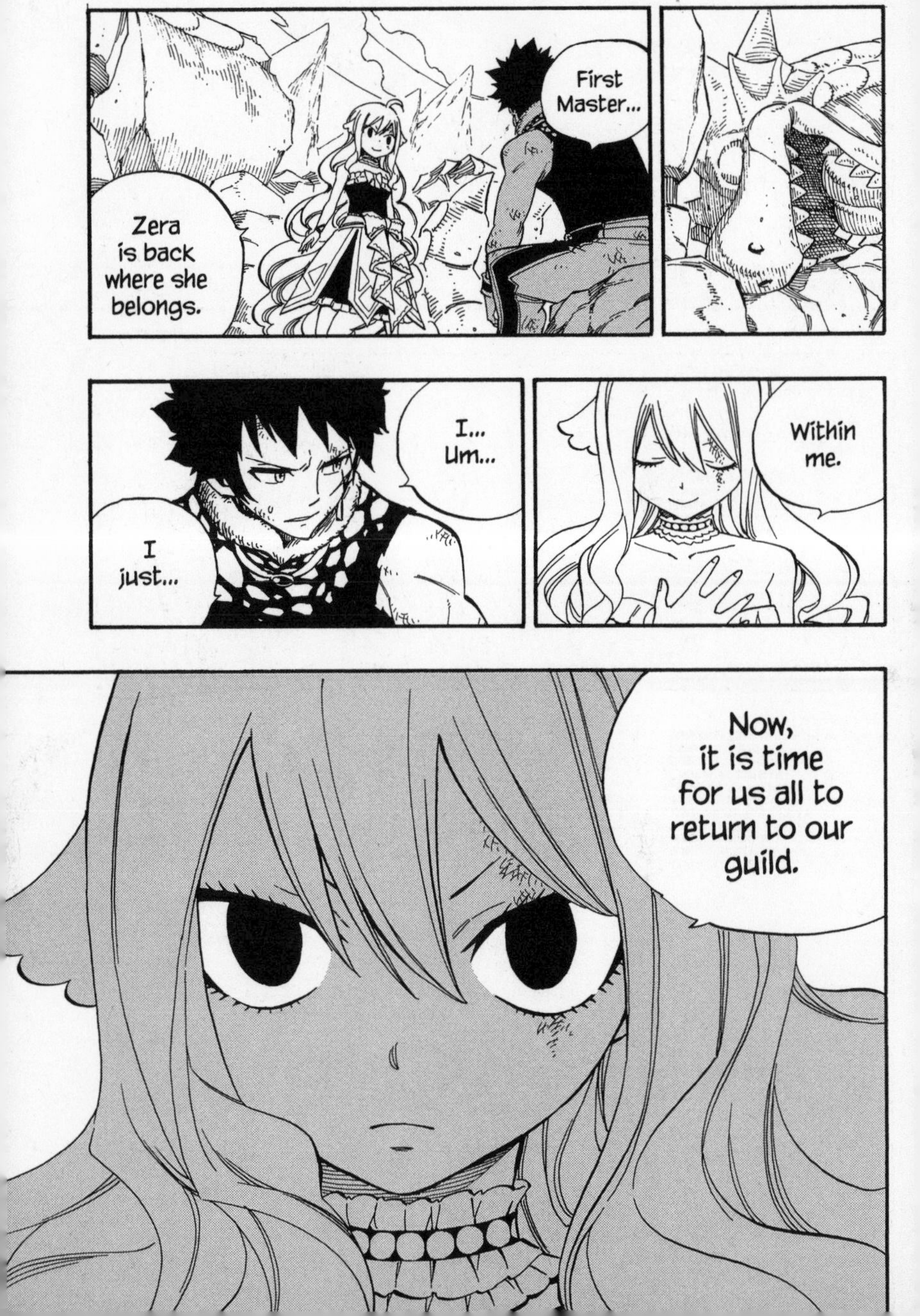
First Master...
Zera is back where she belongs.
Within me.
I... Um...
I just...
Now, it is time for us all to return to our guild.

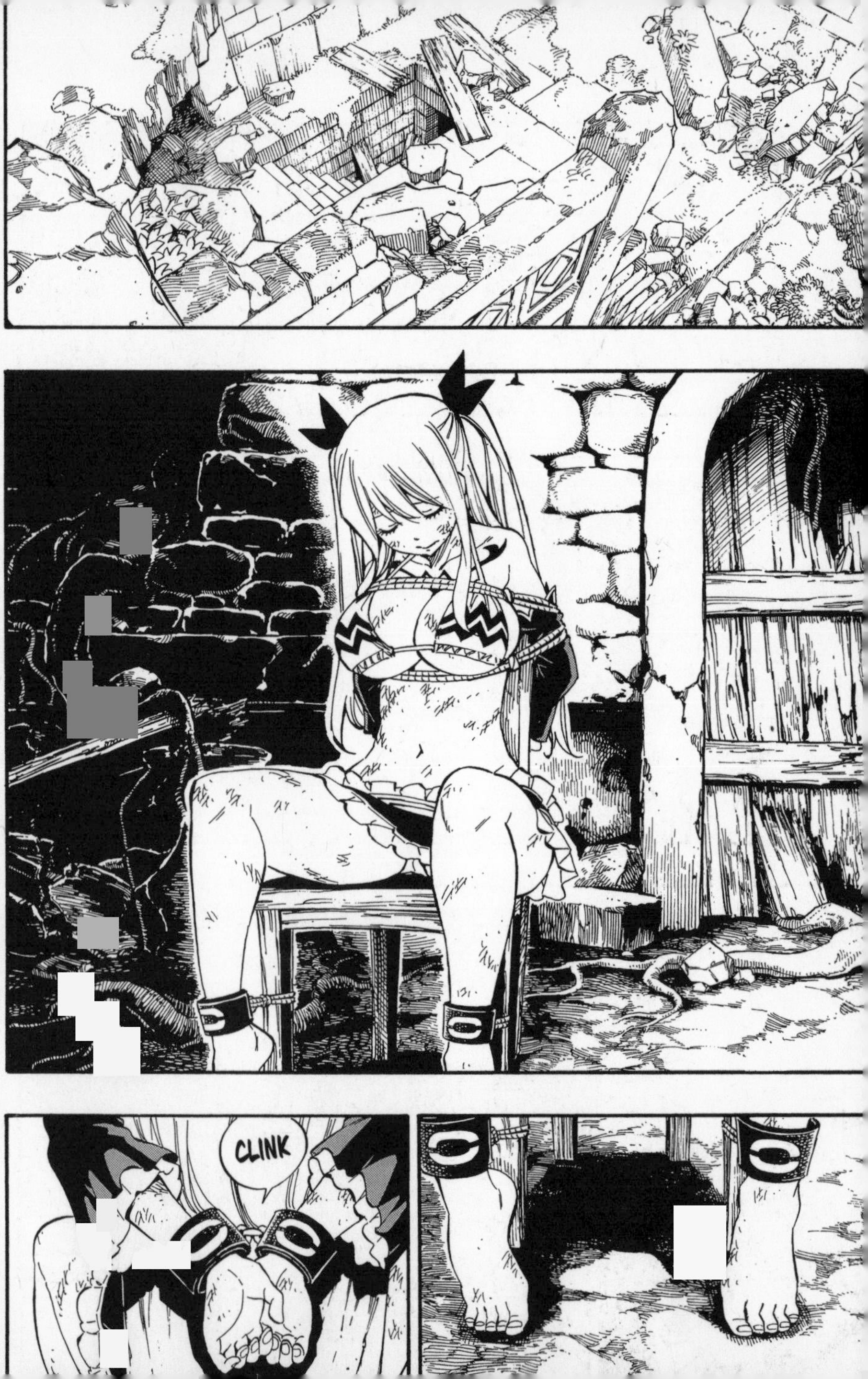
CLINK

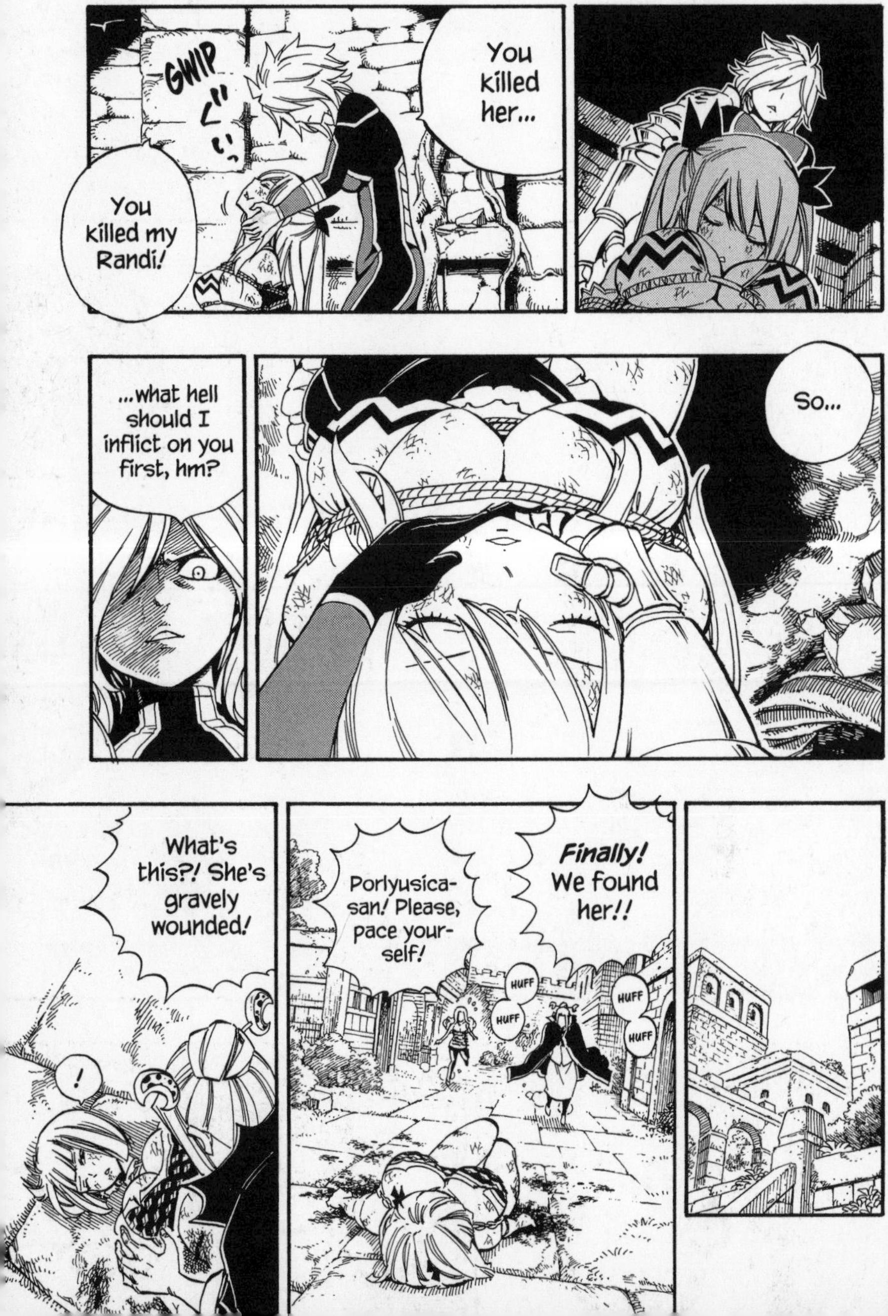
You killed her...
GWIP
ぐいっ
You killed my Randi!
So...
...what hell should I inflict on you first, hm?
Finally! We found her!!
Porlyusica-san! Please, pace yourself!
HUFF
HUFF
HUFF
HUFF
What's this?! She's gravely wounded!
!

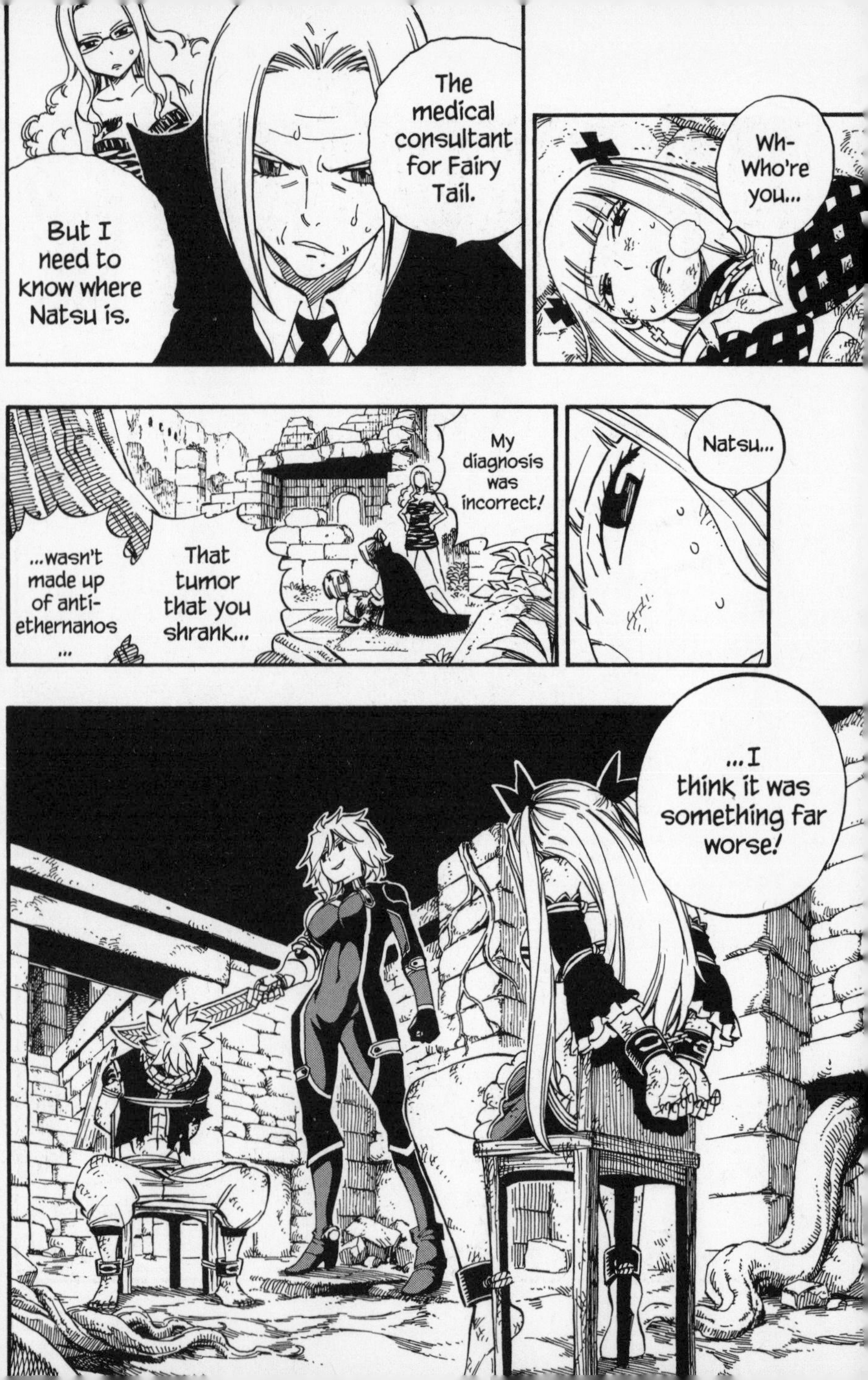
Wh- Who're you...
The medical consultant for Fairy Tail.
But I need to know where Natsu is.
Natsu...
My diagnosis was incorrect!
That tumor that you shrank...
...wasn't made up of anti-ethernanos ...
...I think it was something far worse!

FAIRY TAIL

フェアリーテイル

Chapter 503: The Last Sight Seen

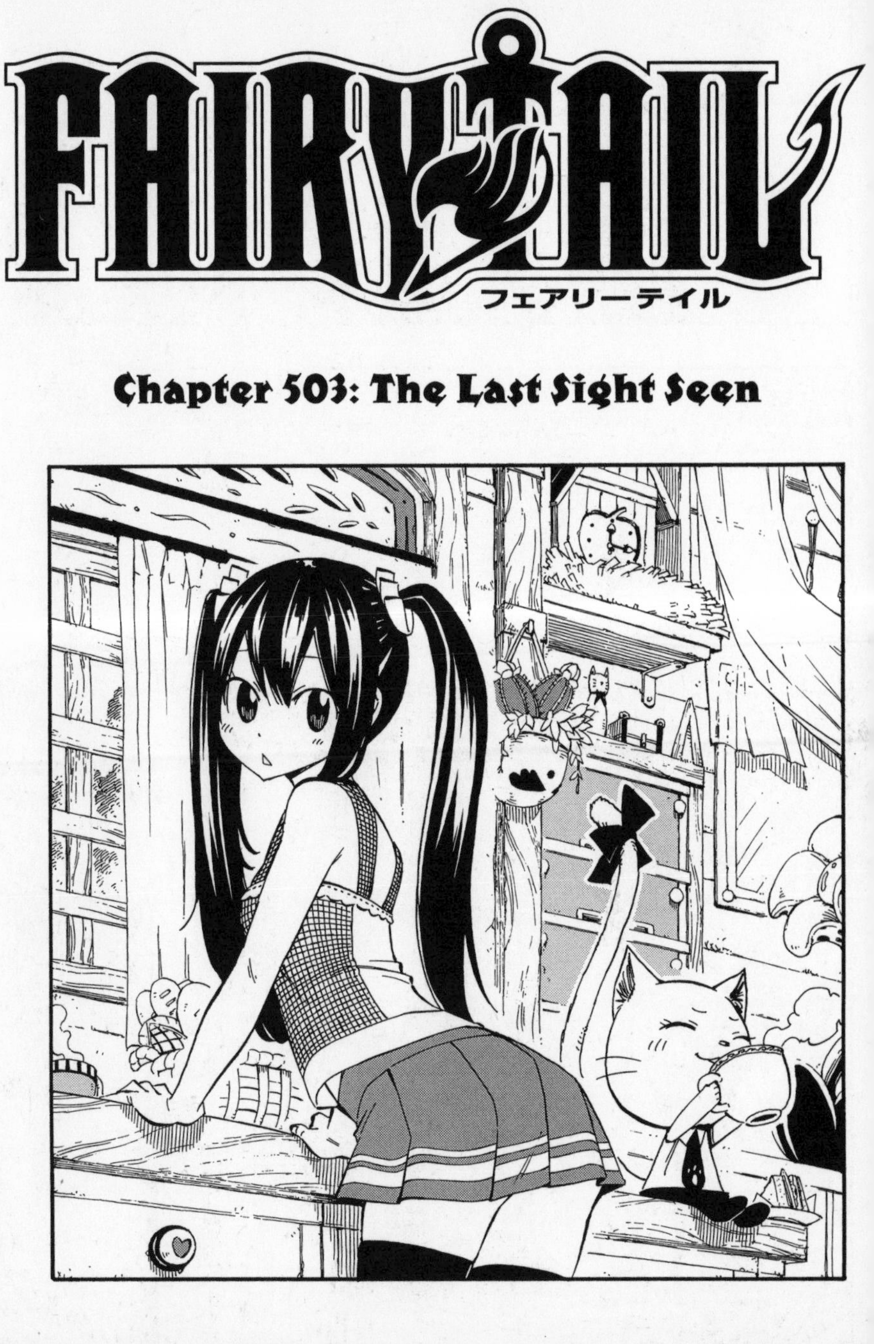

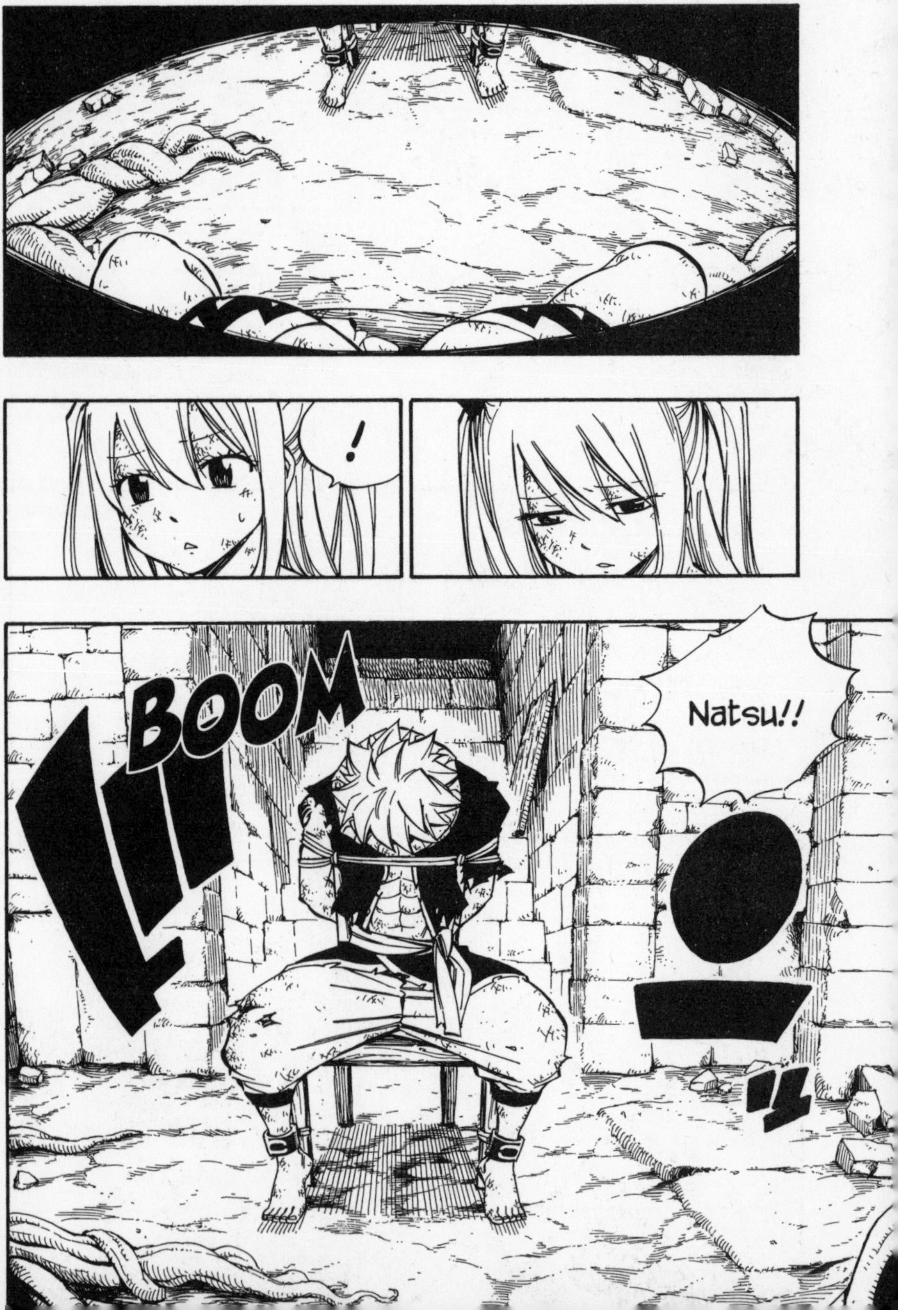
!
Natsu!!
BOOM

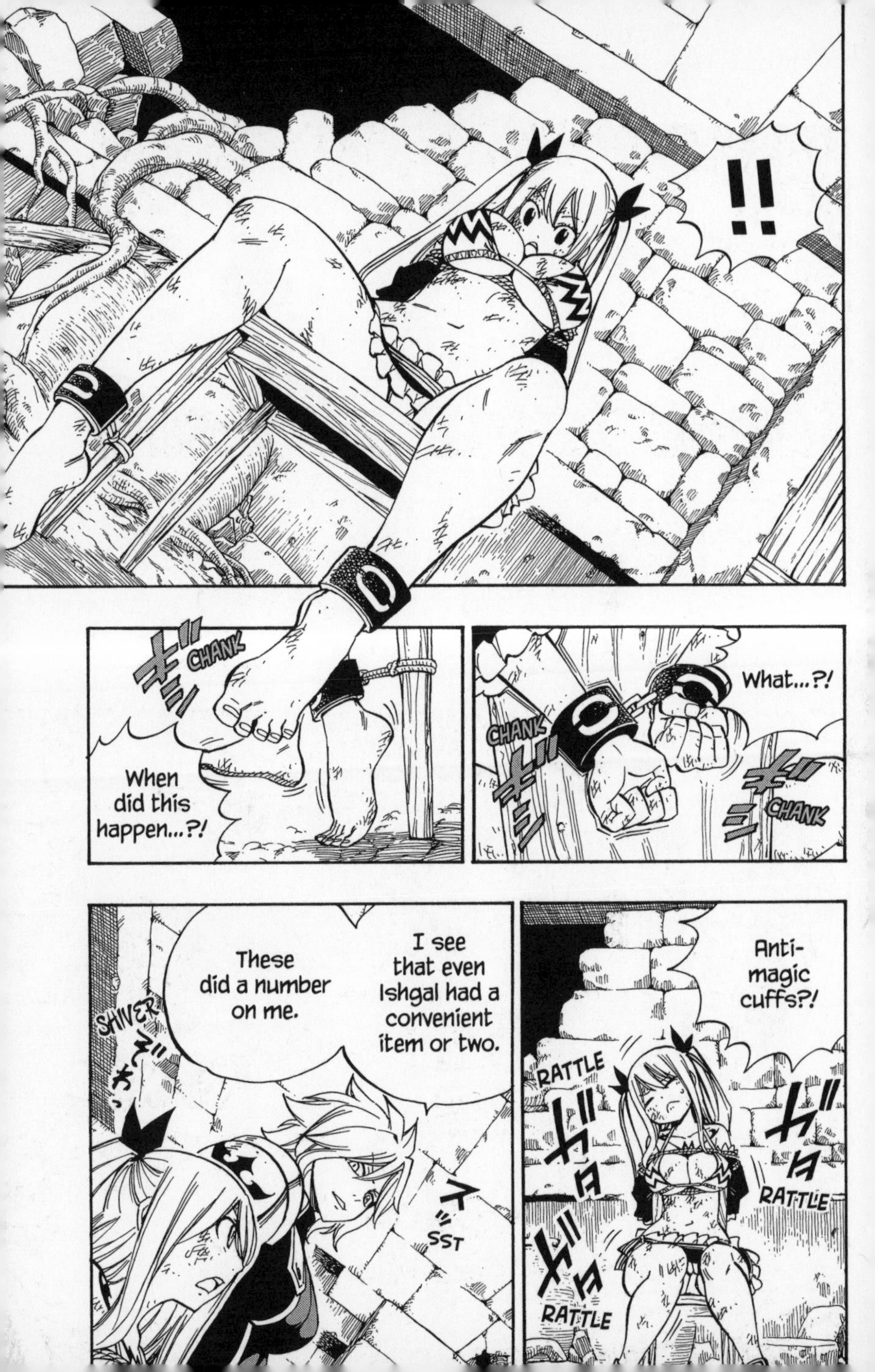
!!
What...?!
CHANK
CHANK
CHANK
When did this happen...?!
Anti-magic cuffs?!
RATTLE
RATTLE
RATTLE
I see that even Ishgal had a convenient item or two.
These did a number on me.
SHIVER
SST

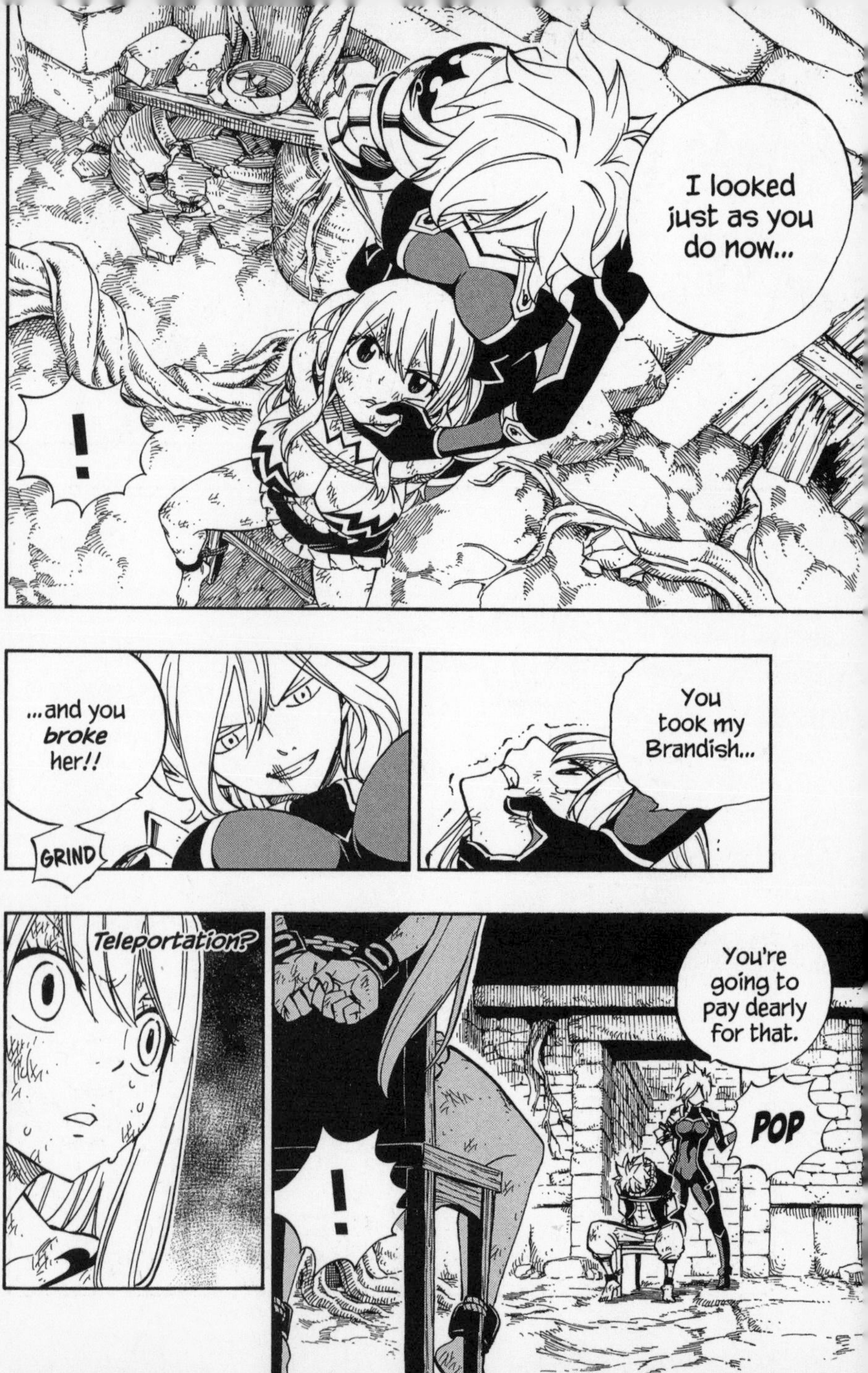
I looked just as you do now...
!
You took my Brandish...
...and you *broke* her!!
GRIND
You're going to pay dearly for that.
POP
!
Teleportation?

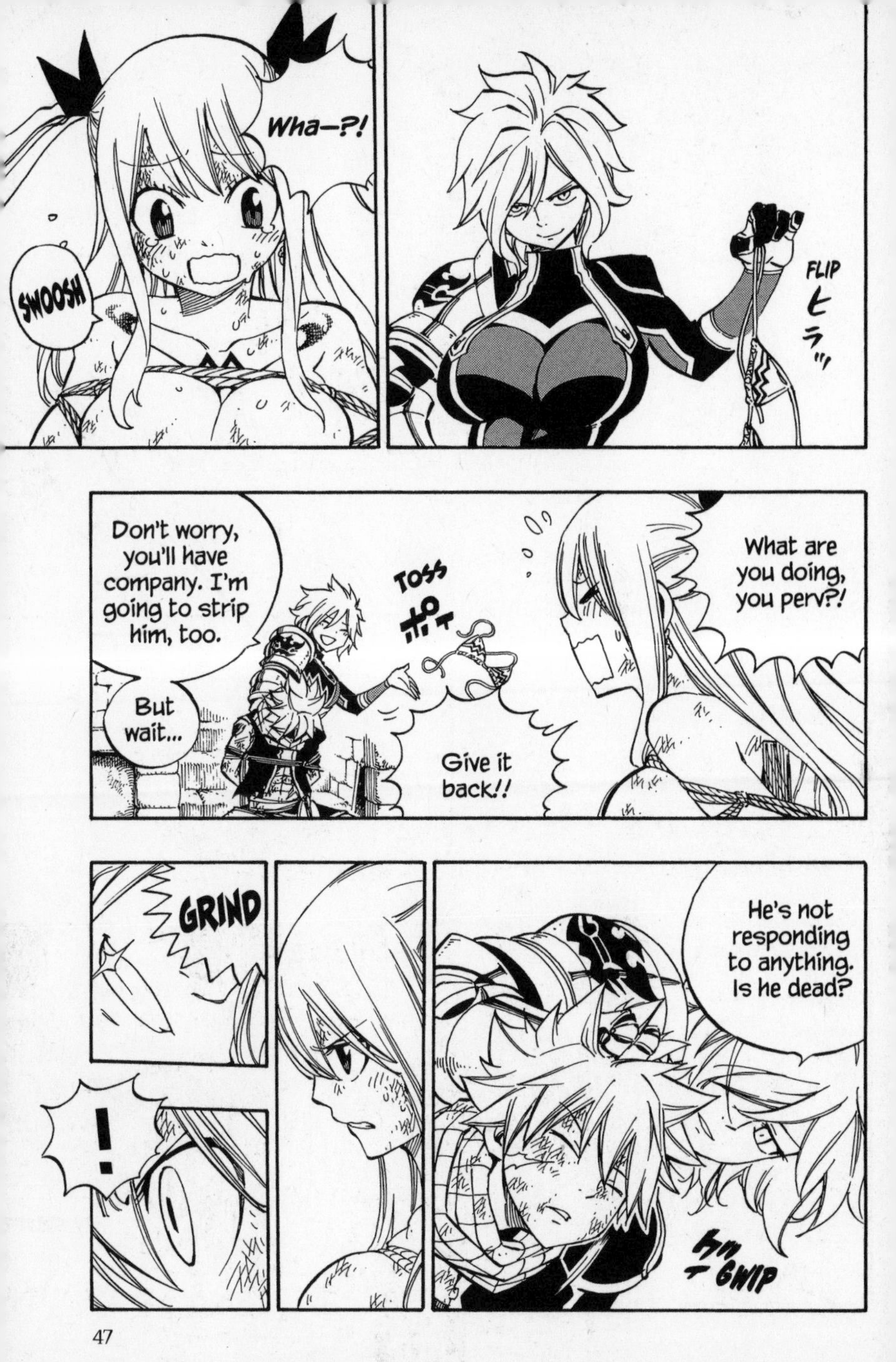
FLIP
ヒラッ
Wha-?!
SWOOSH
What are you doing, you perv?!
Give it back!!
TOSS
Don't worry, you'll have company. I'm going to strip him, too.
But wait...
He's not responding to anything. Is he dead?
GWIP
GRIND
!

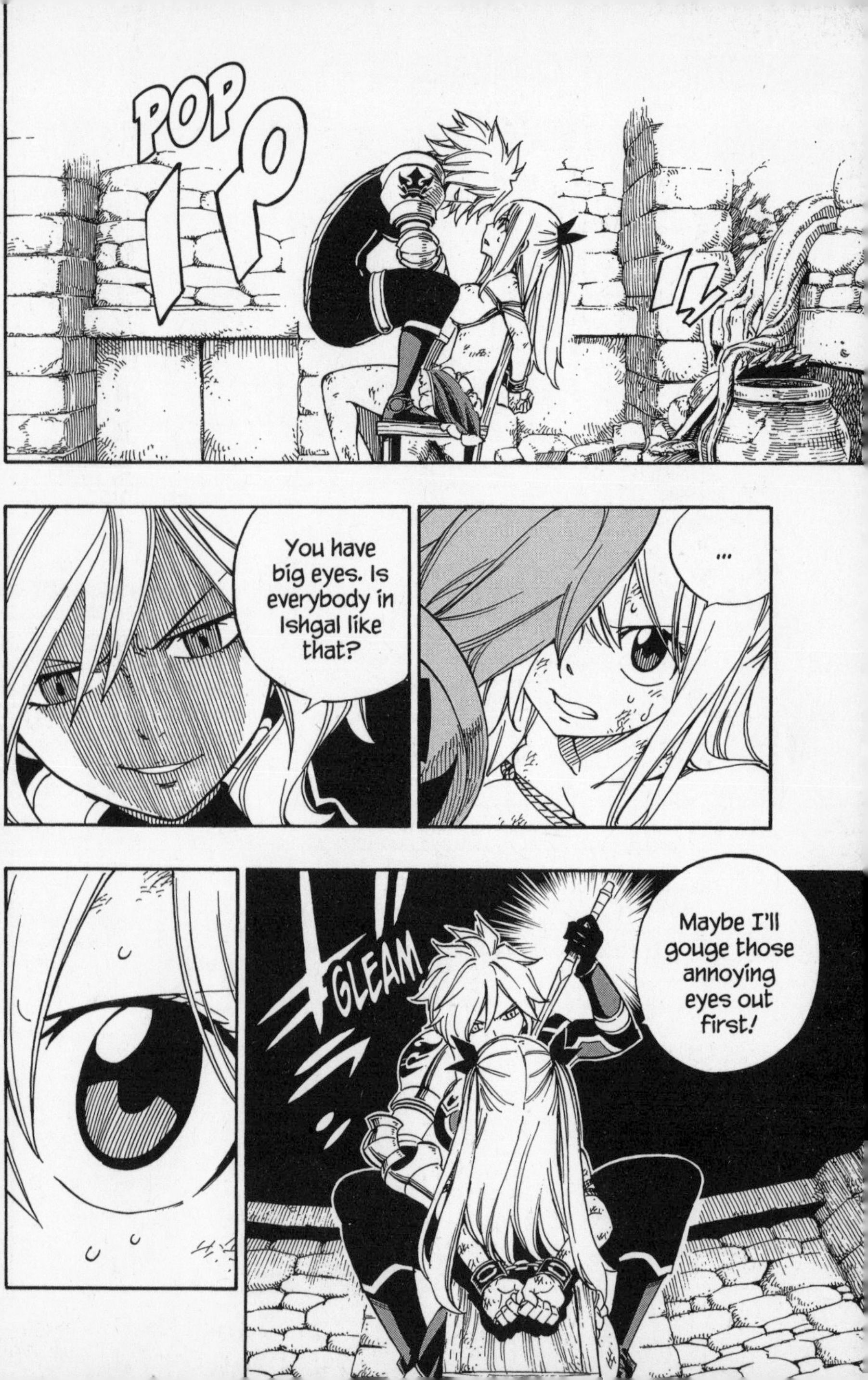
POP
...
You have big eyes. Is everybody in Ishgal like that?
GLEAM
Maybe I'll gouge those annoying eyes out first!

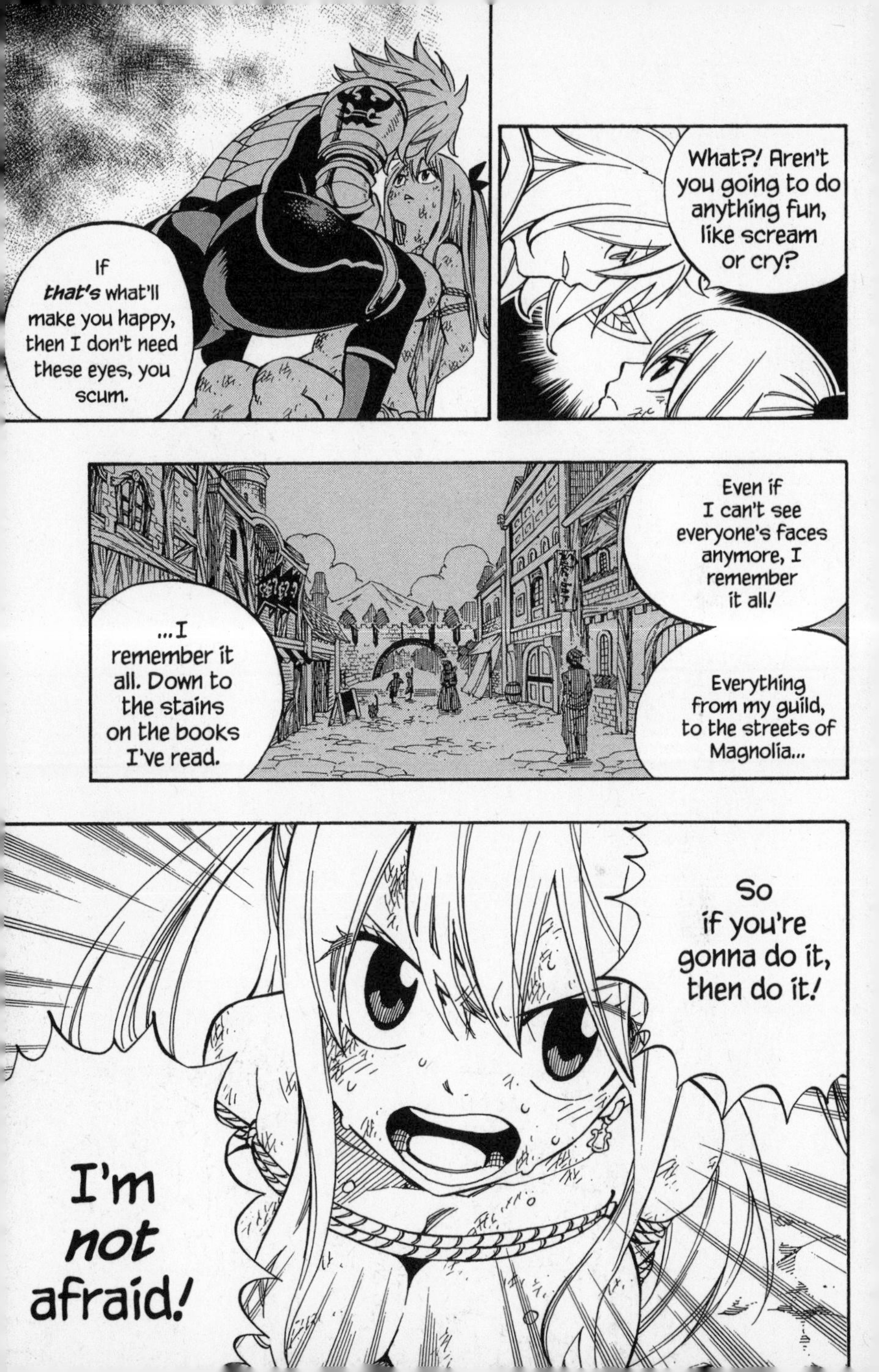
What?! Aren't you going to do anything fun, like scream or cry?
If *that's* what'll make you happy, then I don't need these eyes, you scum.
Even if I can't see everyone's faces anymore, I remember it all!
Everything from my guild, to the streets of Magnolia...
...I remember it all. Down to the stains on the books I've read.
So if you're gonna do it, then do it!
I'm *not* afraid!

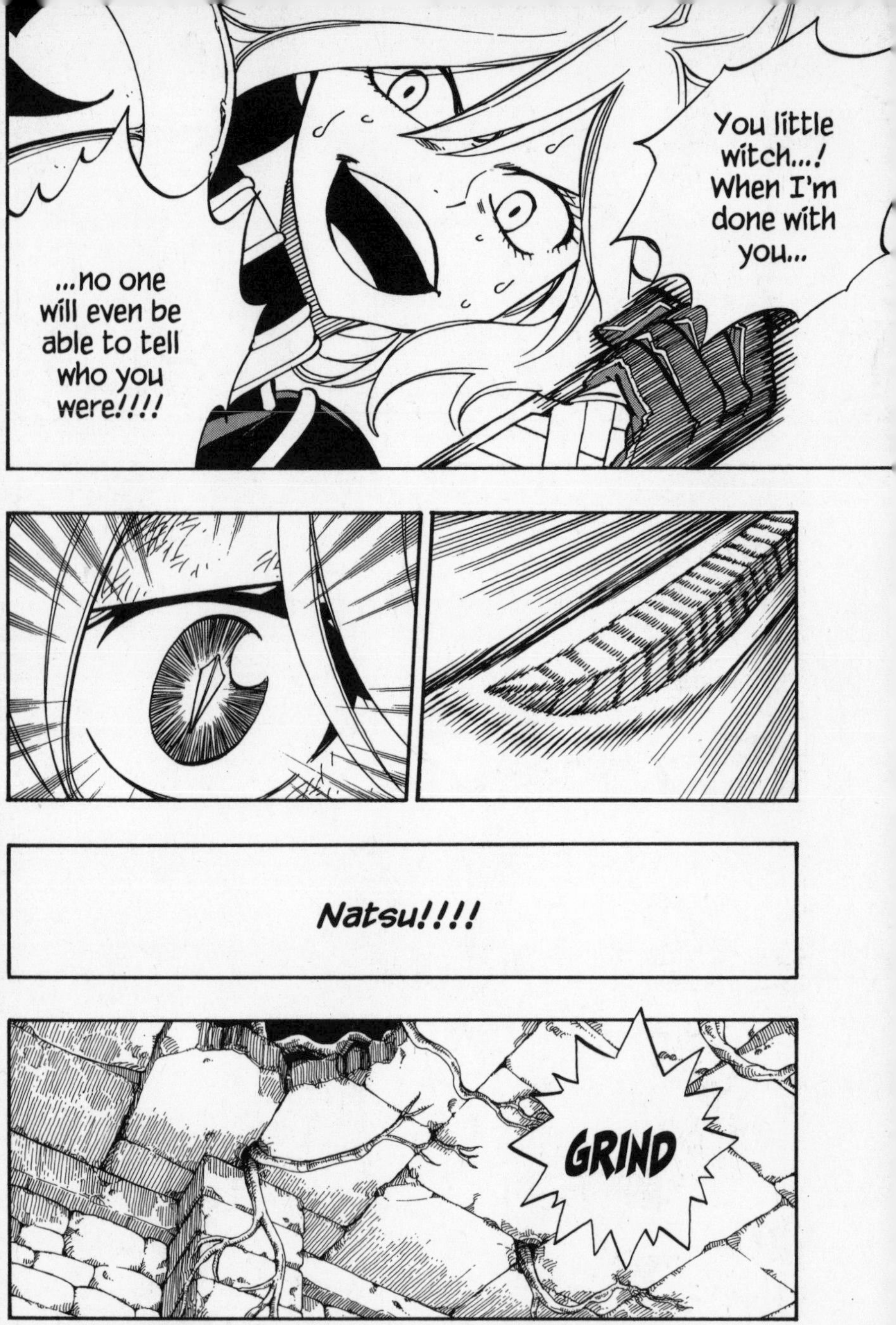
You little witch...! When I'm done with you...
...no one will even be able to tell who you were!!!!
Natsu!!!!
GRIND

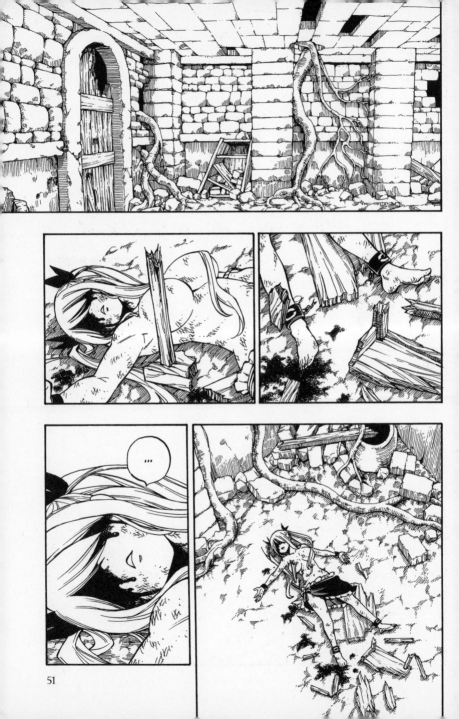

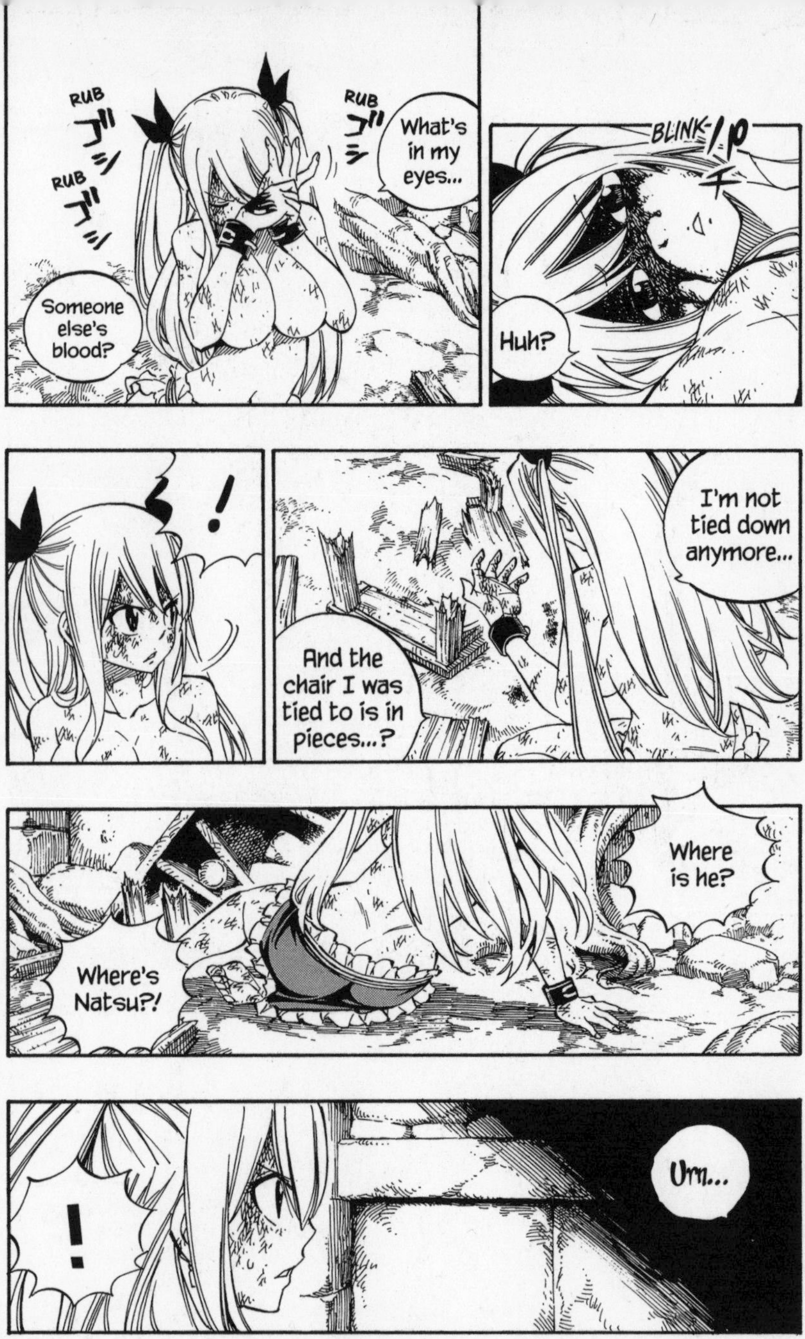
BLINK
Huh?
RUB
What's in my eyes...
RUB
RUB
Someone else's blood?
I'm not tied down anymore...
And the chair I was tied to is in pieces...?
!
Where is he?
Where's Natsu?!
Urn...
!

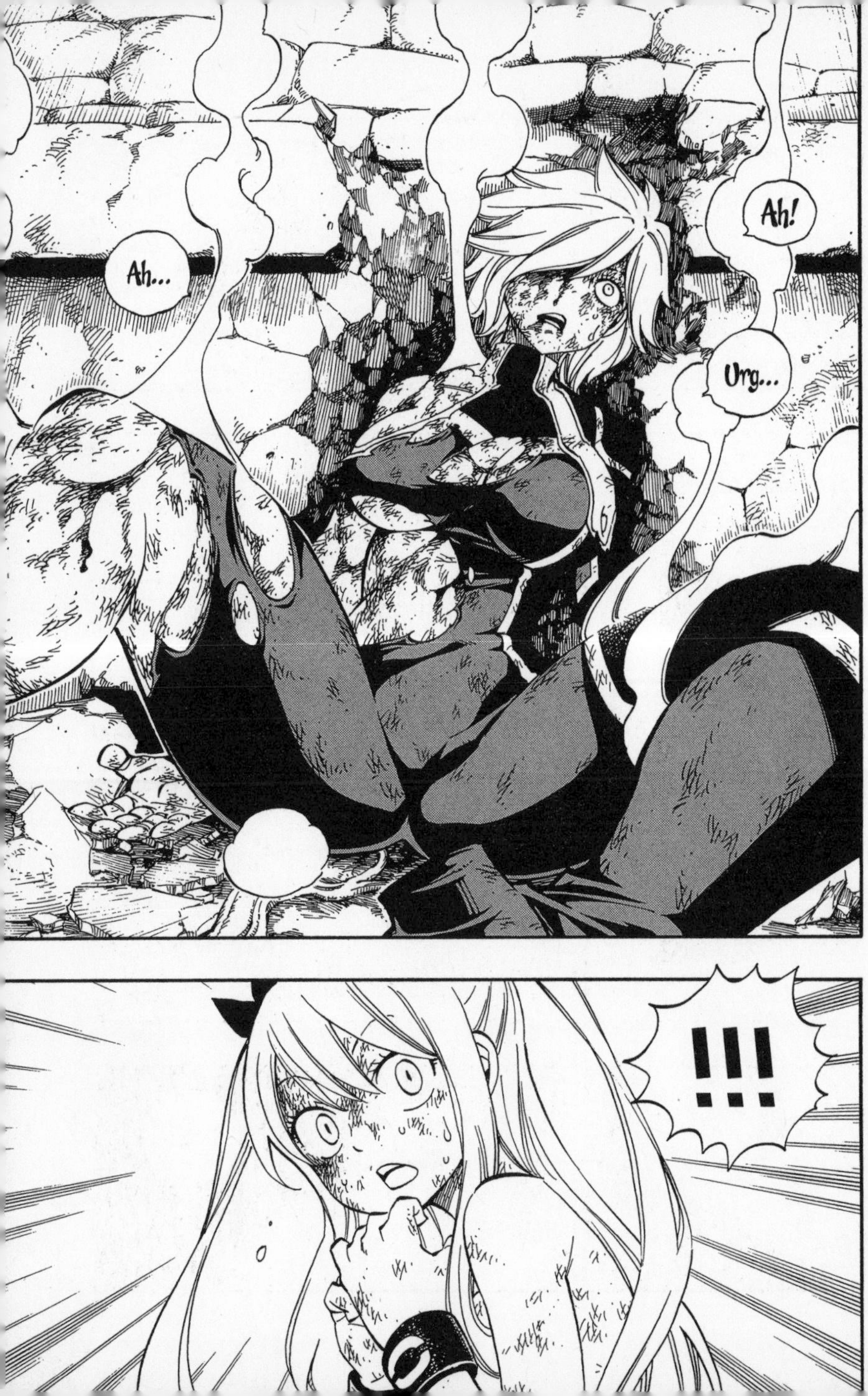
Ah!
Ah...
Urg...
!!!

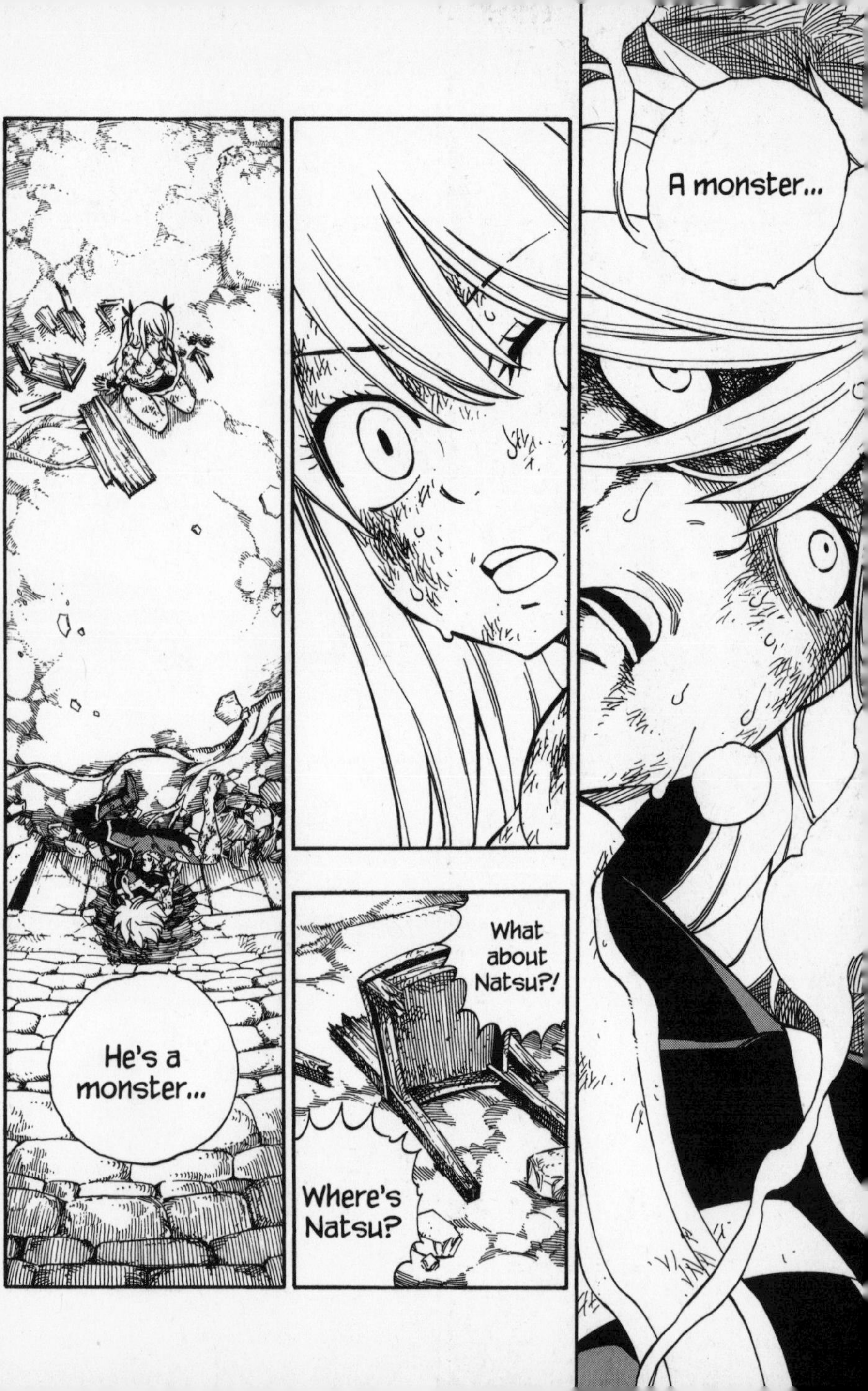
A monster...
What about Natsu?!
Where's Natsu?
He's a monster...

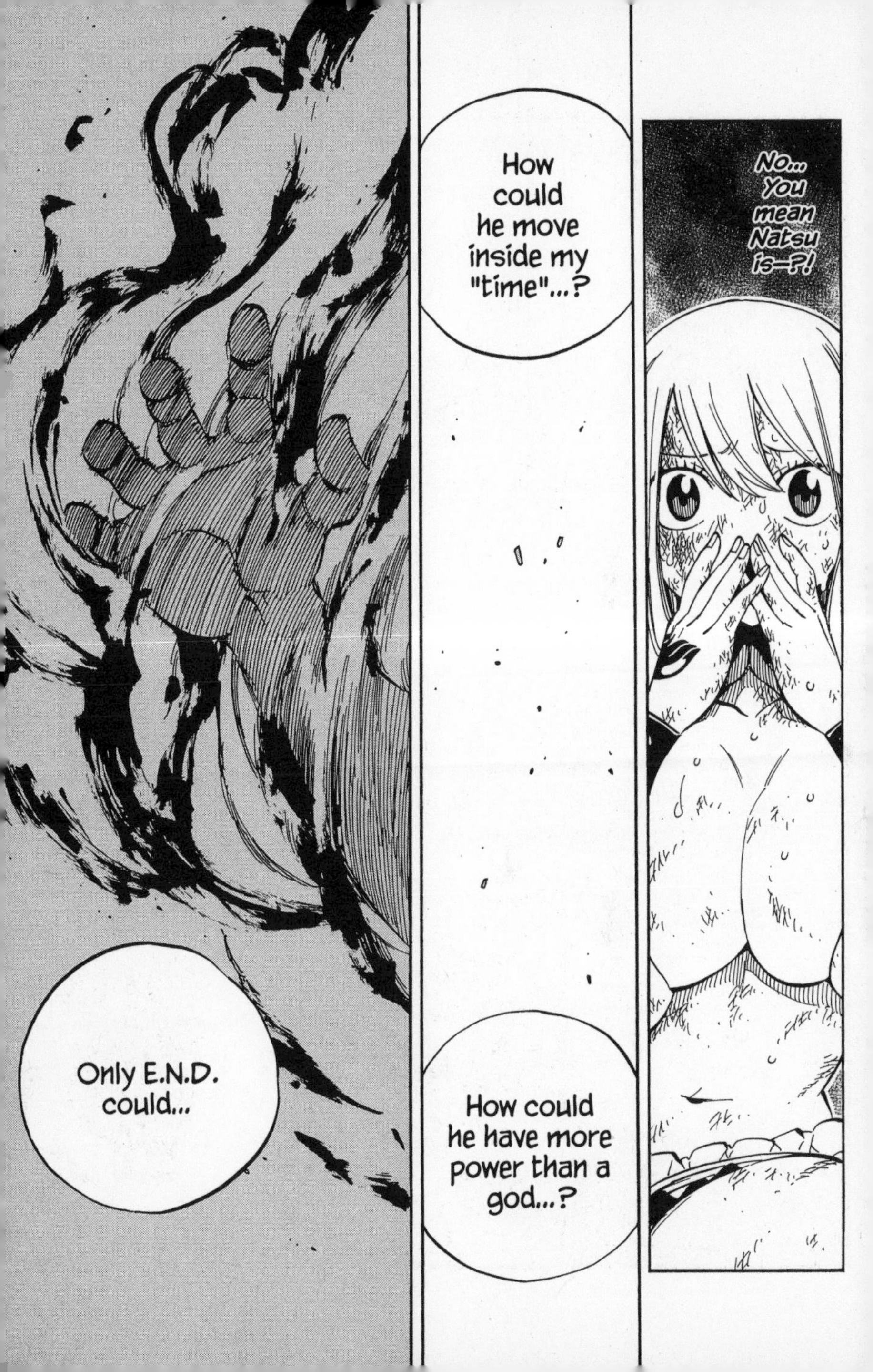
No... You mean Natsu is—?!
How could he move inside my "time"...?
How could he have more power than a god...?
Only E.N.D. could...

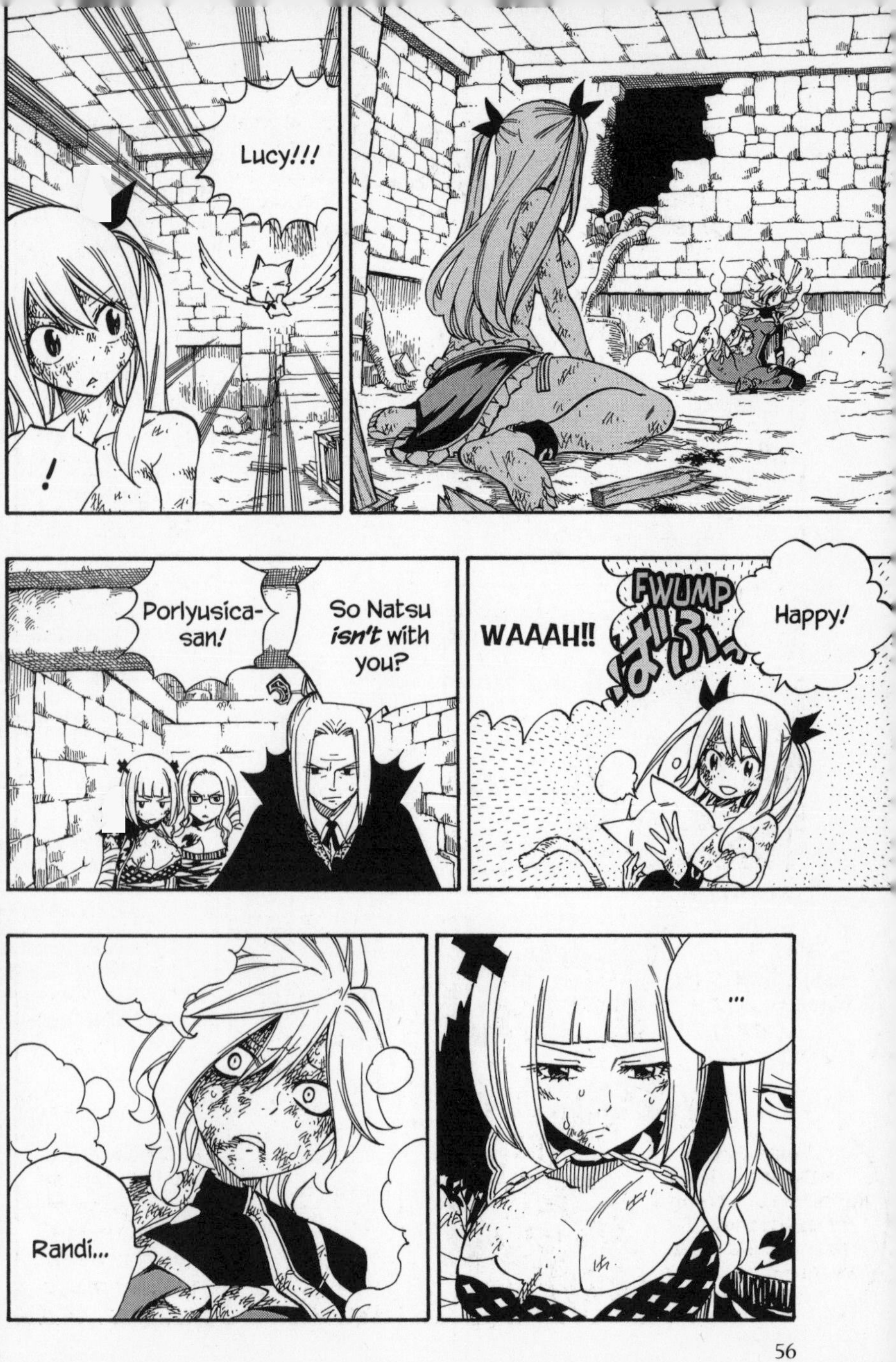
Lucy!!!
!
Happy!
FWUMP
WAAAH!!
So Natsu *isn't* with you?
Porlyusica-san!
...
Randi...

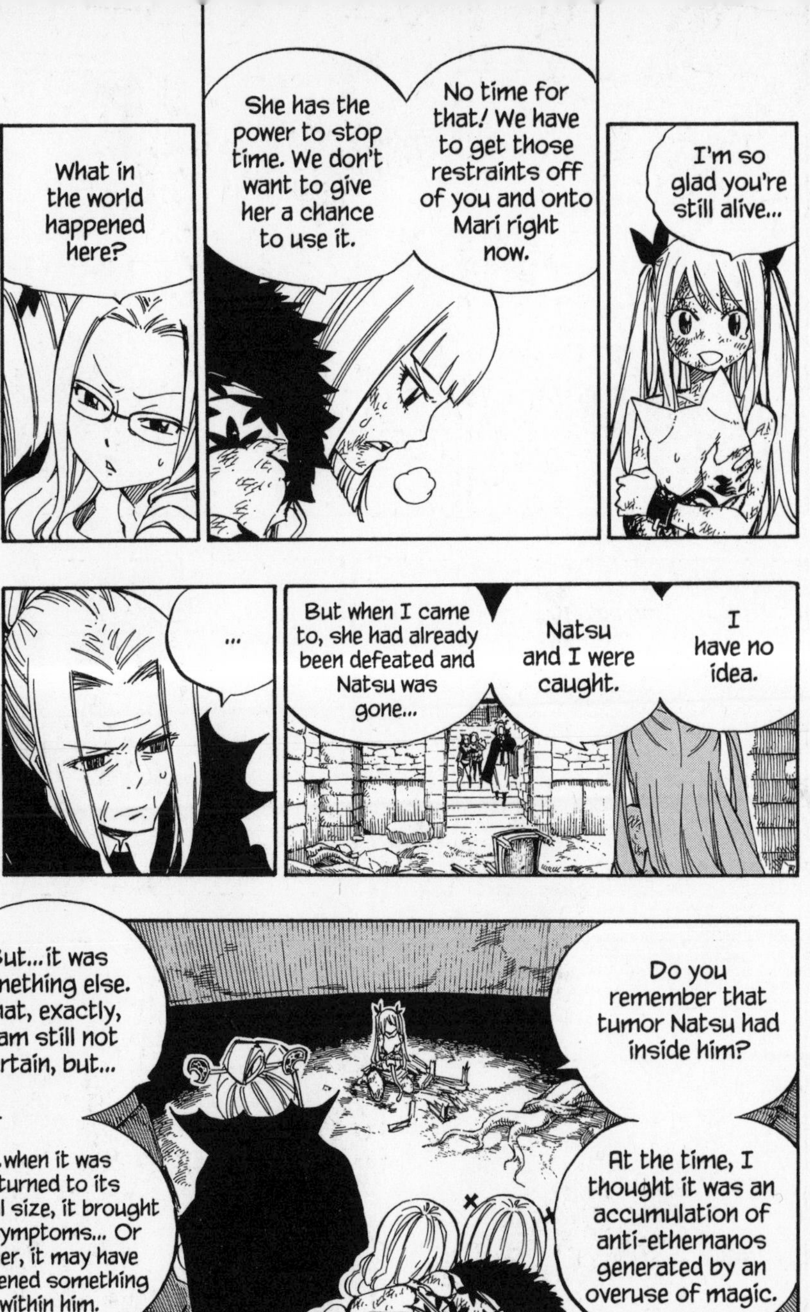
I'm so glad you're still alive...
No time for that! We have to get those restraints off of you and onto Mari right now.
She has the power to stop time. We don't want to give her a chance to use it.
What in the world happened here?
I have no idea.
Natsu and I were caught.
But when I came to, she had already been defeated and Natsu was gone...
...
Do you remember that tumor Natsu had inside him?
At the time, I thought it was an accumulation of anti-ethernanos generated by an overuse of magic.
But...it was something else. What, exactly, I am still not certain, but...
...when it was returned to its normal size, it brought on symptoms... Or rather, it may have awakened something within him.

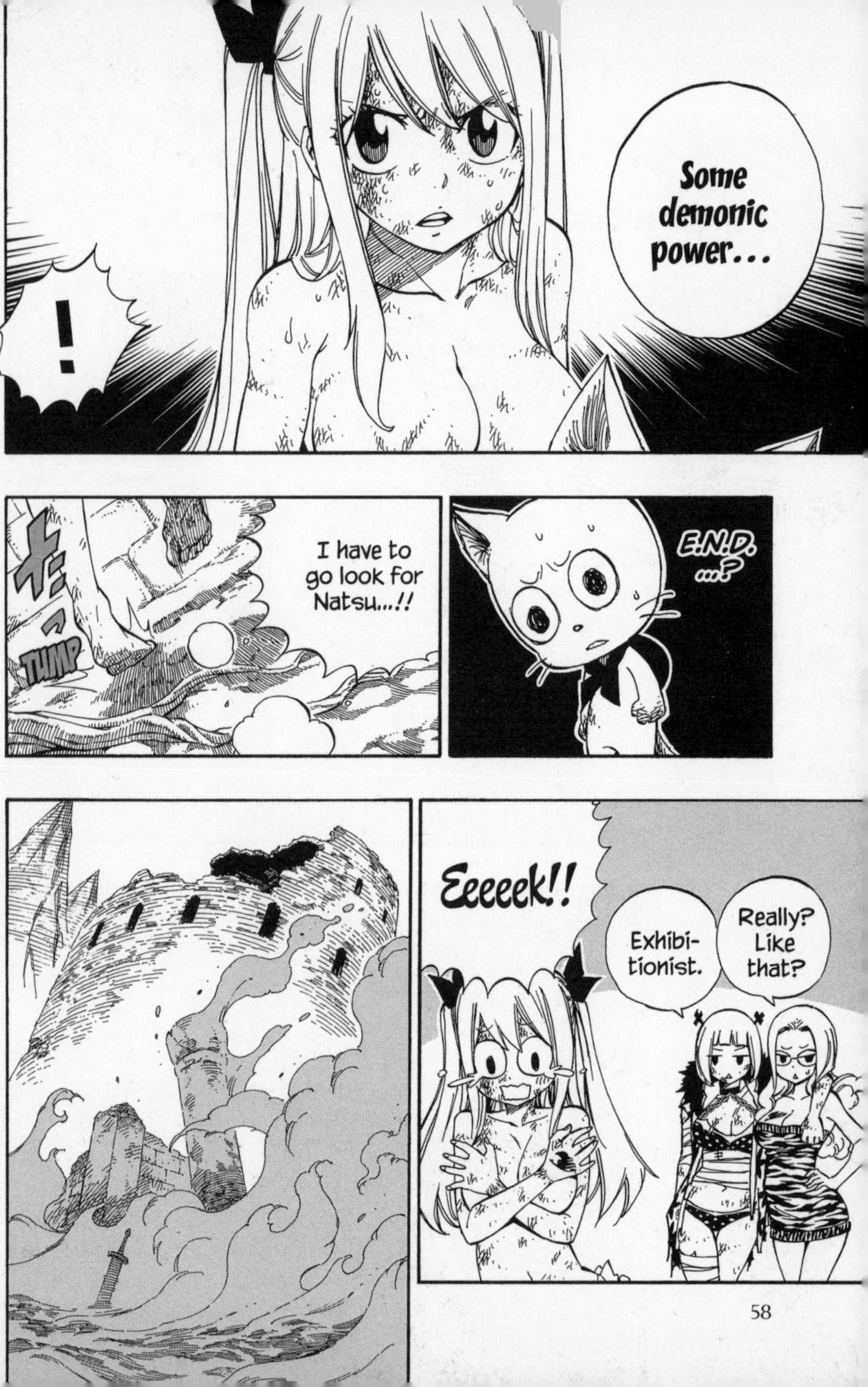

Some demonic power...
!
E.N.D. ...?
I have to go look for Natsu...!!
TUMP
Eeeeek!!
Really? Like that?
Exhibi-tionist.

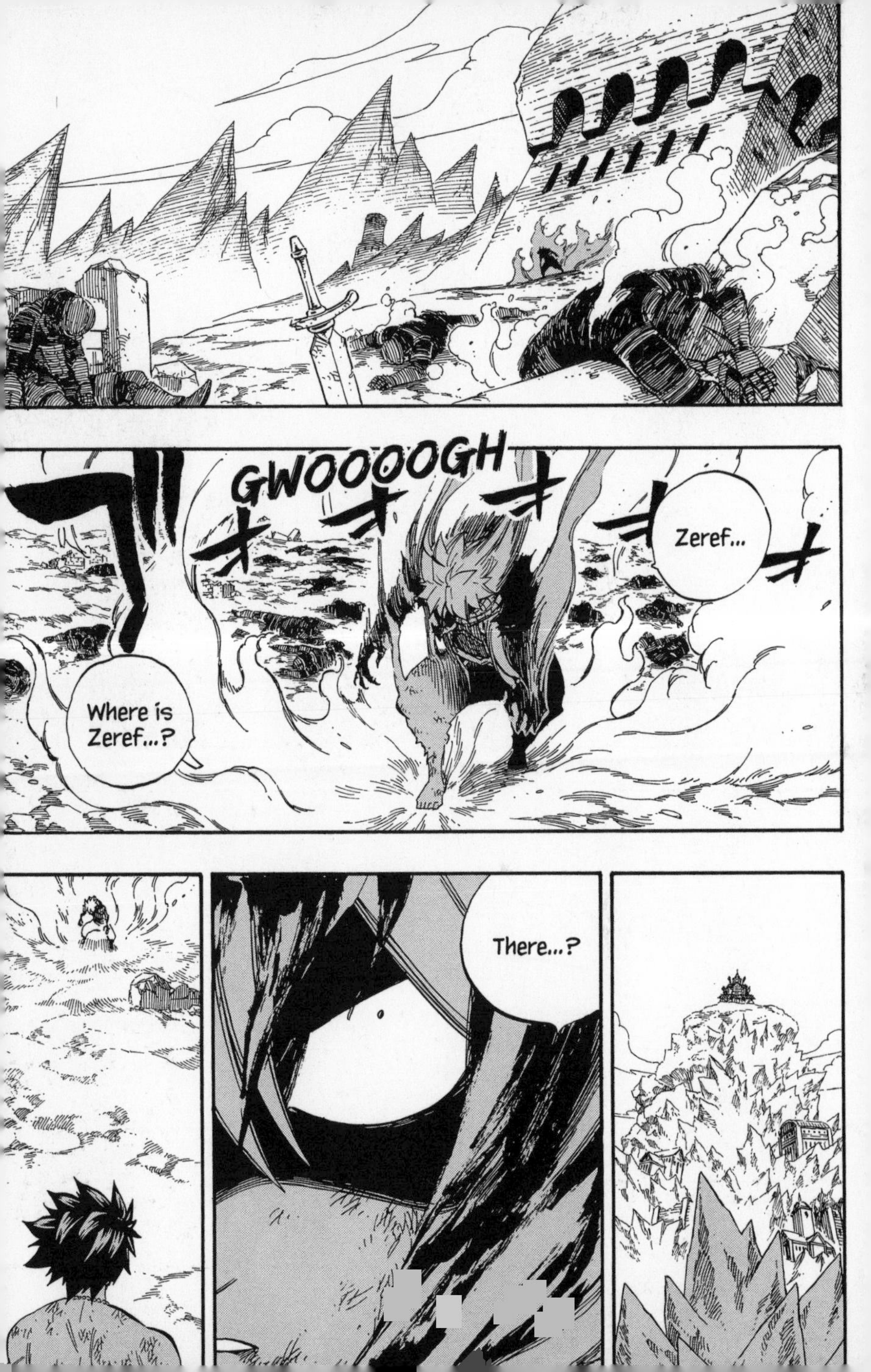
GWOOOOGH
Zeref...
Where is Zeref...?
There...?

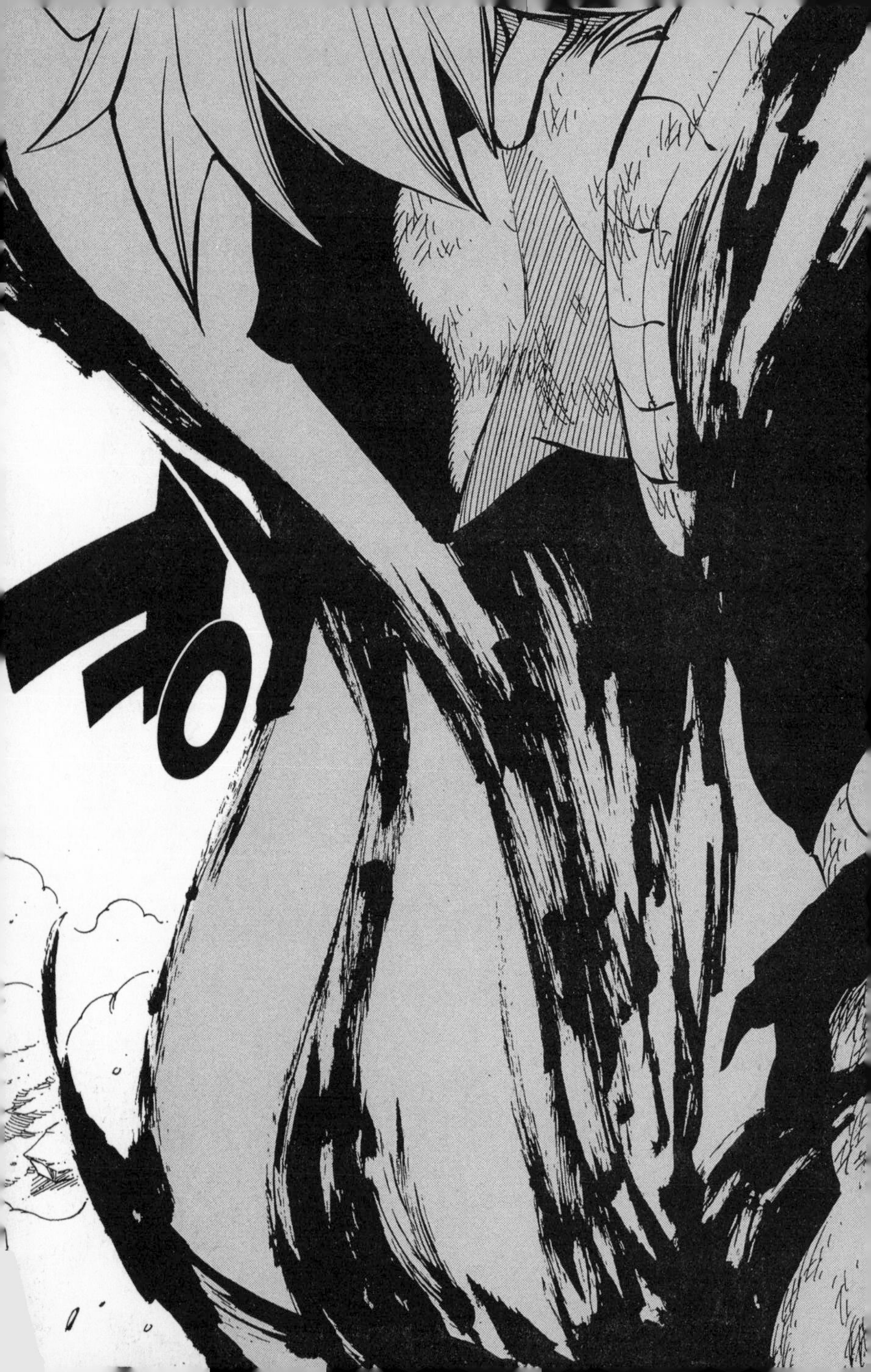
FO

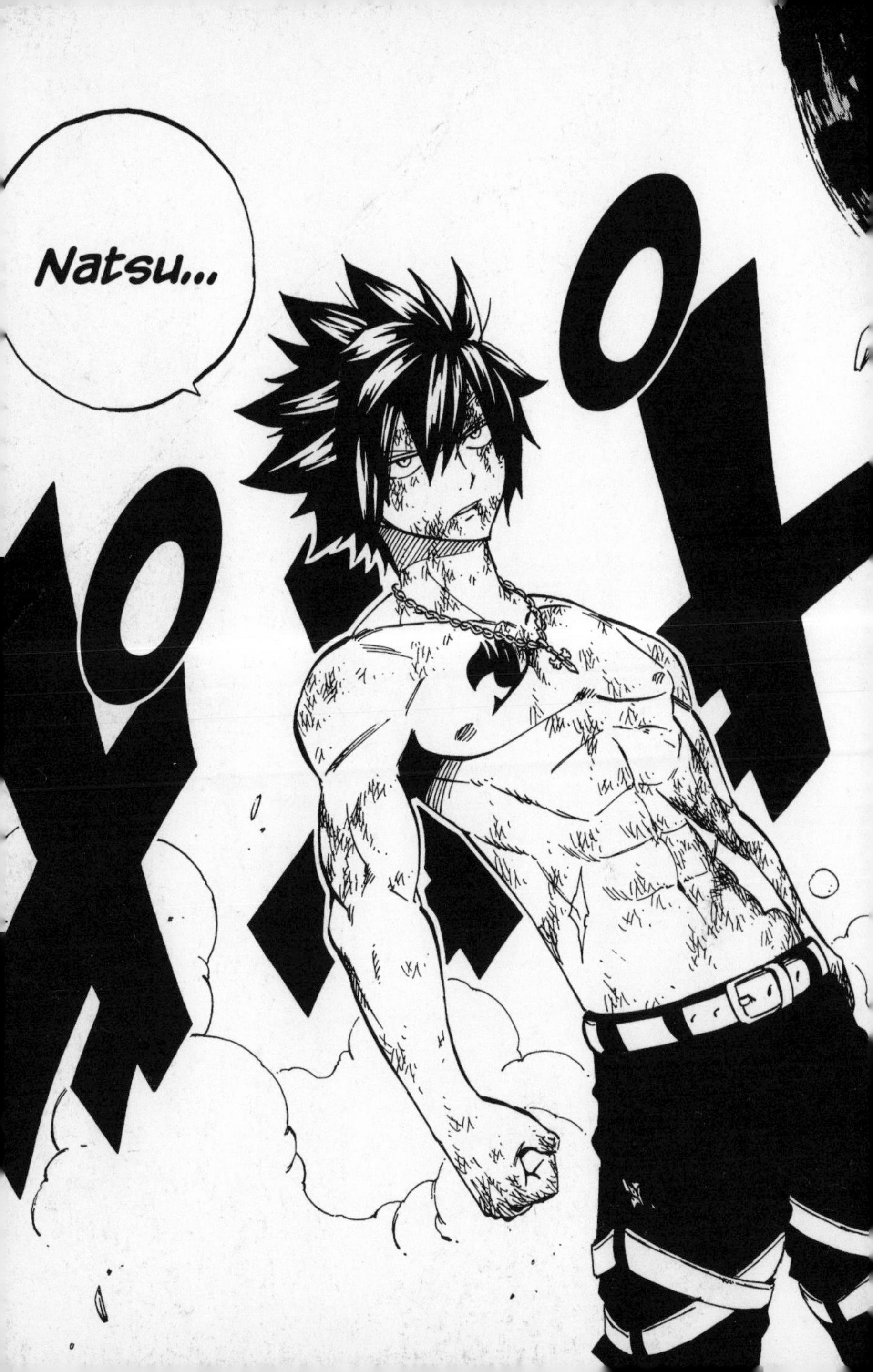
Natsu...

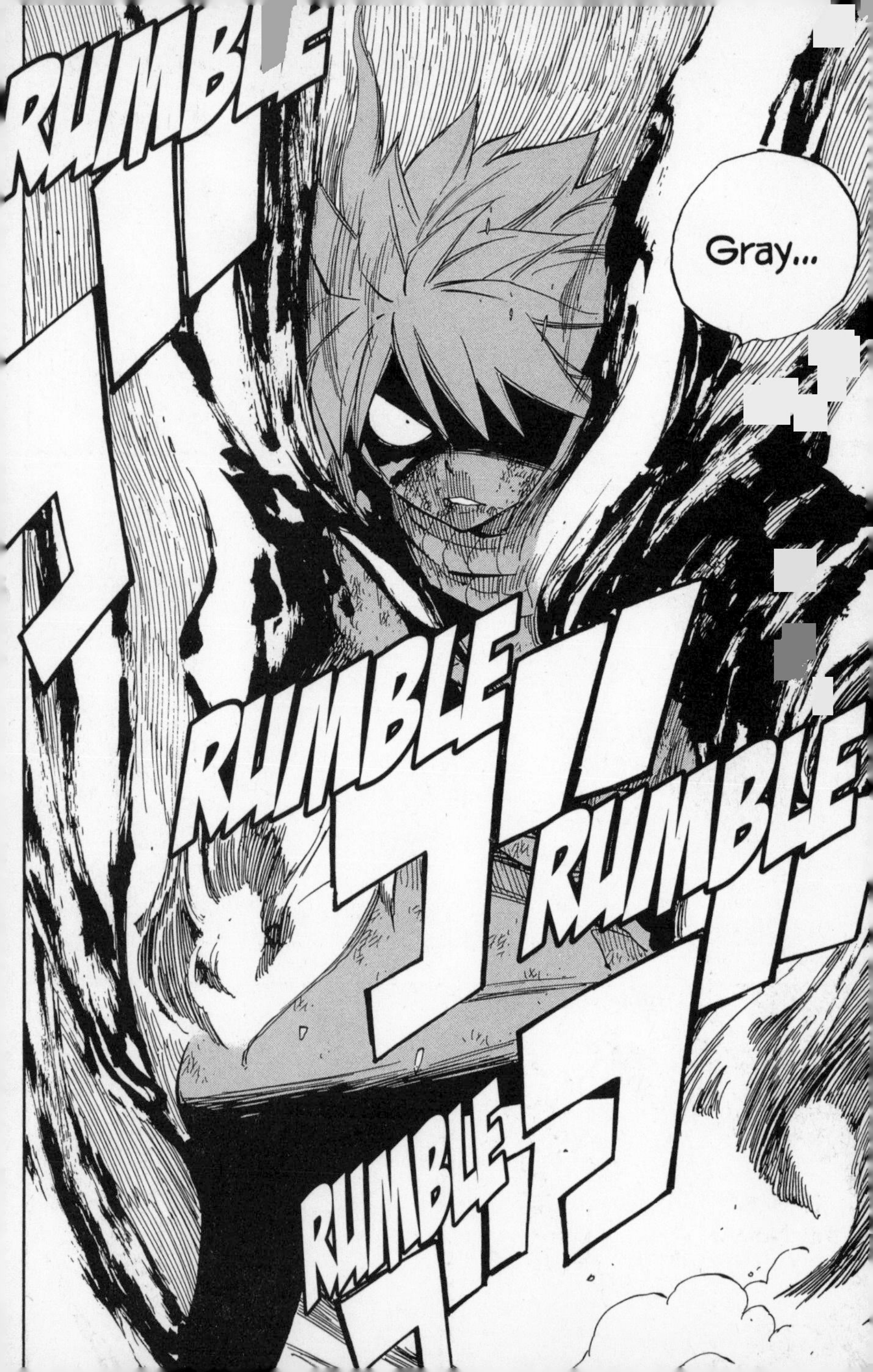
Gray...
RUMBLE
RUMBLE
RUMBLE
RUMBLE

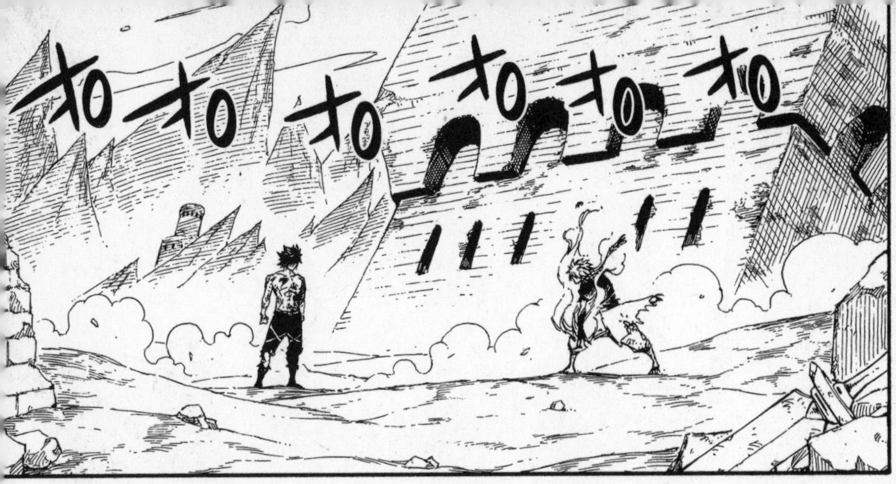

FAIRY TAIL

Chapter 504: The Gash

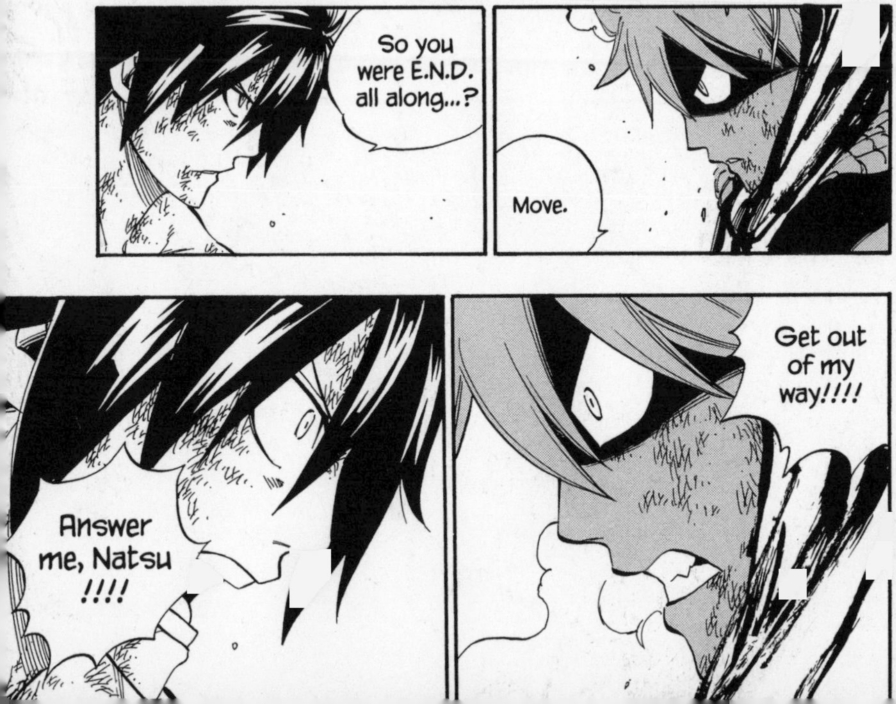
Move.
So you were E.N.D. all along...?
Get out of my way!!!!
Answer me, Natsu !!!!

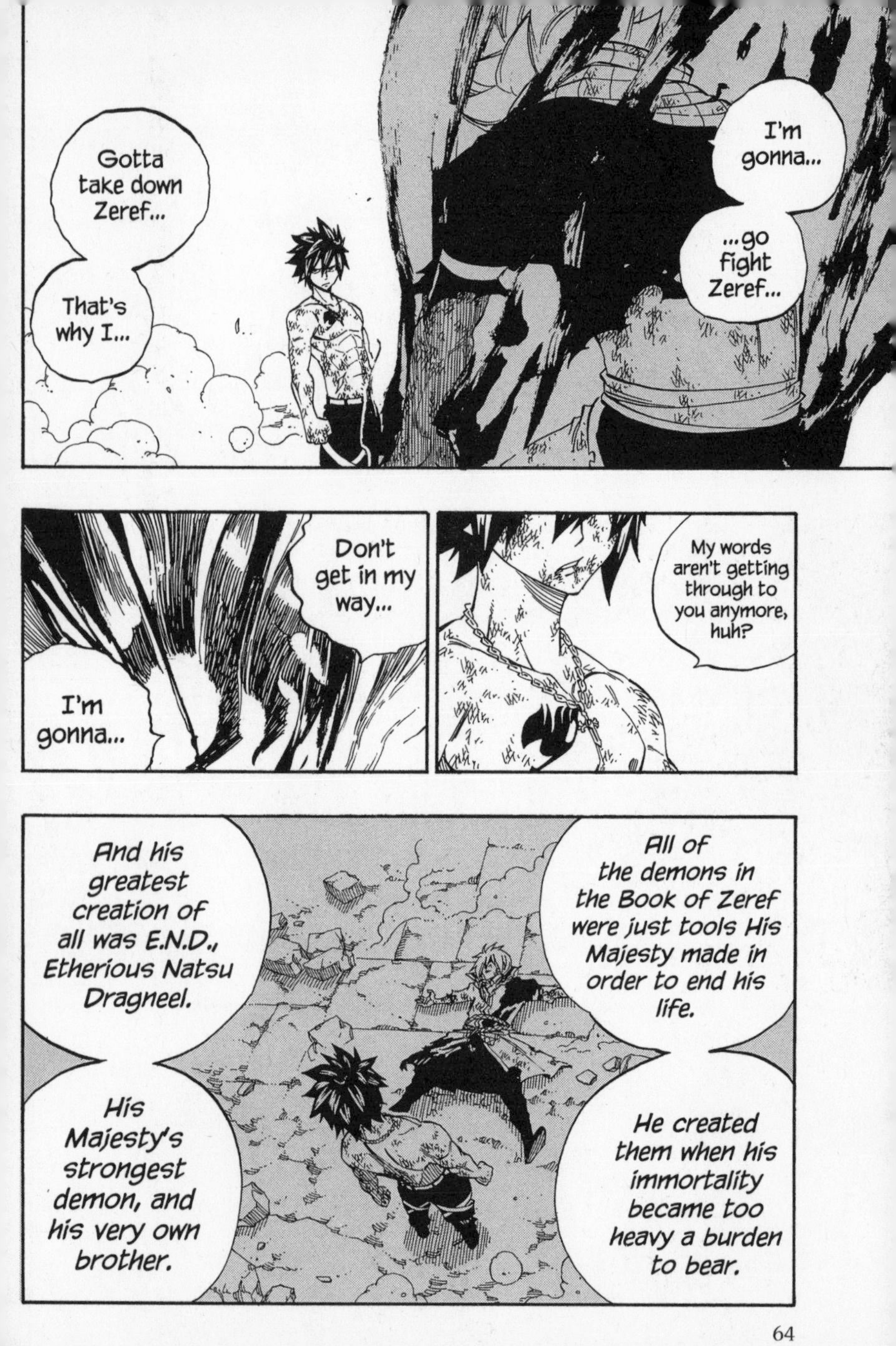
I'm gonna...
...go fight Zeref...
Gotta take down Zeref...
That's why I...
My words aren't getting through to you anymore, huh?
Don't get in my way...
I'm gonna...
All of the demons in the Book of Zeref were just tools His Majesty made in order to end his life.
He created them when his immortality became too heavy a burden to bear.
And his greatest creation of all was E.N.D., Etherious Natsu Dragneel.
His Majesty's strongest demon, and his very own brother.

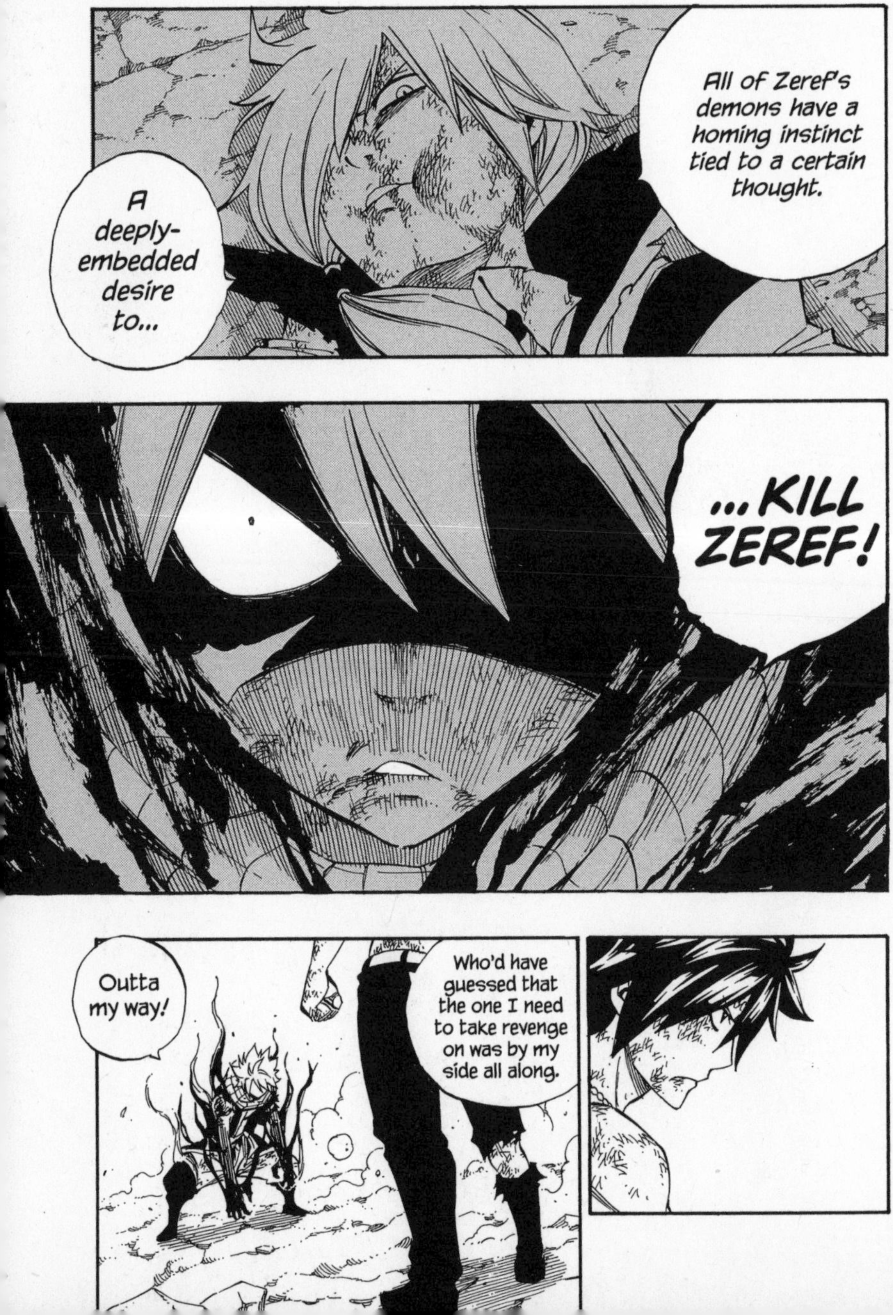
All of Zeref's demons have a homing instinct tied to a certain thought.
A deeply-embedded desire to...
...KILL ZEREF!
Who'd have guessed that the one I need to take revenge on was by my side all along.
Outta my way!

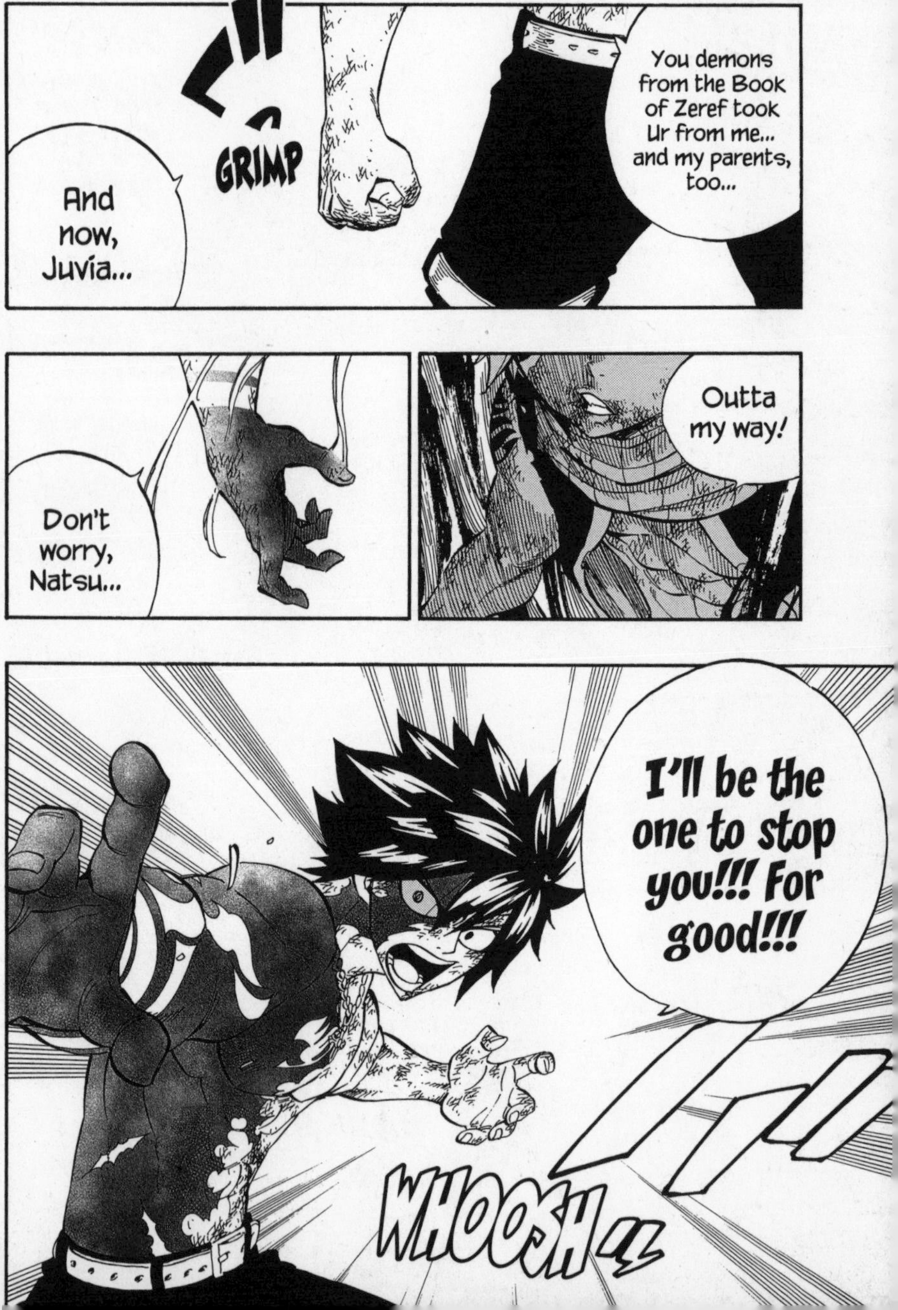
You demons from the Book of Zeref took Ur from me... and my parents, too...
GRIMP
And now, Juvia...
Outta my way!
Don't worry, Natsu...
I'll be the one to stop you!!! For good!!!
WHOOSH

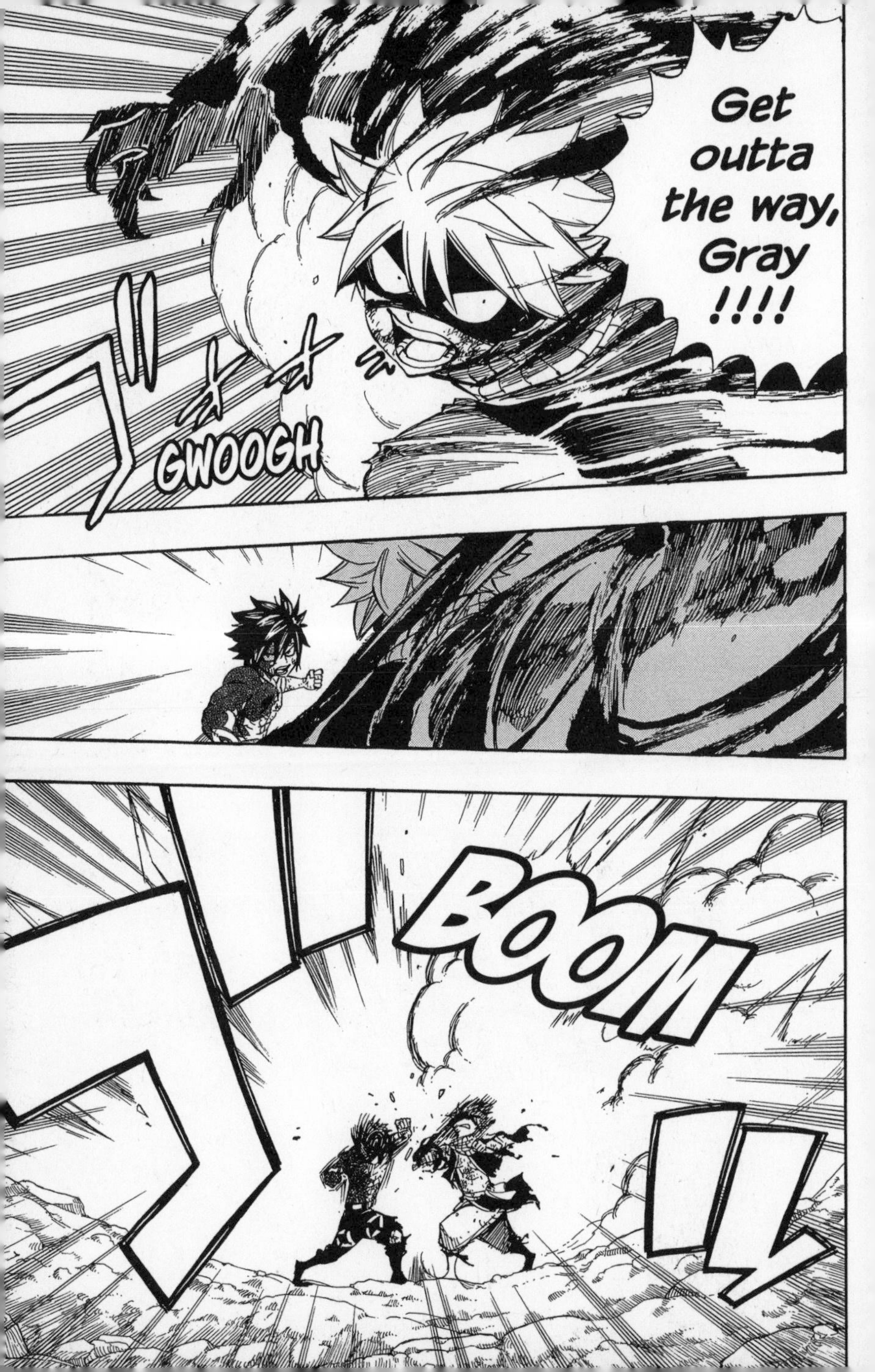

Get outta the way, Gray !!!!
GWOOGH
BOOM

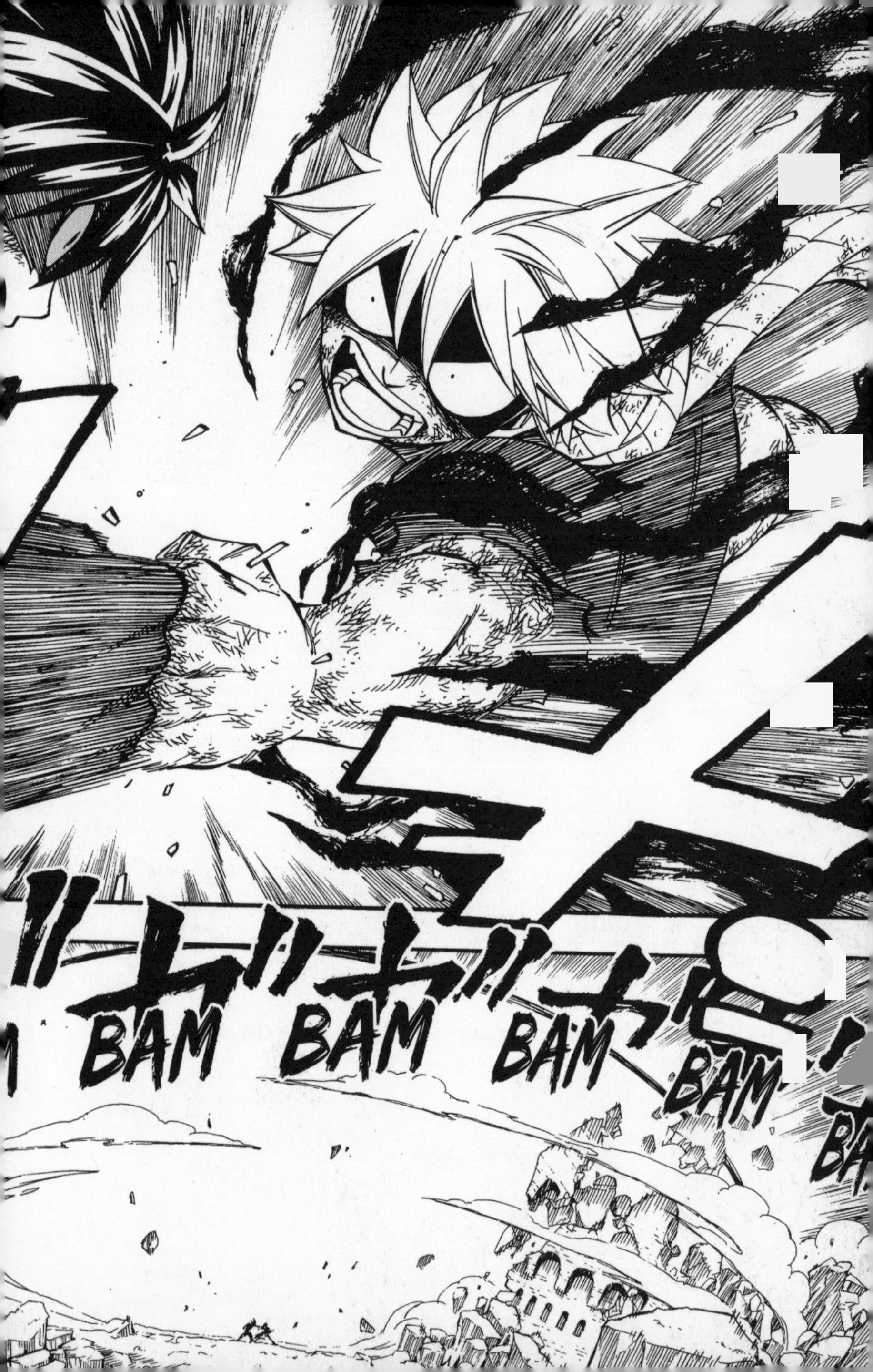
BAM BAM BAM BAM

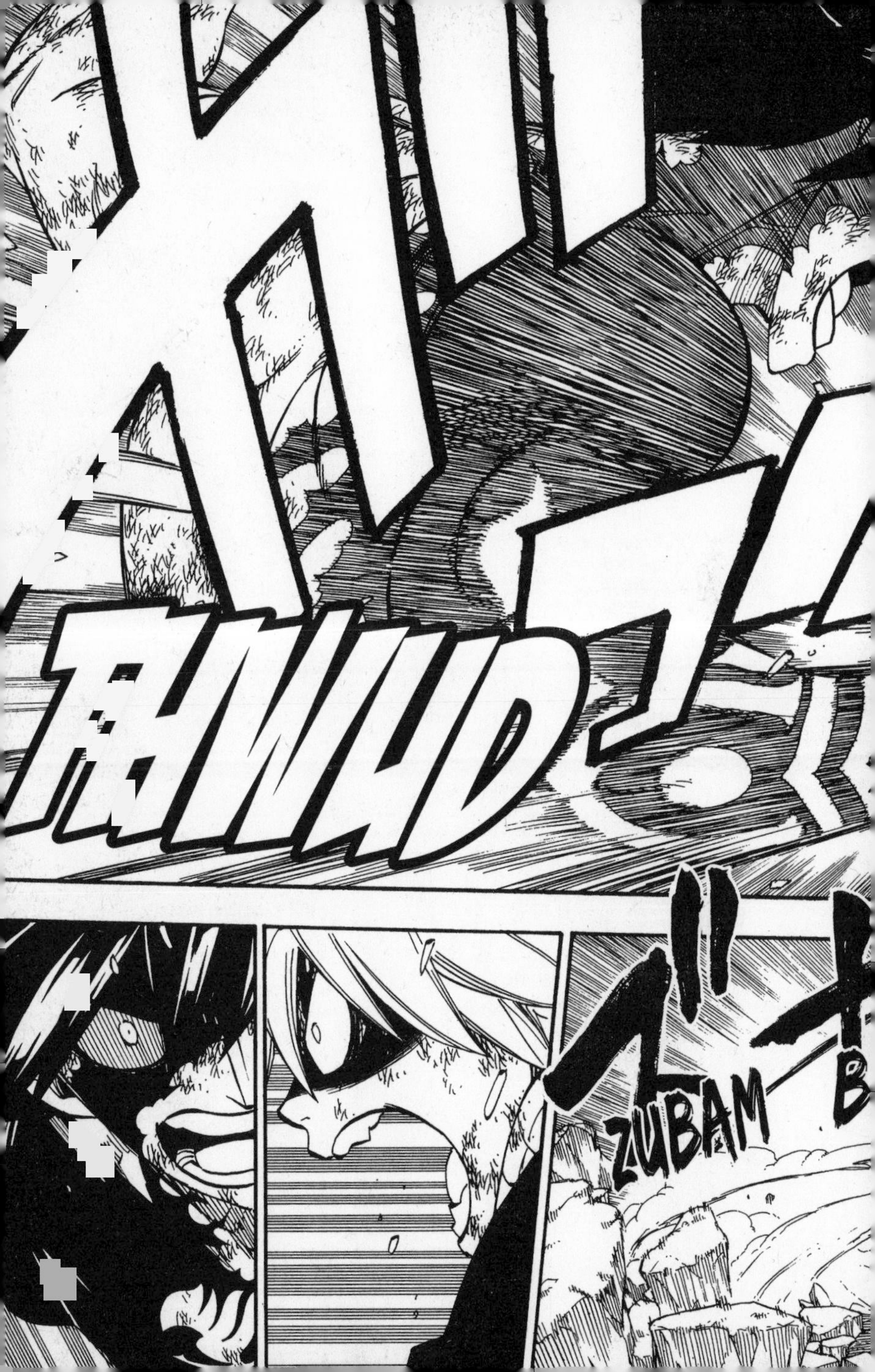
THUD
ZUBAM

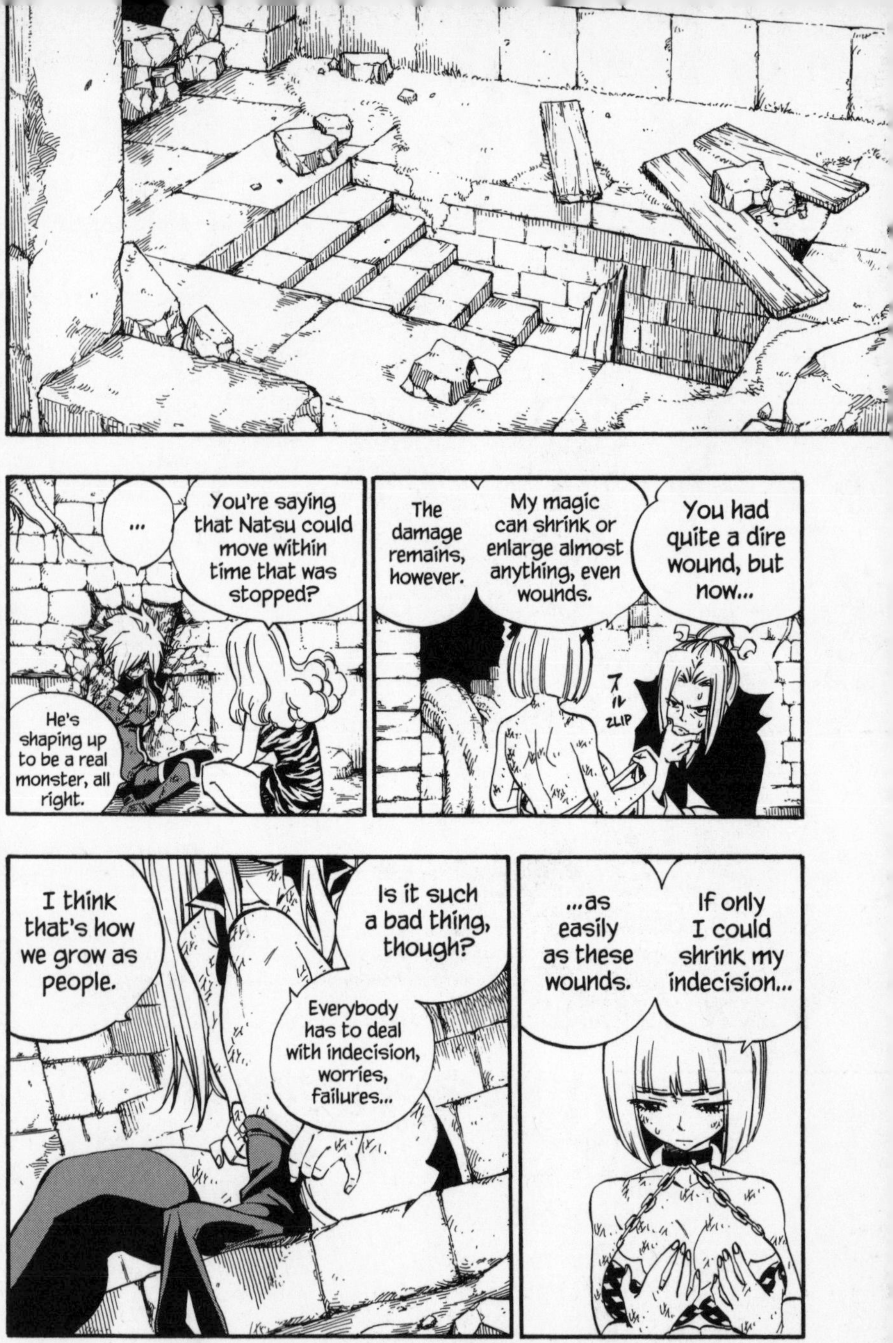
You had quite a dire wound, but now...
My magic can shrink or enlarge almost anything, even wounds.
The damage remains, however.
ZLIP
You're saying that Natsu could move within time that was stopped?
...
He's shaping up to be a real monster, all right.
If only I could shrink my indecision...
...as easily as these wounds.
Is it such a bad thing, though?
Everybody has to deal with indecision, worries, failures...
I think that's how we grow as people.

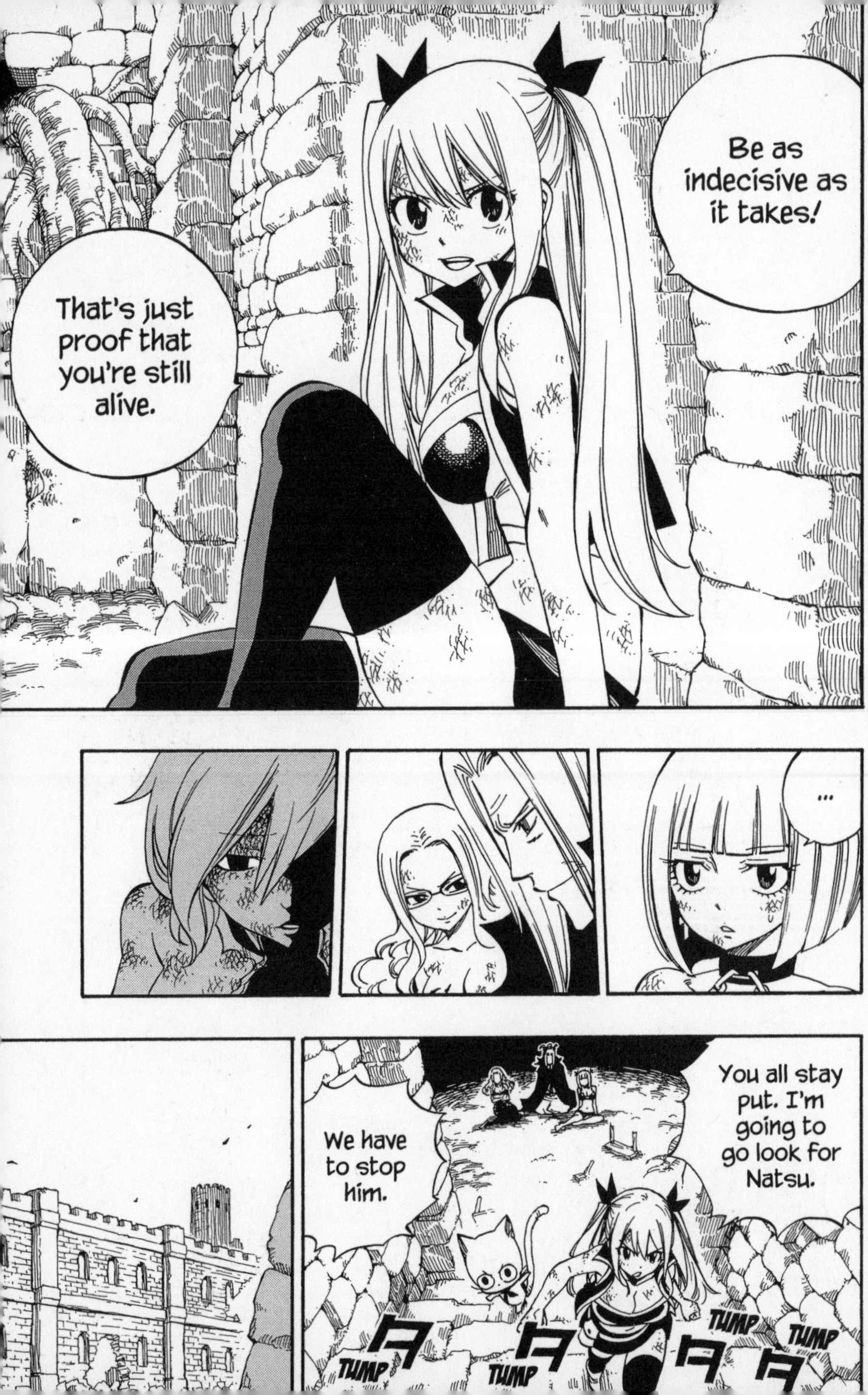
Be as indecisive as it takes!
That's just proof that you're still alive.
...
You all stay put. I'm going to go look for Natsu.
We have to stop him.
TUMP
TUMP
TUMP
TUMP

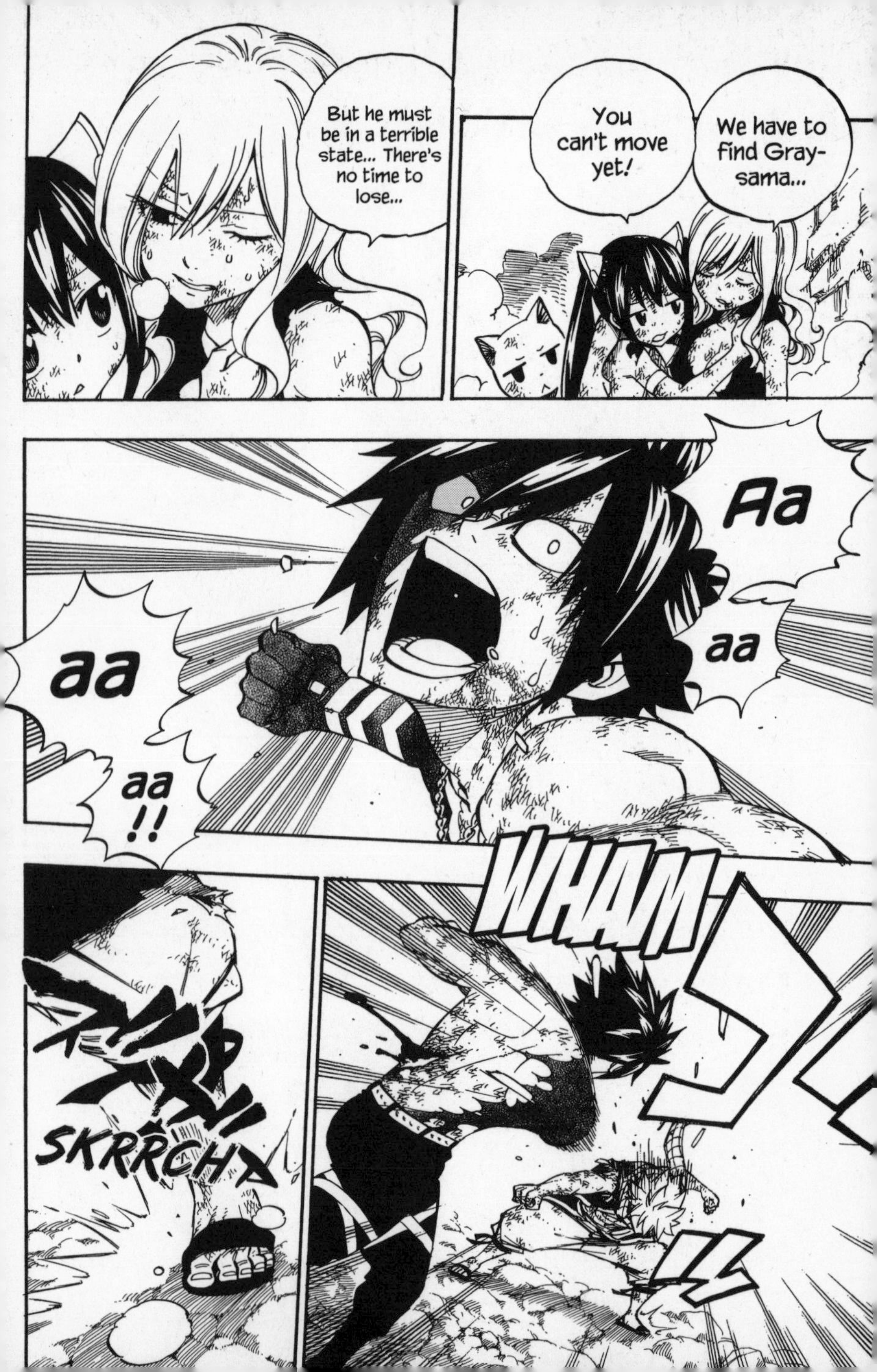
We have to find Gray-sama...
You can't move yet!
But he must be in a terrible state... There's no time to lose...
Aa
aa
aa
aa !!
WHAM
SKRRCH

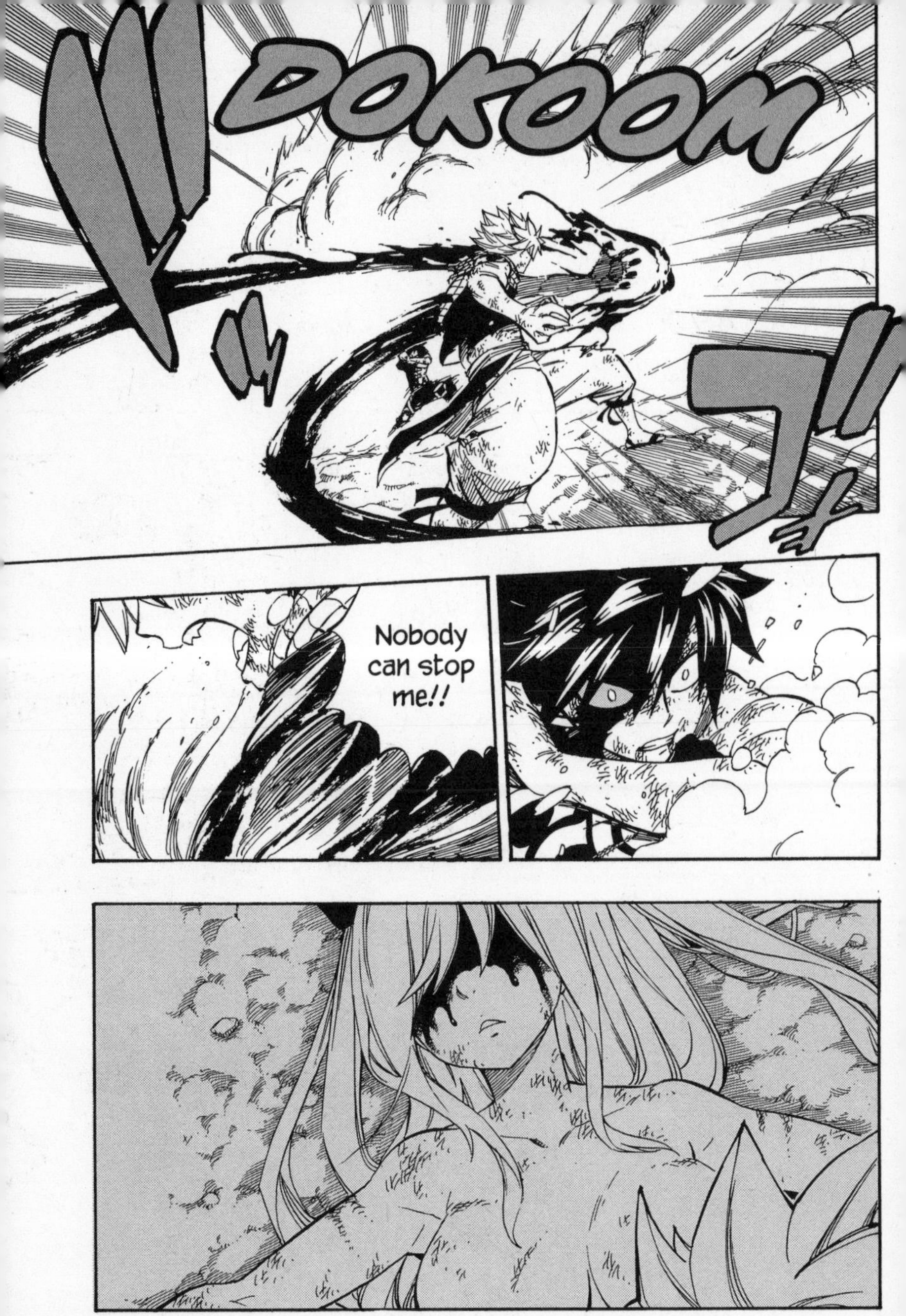
DOKOOM
Nobody can stop me!!

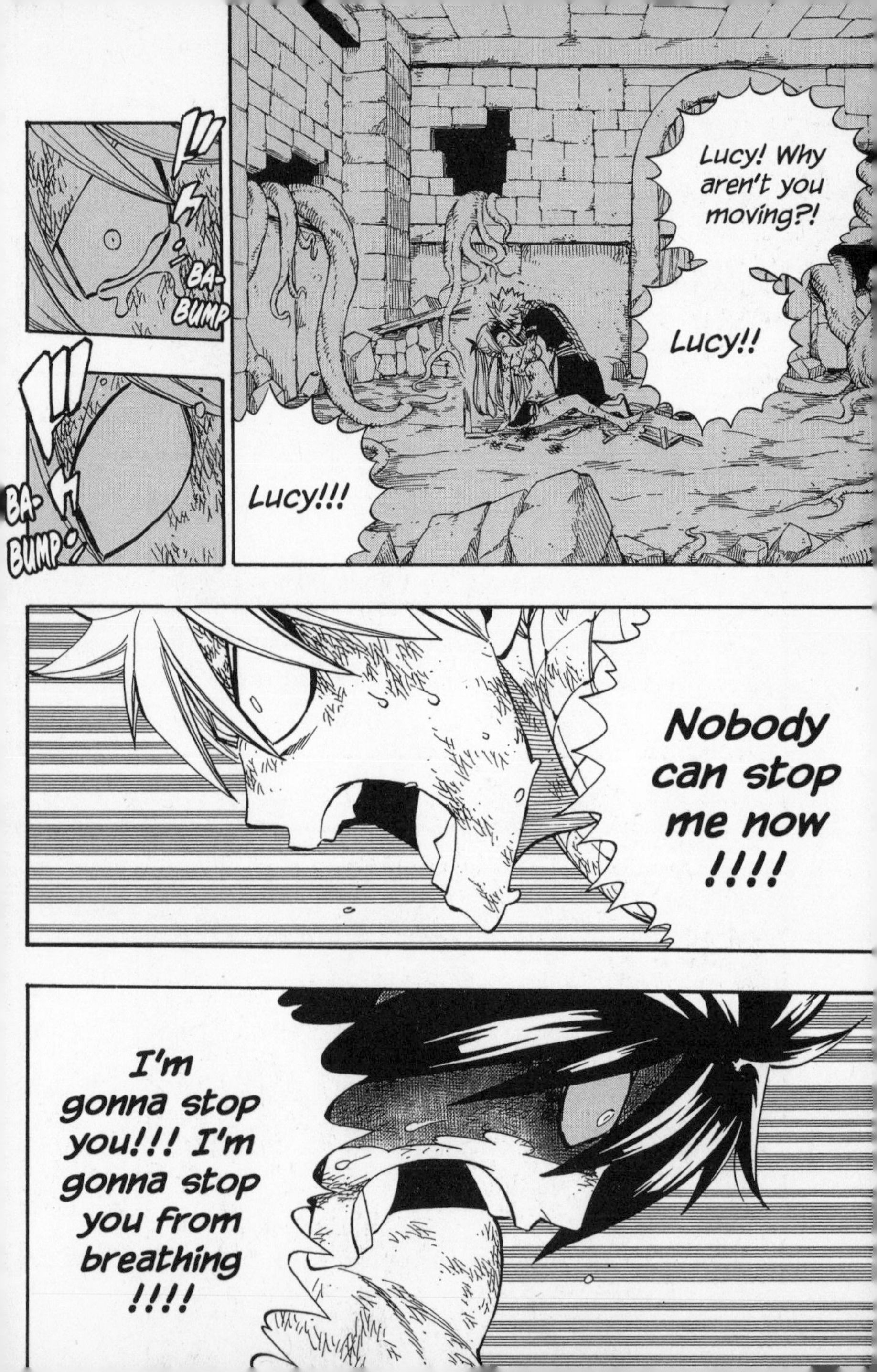
Lucy! Why aren't you moving?!
Lucy!!
Lucy!!!
BA-BUMP
BA-BUMP
Nobody can stop me now !!!!
I'm gonna stop you!!! I'm gonna stop you from breathing !!!!

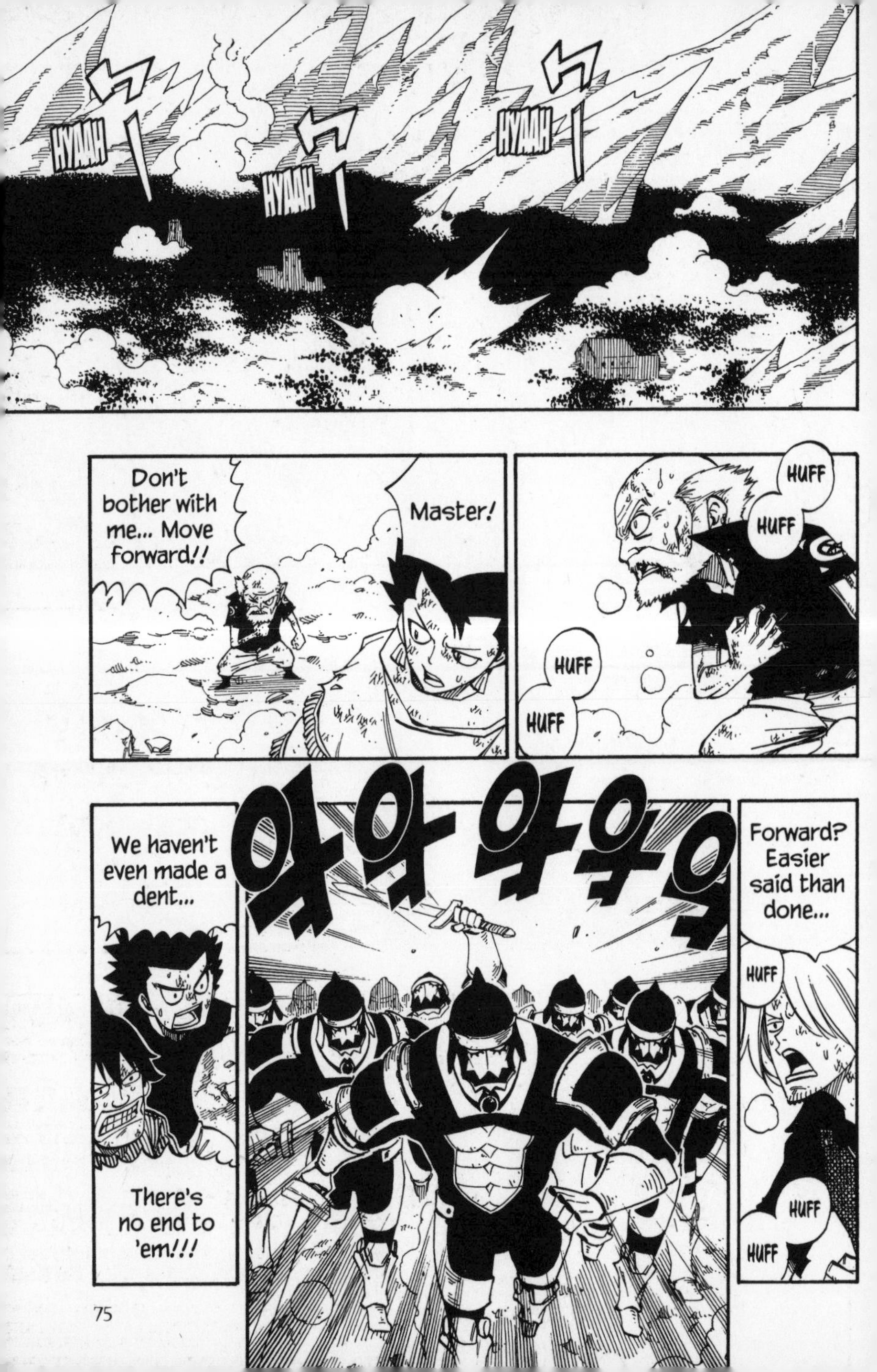
HYAAH
HYAAH
HYAAH
HUFF
HUFF
HUFF
HUFF
Master!
Don't bother with me... Move forward!!
Forward? Easier said than done...
HUFF
HUFF
HUFF
We haven't even made a dent...
There's no end to 'em!!!

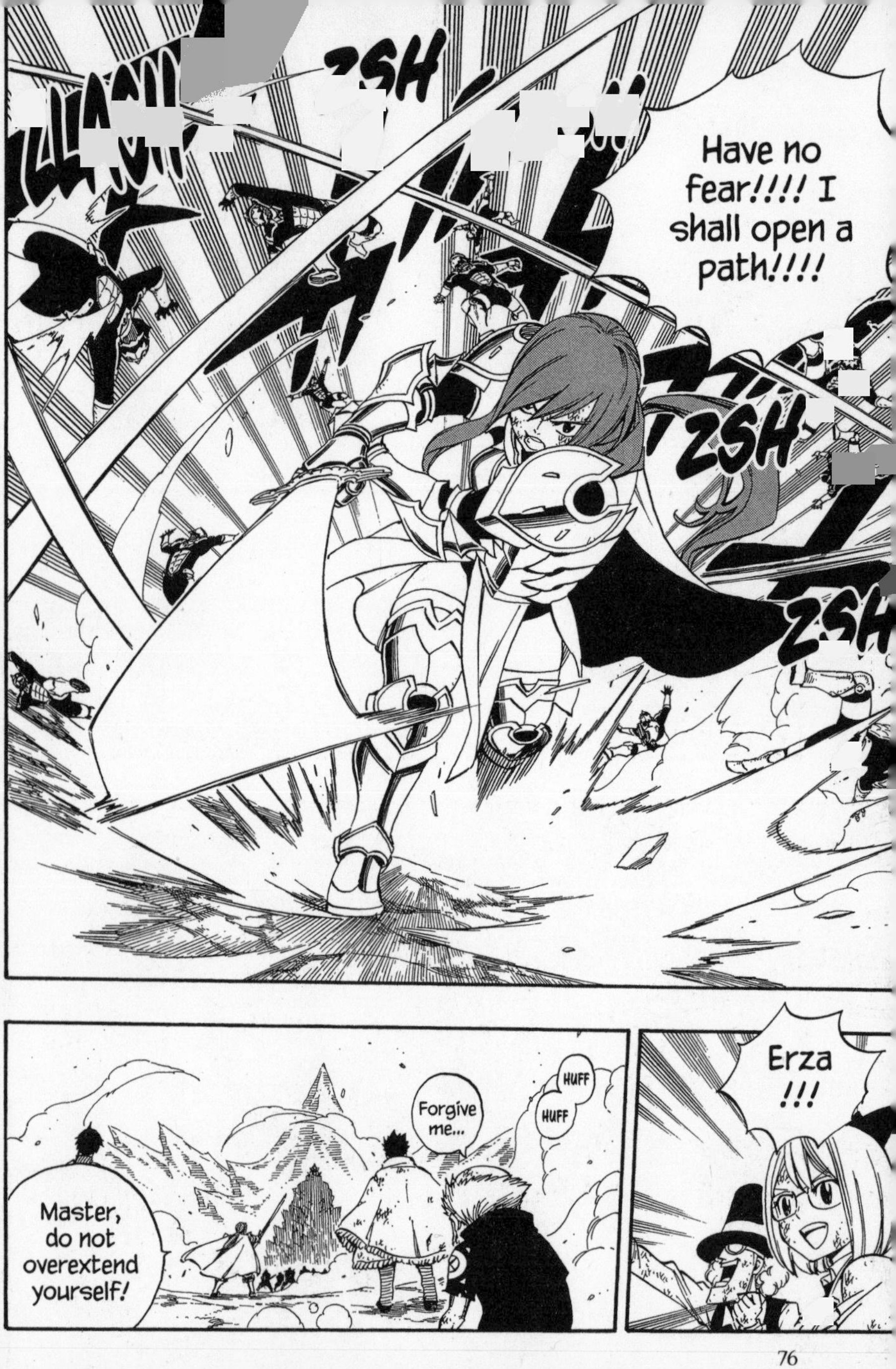
Have no fear!!!! I shall open a path!!!!
ZSH
ZSH
ZSH
Erza !!!
HUFF
HUFF
Forgive me...
Master, do not overextend yourself!

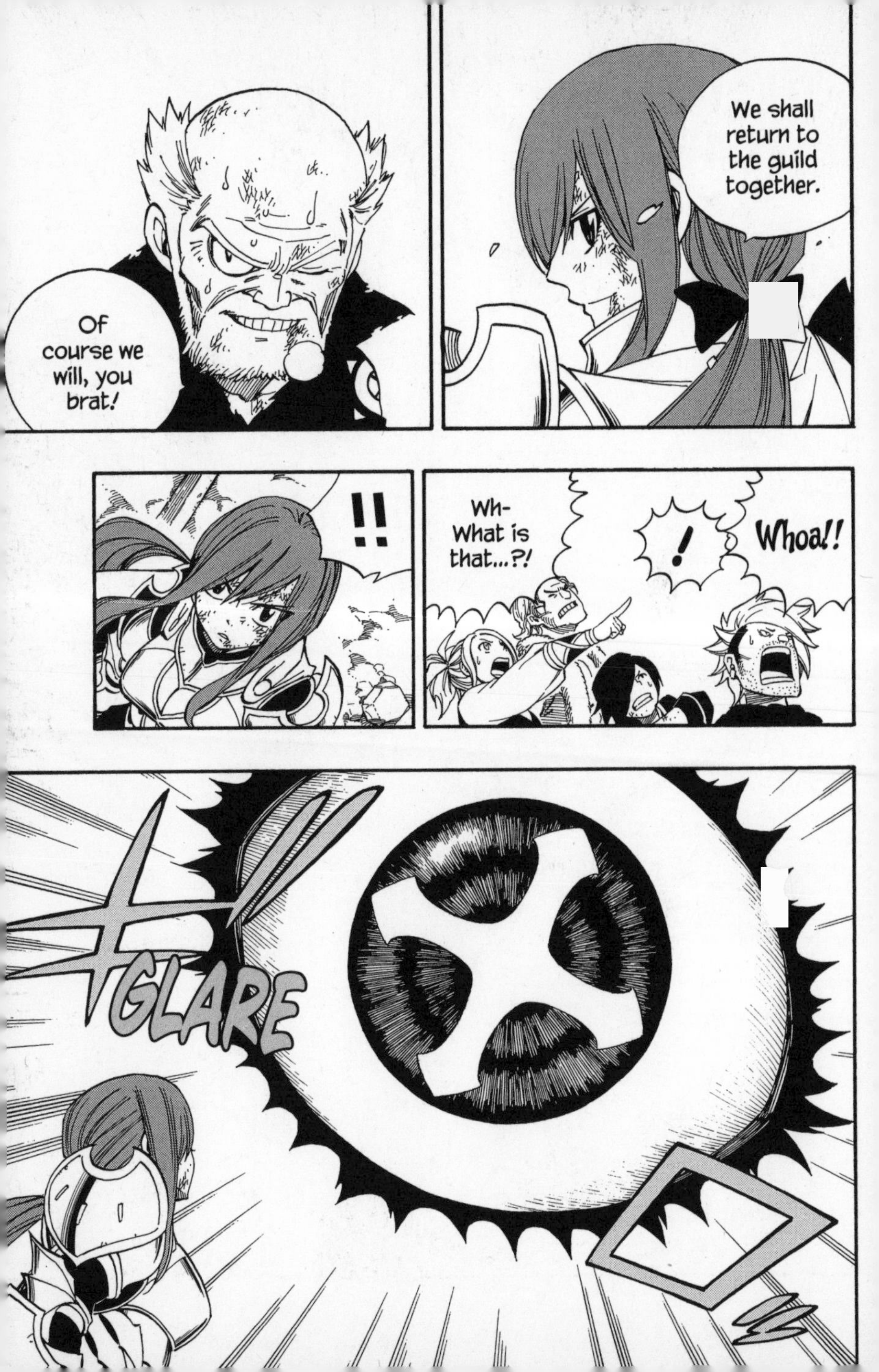
We shall return to the guild together.
Of course we will, you brat!
Whoa!!
!
Wh- What is that...?!
!!
GLARE

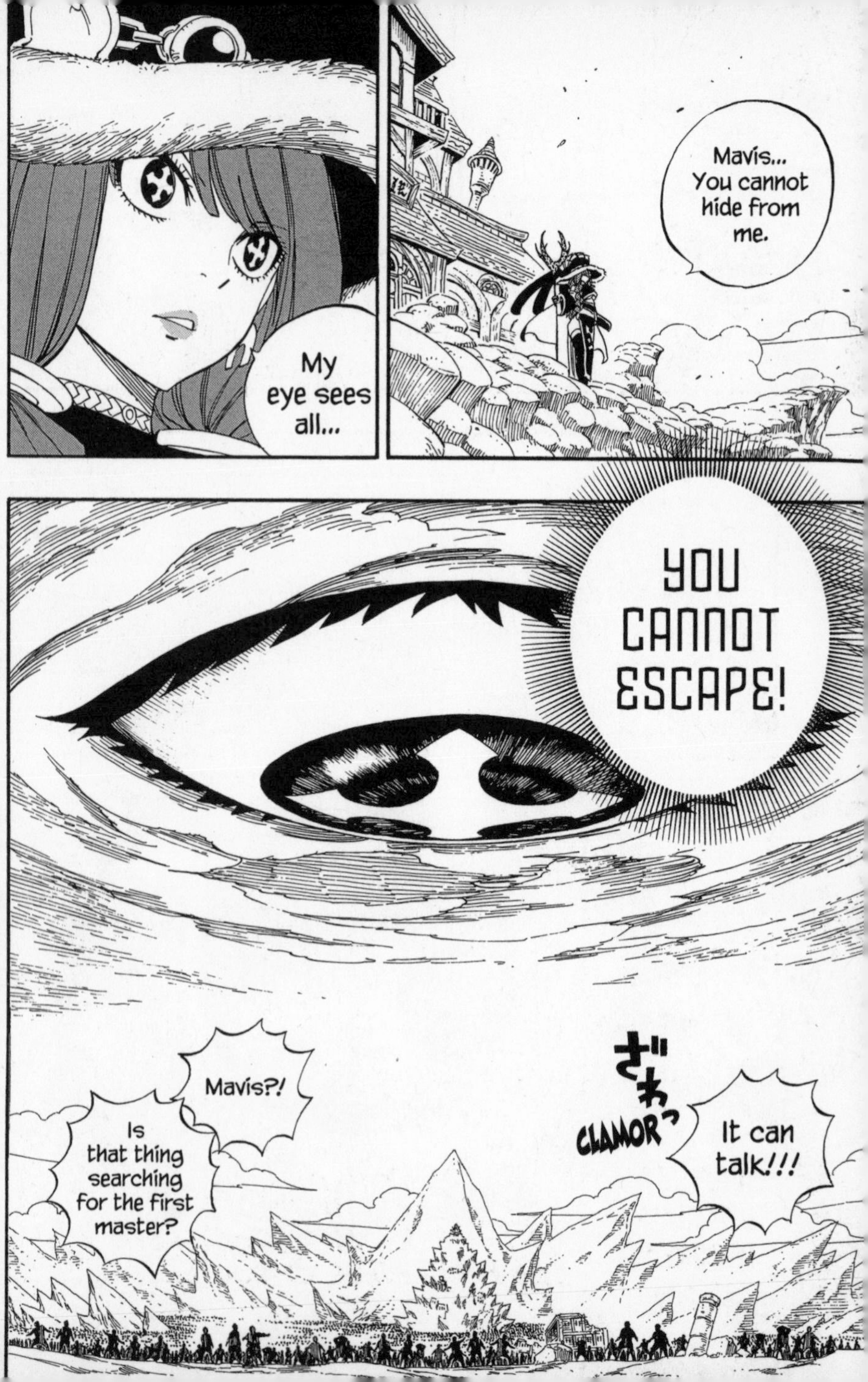
Mavis... You cannot hide from me.
My eye sees all...
YOU CANNOT ESCAPE!
ざわっ
CLAMOR
It can talk!!!
Mavis?!
Is that thing searching for the first master?

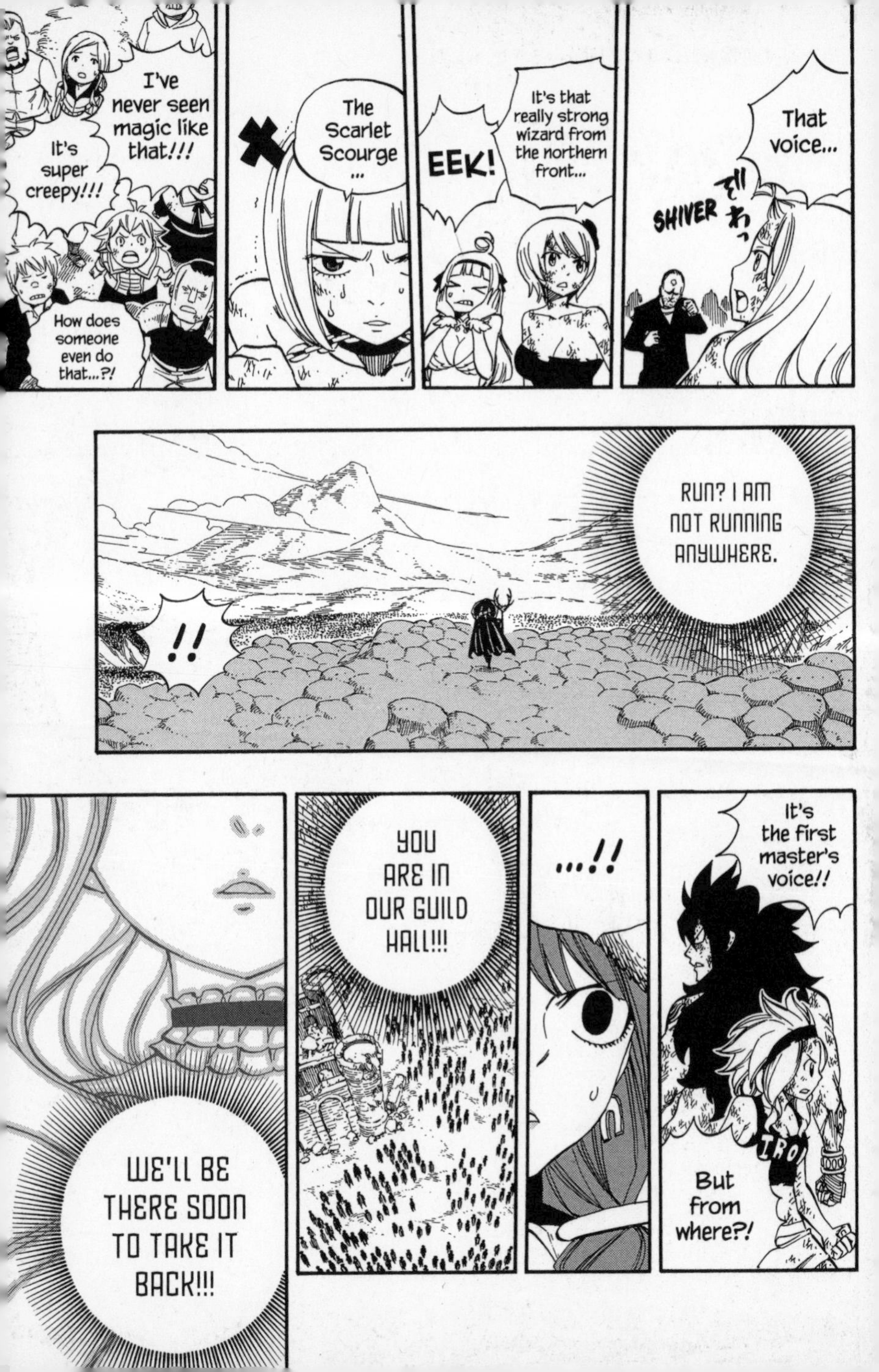
That voice...
SHIVER
It's that really strong wizard from the northern front...
EEK!
The Scarlet Scourge ...
I've never seen magic like that!!!
It's super creepy!!!
How does someone even do that...?!
RUN? I AM NOT RUNNING ANYWHERE.
!!
It's the first master's voice!!
But from where?!
...!!
YOU ARE IN OUR GUILD HALL!!!
WE'LL BE THERE SOON TO TAKE IT BACK!!!

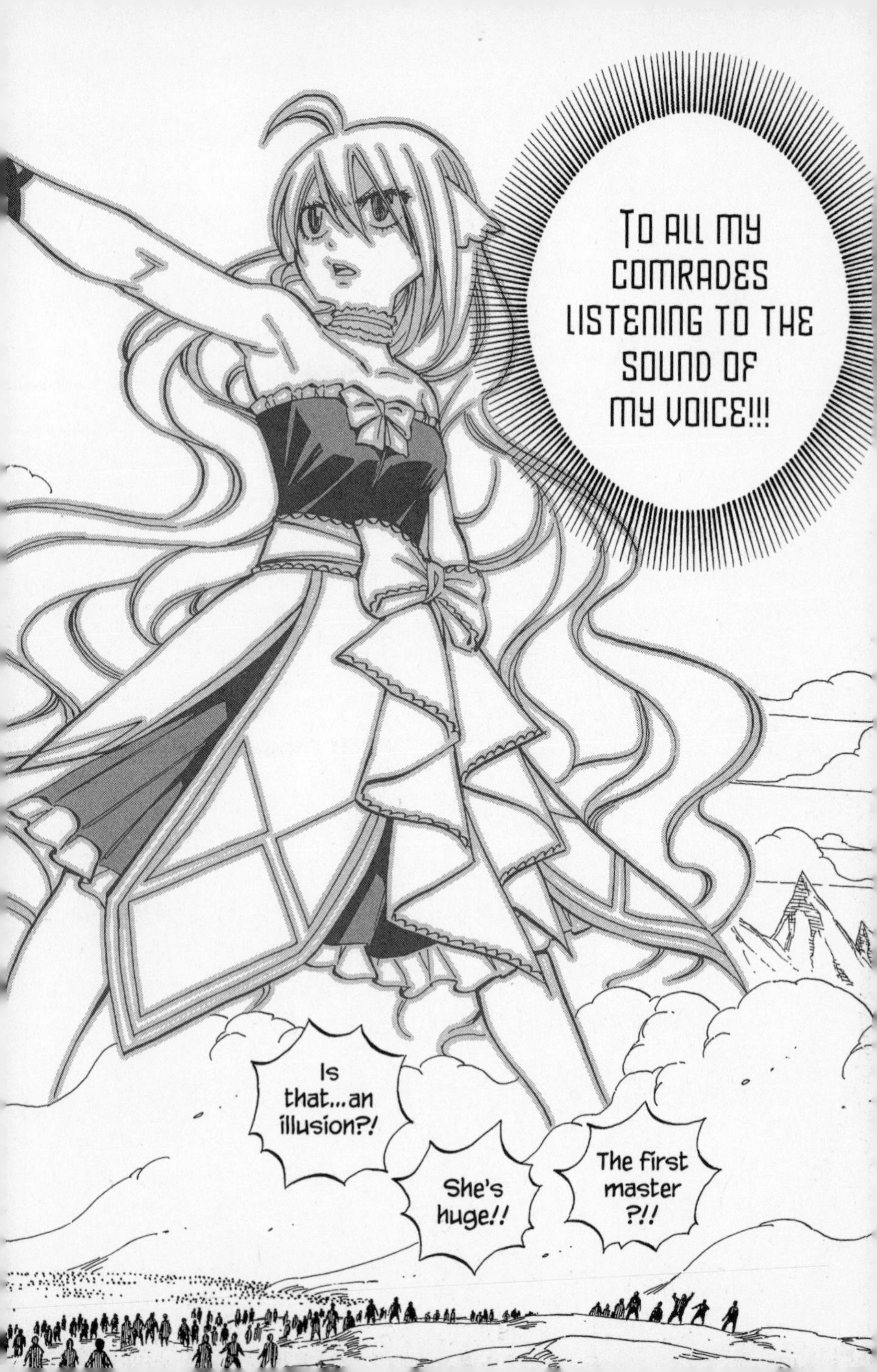
TO ALL MY COMRADES LISTENING TO THE SOUND OF MY VOICE!!!
The first master ?!!
She's huge!!
Is that...an illusion?!

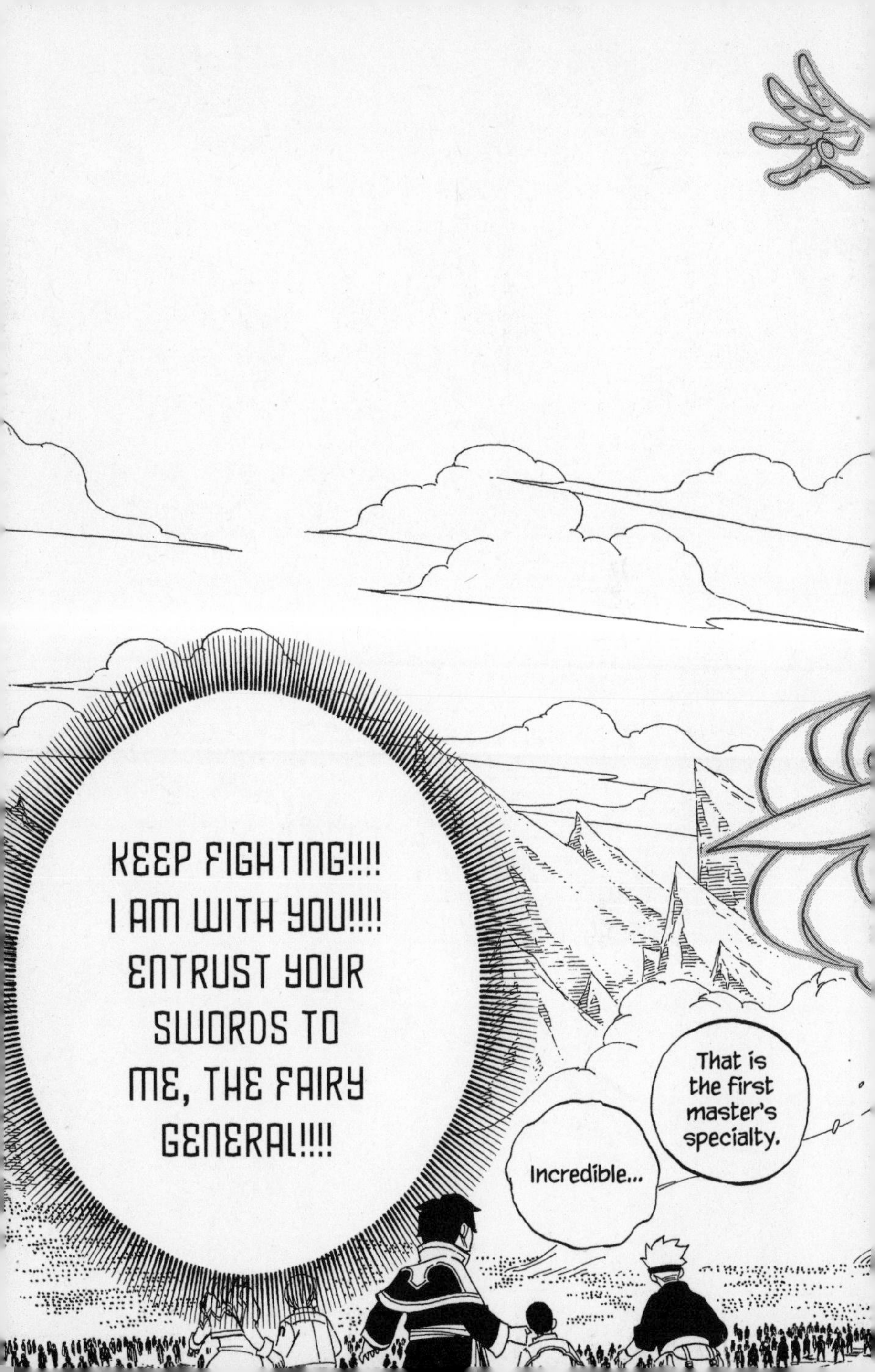
KEEP FIGHTING!!!! I AM WITH YOU!!!! ENTRUST YOUR SWORDS TO ME, THE FAIRY GENERAL!!!!
That is the first master's specialty.
Incredible...

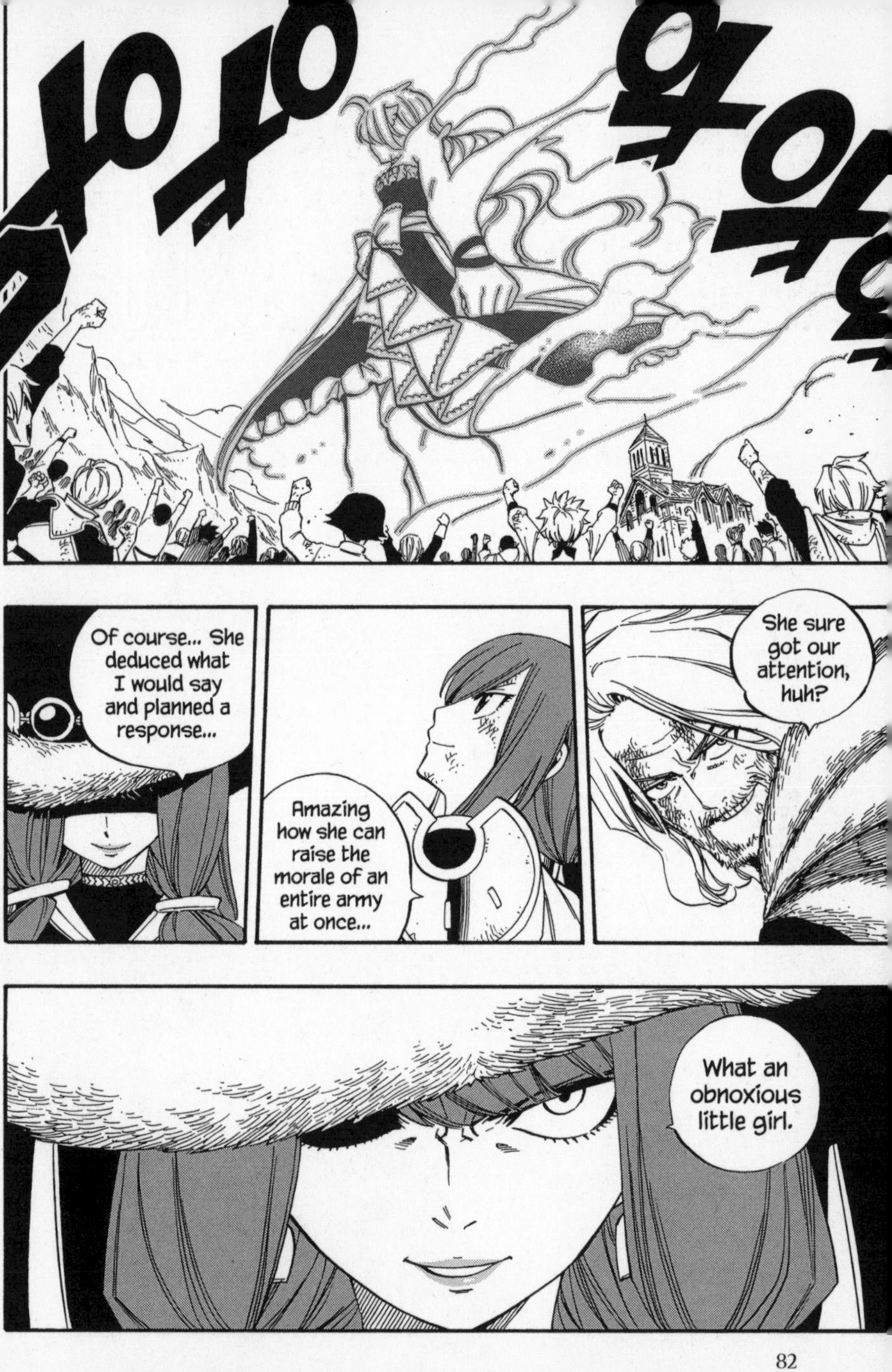
She sure got our attention, huh?
Amazing how she can raise the morale of an entire army at once...
Of course... She deduced what I would say and planned a response...
What an obnoxious little girl.

FAIRY TAIL

フェアリーテイル

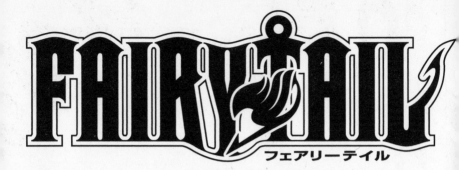

Chapter 505: Trump Card

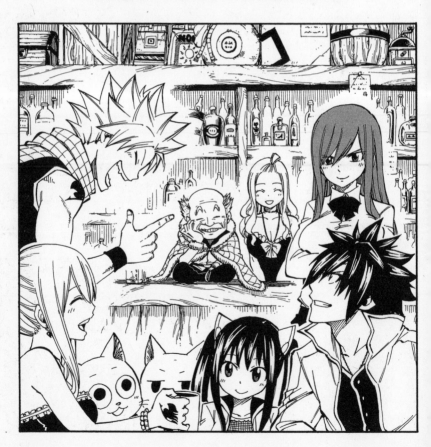

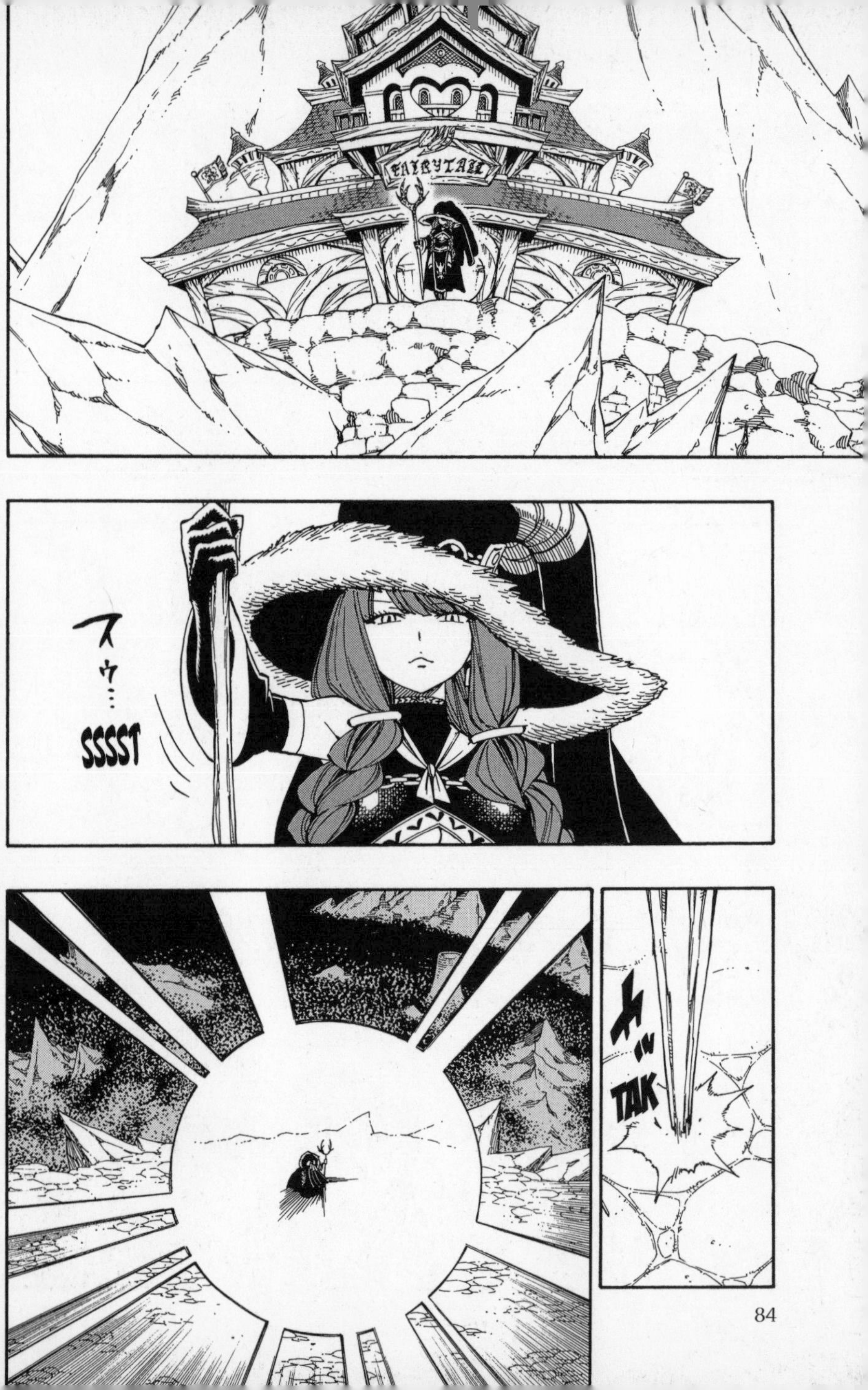
FAIRYTAIL
スゥ…
SSSST
トッ
TAK

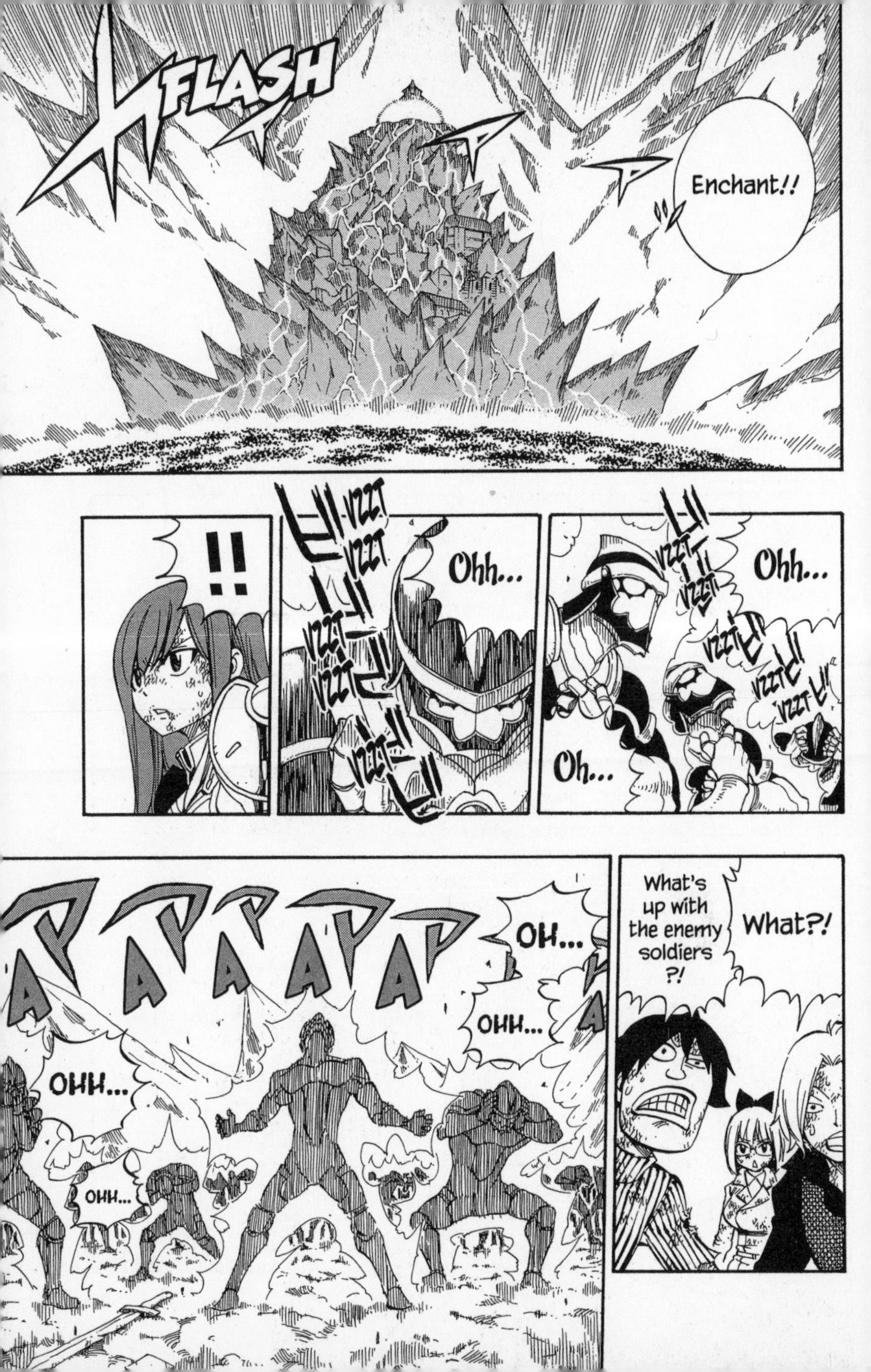
FLASH
Enchant!!
Ohh...
Oh...
VZZT
Ohh...
VZZT
!!
What?!
What's up with the enemy soldiers ?!
OH...
OHH...
OHH...
OHH...
PAPAPAPAPA

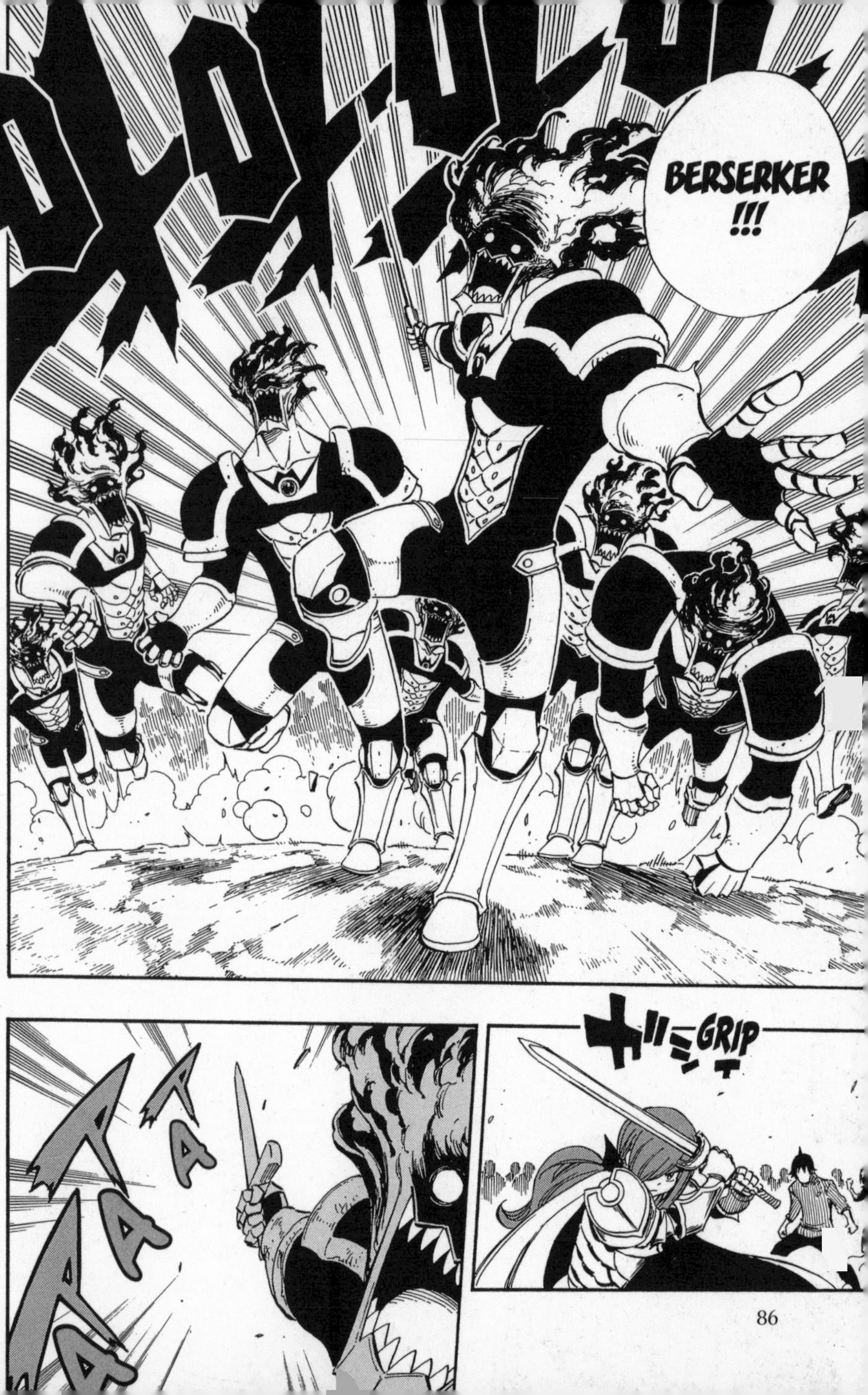
BERSERKER !!!
GRIP

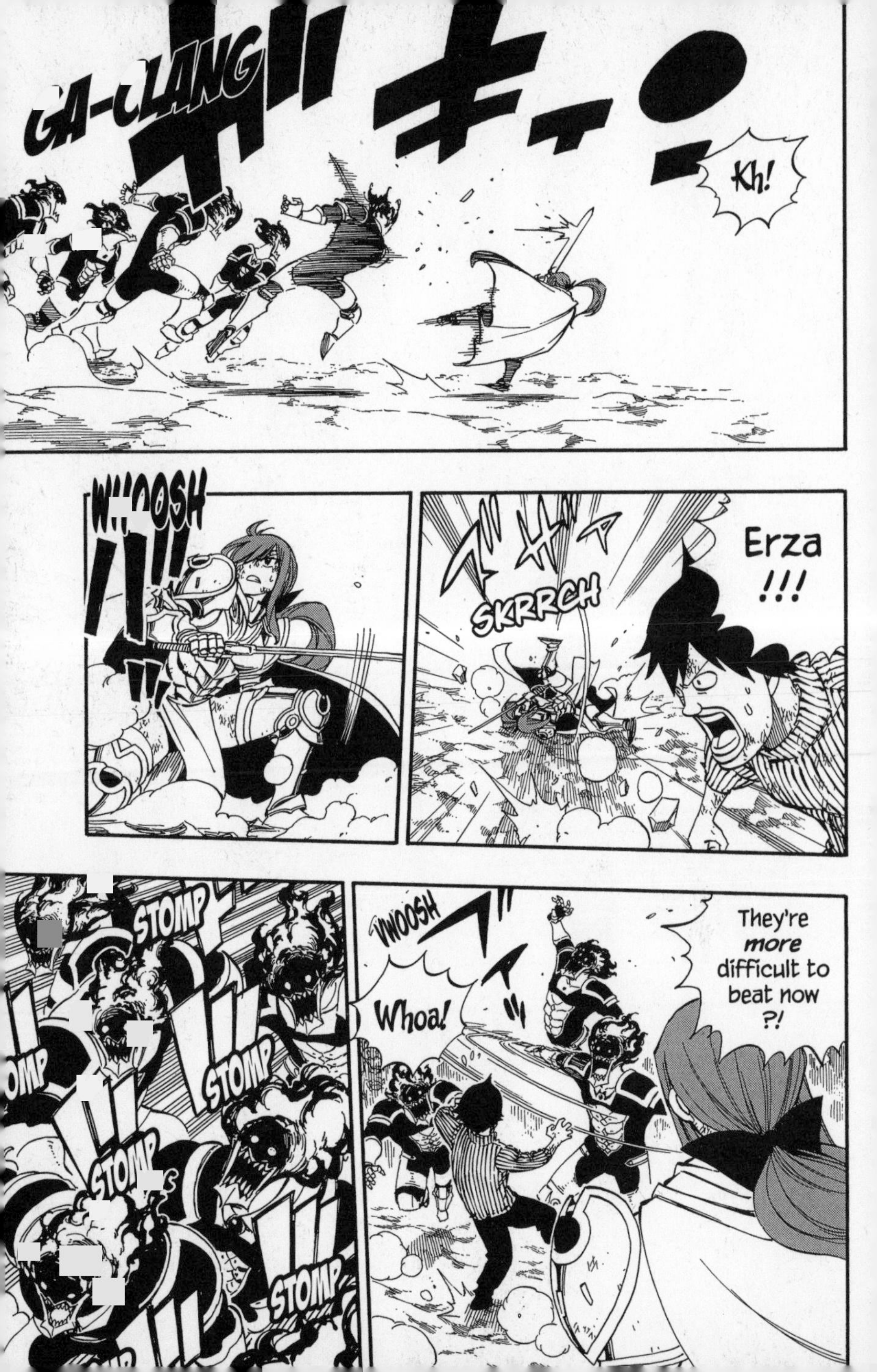
GA-CLANG
Kh!
Erza
!!!
SKRRCH
WHOOSH
They're *more* difficult to beat now?!
Whoa!
VWOOSH
STOMP
OMP
STOMP
STOMP
STOMP

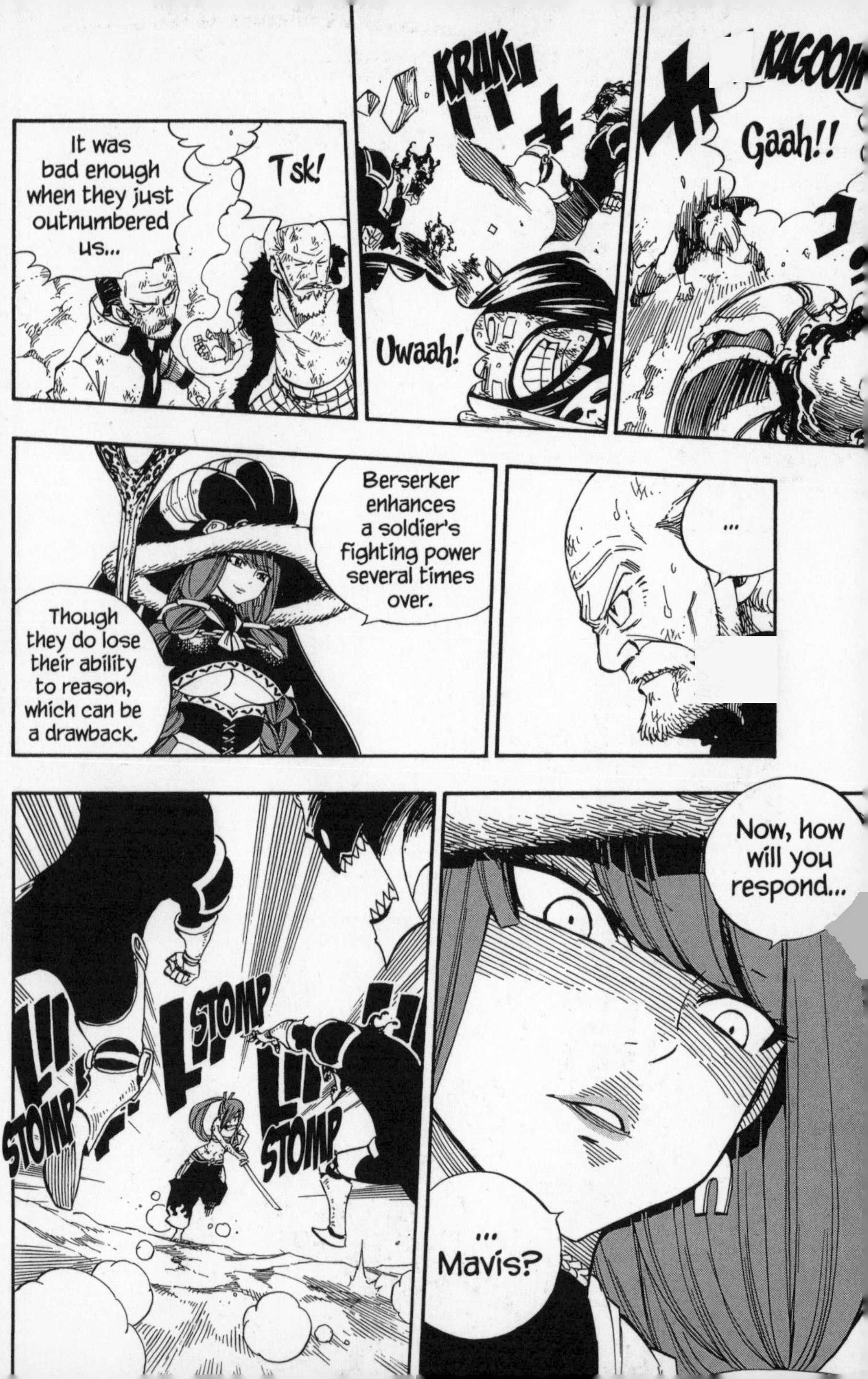
KAGOOM
Gaah!!
KRAK
Uwaah!
Tsk!
It was bad enough when they just outnumbered us...
...
Berserker enhances a soldier's fighting power several times over.
Though they do lose their ability to reason, which can be a drawback.
Now, how will you respond...
... Mavis?
STOMP
STOMP
STOMP
STOMP

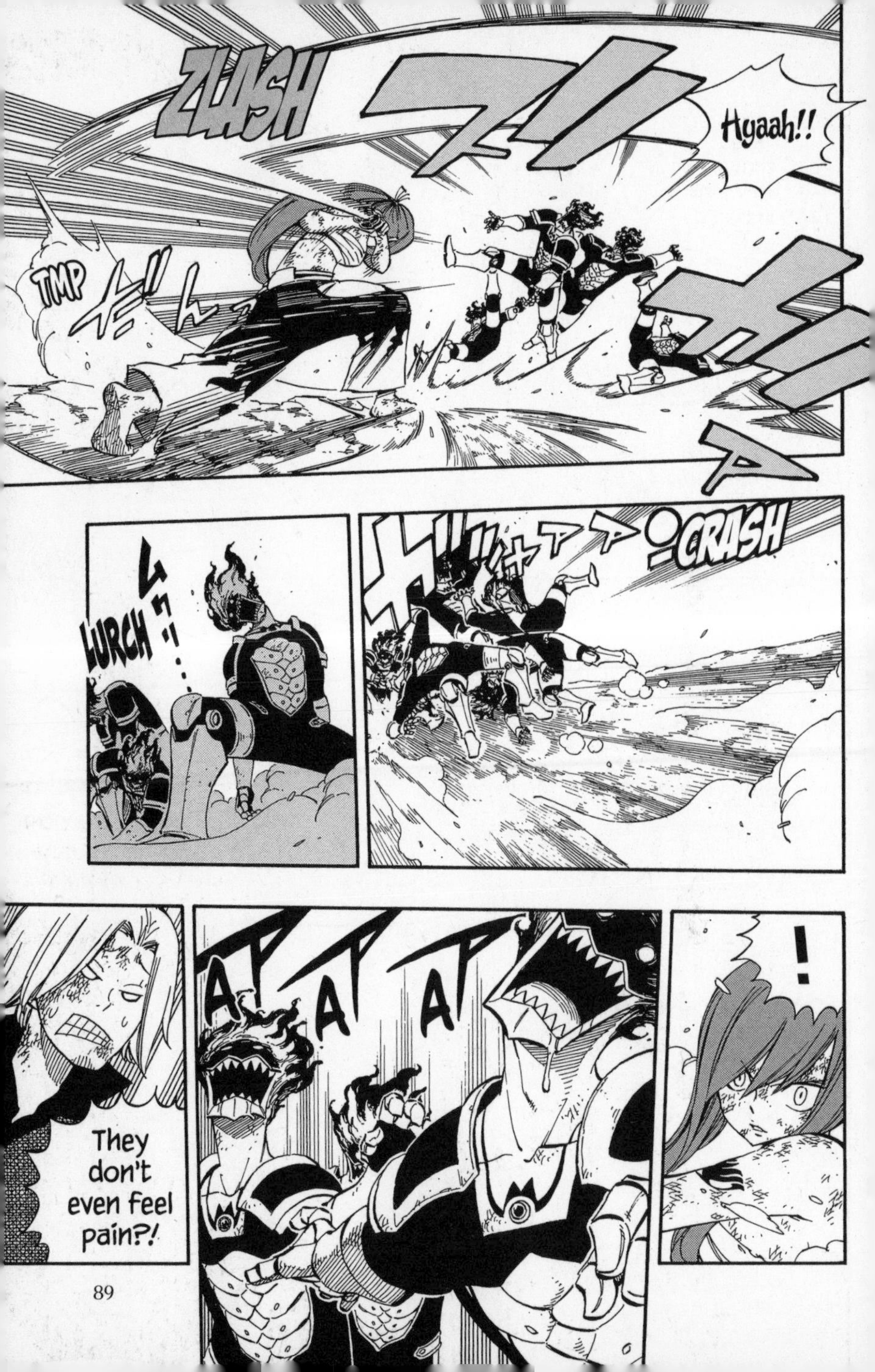
Hyaah!!
ZLASH
TMP
CRASH
LURCH
!
A A A
They don't even feel pain?!

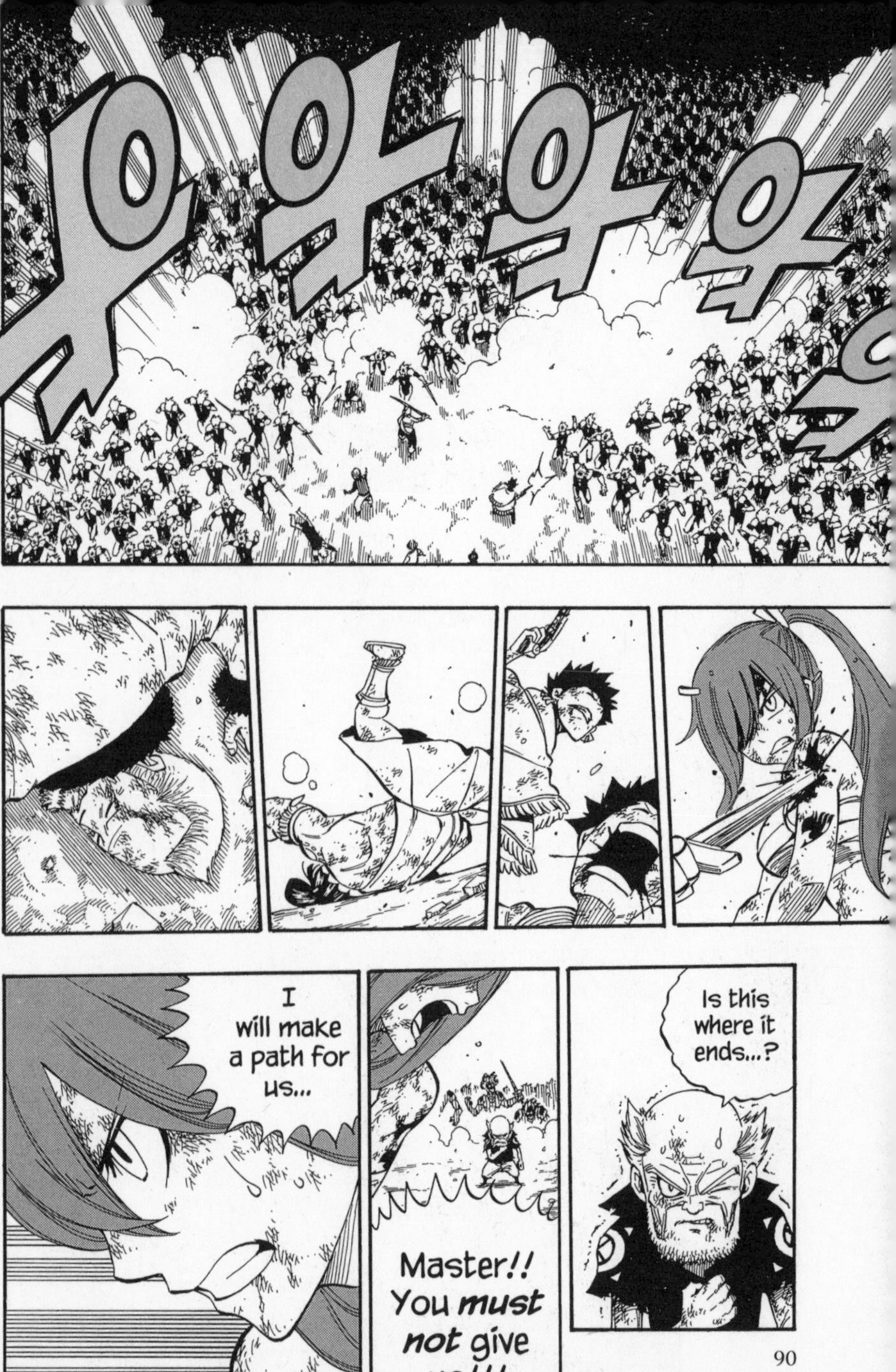
Is this where it ends...?
Master!! You *must* *not* give up!!!
I will make a path for us...

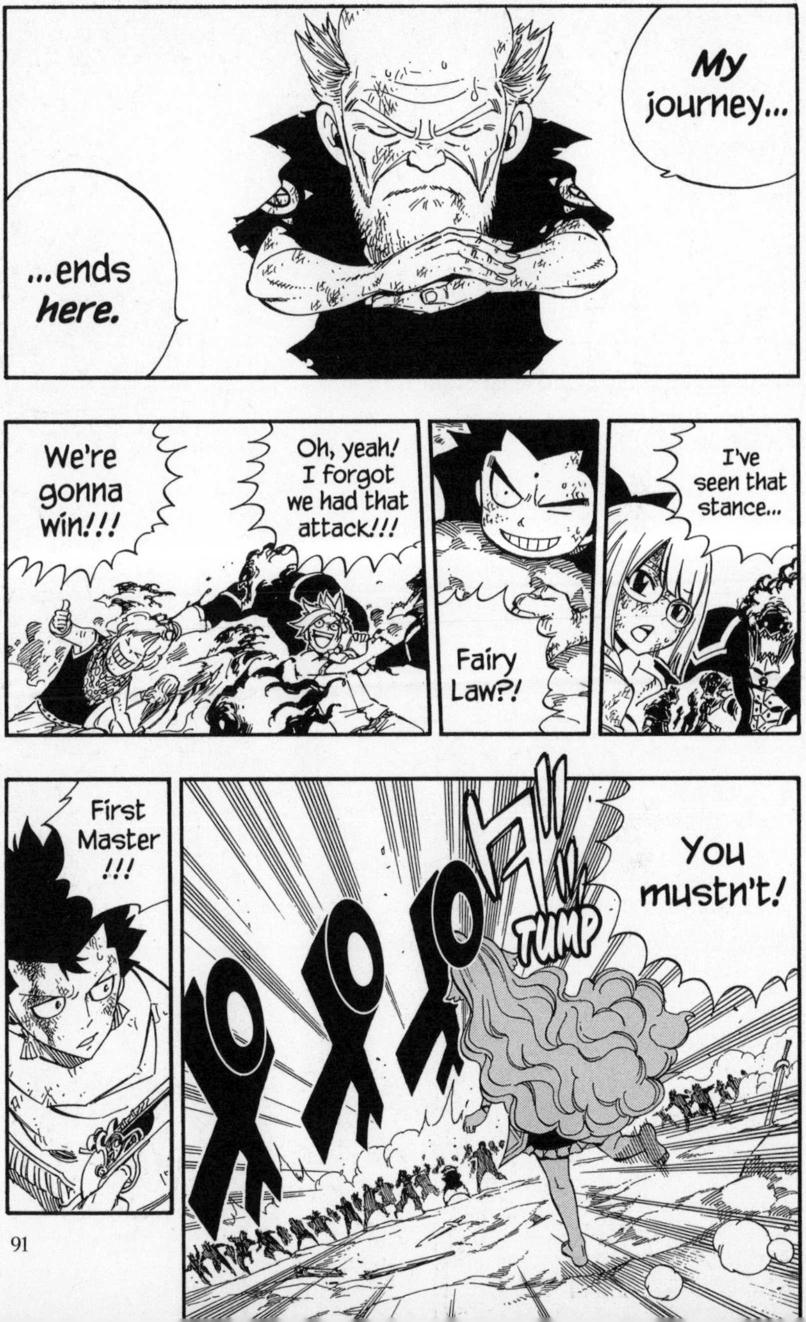
My journey...
...ends here.
I've seen that stance...
Fairy Law?!
Oh, yeah! I forgot we had that attack!!!
We're gonna win!!!
You mustn't!
TUMP
First Master!!!

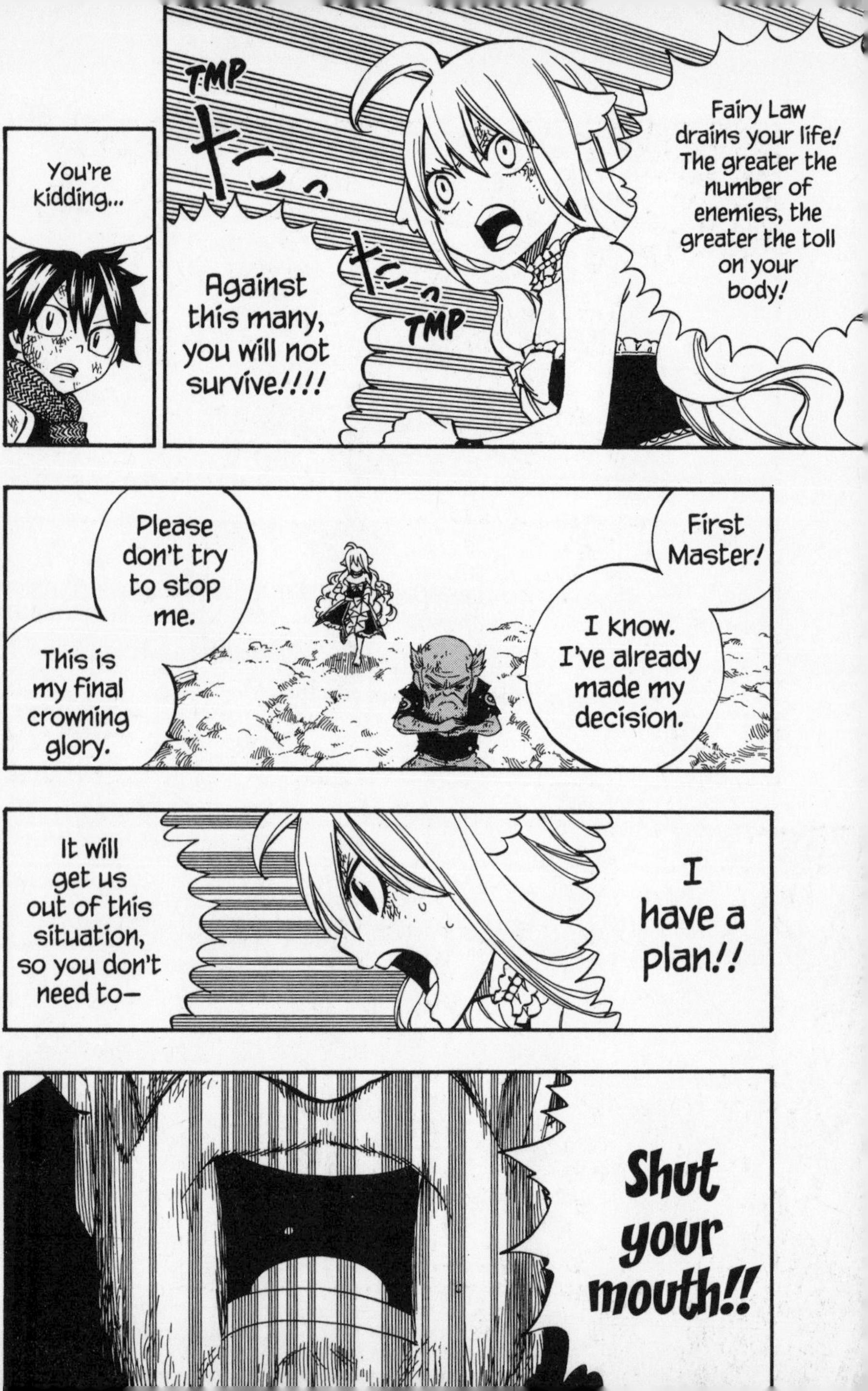
Fairy Law drains your life! The greater the number of enemies, the greater the toll on your body!
TMP
TMP
Against this many, you will not survive!!!!
You're kidding...
First Master!
I know. I've already made my decision.
Please don't try to stop me.
This is my final crowning glory.
I have a plan!!
It will get us out of this situation, so you don't need to—
Shut your mouth!!

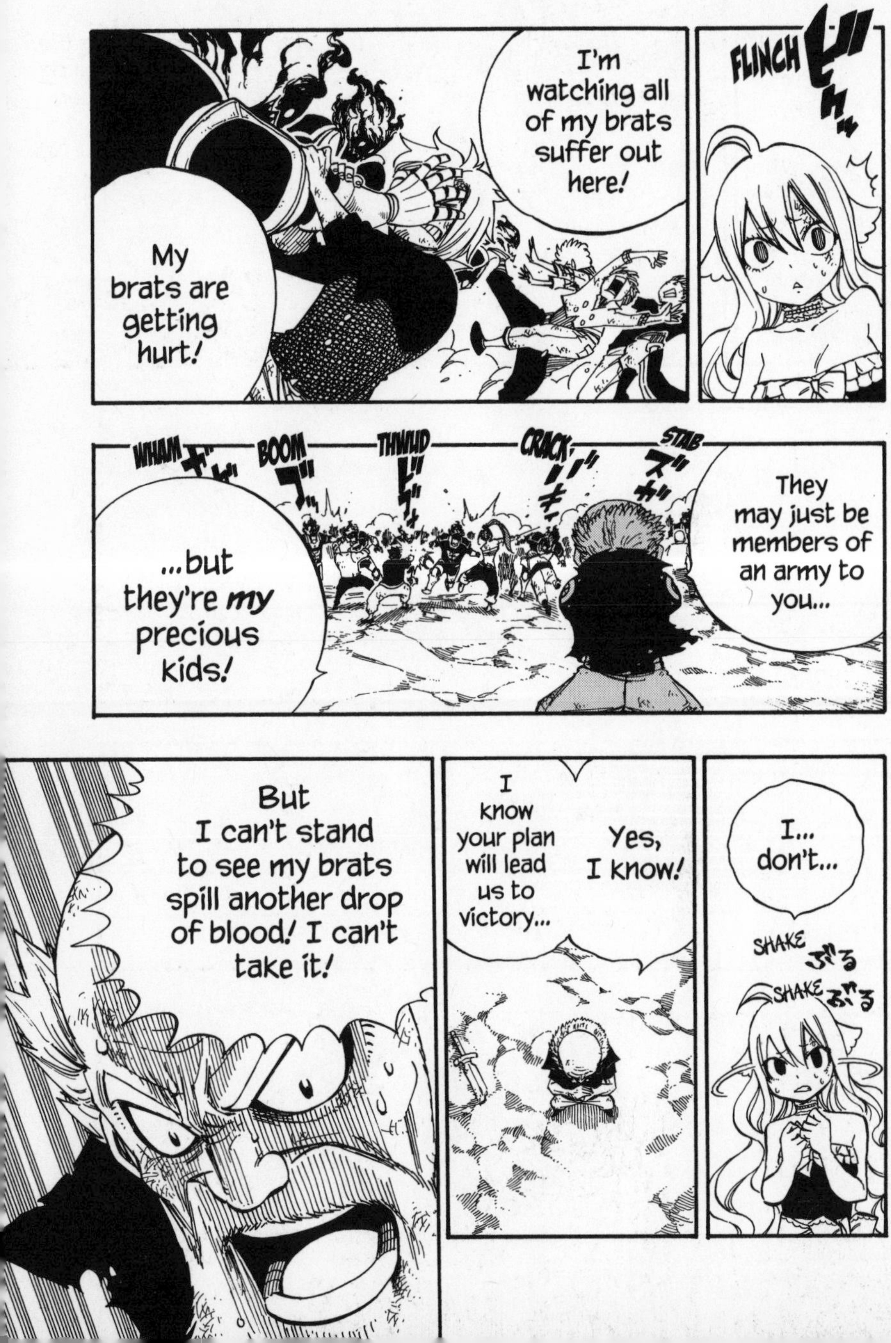
FLINCH
I'm watching all of my brats suffer out here!
My brats are getting hurt!
STAB
CRACK
THWUD
BOOM
WHAM
They may just be members of an army to you...
...but they're *my* precious kids!
I... don't...
SHAKE
SHAKE
Yes, I know!
I know your plan will lead us to victory...
But I can't stand to see my brats spill another drop of blood! I can't take it!

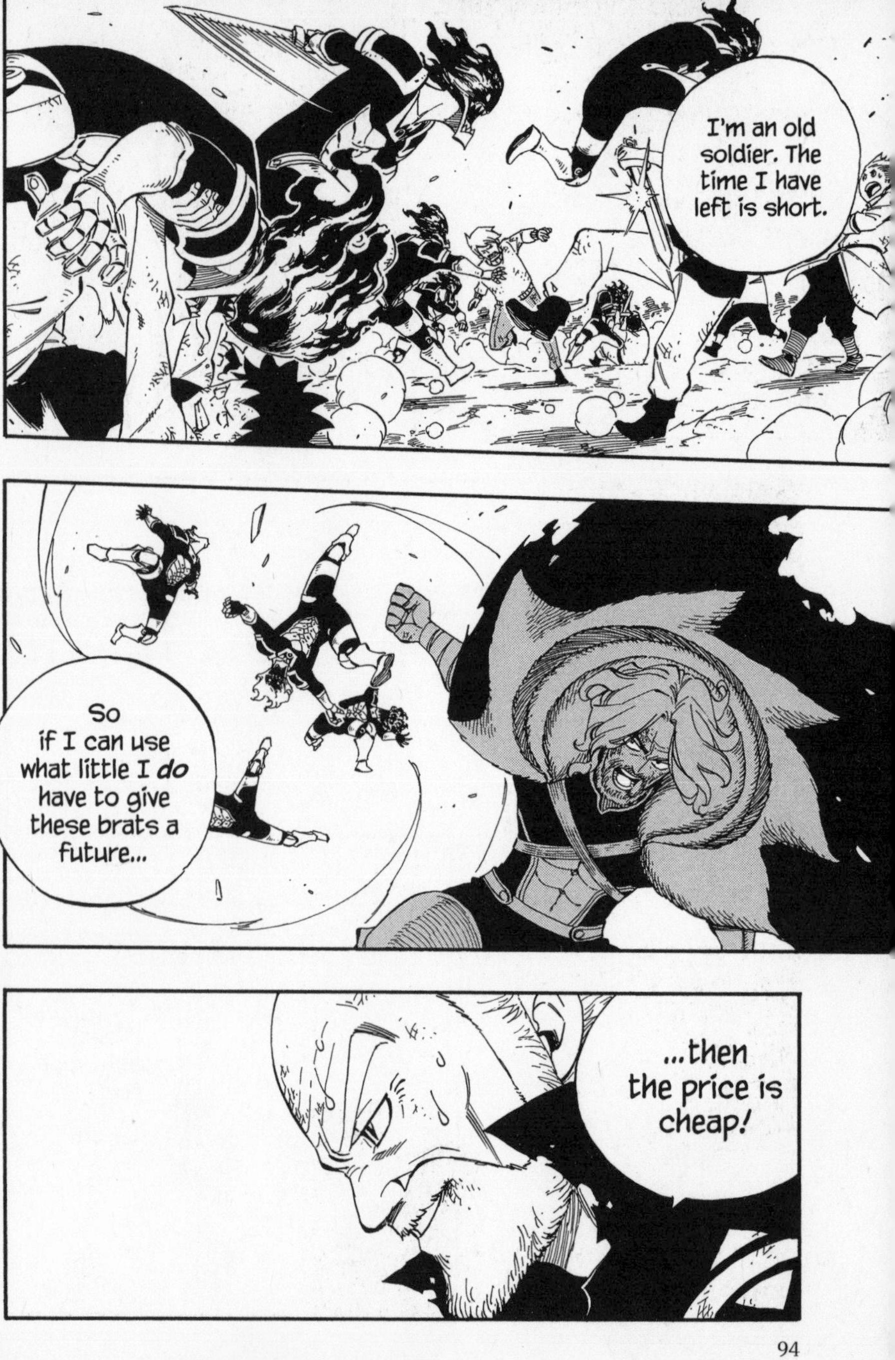
I'm an old soldier. The time I have left is short.
So if I can use what little I *do* have to give these brats a future...
...then the price is cheap!

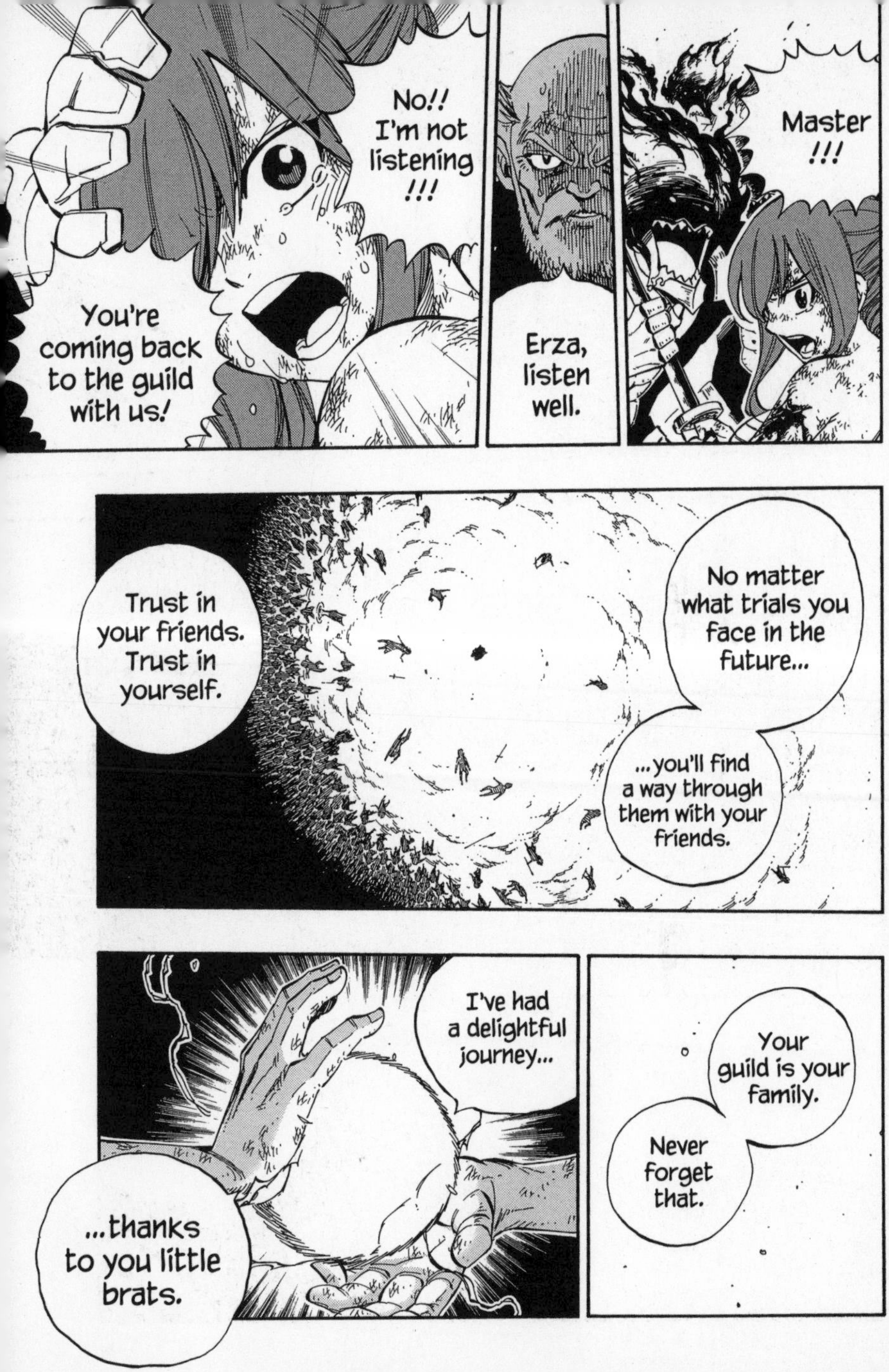
Master!!!
Erza, listen well.
No!! I'm not listening!!!
You're coming back to the guild with us!
No matter what trials you face in the future...
...you'll find a way through them with your friends.
Trust in your friends. Trust in yourself.
Your guild is your family.
Never forget that.
I've had a delightful journey...
...thanks to you little brats.

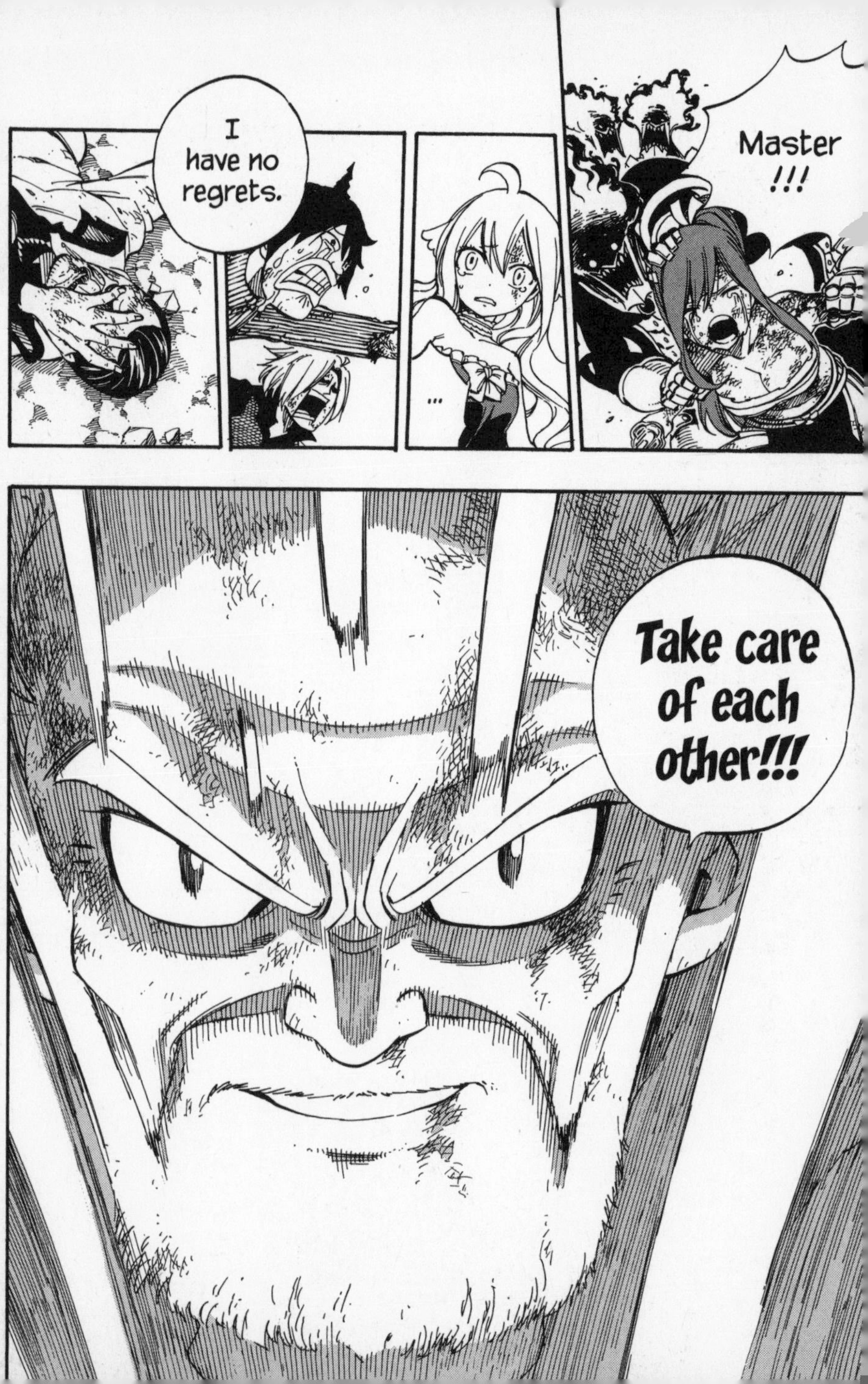
Master !!!
...
I have no regrets.
Take care of each other!!!

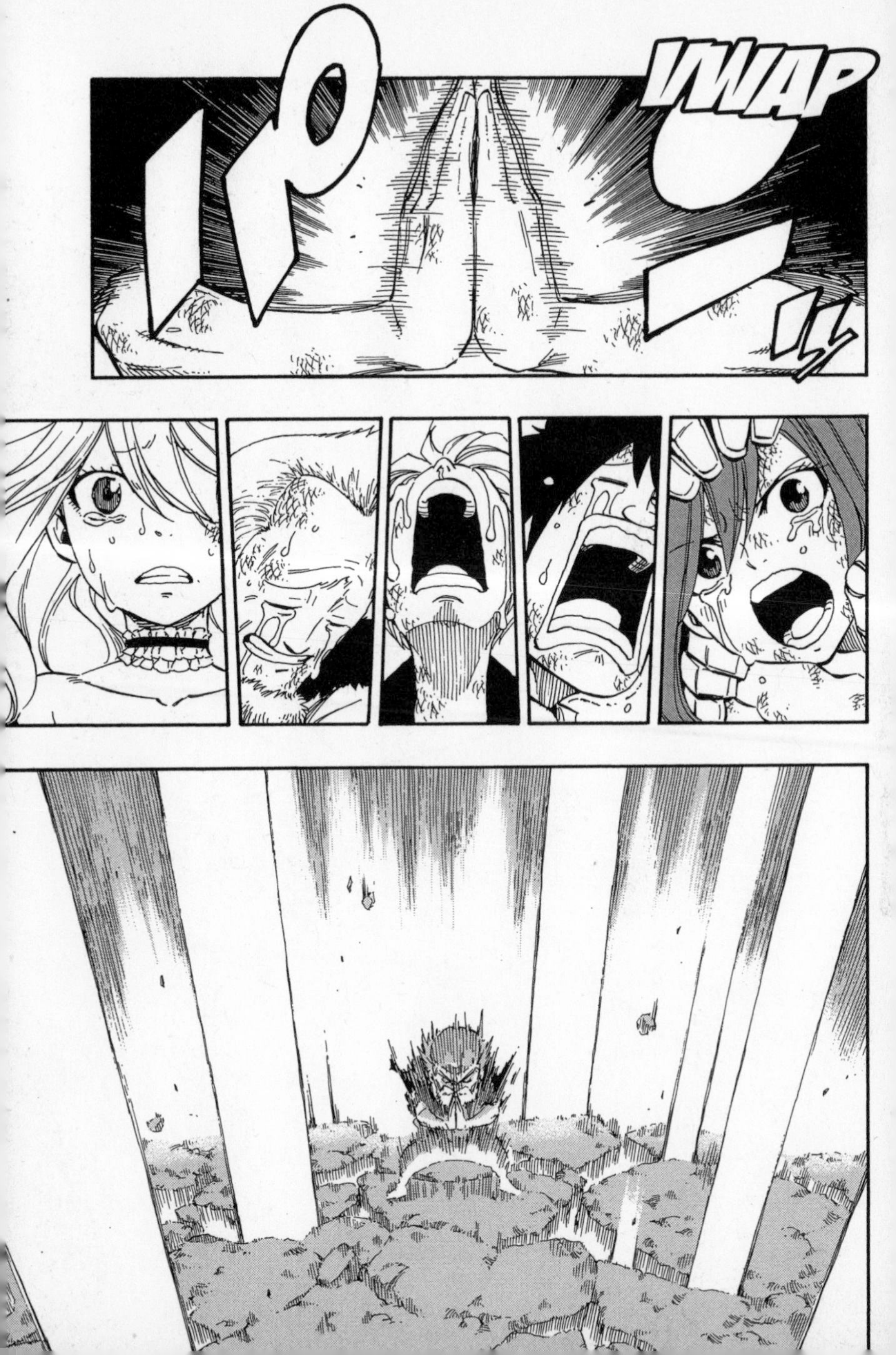
VWAP

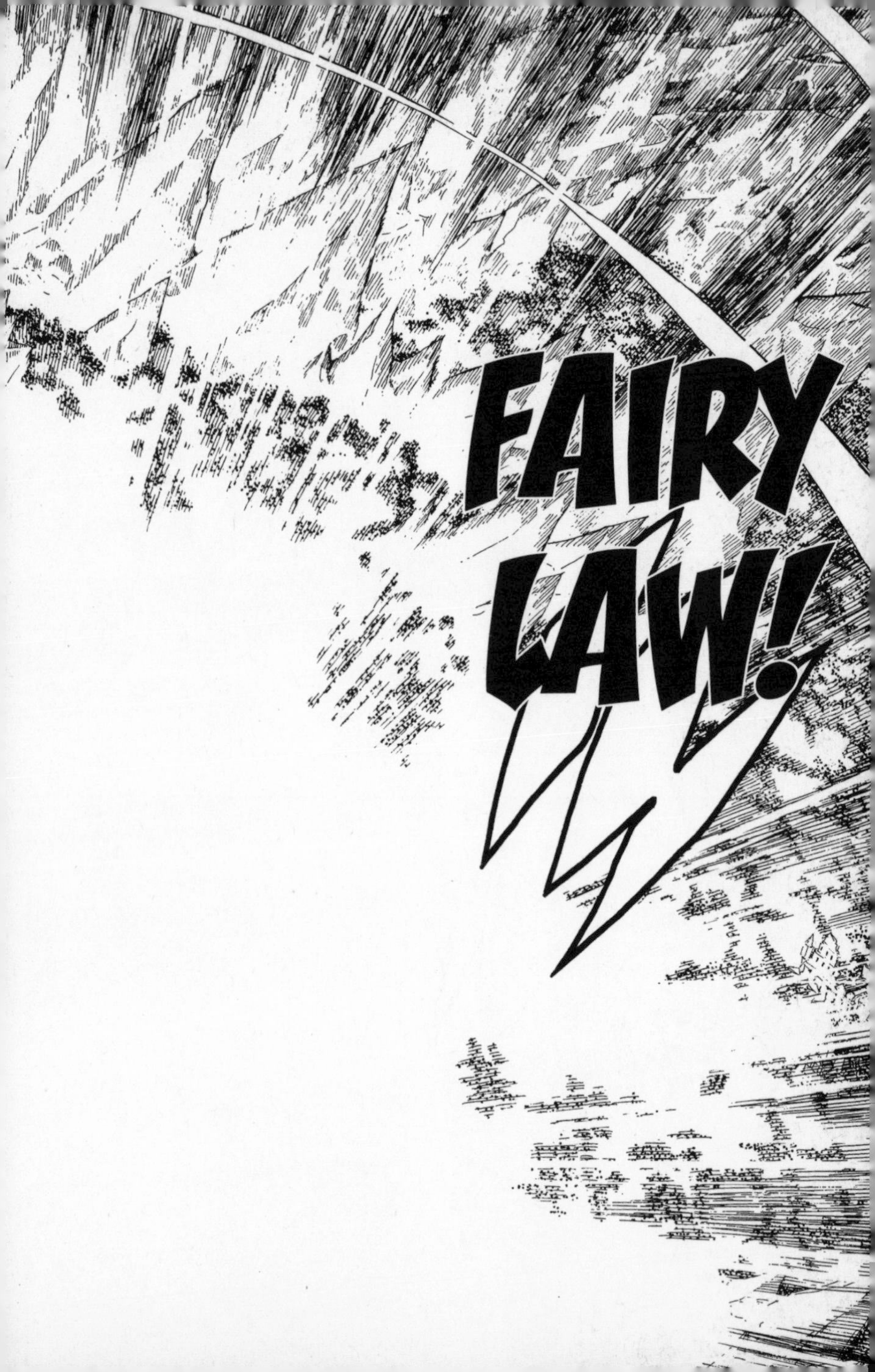
FAIRY LAW!

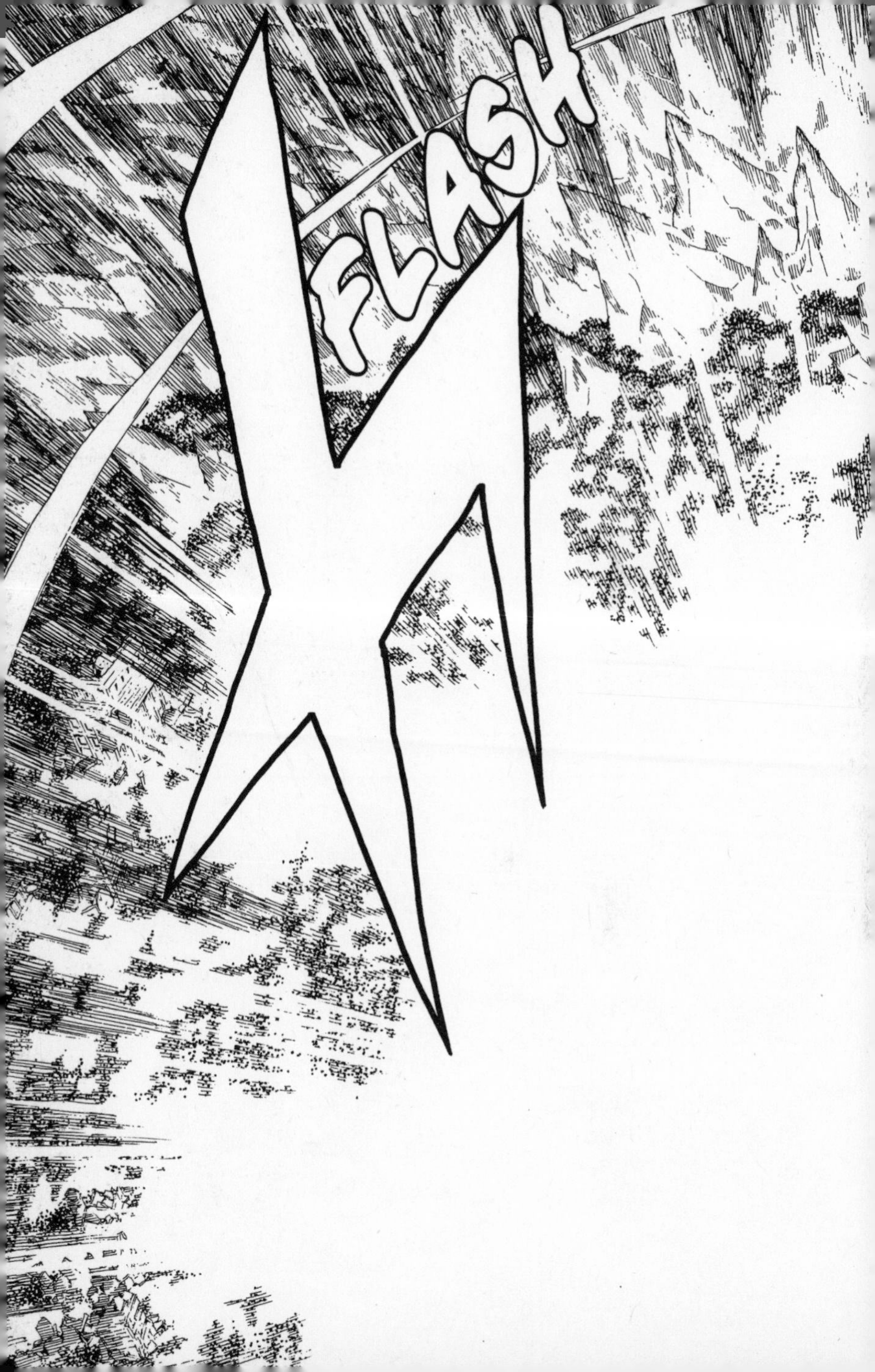
FLASH

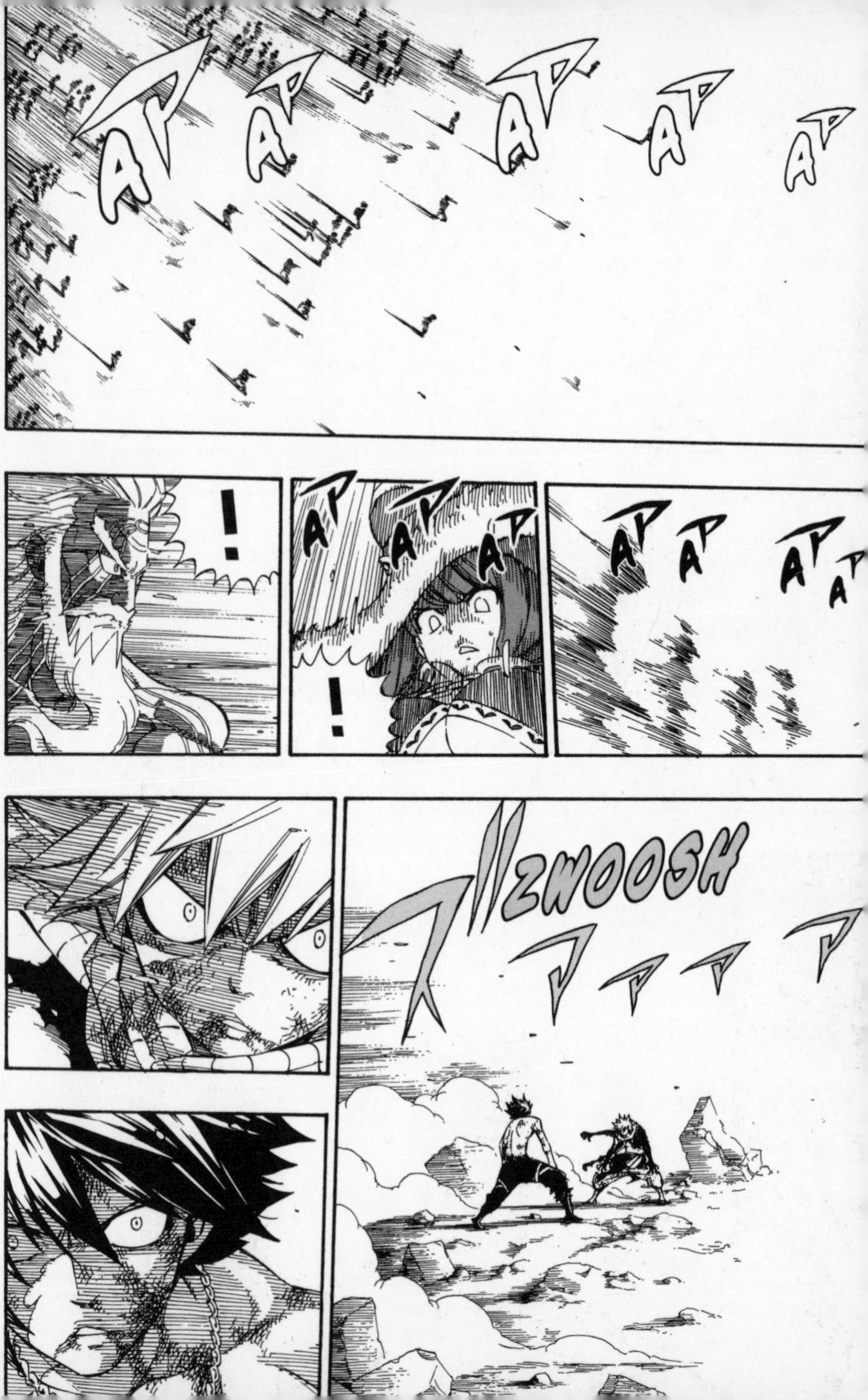
AP AP AP AP AP
AP AP AP AP
AP AP AP
!
!
ZWOOSH

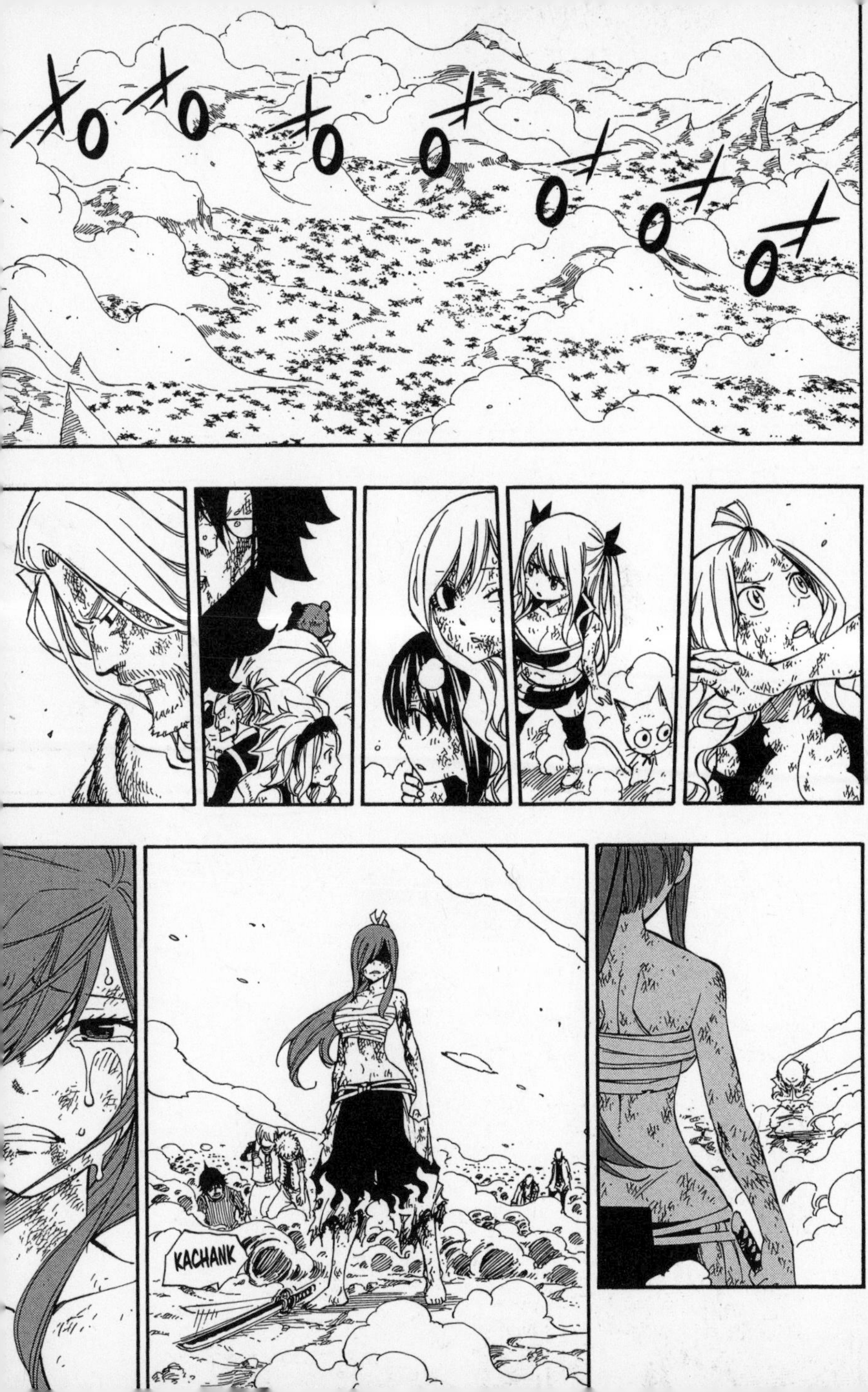
KACHANK

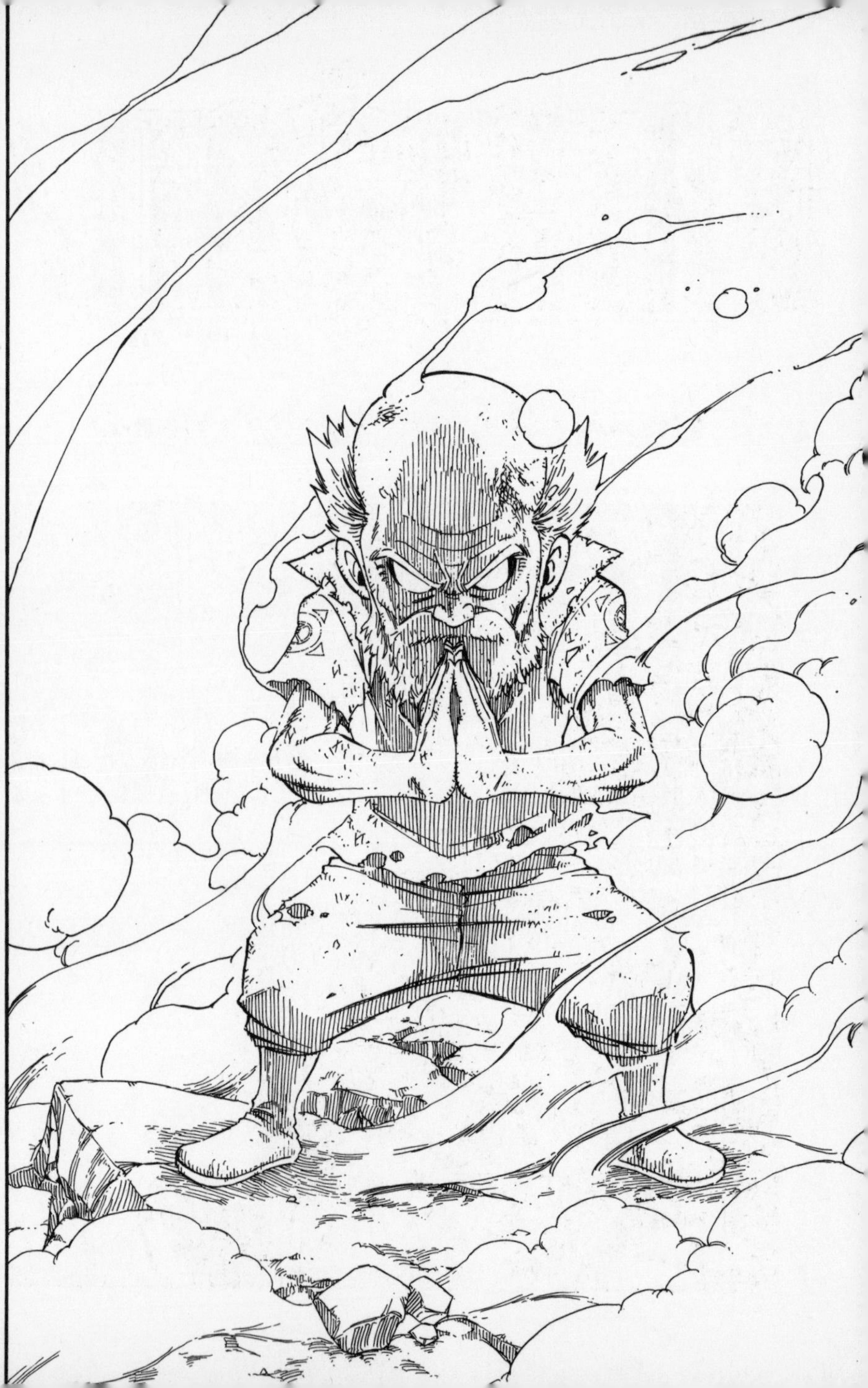

FAIRY TAIL

フェアリーテイル

Chapter 506: The Broken Bond

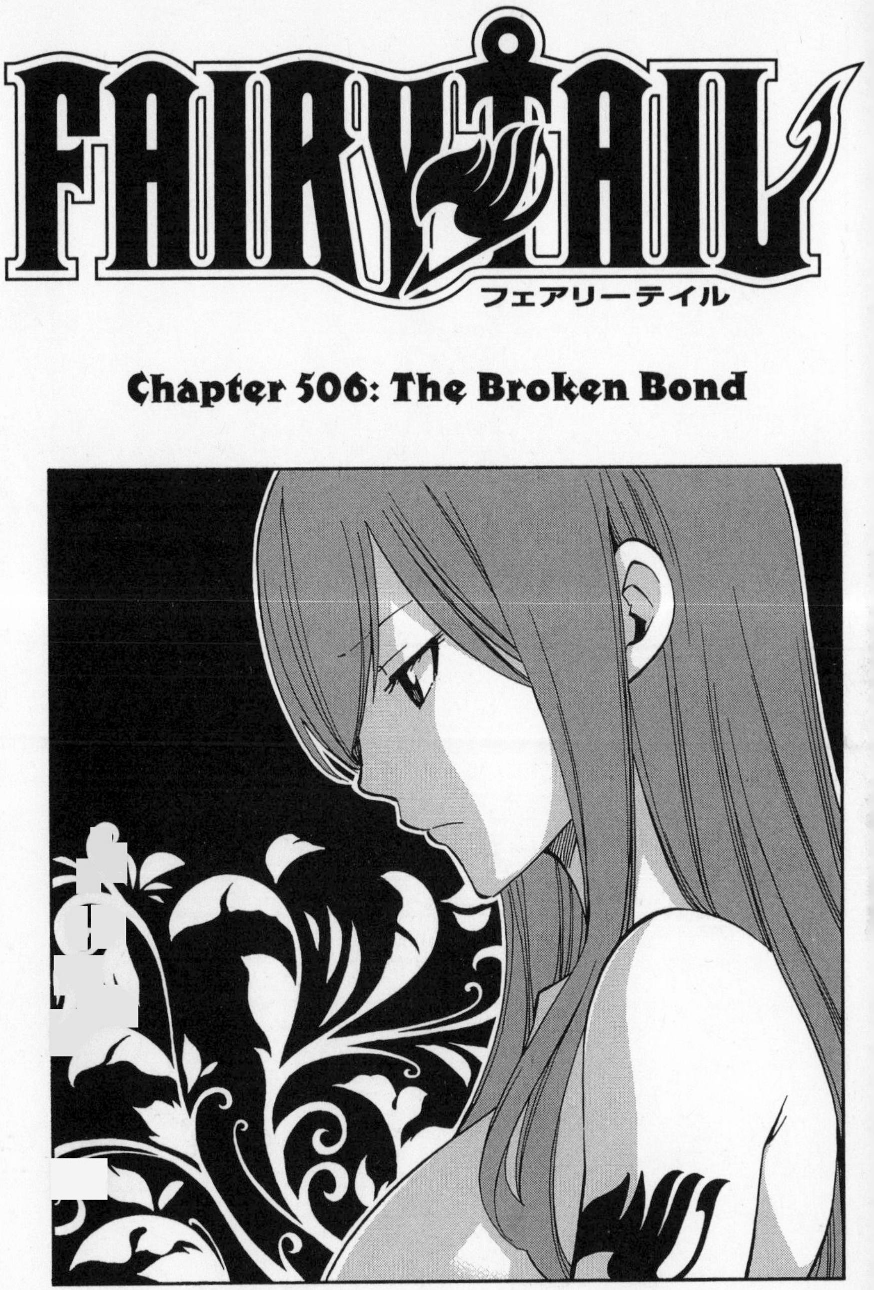

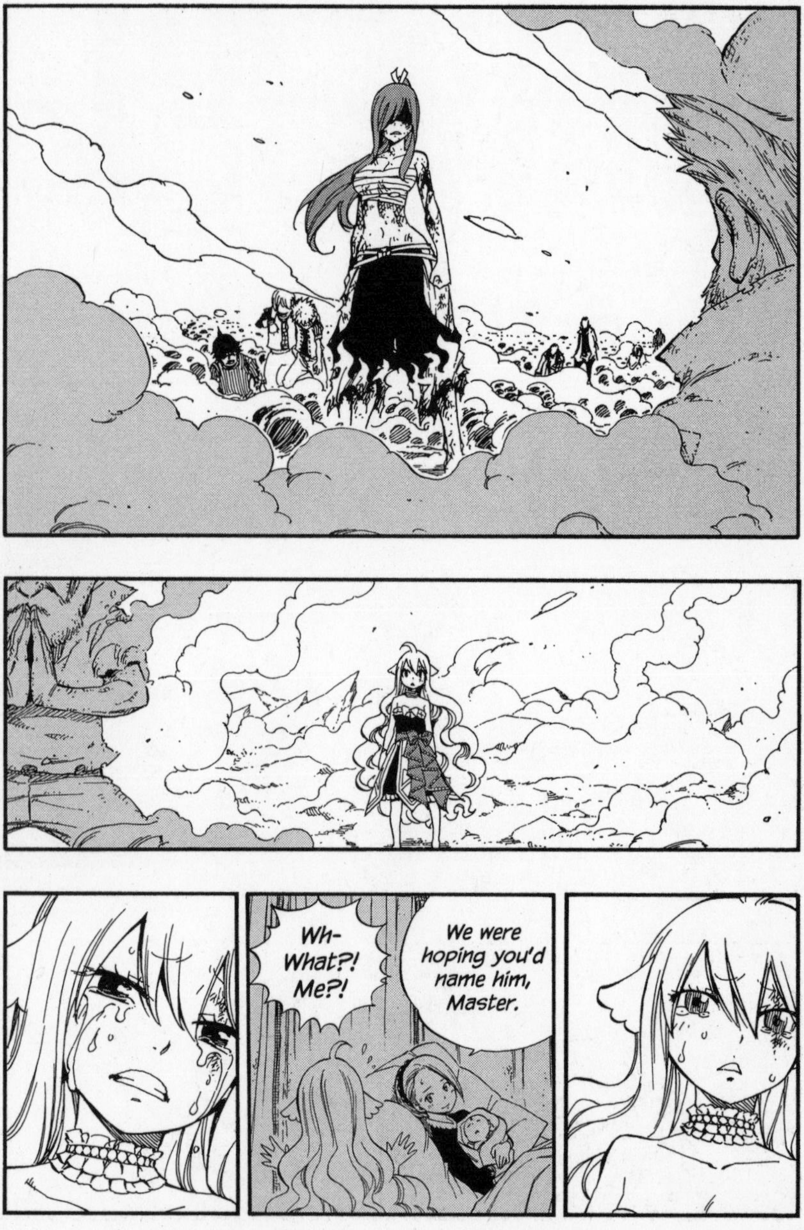
We were hoping you'd name him, Master.
Wh- What?! Me?!

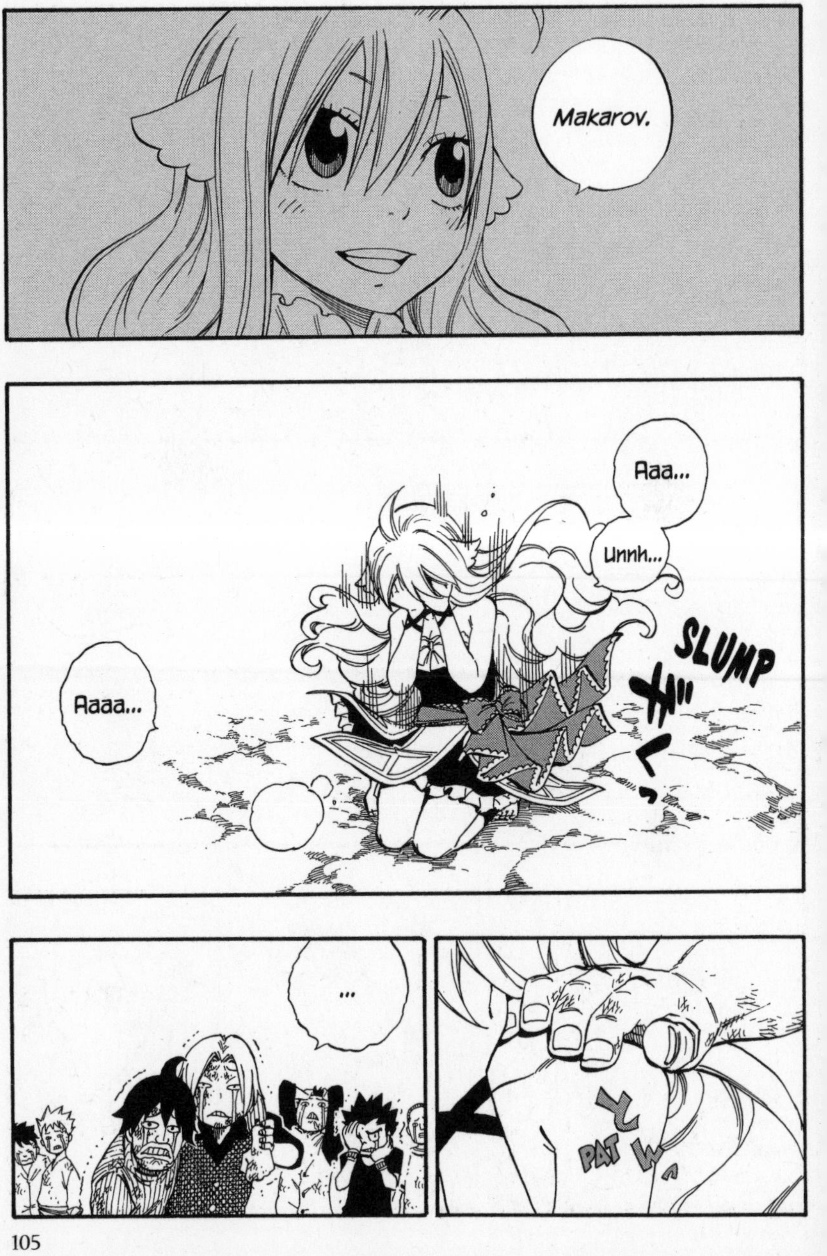
Makarov.
Aaa...
Unnh...
SLUMP
Aaaa...
PAT
...

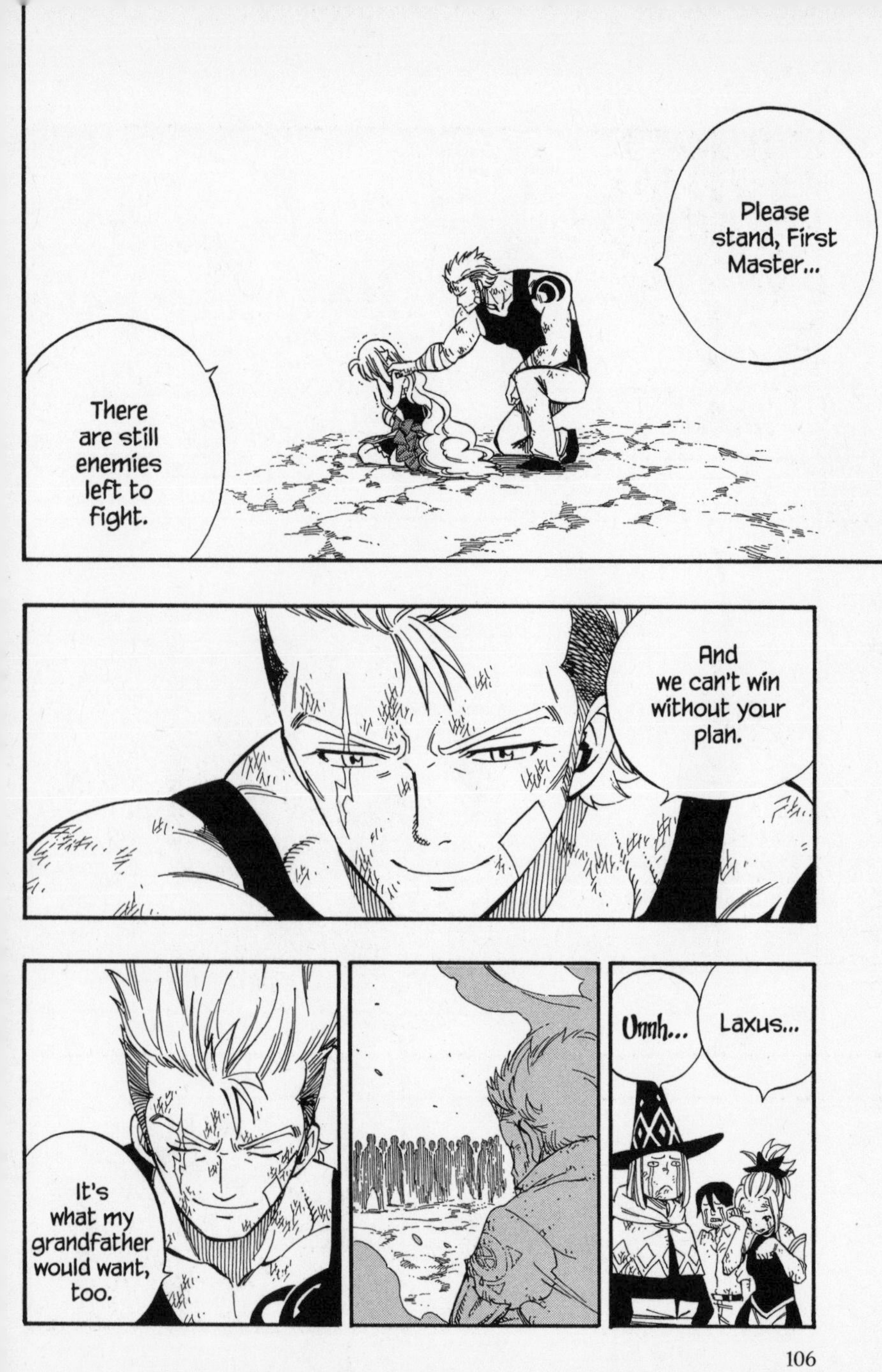
Please stand, First Master...
There are still enemies left to fight.
And we can't win without your plan.
Laxus...
Unnh...
It's what my grandfather would want, too.

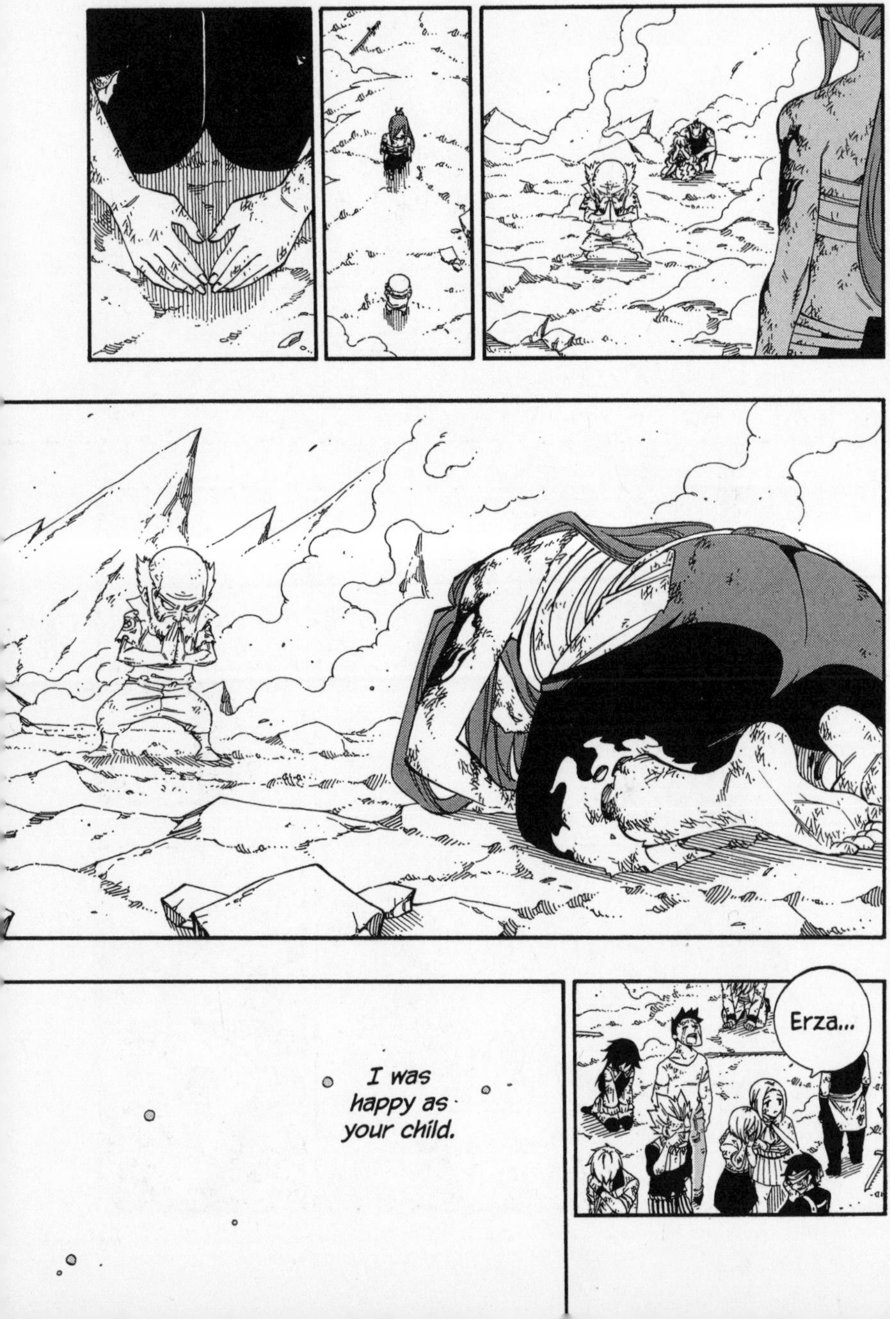
Erza...
I was happy as your child.

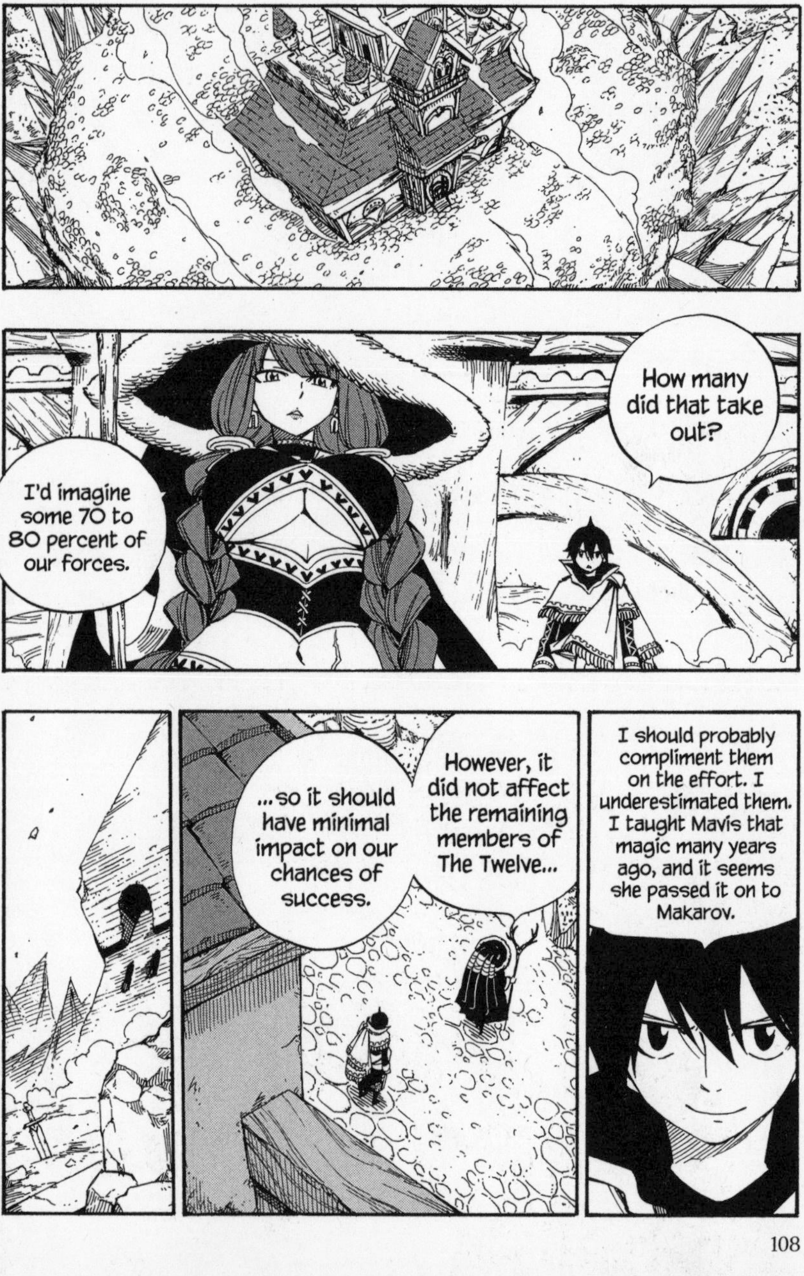
How many did that take out?
I'd imagine some 70 to 80 percent of our forces.
I should probably compliment them on the effort. I underestimated them. I taught Mavis that magic many years ago, and it seems she passed it on to Makarov.
However, it did not affect the remaining members of The Twelve...
...so it should have minimal impact on our chances of success.

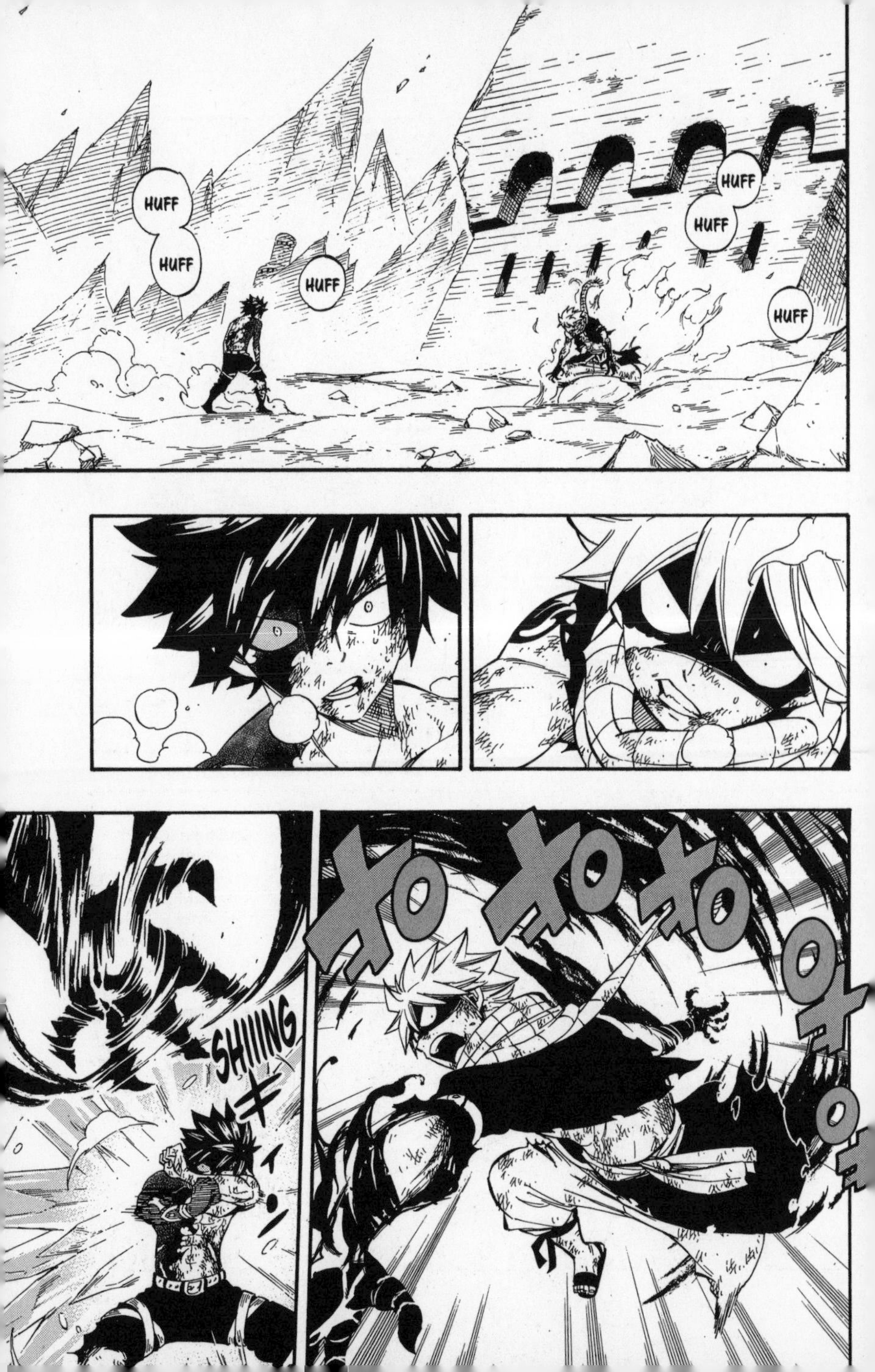
HUFF
HUFF
HUFF
HUFF
HUFF
HUFF
SHIIING

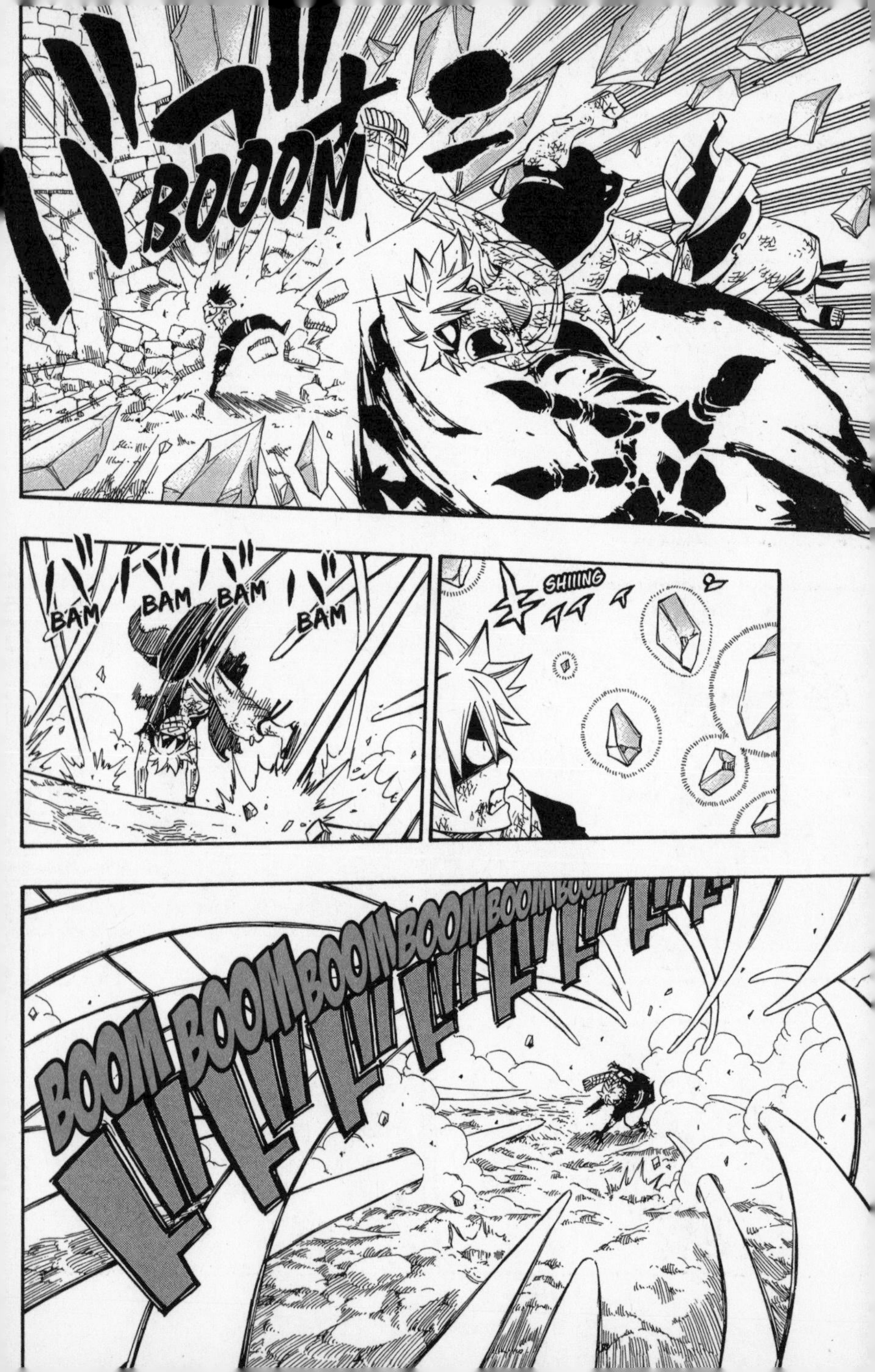
BOOOM
SHIIING
BAM
BAM
BAM
BAM
BOOM BOOM BOOM BOOM BOOM BOOM

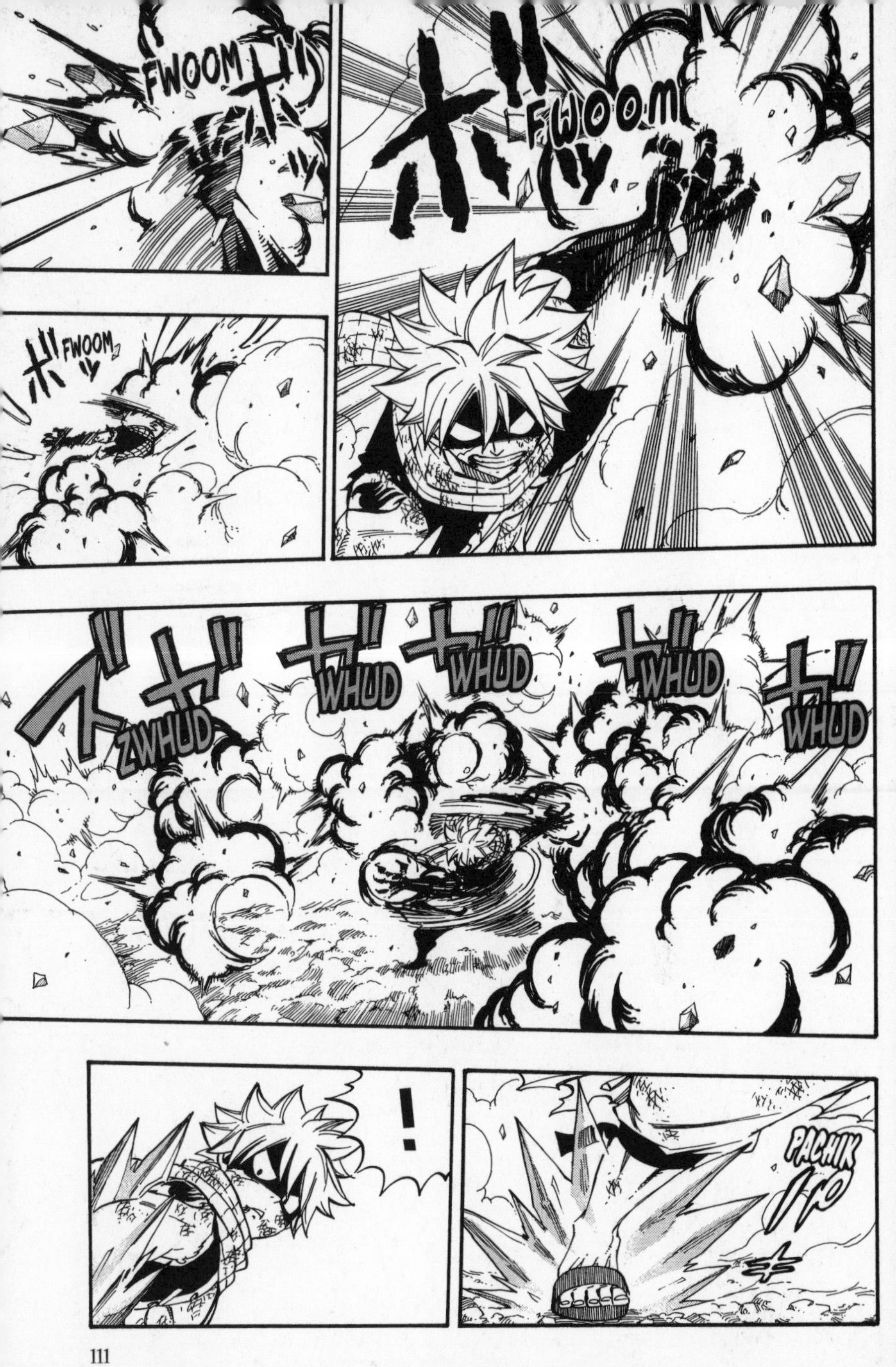
FWOOM
FWOOM
FWOOM
WHUD
WHUD
WHUD
WHUD
ZWHUD
PACHIK
!

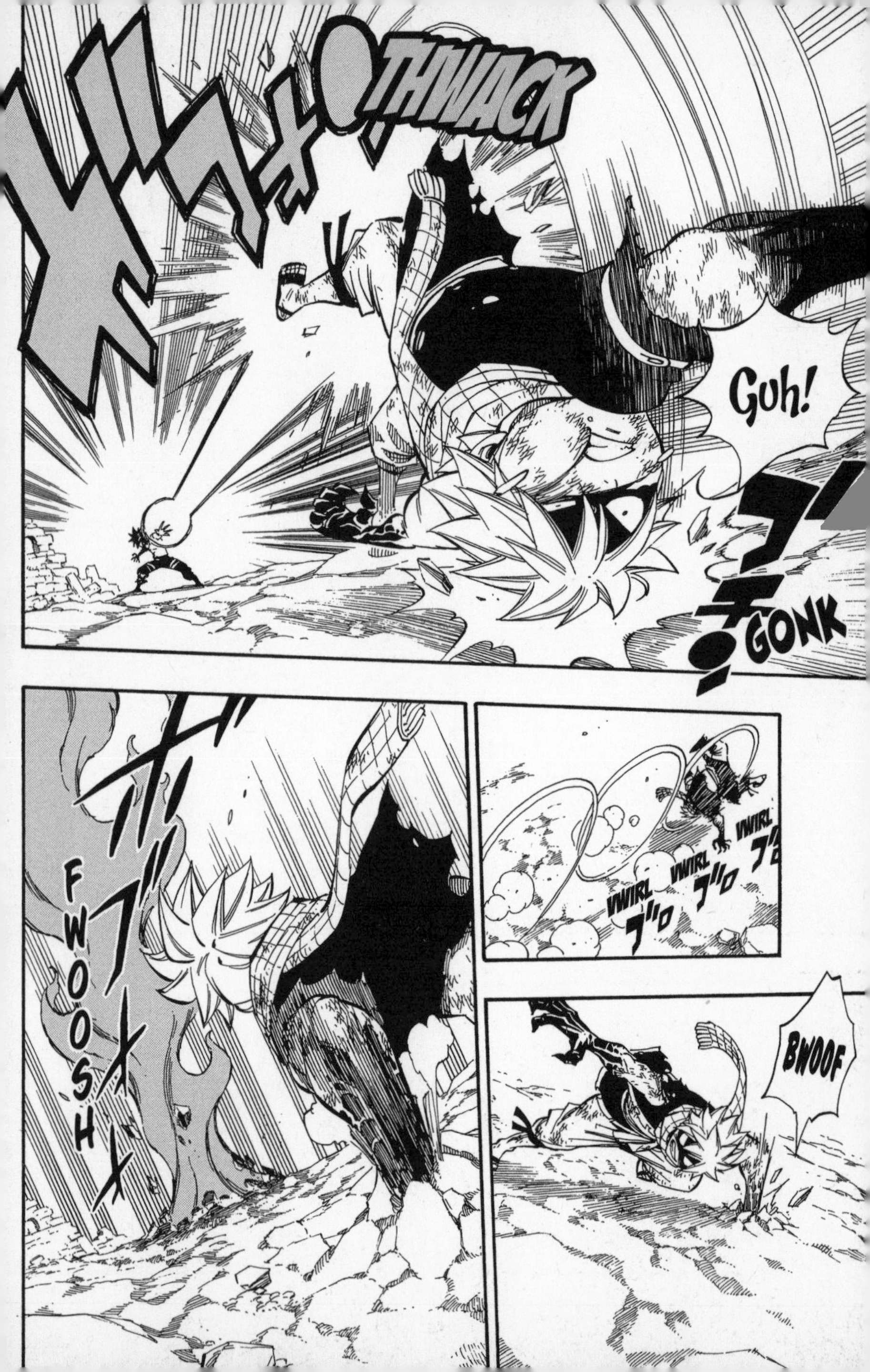
THWACK
Guh!
GONK
VWIRL
VWIRL
VWIRL
BWOOF
FWOOSH

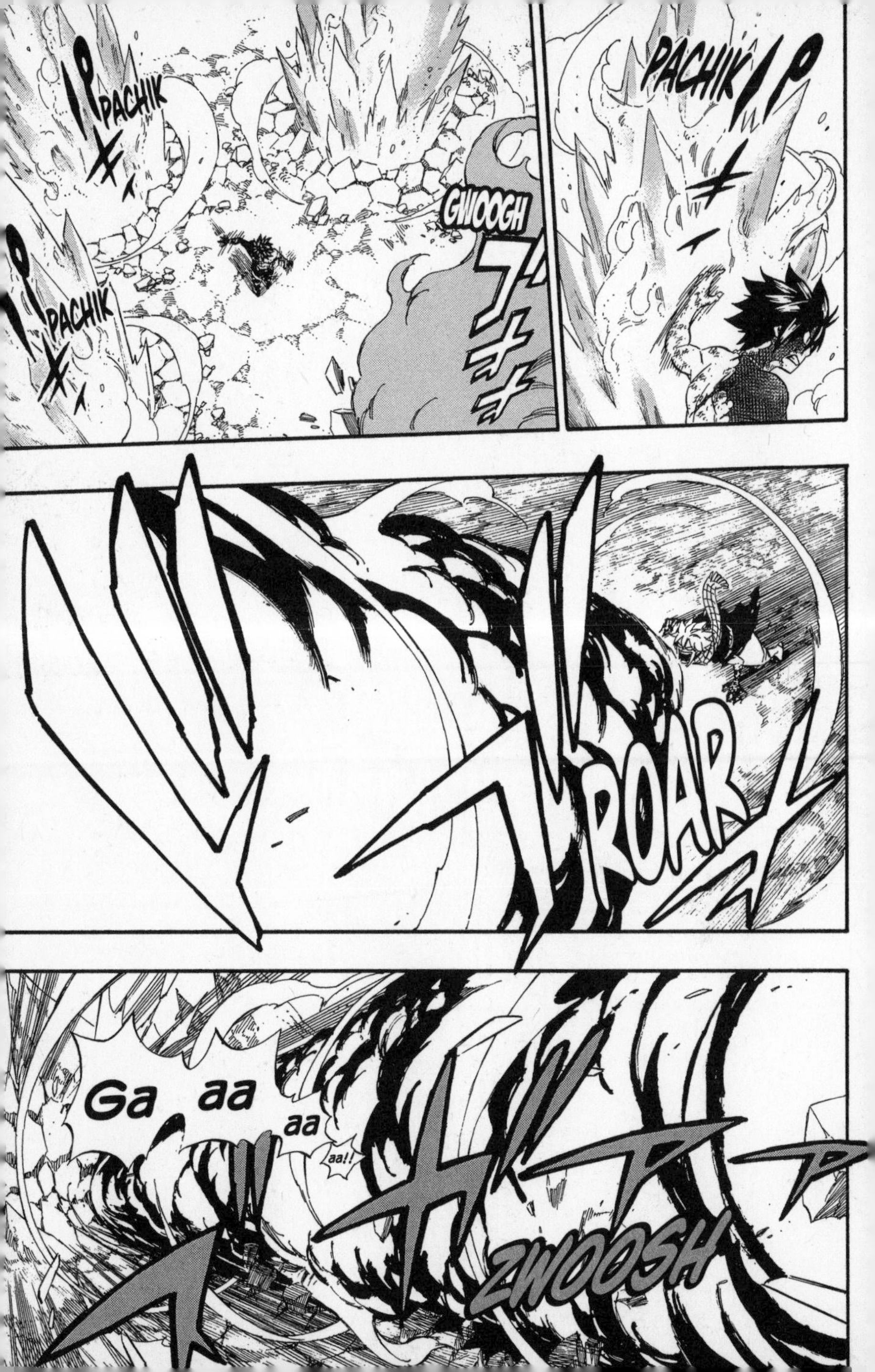
PACHIK
GWOOGH
PACHIK
PACHIK
ROAR
Ga aa aa aa!!
ZWOOSH

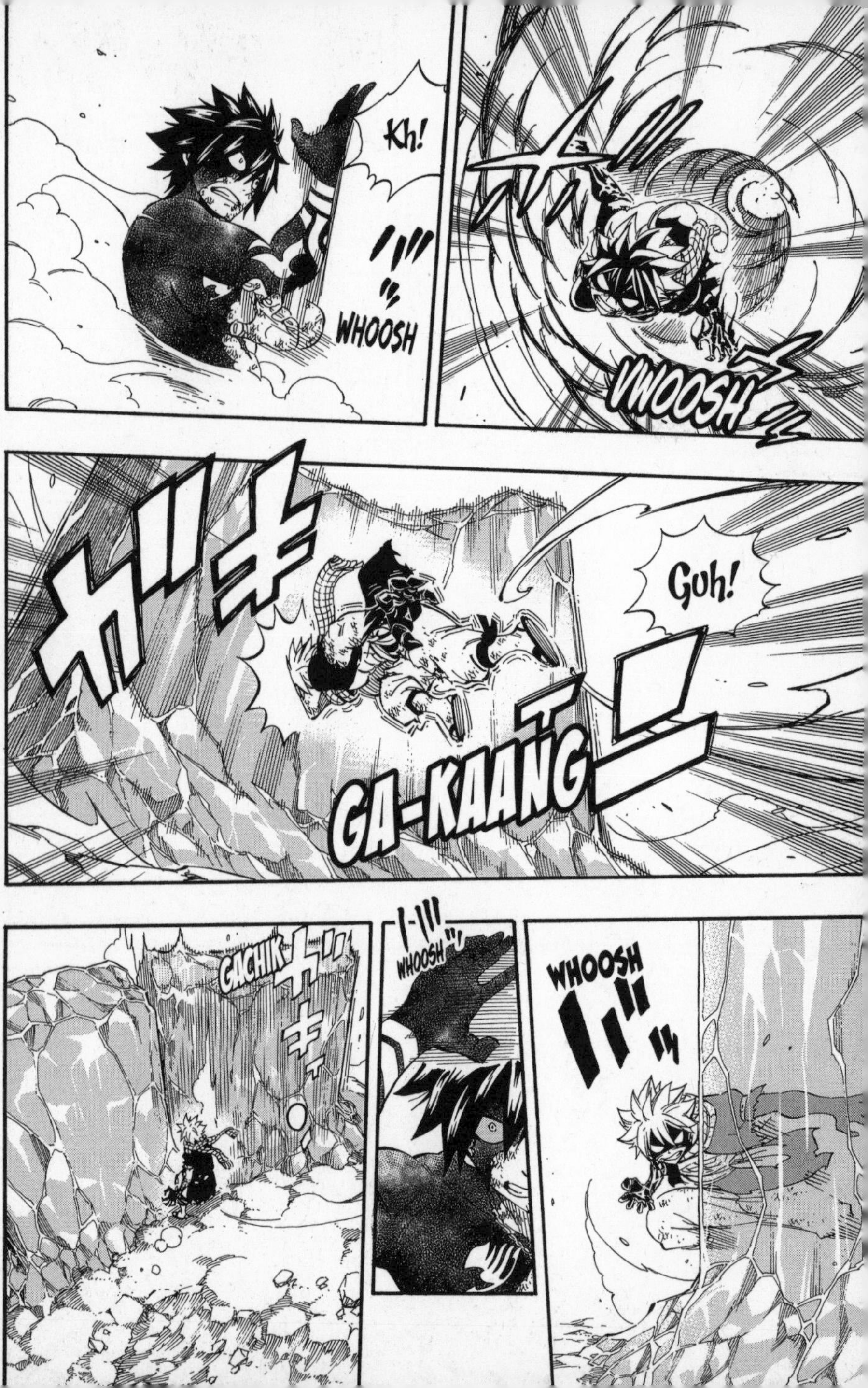
VWOOSH
Kh!
WHOOSH
Guh!
GA-KAANG
WHOOSH
WHOOSH
GACHIK

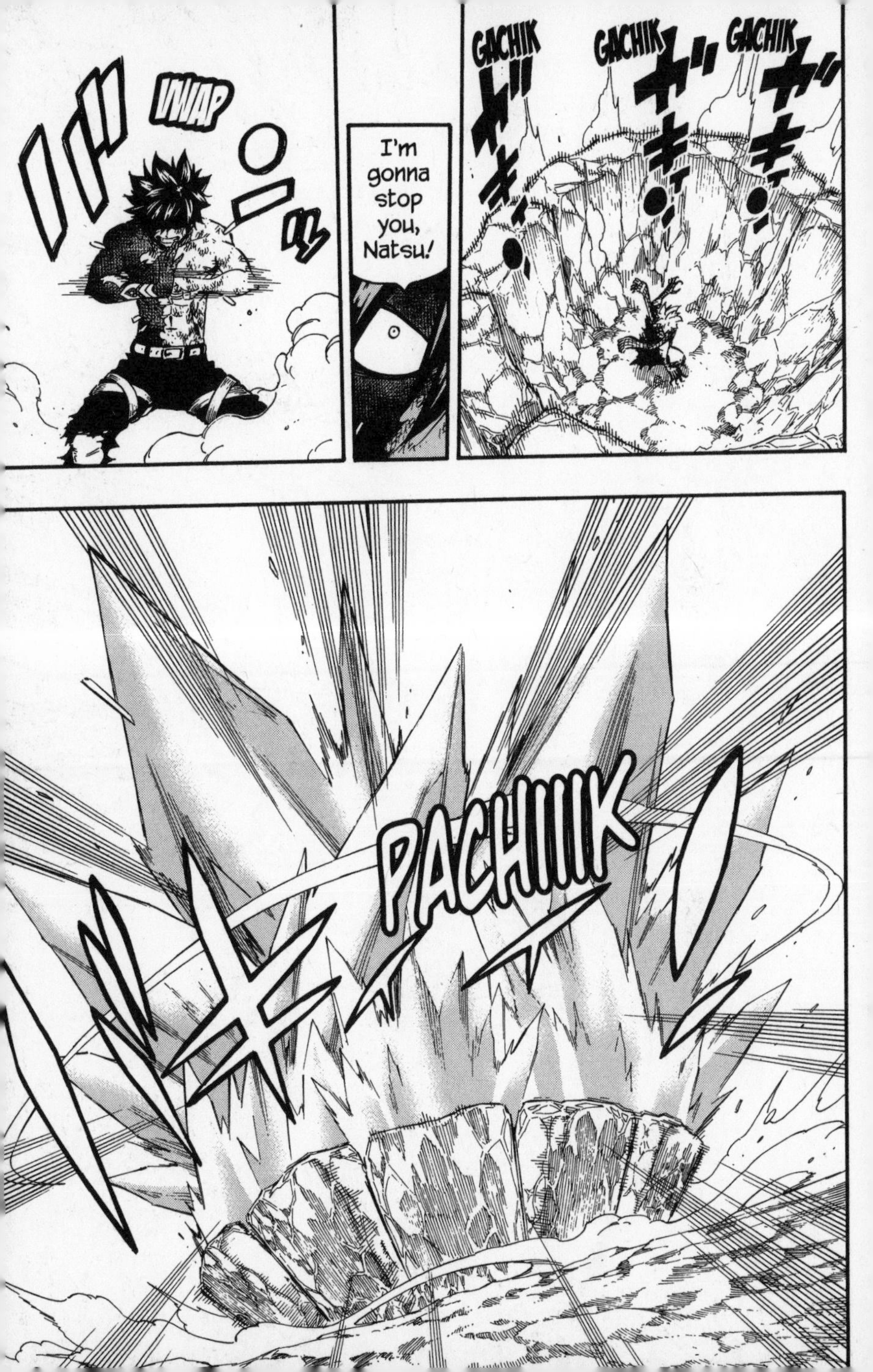
GACHIK
GACHIK
GACHIK
I'm gonna stop you, Natsu!
VWAP
PACHIIIK

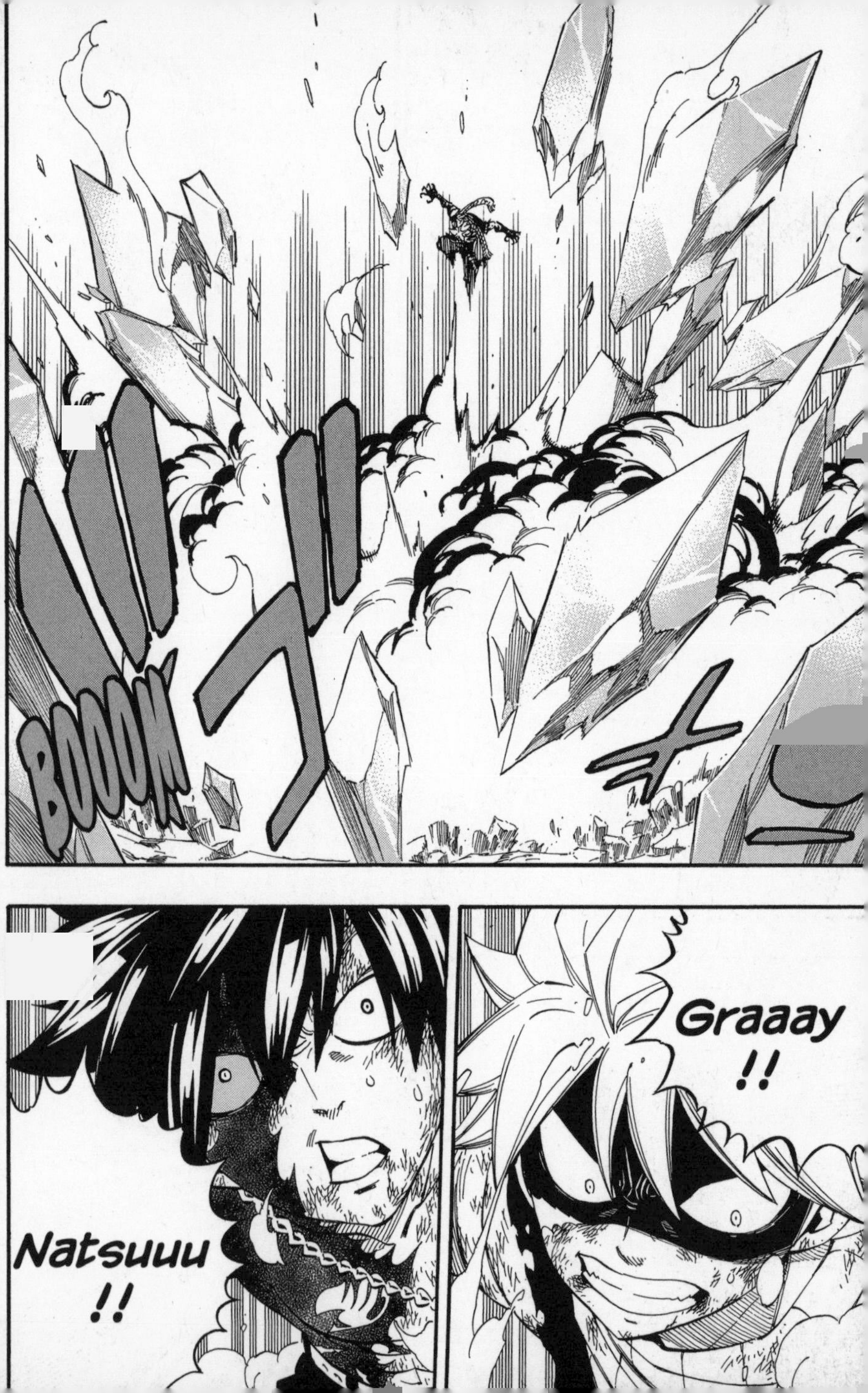
BOOOM
Graaay !!
Natsuuu !!

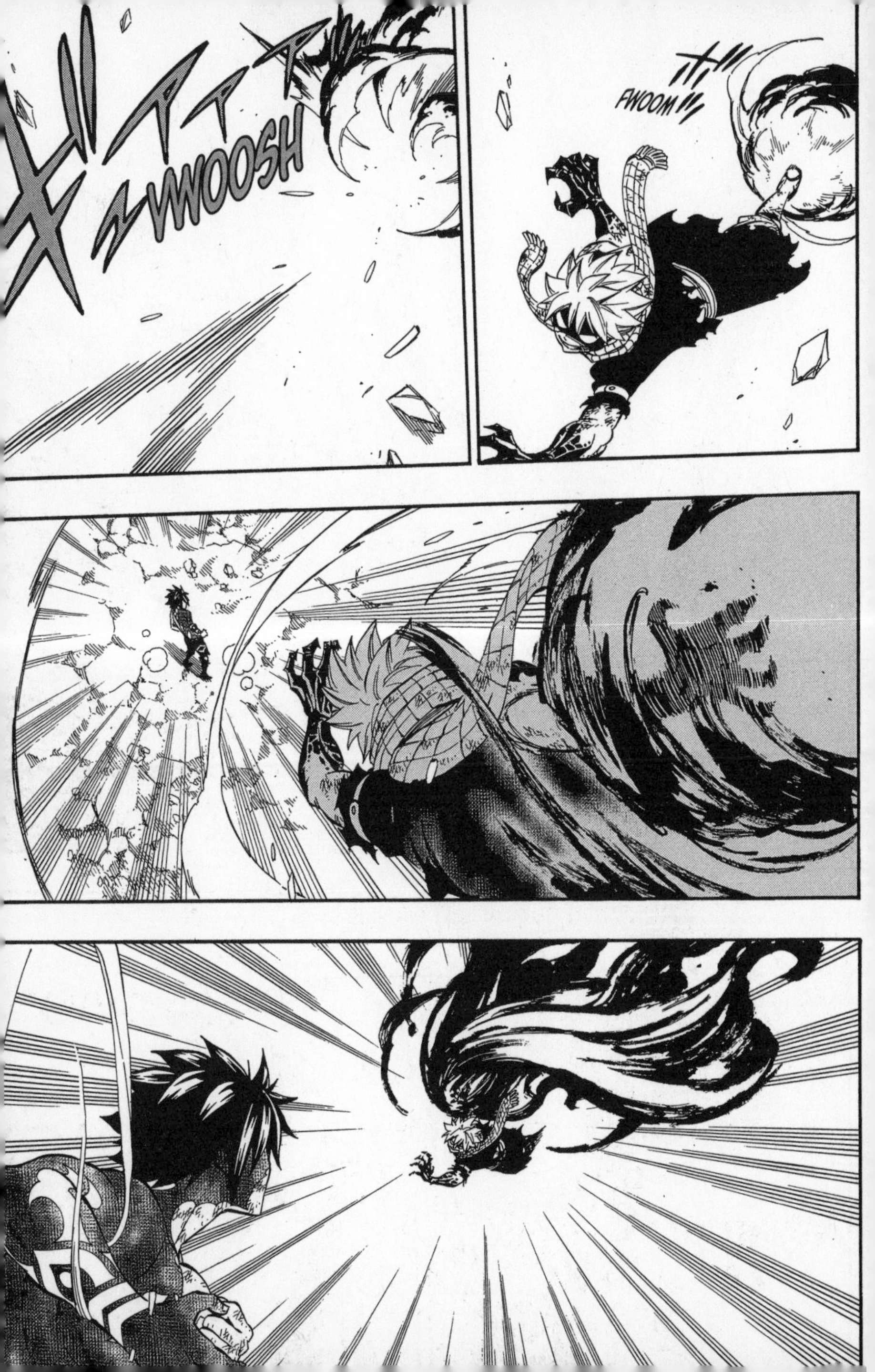
FWOOM!!
WHOOSH

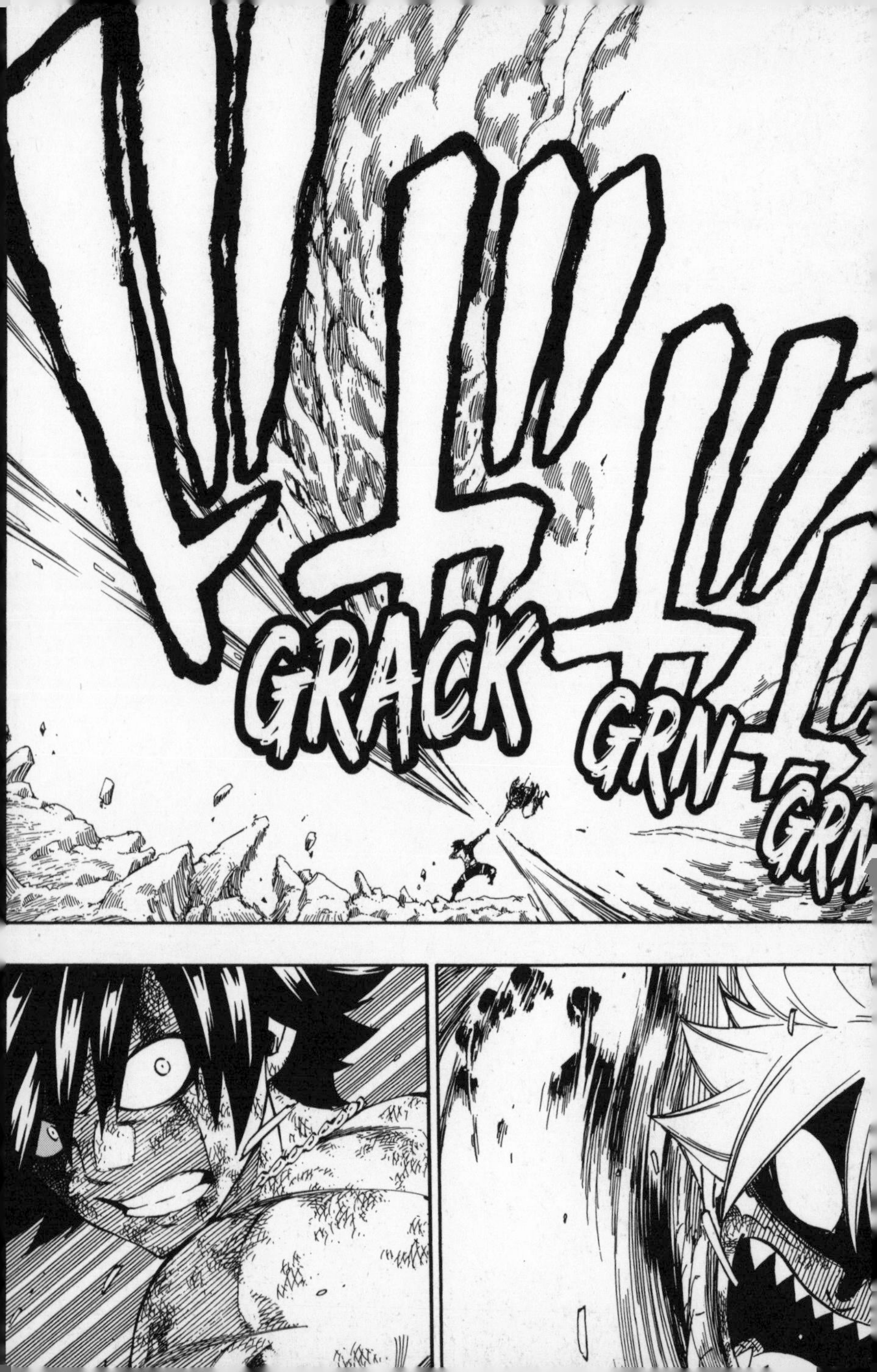
GRACK
GRN

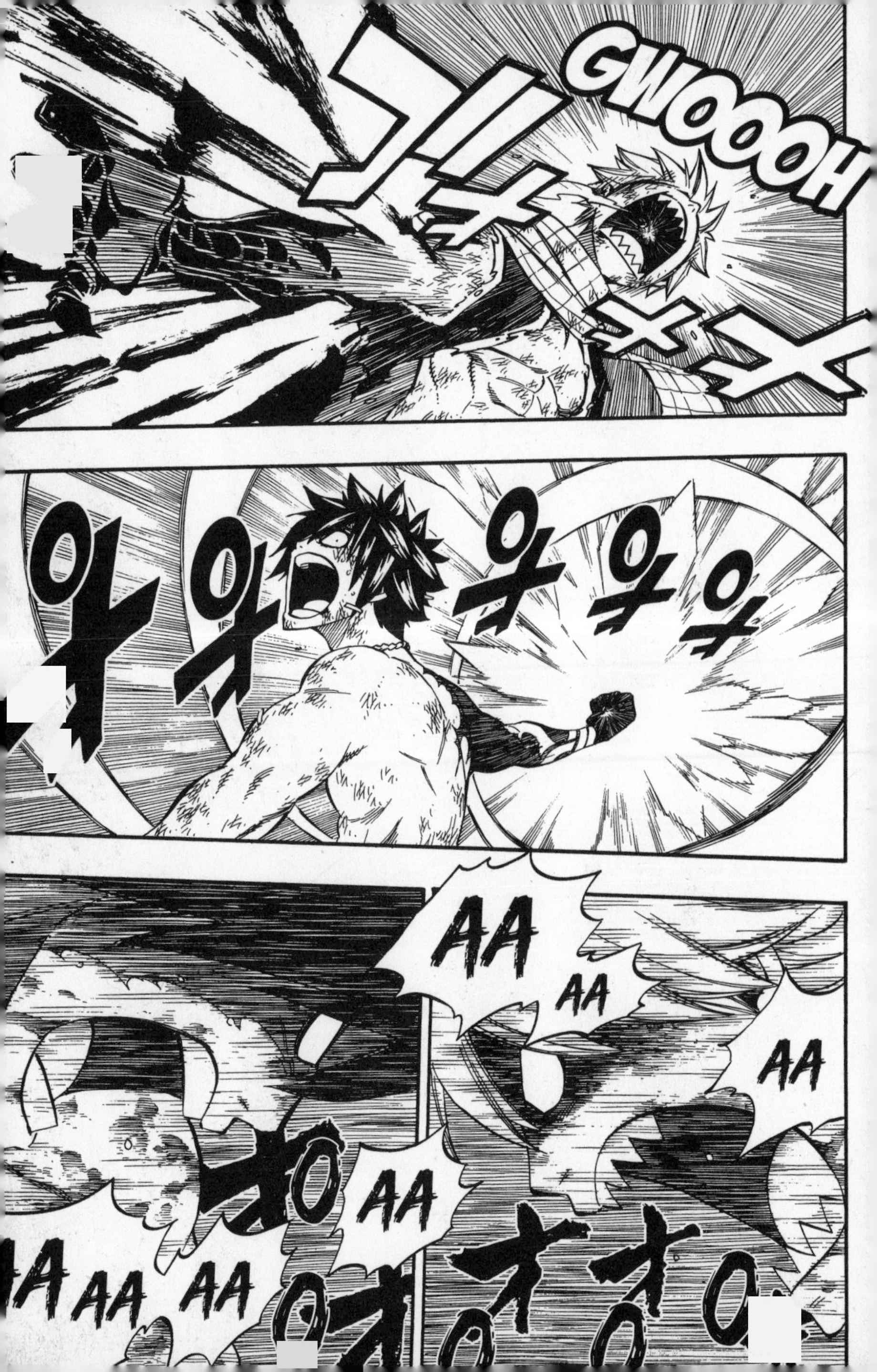
GWOOOOH
AA
AA
AA
AA
AA
AA
AA

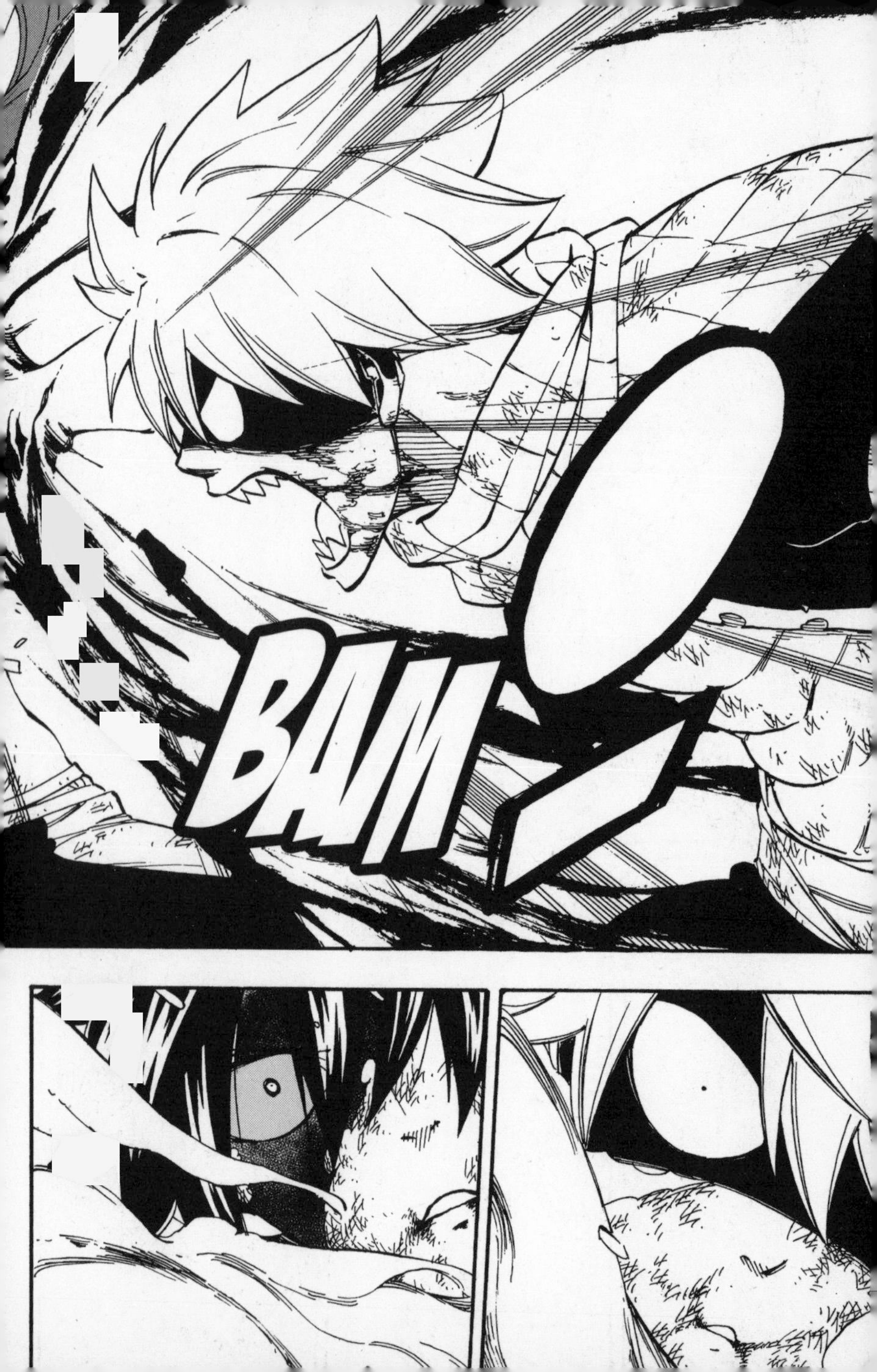
BAM

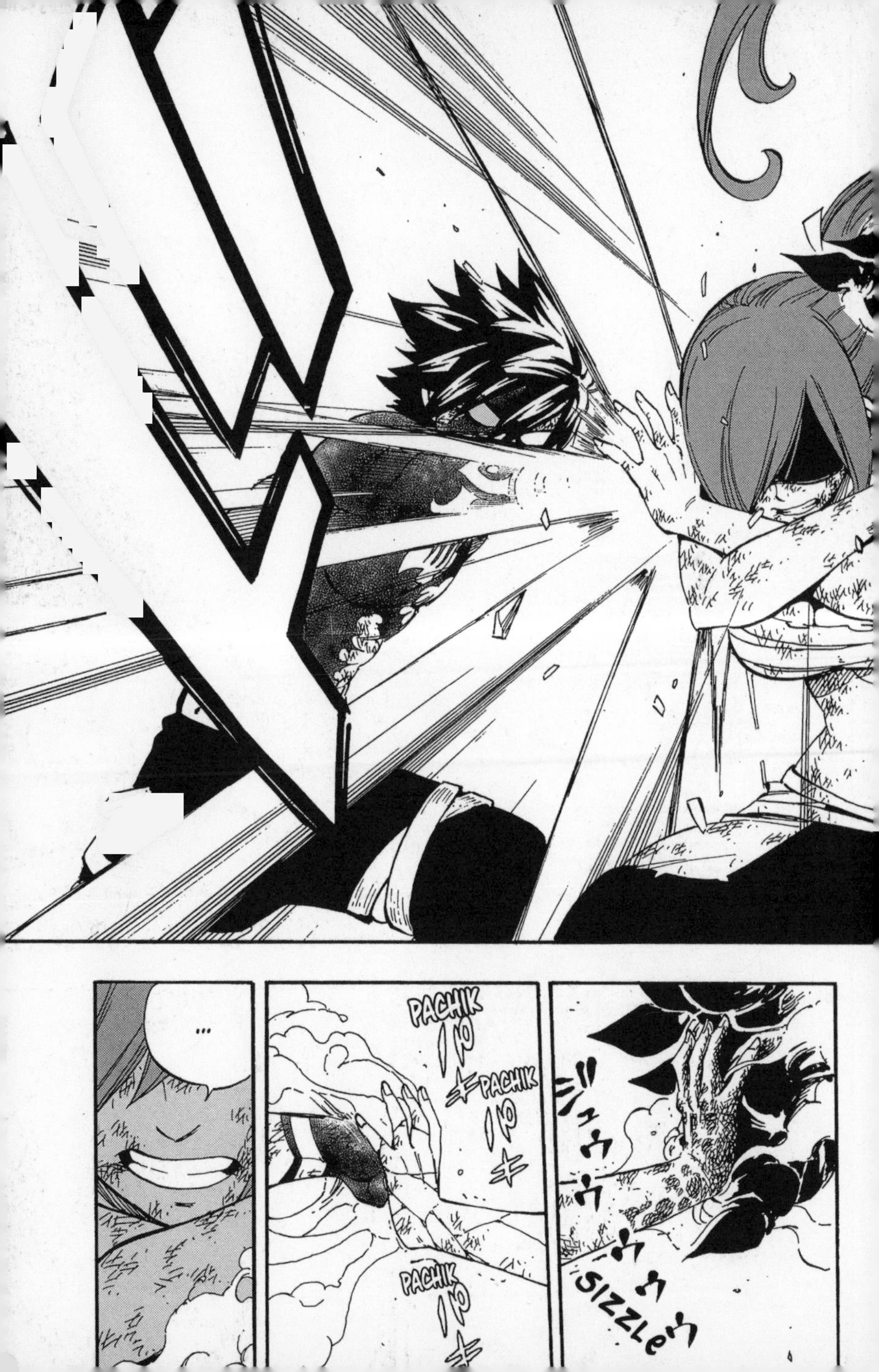
SIZZLE
PACHIK
PACHIK
PACHIK
...

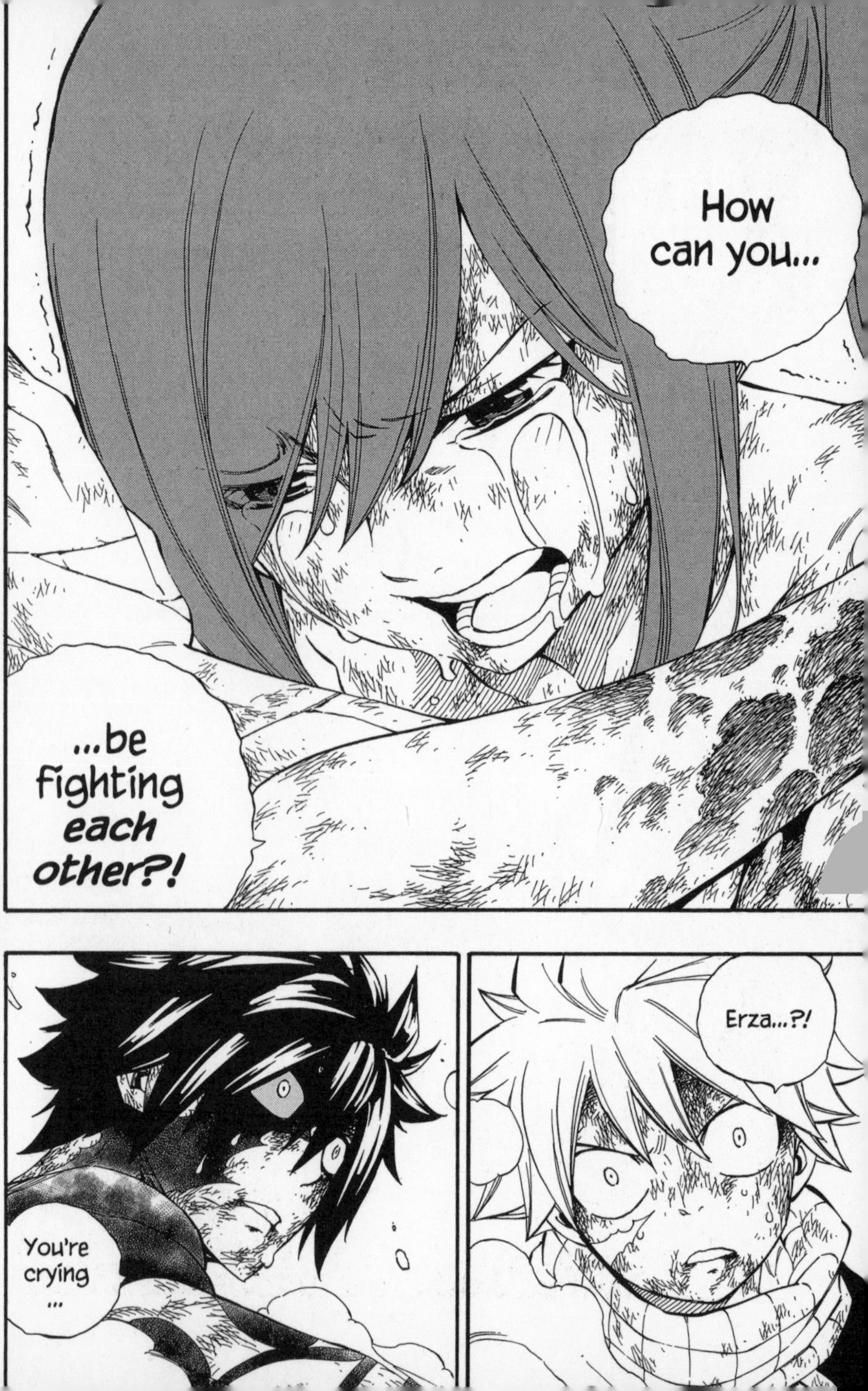
How can you...
...be fighting each other?!
Erza...?!
You're crying ...

FAIRY TAIL

フェアリーテイル

Chapter 507: Voice

OSAKANA FEST!!
Wonder Nyawn

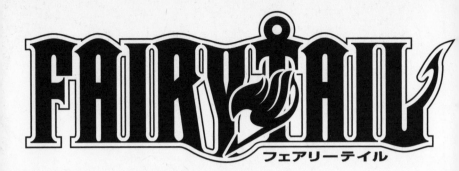

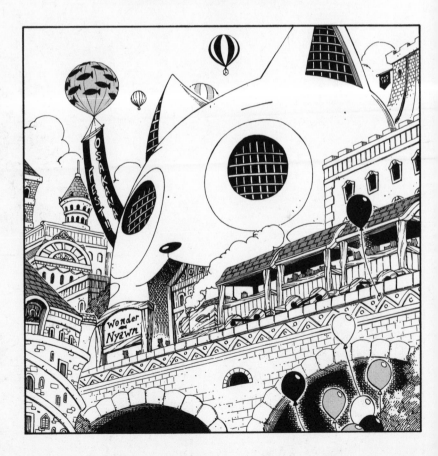

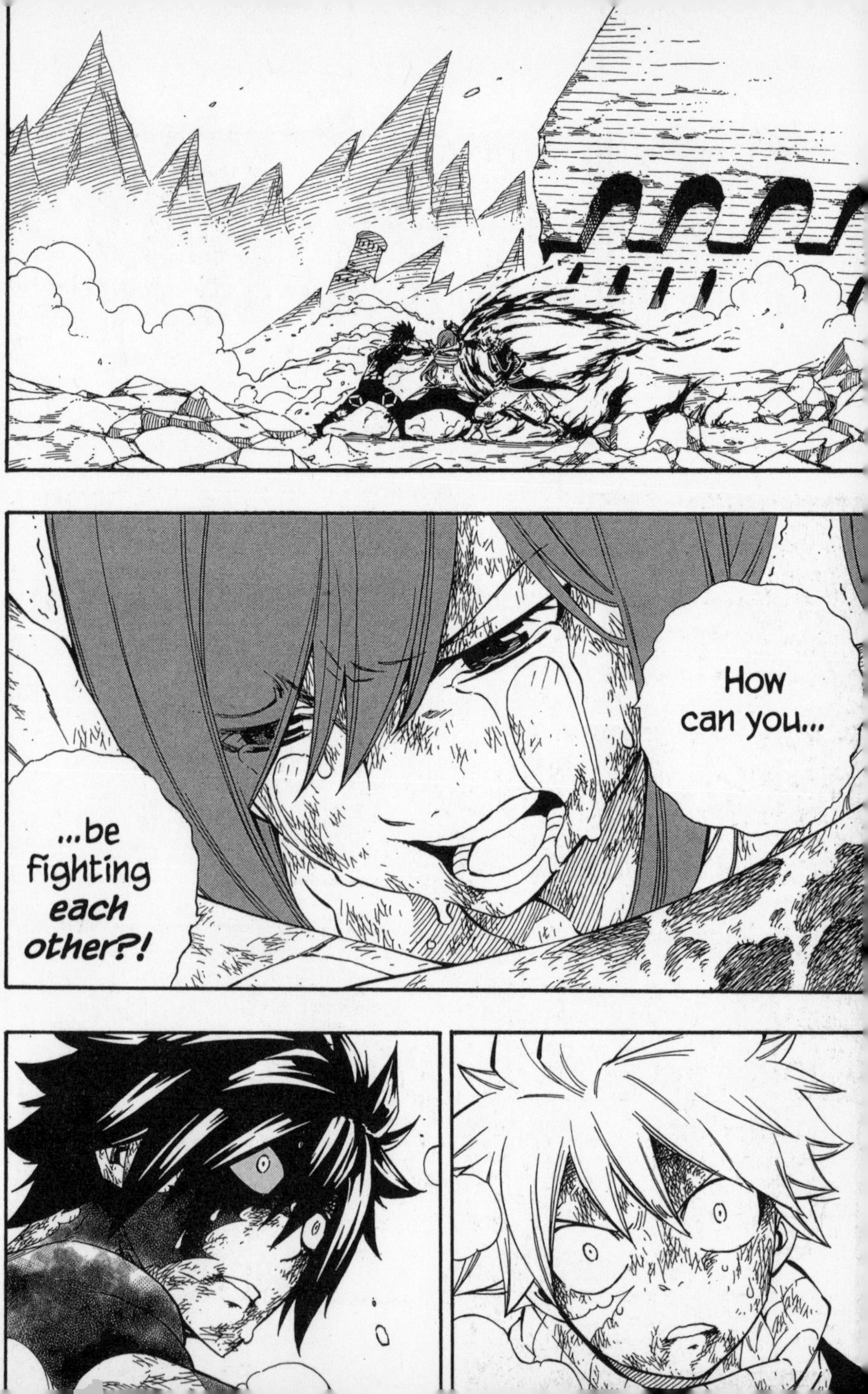
How can you...
...be fighting each other?!

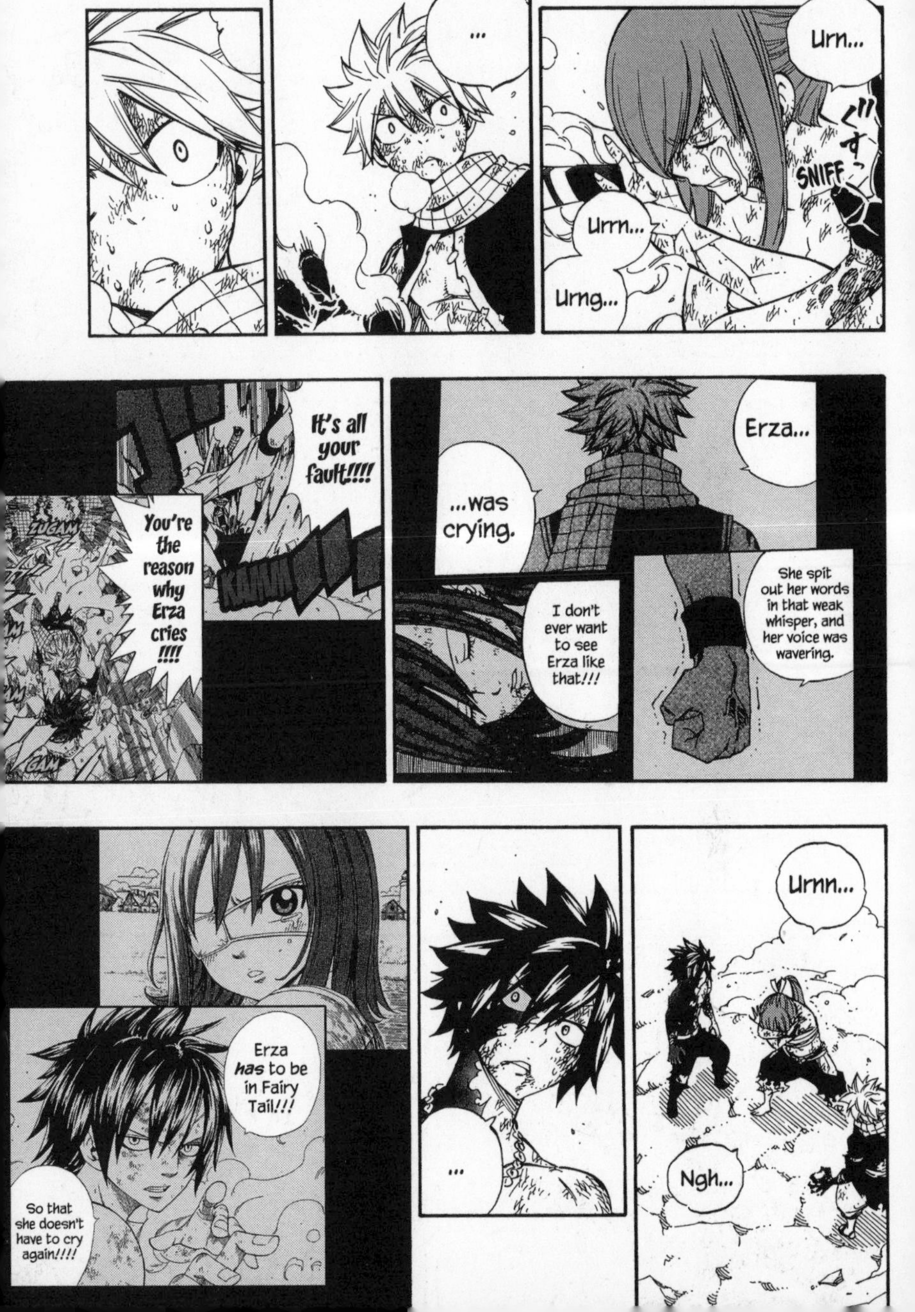

Urn...
SNIFF
Urrn...
Urng...
...
Erza...
...was crying.
She spit out her words in that weak whisper, and her voice was wavering.
I don't ever want to see Erza like that!!!
It's all your fault!!!!
You're the reason why Erza cries!!!!
ZUGAM
KAMM
GAM
Urnn...
Ngh...
...
Erza *has* to be in Fairy Tail!!!
So that she doesn't have to cry again!!!!

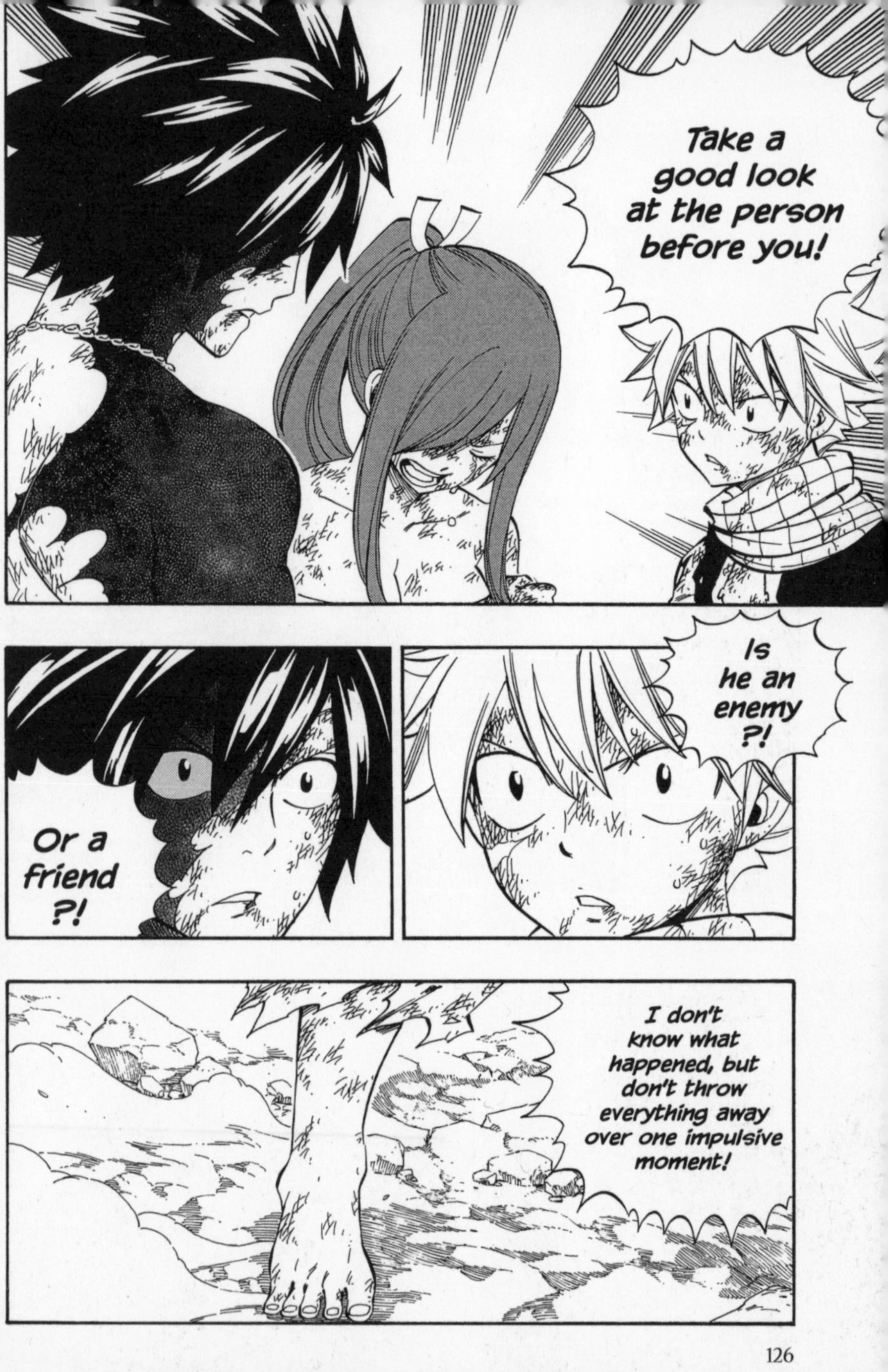
Take a good look at the person before you!
Is he an enemy ?!
Or a friend ?!
I don't know what happened, but don't throw everything away over one impulsive moment!

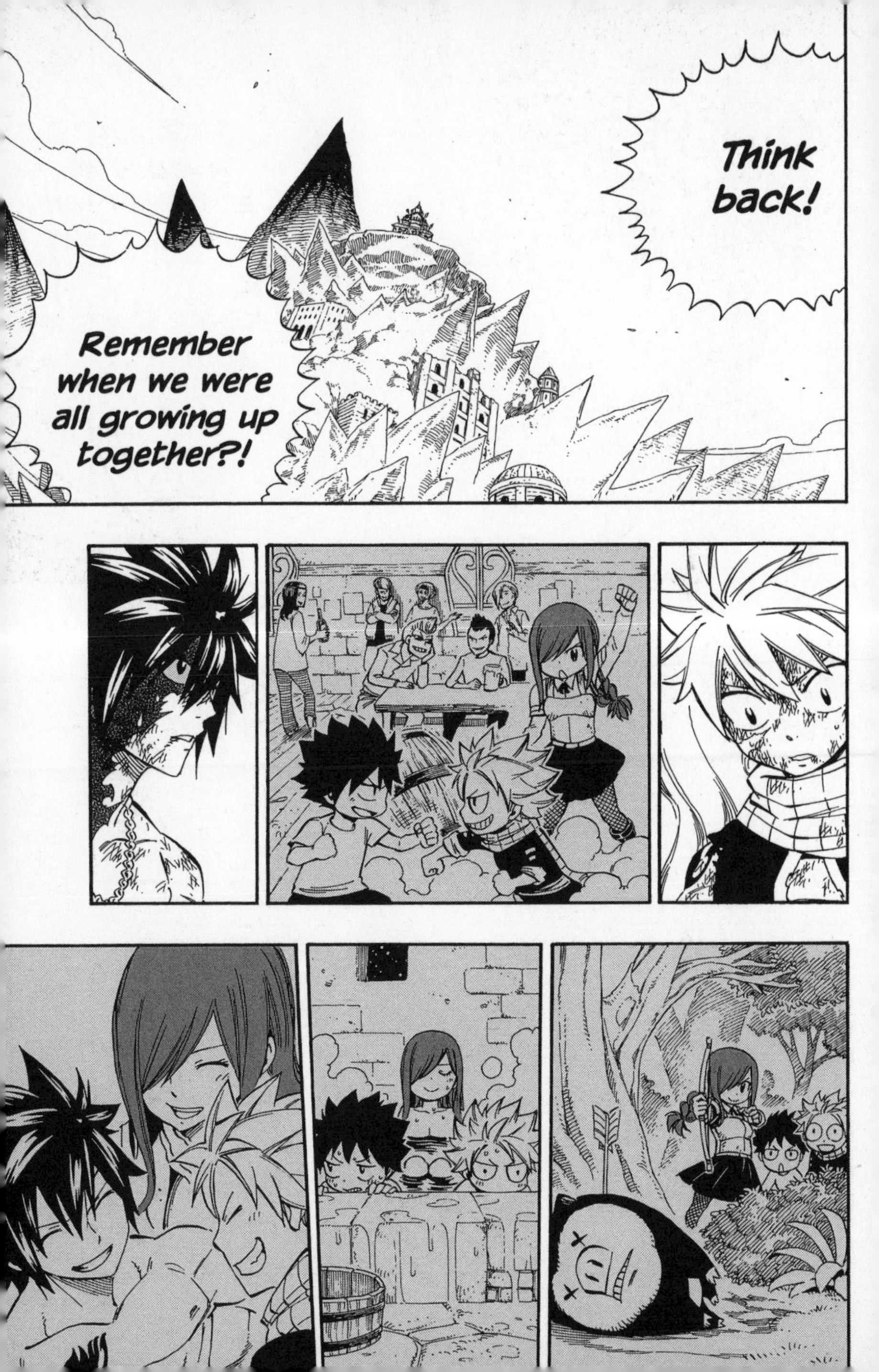
Think back!
Remember when we were all growing up together?!

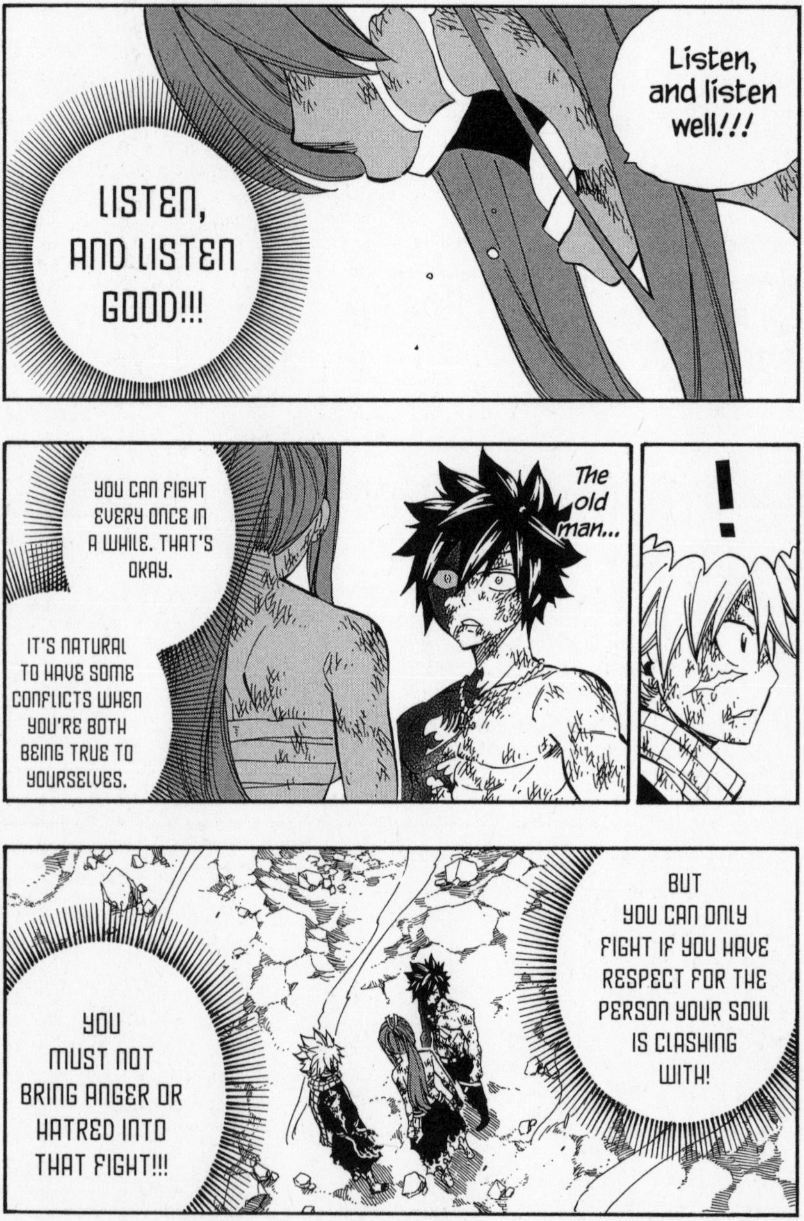
Listen, and listen well!!!
LISTEN, AND LISTEN GOOD!!!
!
The old man...
YOU CAN FIGHT EVERY ONCE IN A WHILE. THAT'S OKAY.
IT'S NATURAL TO HAVE SOME CONFLICTS WHEN YOU'RE BOTH BEING TRUE TO YOURSELVES.
BUT YOU CAN ONLY FIGHT IF YOU HAVE RESPECT FOR THE PERSON YOUR SOUL IS CLASHING WITH!
YOU MUST NOT BRING ANGER OR HATRED INTO THAT FIGHT!!!

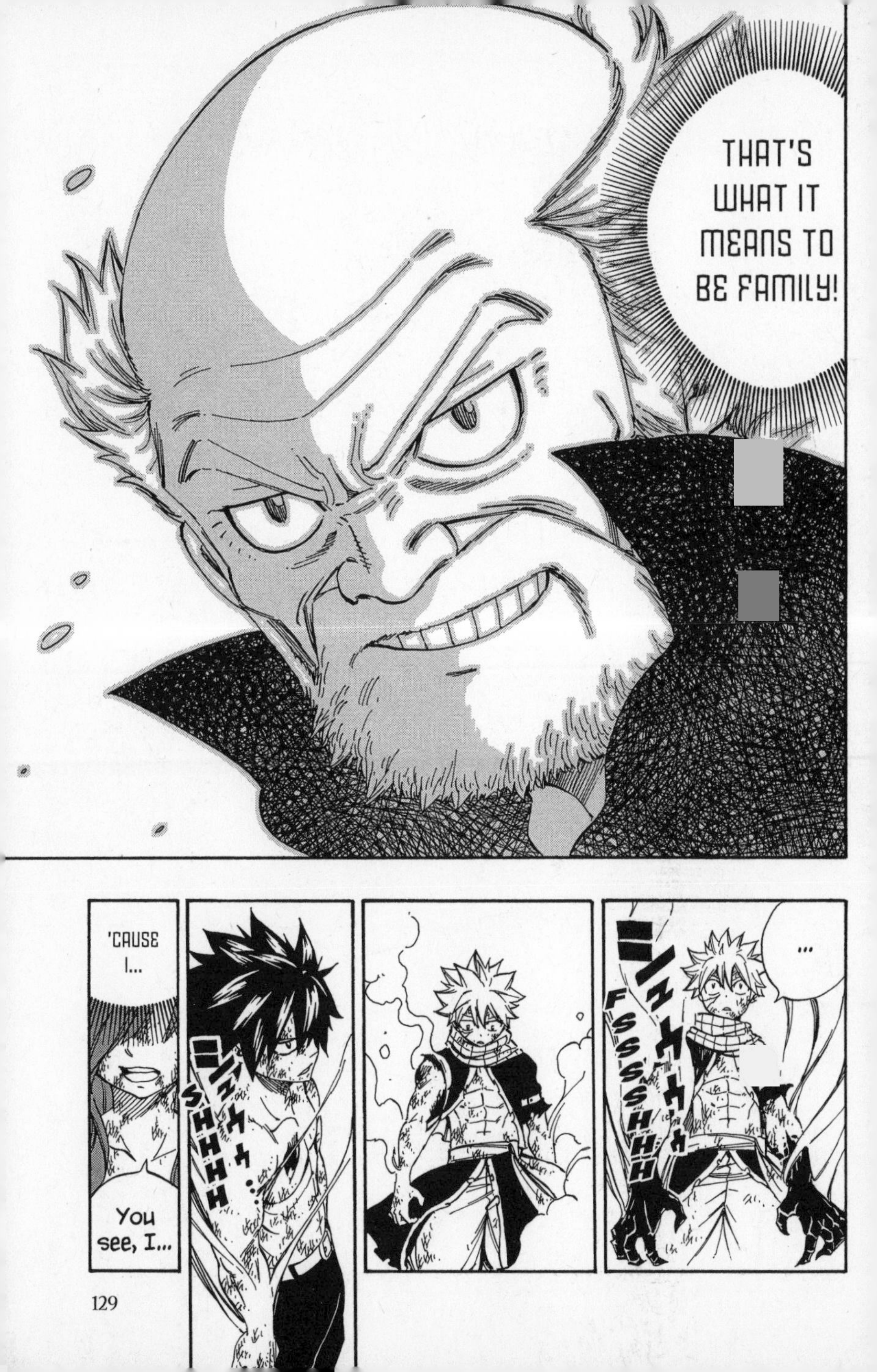
THAT'S WHAT IT MEANS TO BE FAMILY!
...
FSSSSHHH
SHHHH
'CAUSE I...
You see, I...

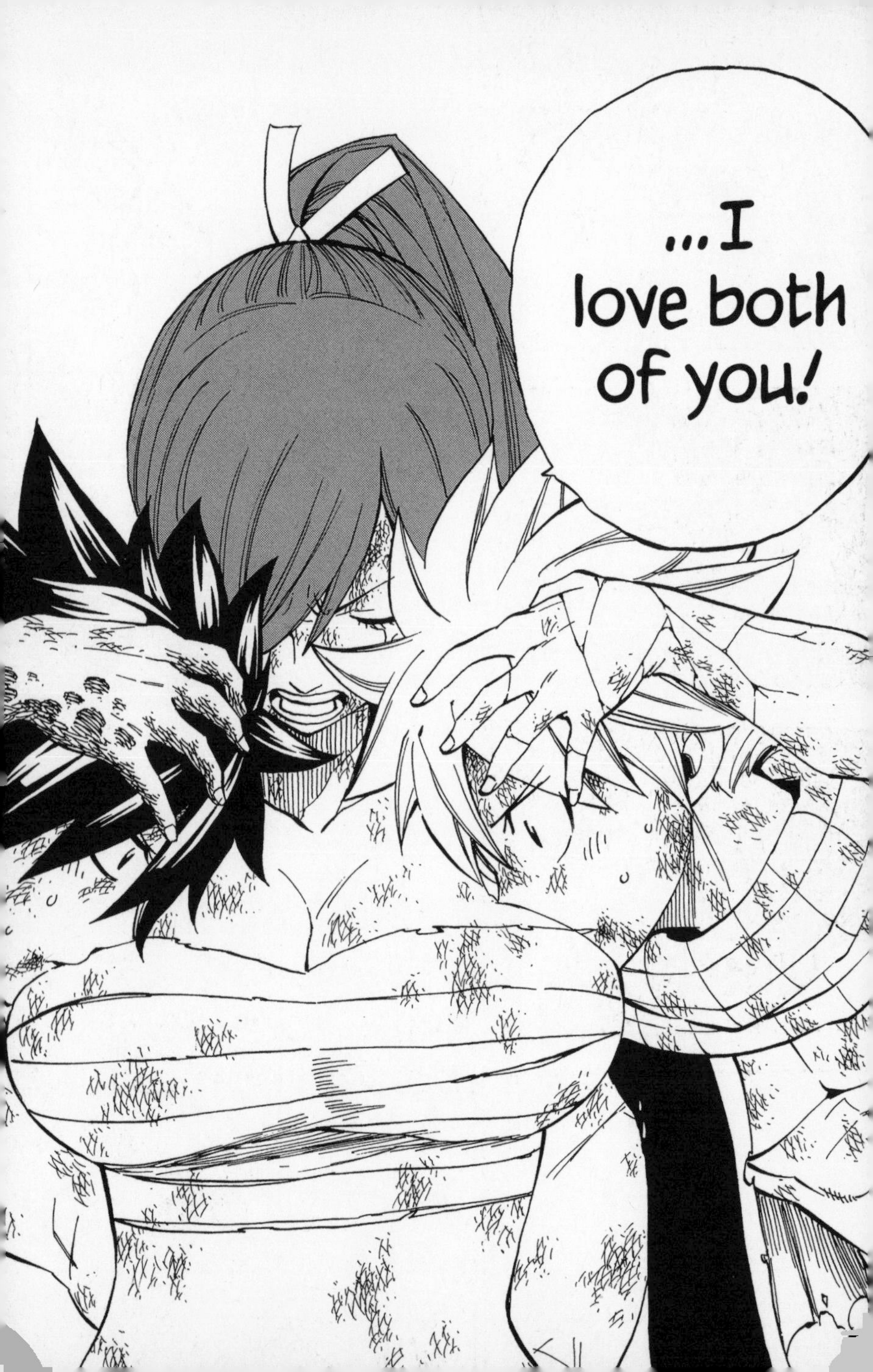
...I love both of you!

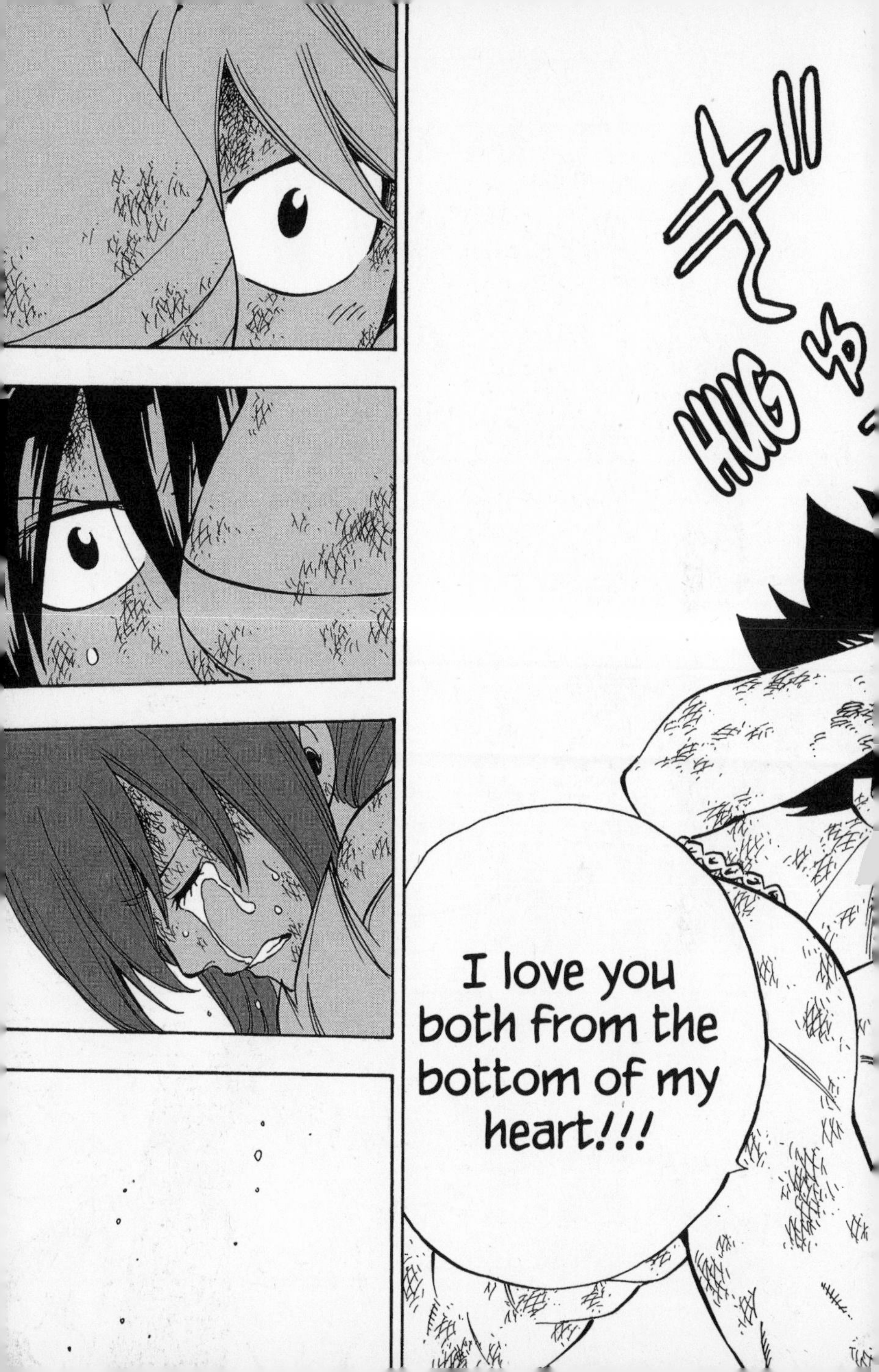
HUG
I love you both from the bottom of my heart!!!

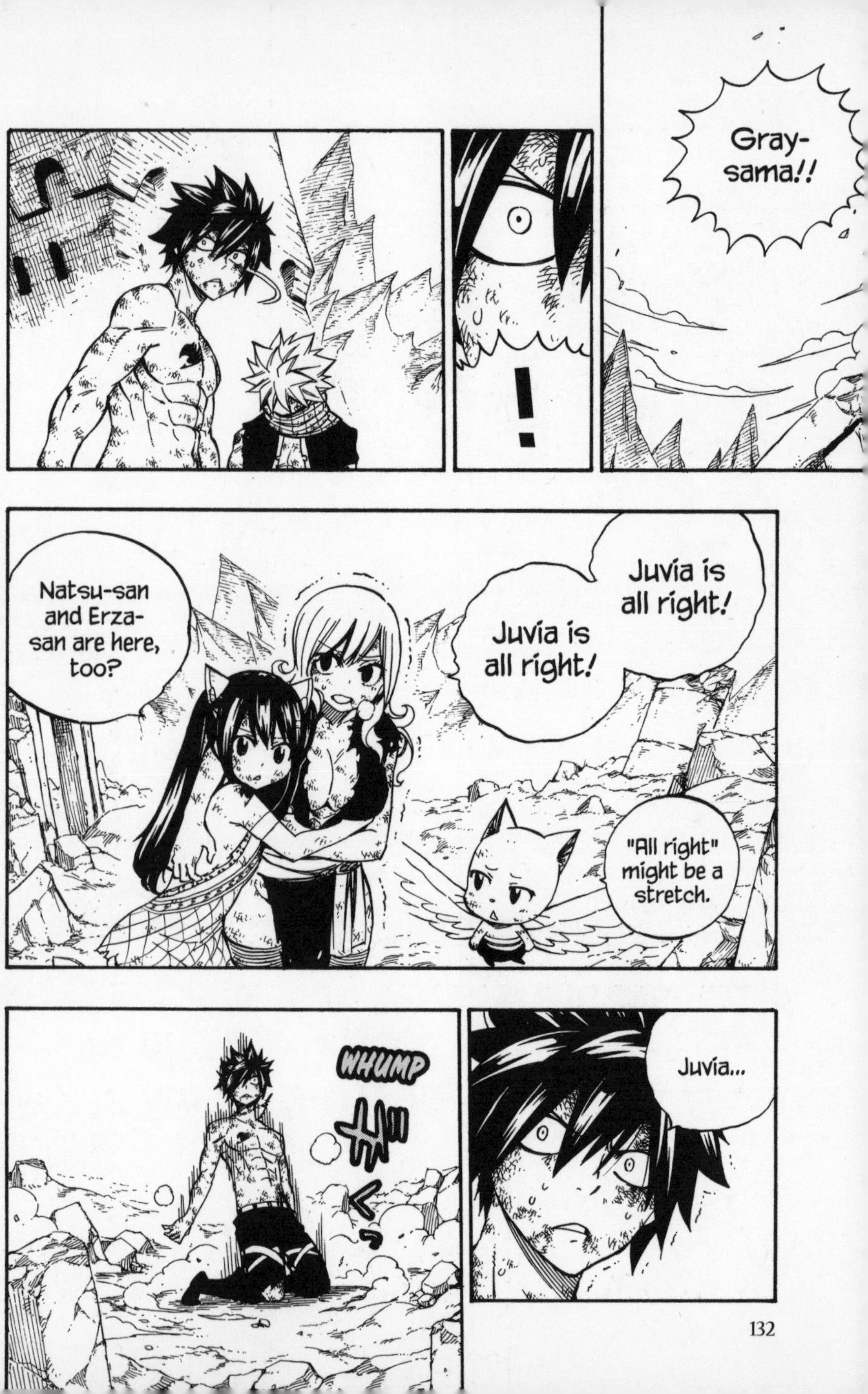
Gray-sama!!
!
Juvia is all right!
Juvia is all right!
Natsu-san and Erza-san are here, too?
"All right" might be a stretch.
Juvia...
WHUMP

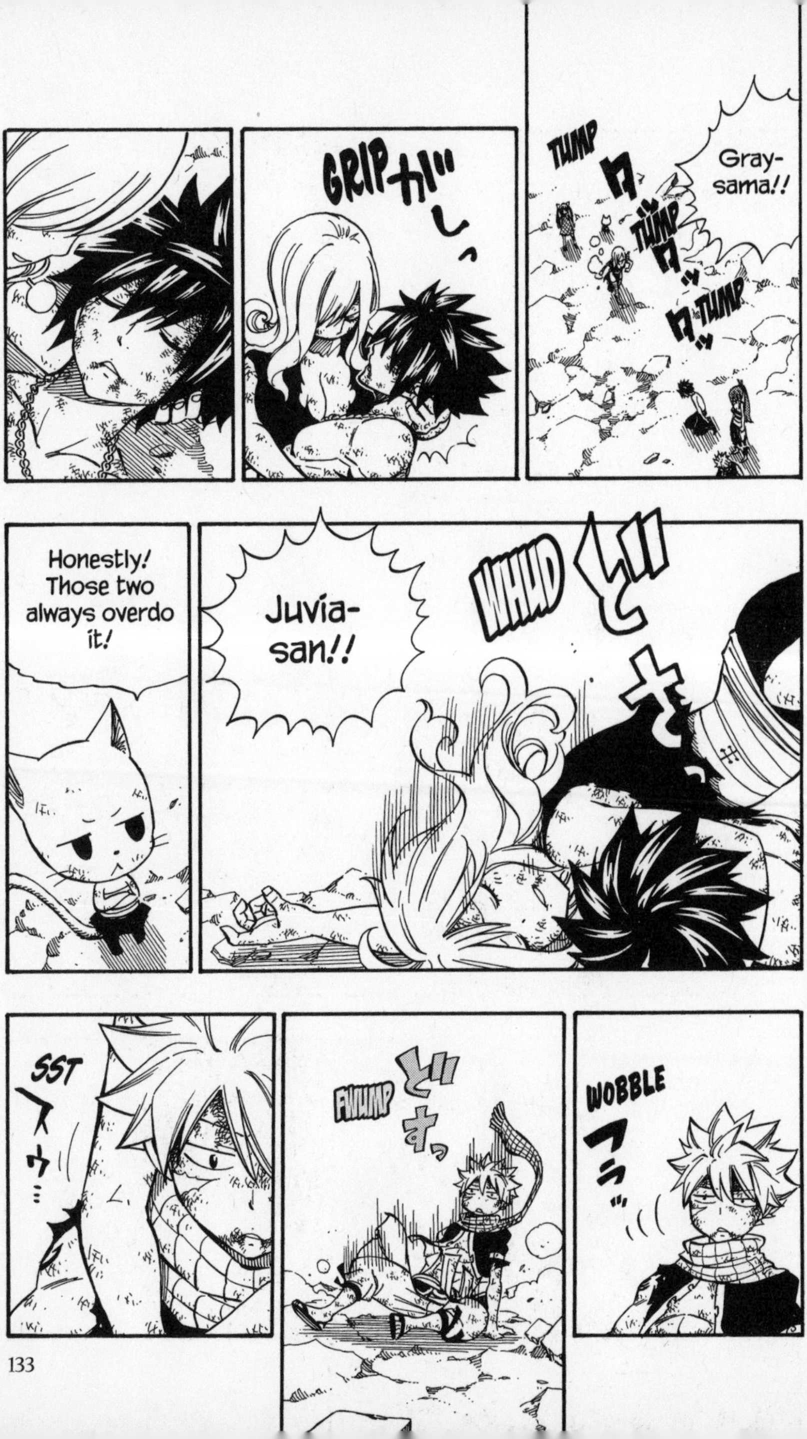
Gray-sama!!
TUMP
TUMP
TUMP
GRIP
がしっ
WHUD
どさっ
Juvia-san!!
Honestly! Those two always overdo it!
WOBBLE
フラッ
FWUMP
どすっ
SST
スゥー

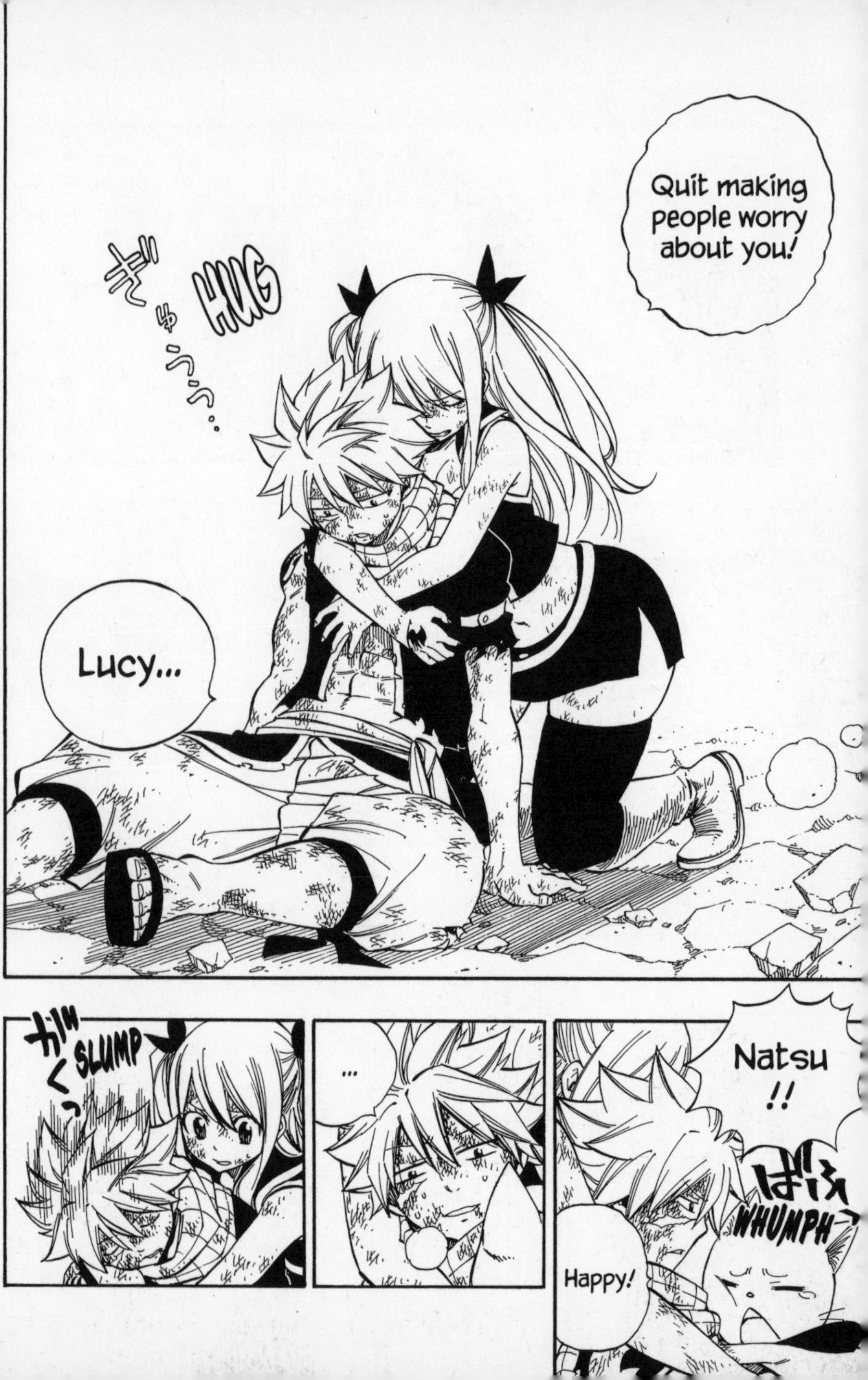
Quit making people worry about you!
ぎゅうう..
HUG
Lucy...
Natsu !!
ぱふっ
WHUMPH
Happy!
...
がくっ
SLUMP

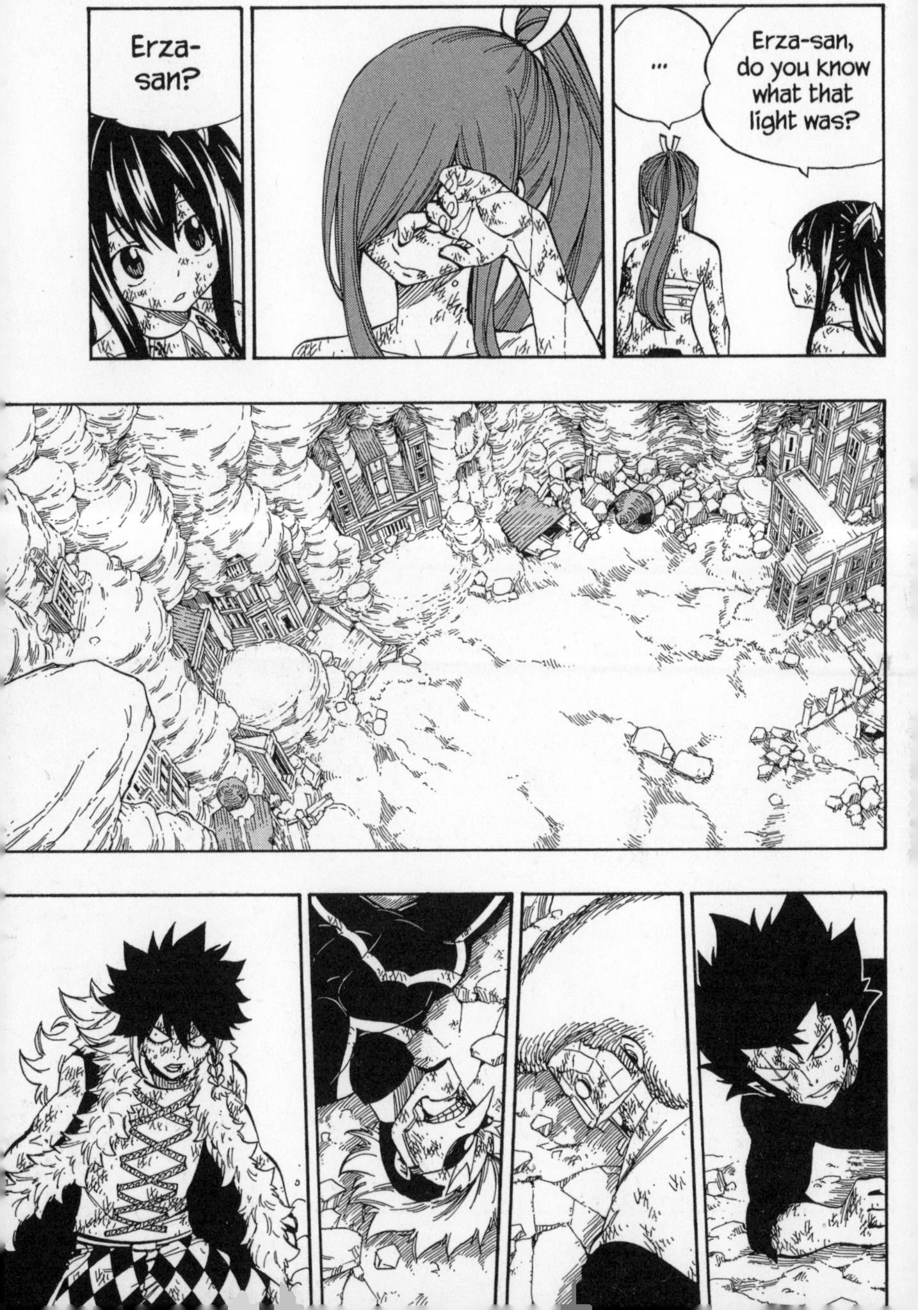
Erza-san, do you know what that light was?
...
Erza-san?

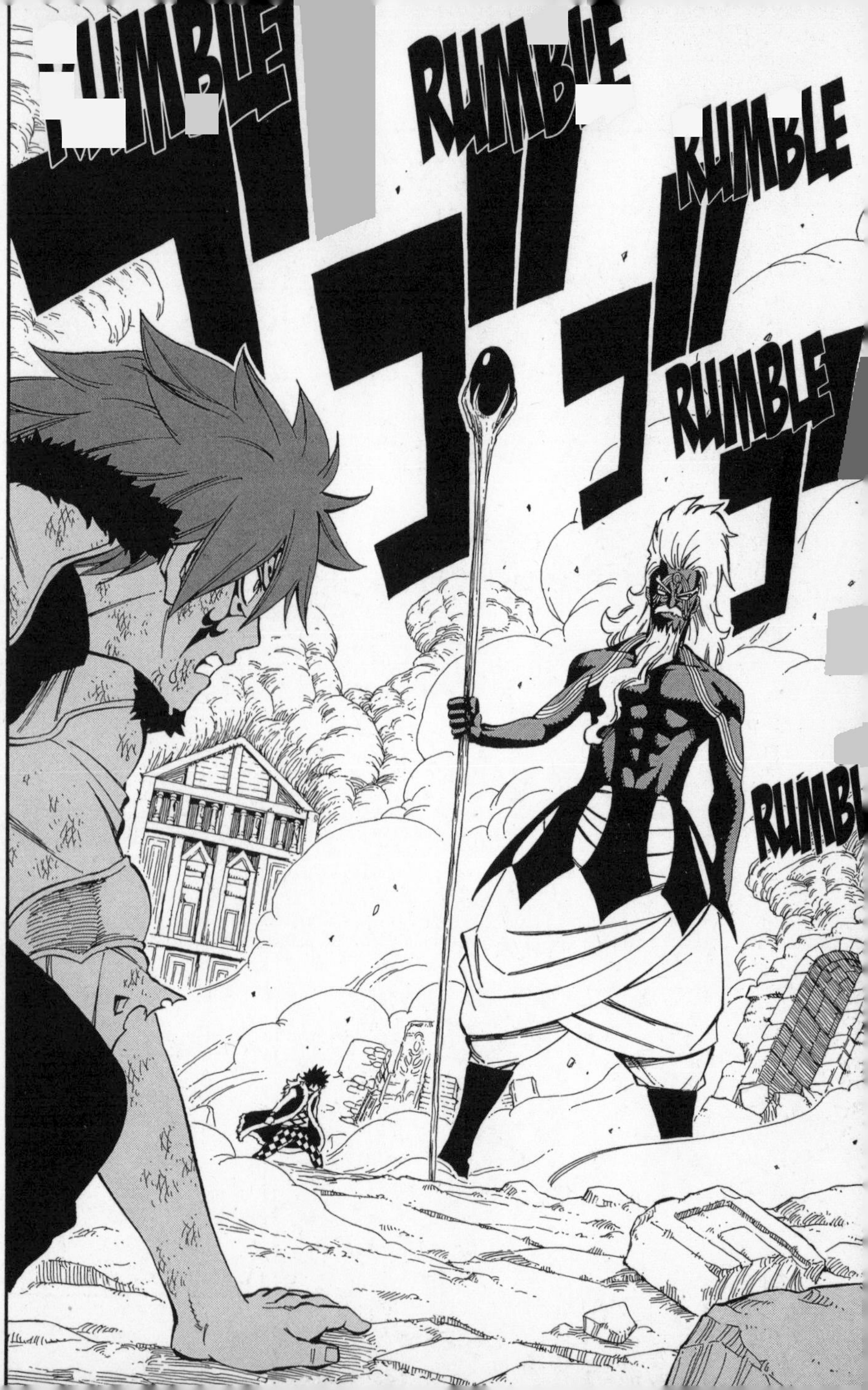
RUMBLE
RUMBLE
RUMB

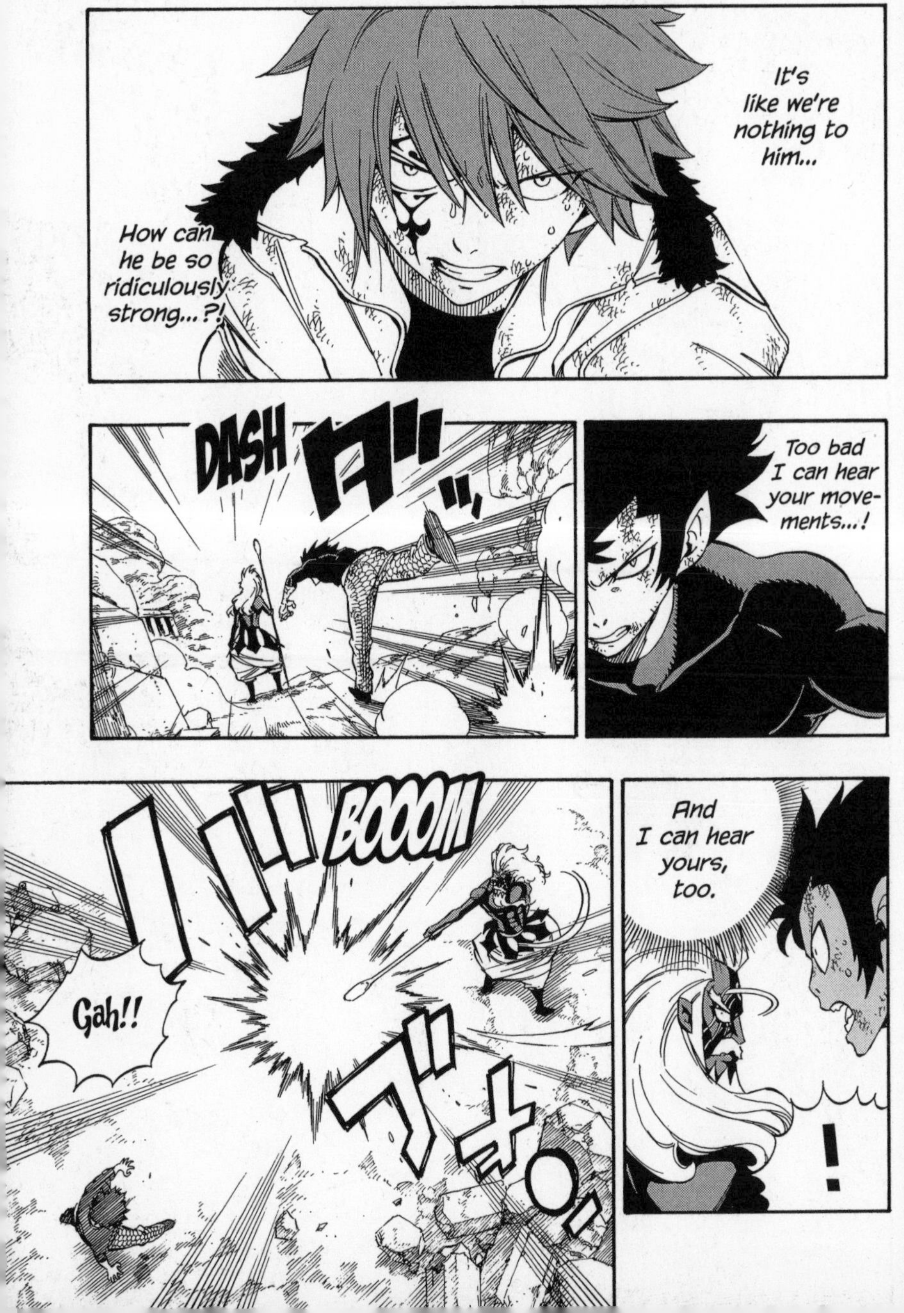
It's like we're nothing to him...
How can he be so ridiculously strong...?!
Too bad I can hear your movements...!
DASH
And I can hear yours, too.
!
BOOOM
Gah!!

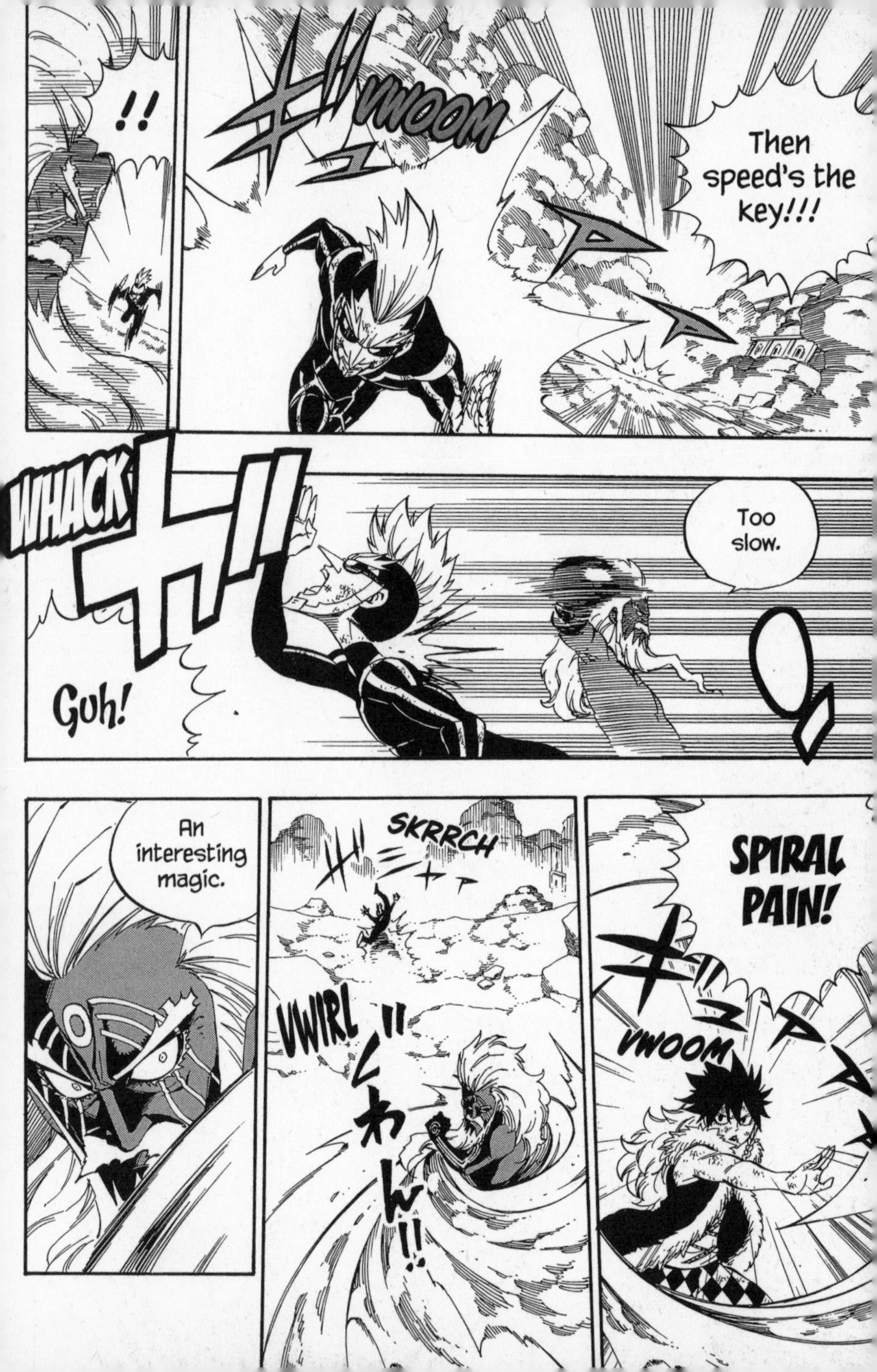
VWOOM
Then speed's the key!!!
!!
Too slow.
WHACK
Guh!
SPIRAL PAIN!
VWOOM
SKRRCH
VWIRL
An interesting magic.

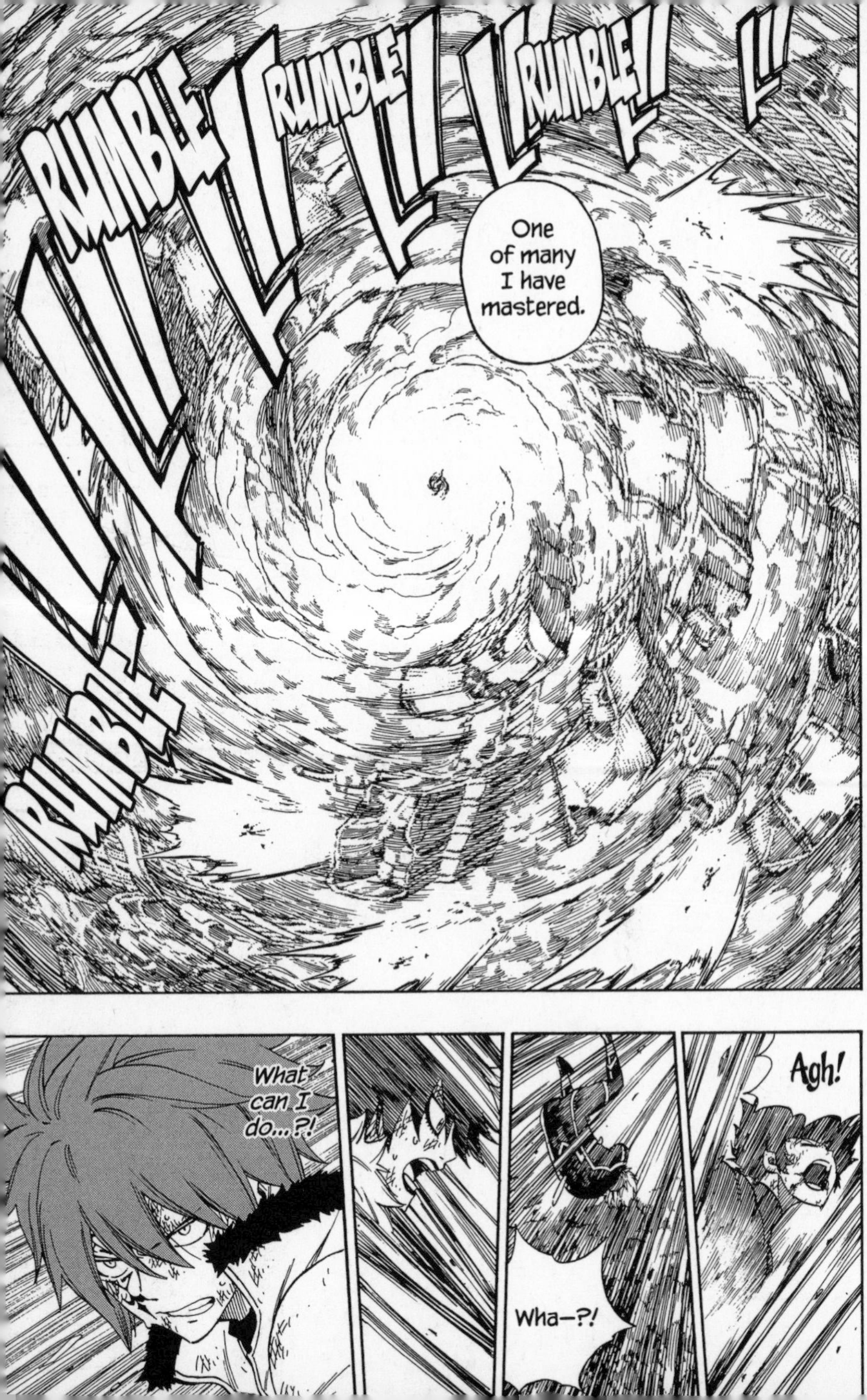
RUMBLE!!
One of many I have mastered.
RUMBLE!!
RUMBLE!!
RUMBLE
Agh!
Wha–?!
What can I do...?!

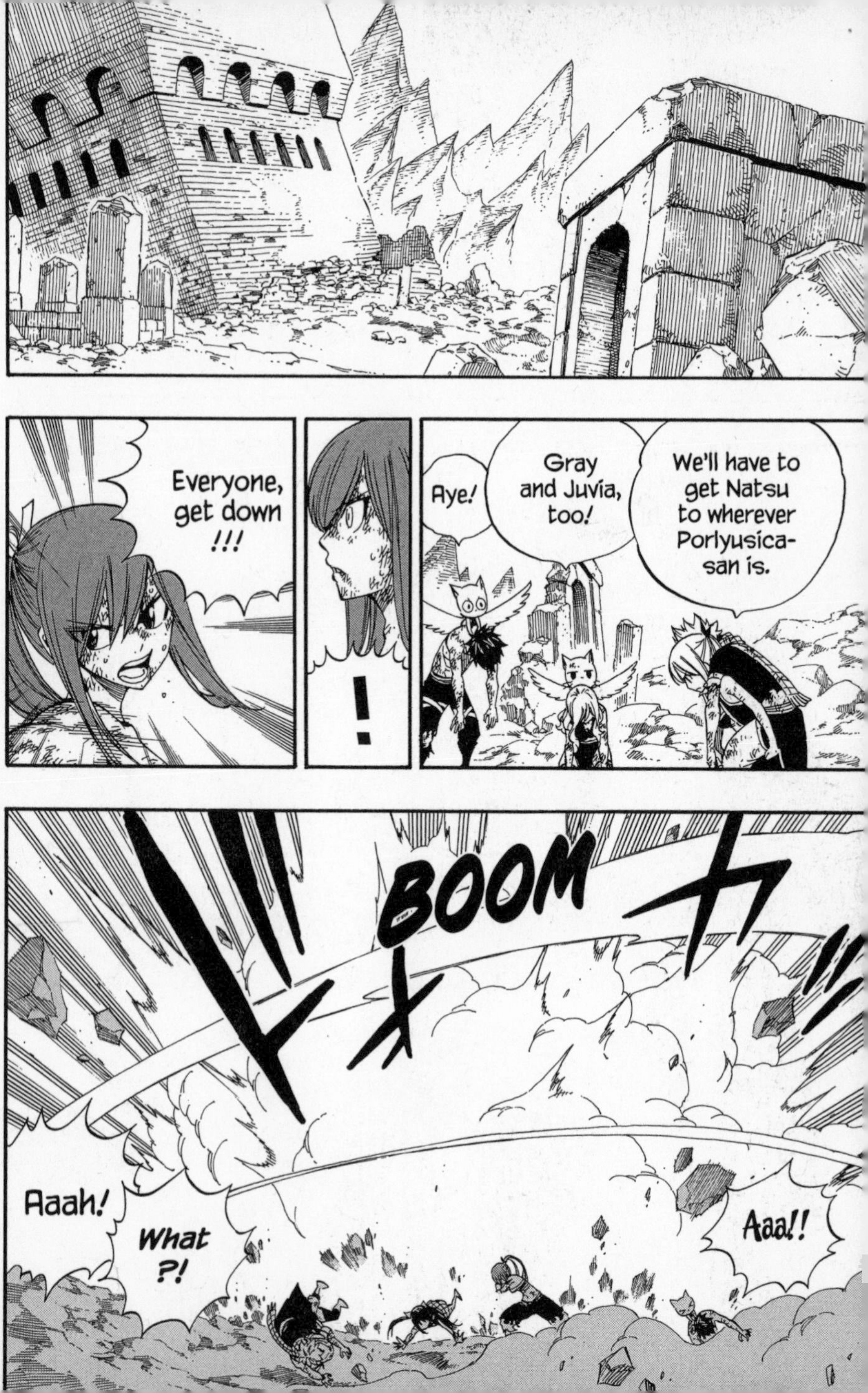
We'll have to get Natsu to wherever Porlyusica-san is.
Gray and Juvia, too!
Aye!
!
Everyone, get down !!!
BOOM
Aaa!!
Aaah!
What ?!

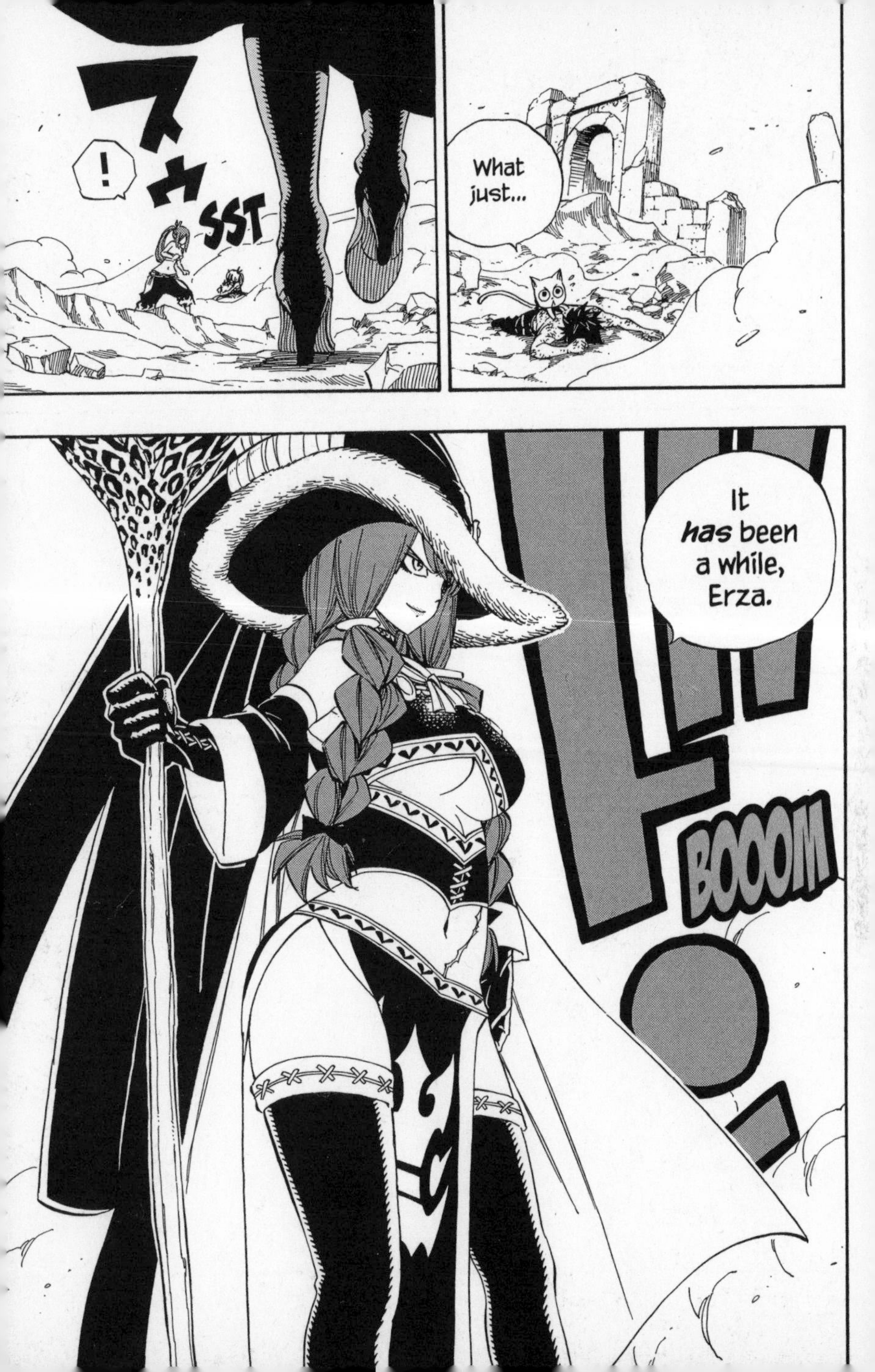
What just...
!
SST
It *has* been a while, Erza.
BOOOM

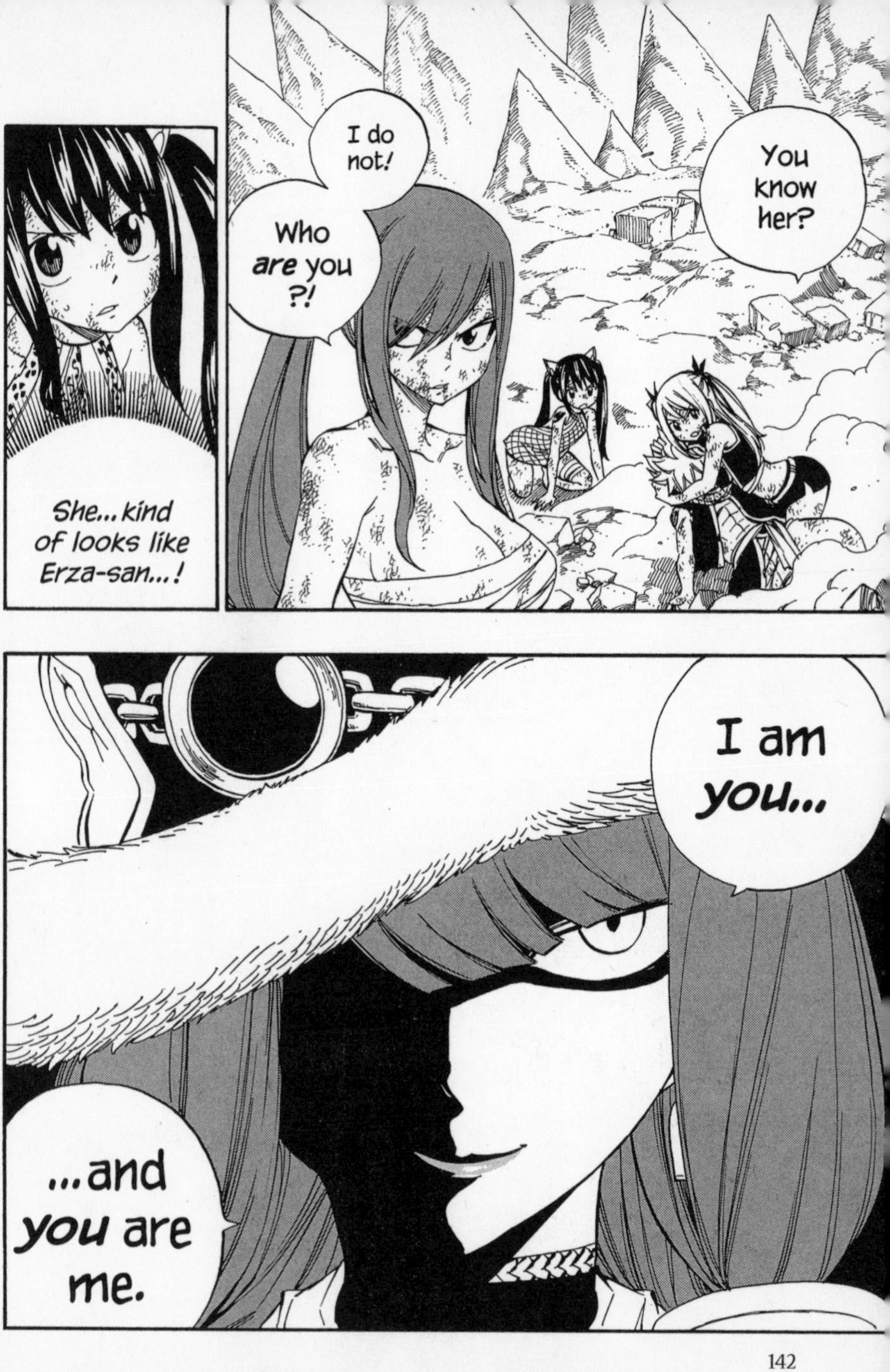
You know her?
I do not!
Who are you ?!
She...kind of looks like Erza-san...!
I am you...
...and you are me.

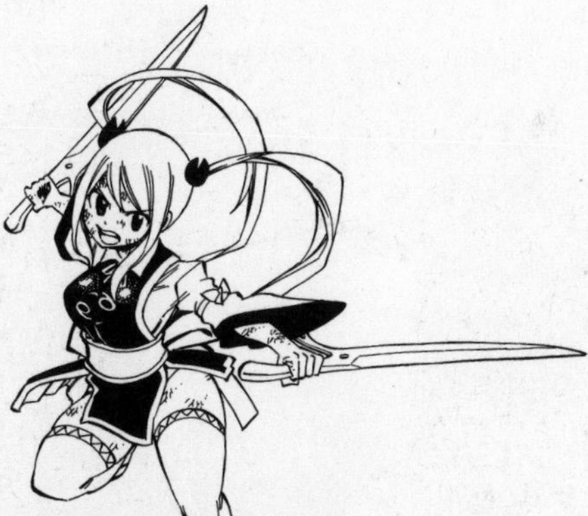

FAIRY TAIL

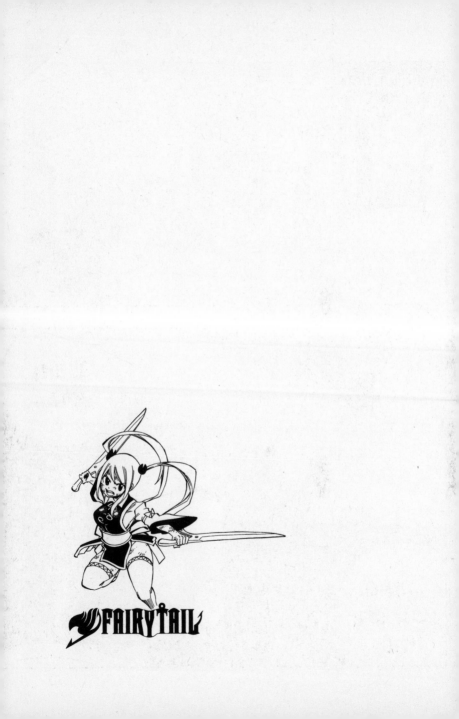

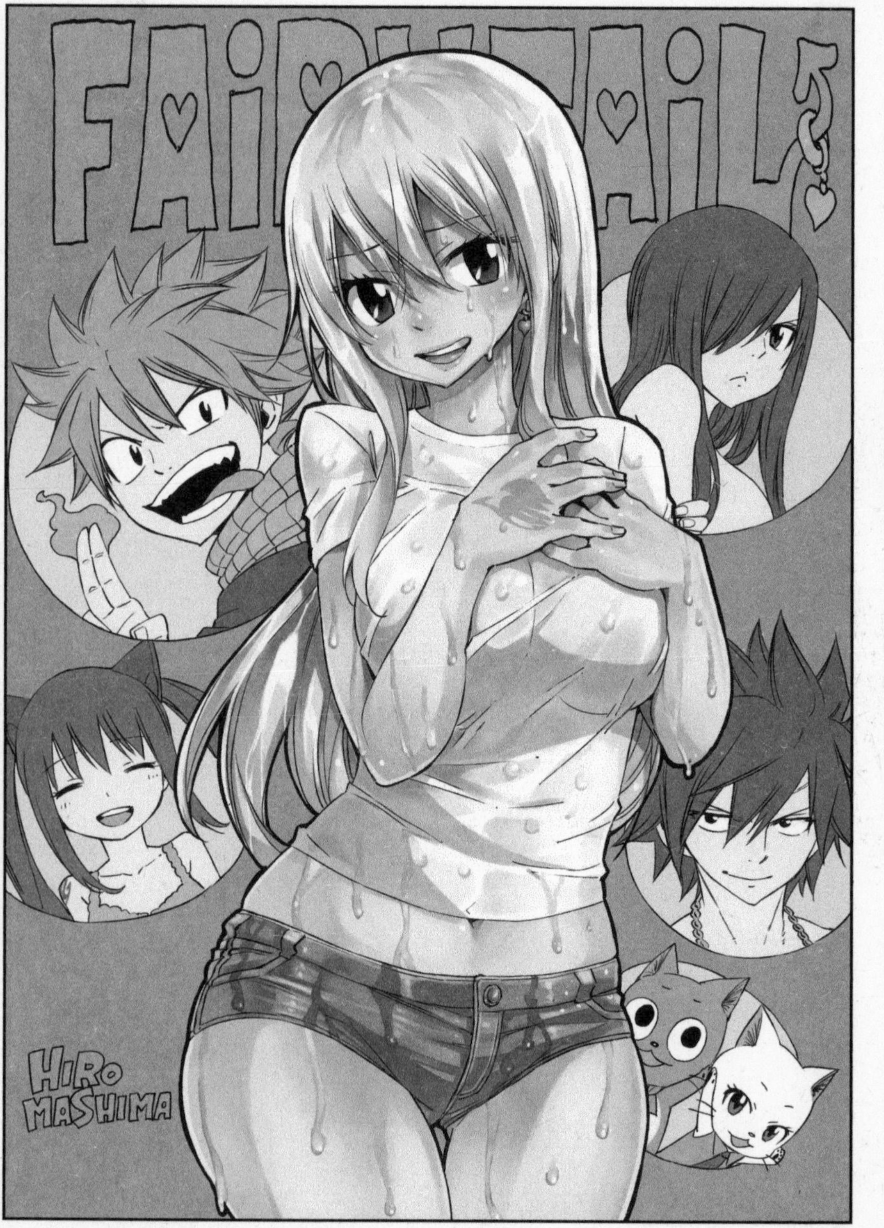
HIRO MASHIMA

Chapter 508: Pleasure and Pain

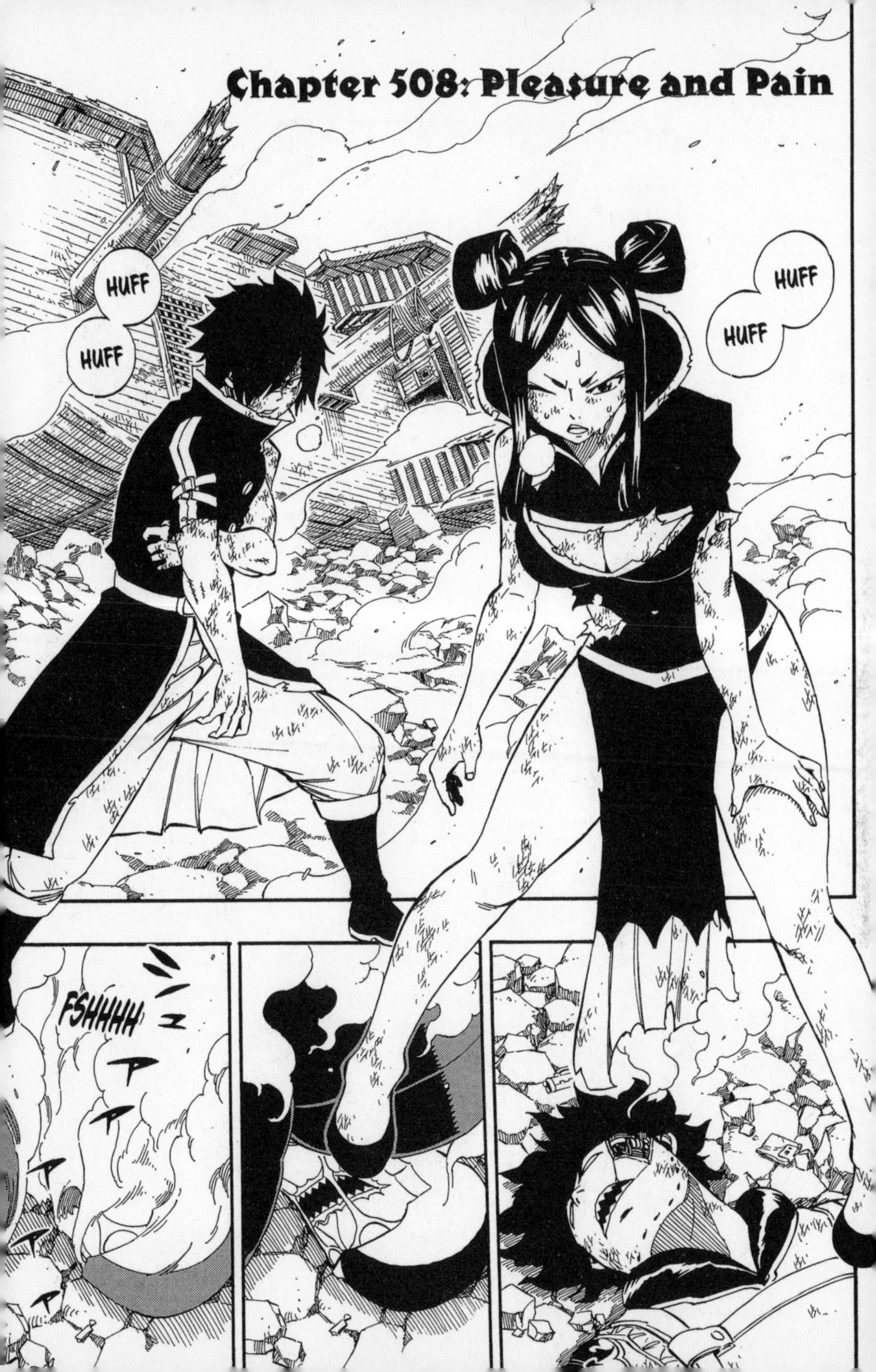
HUFF
HUFF
HUFF
HUFF
FSHHHH

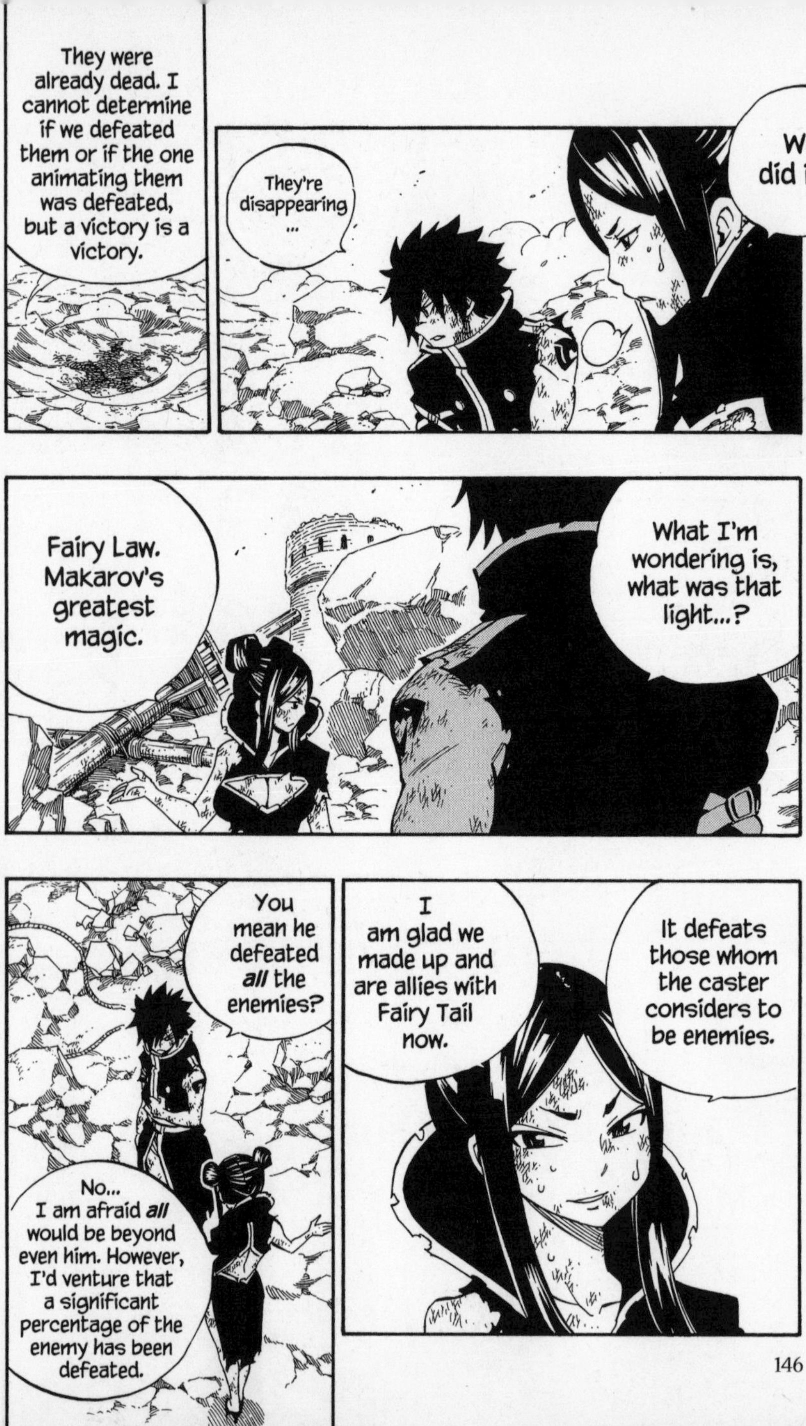
We did it...
They're disappearing ...
They were already dead. I cannot determine if we defeated them or if the one animating them was defeated, but a victory is a victory.
What I'm wondering is, what was that light...?
Fairy Law. Makarov's greatest magic.
It defeats those whom the caster considers to be enemies.
I am glad we made up and are allies with Fairy Tail now.
You mean he defeated *all* the enemies?
No... I am afraid *all* would be beyond even him. However, I'd venture that a significant percentage of the enemy has been defeated.

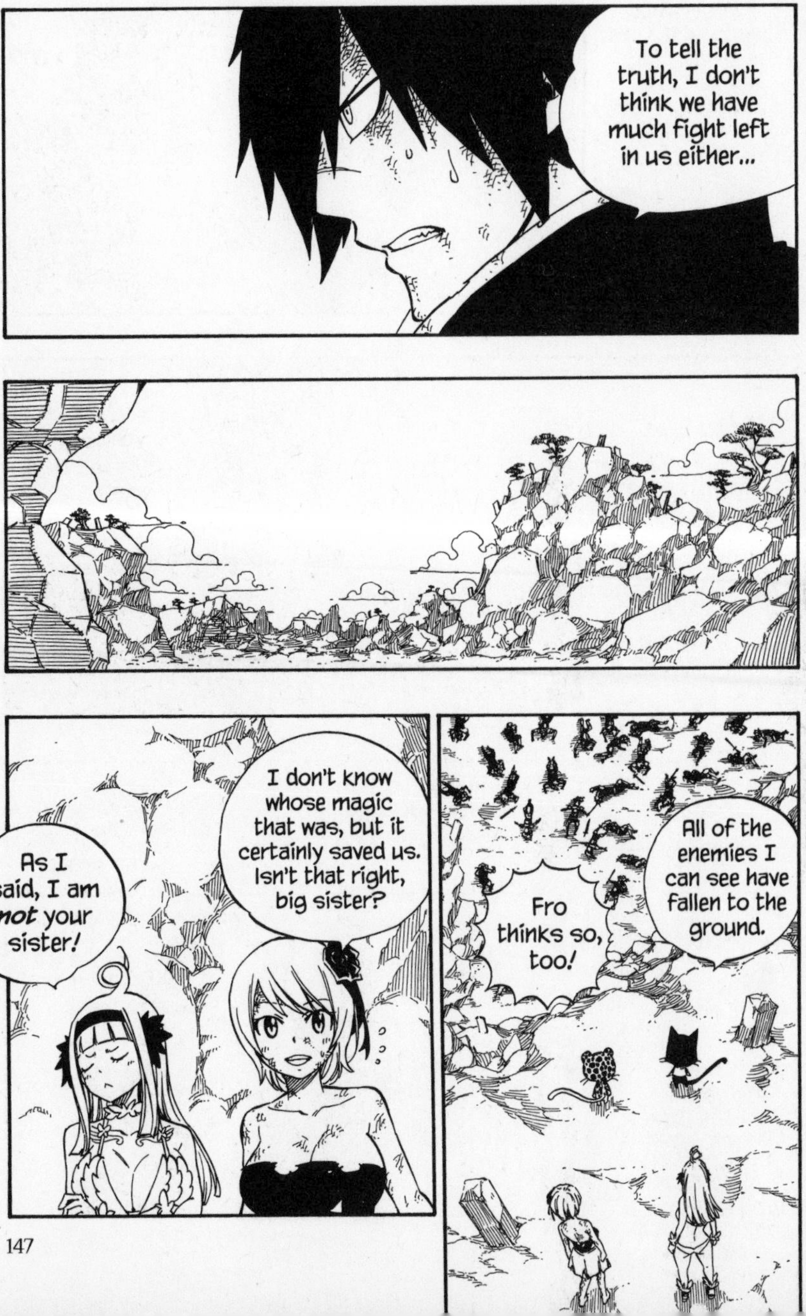
To tell the truth, I don't think we have much fight left in us either...
All of the enemies I can see have fallen to the ground.
Fro thinks so, too!
I don't know whose magic that was, but it certainly saved us. Isn't that right, big sister?
As I said, I am *not* your sister!

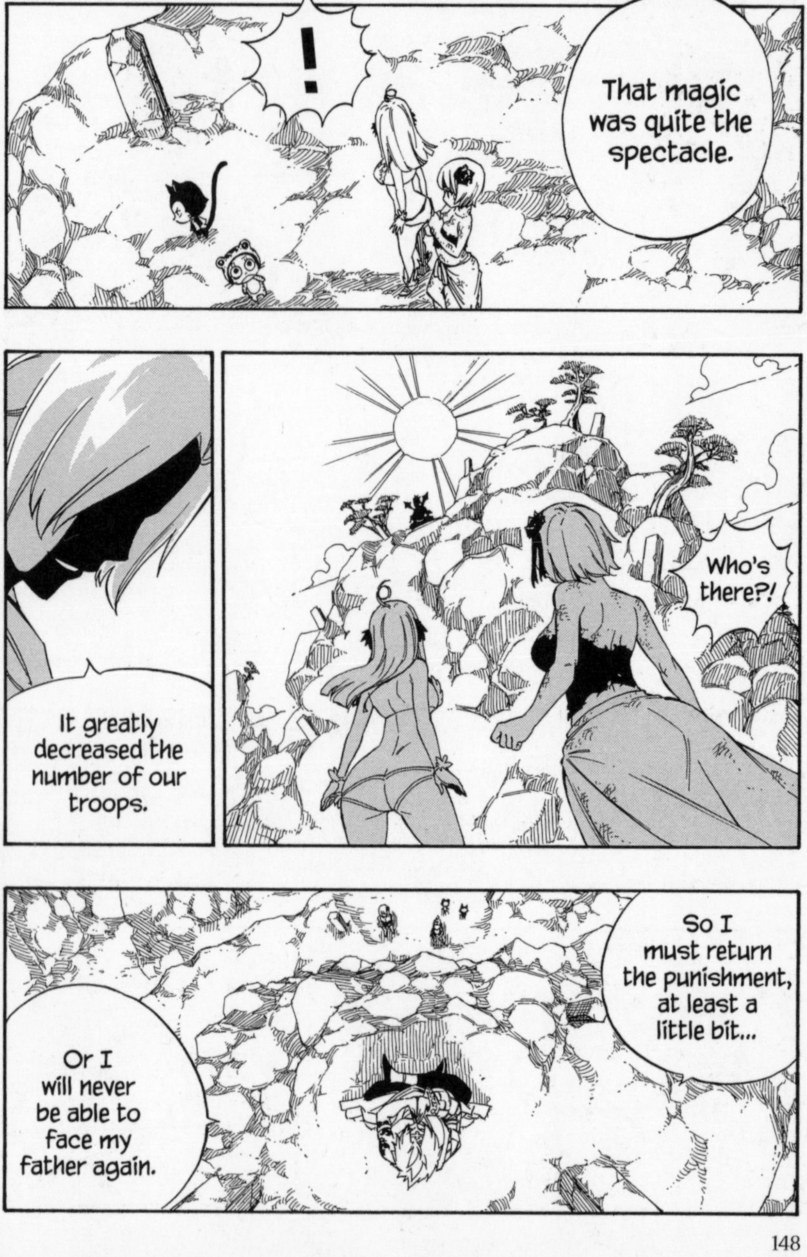
That magic was quite the spectacle.
!
Who's there?!
It greatly decreased the number of our troops.
So I must return the punishment, at least a little bit...
Or I will never be able to face my father again.

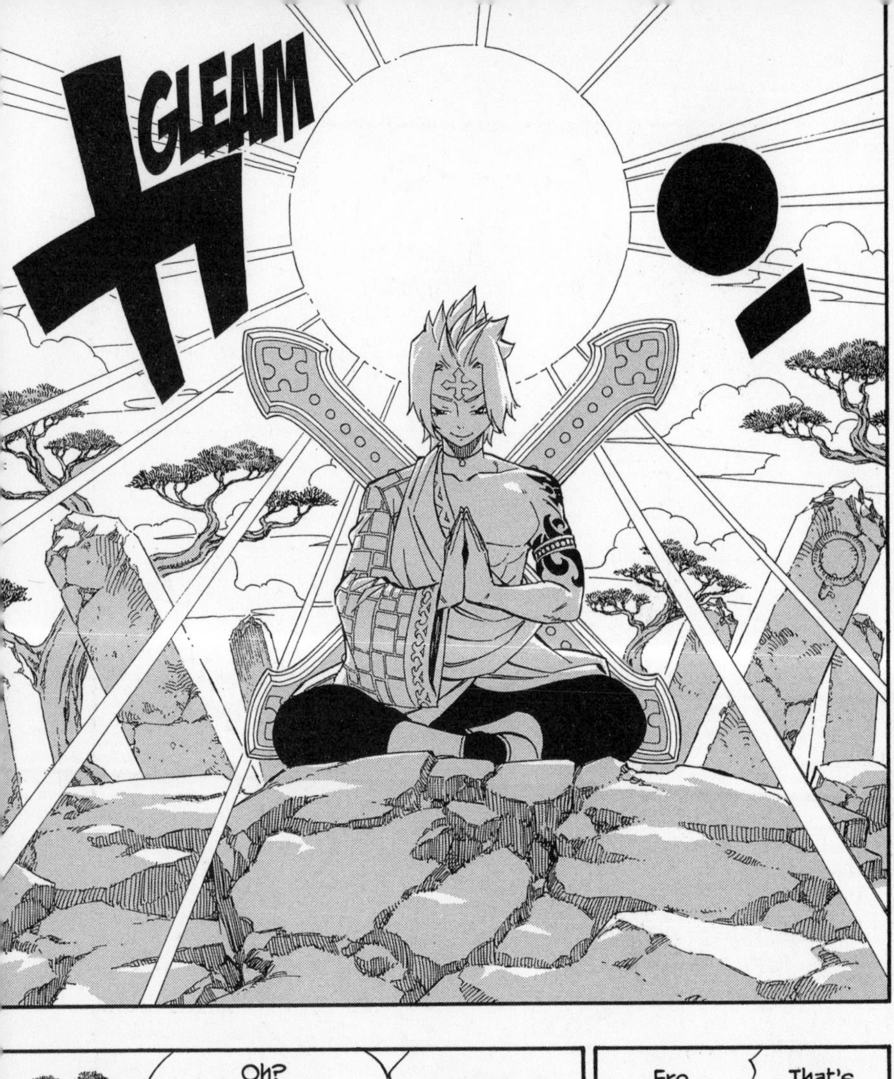
GLEAM

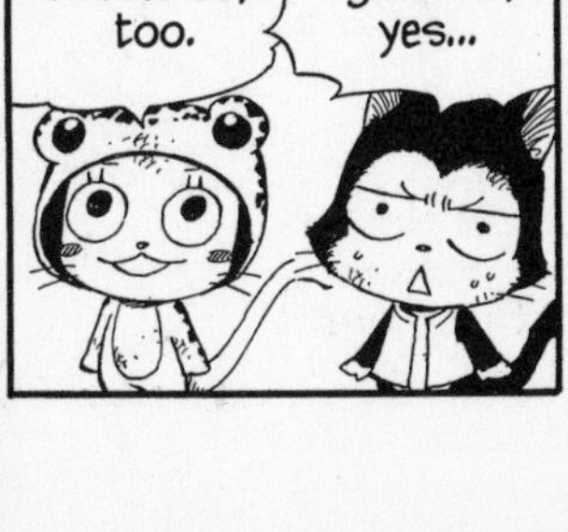
That's god-like, yes...
Fro thinks so, too.

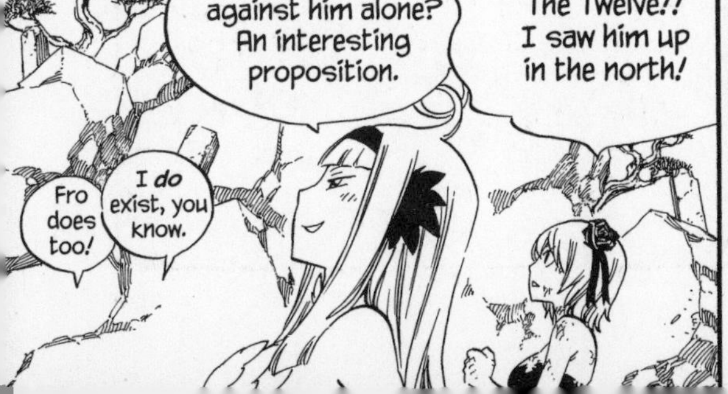
It's one of The Twelve!! I saw him up in the north!
Oh? The two of us against him alone? An interesting proposition.
I *do* exist, you know.
Fro does too!

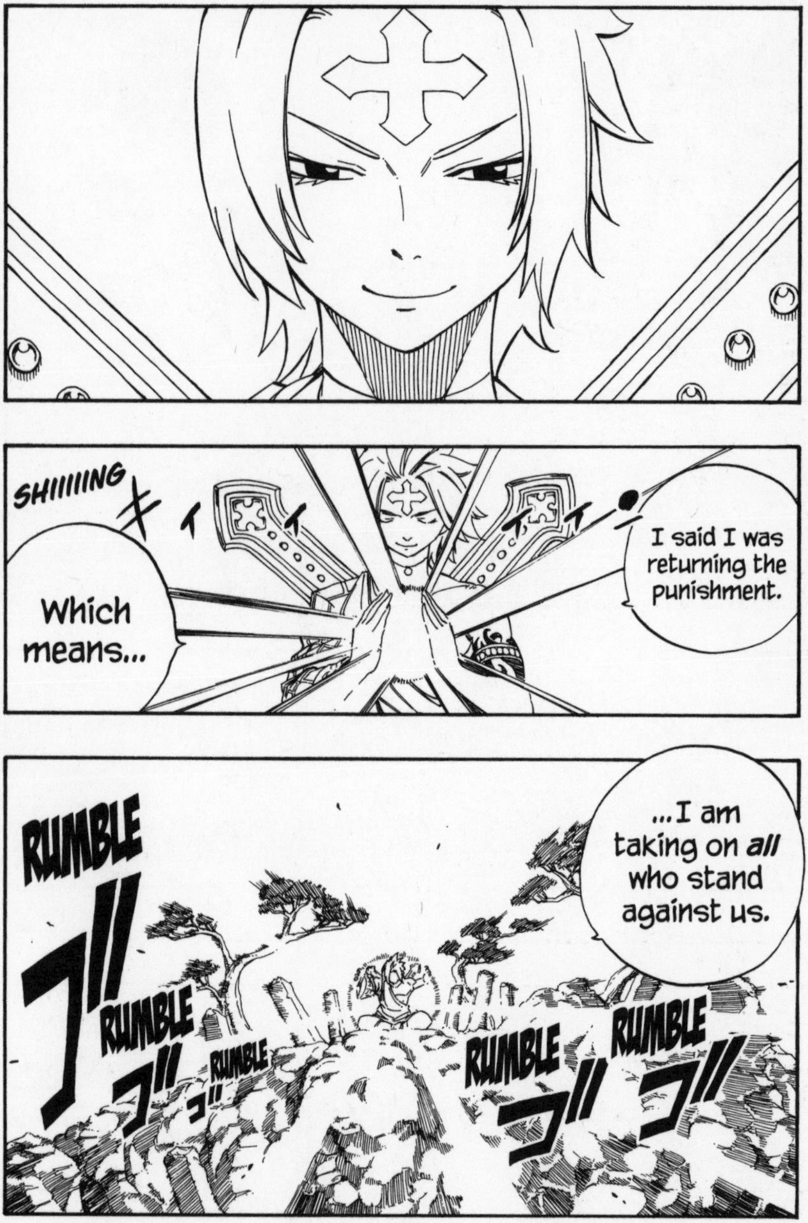

I said I was returning the punishment.
SHIIIIING
Which means...
...I am taking on *all* who stand against us.
RUMBLE
RUMBLE
RUMBLE
RUMBLE
RUMBLE

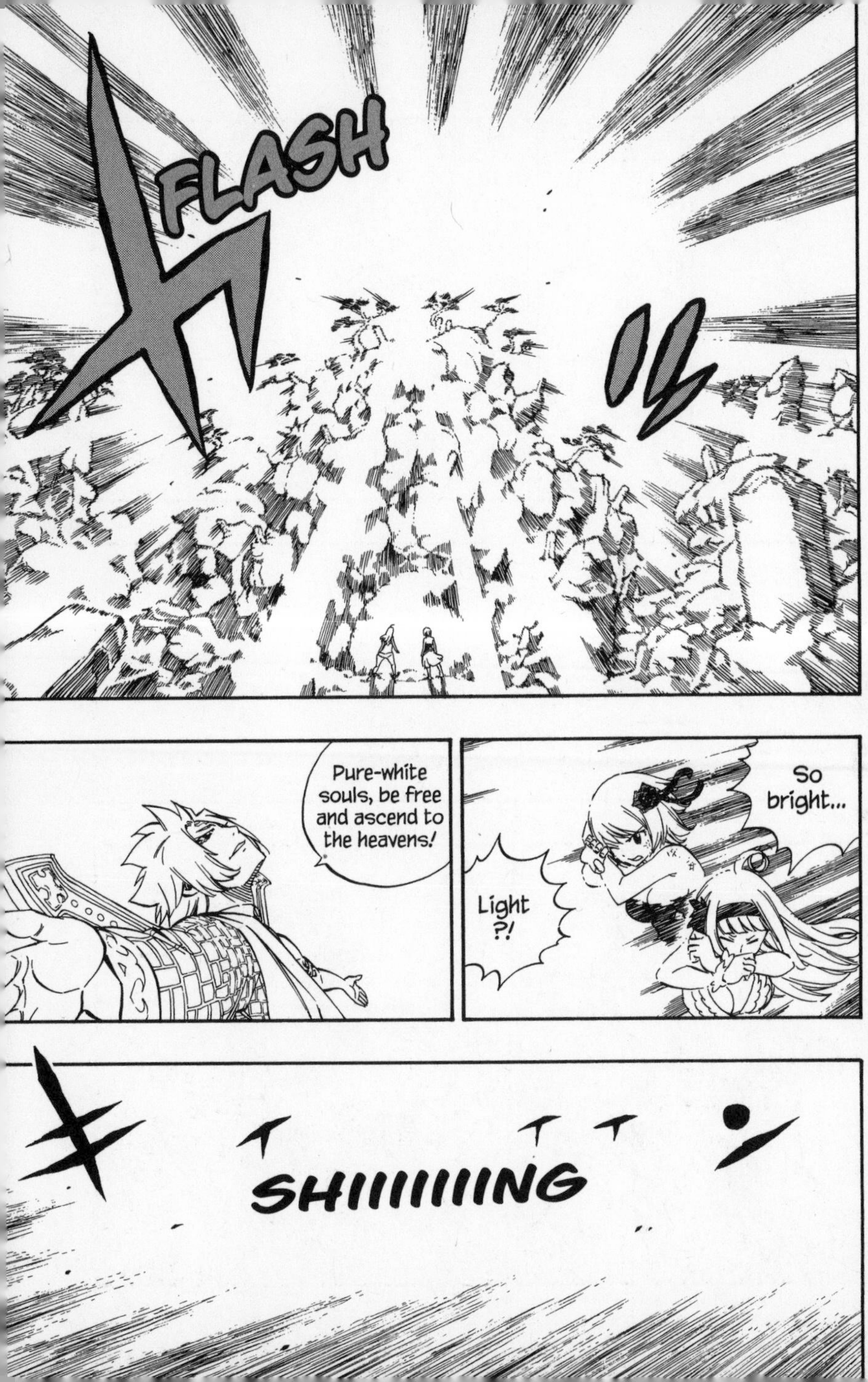
FLASH
So bright...
Light ?!
Pure-white souls, be free and ascend to the heavens!
SHIIIIIING

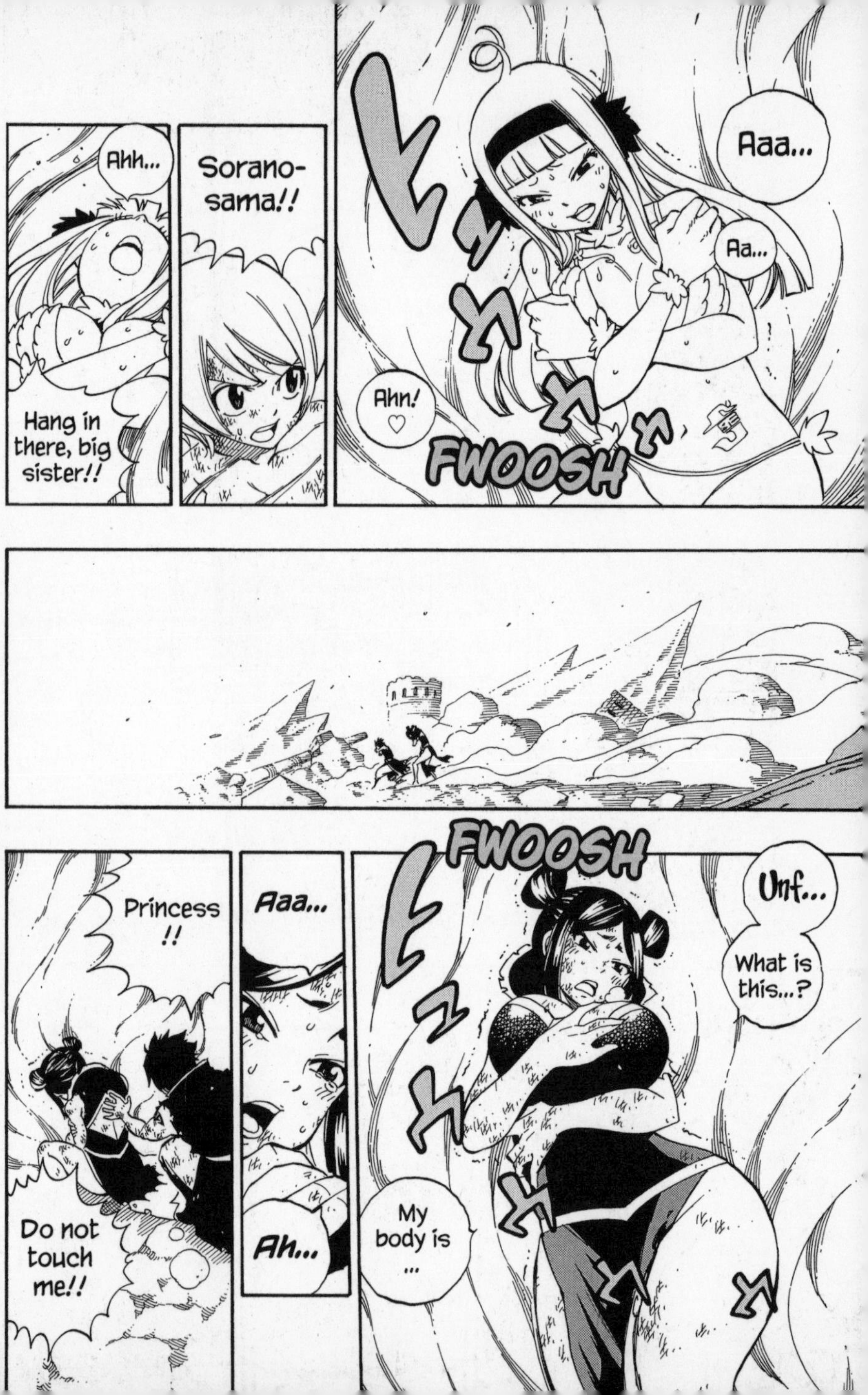
Aaa...
Aa...
Ahn! ♡
FWOOSH
Sorano-sama!!
Ahh...
Hang in there, big sister!!
FWOOSH
Unf...
What is this...?
My body is ...
Aaa...
Ah...
Princess!!
Do not touch me!!

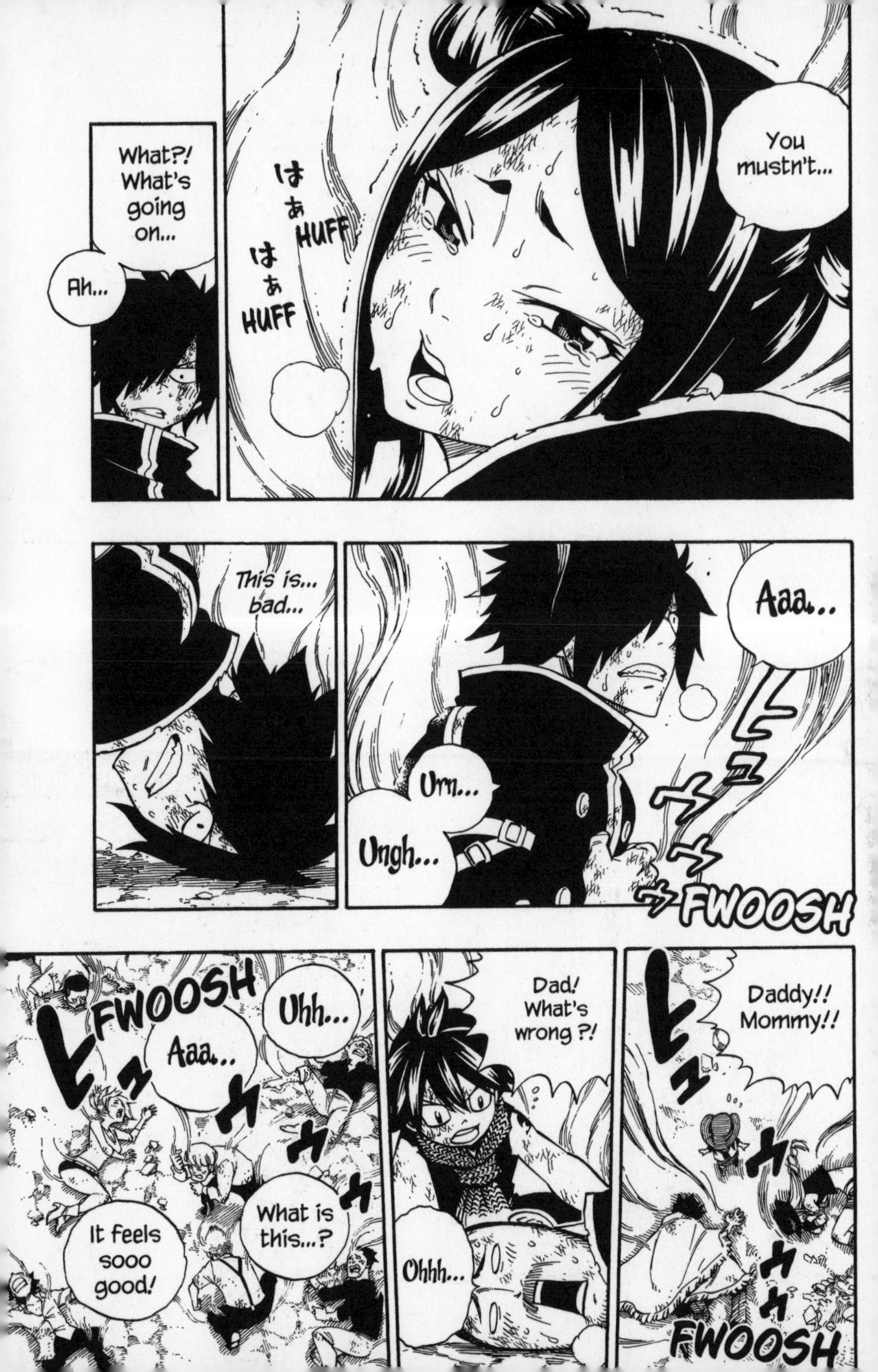
You mustn't...
はぁ HUFF
はぁ HUFF
What?! What's going on...
Ah...
Aaa...
Urn...
Ungh...
ヒュウゥ FWOOSH
This is... bad...
Daddy!! Mommy!!
ヒュウゥ FWOOSH
Dad! What's wrong?!
Ohhh...
ヒュウゥゥゥ FWOOSH
Uhh...
Aaa...
What is this...?
It feels sooo good!

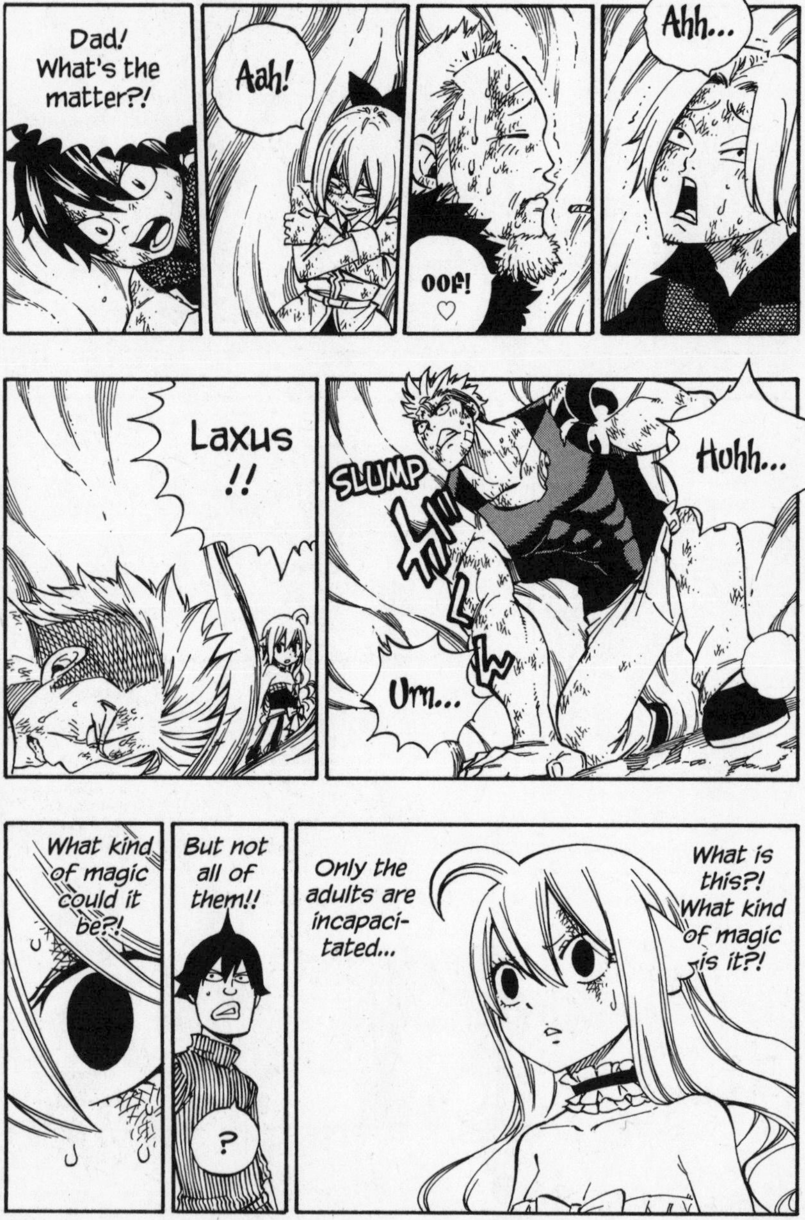
Ahh...
Oof! ♡
Aah!
Dad! What's the matter?!
Huhh...
SLUMP
Urn...
Laxus !!
What is this?! What kind of magic is it?!
Only the adults are incapacitated...
But not all of them!!
?
What kind of magic could it be?!

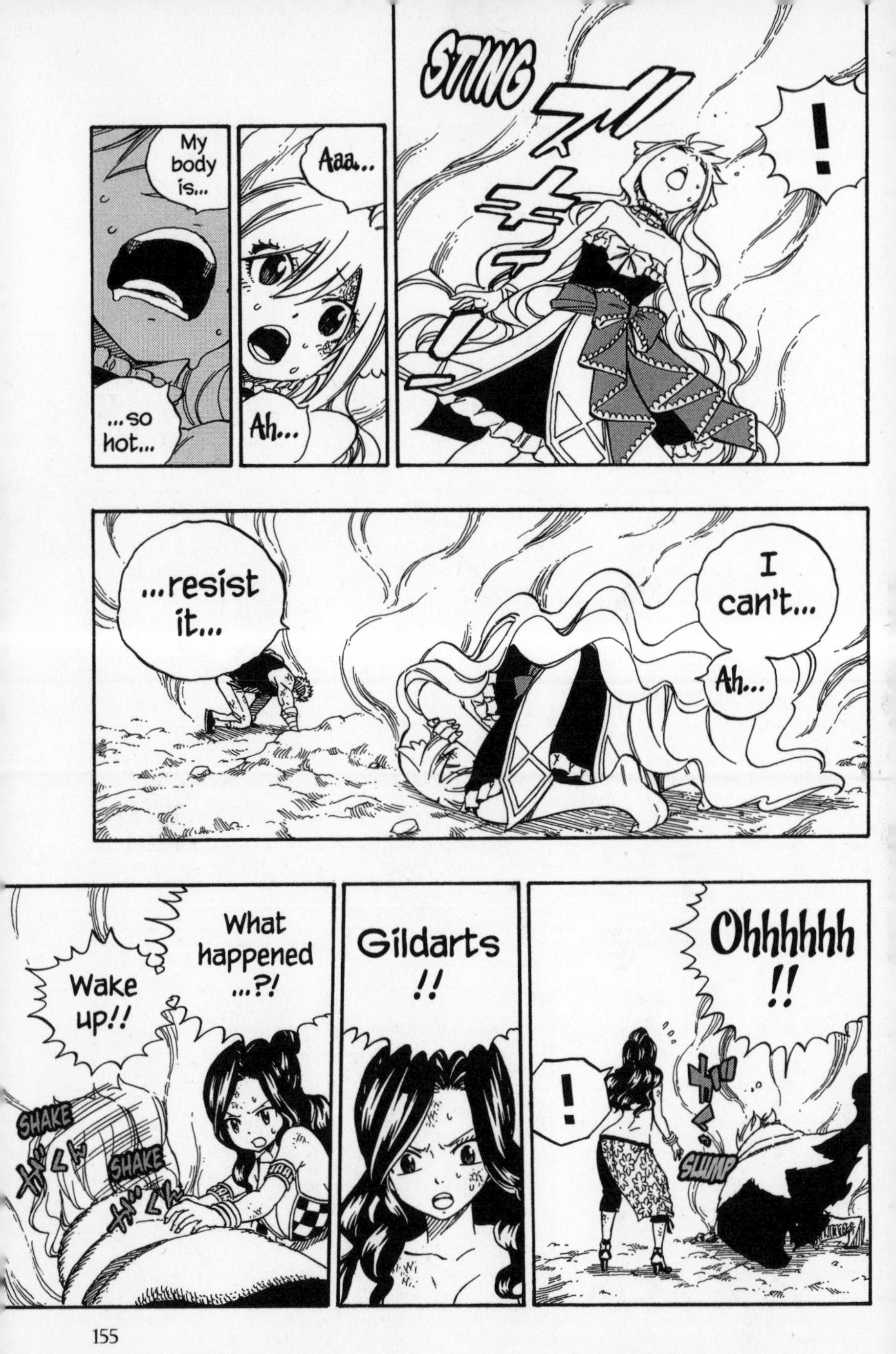
STING
!
Aaa...
Ah...
My body is...
...so hot...
I can't...
Ah...
...resist it...
Ohhhhhh!!
!
SLUMP
Gildarts!!
What happened...?!
Wake up!!
SHAKE
SHAKE

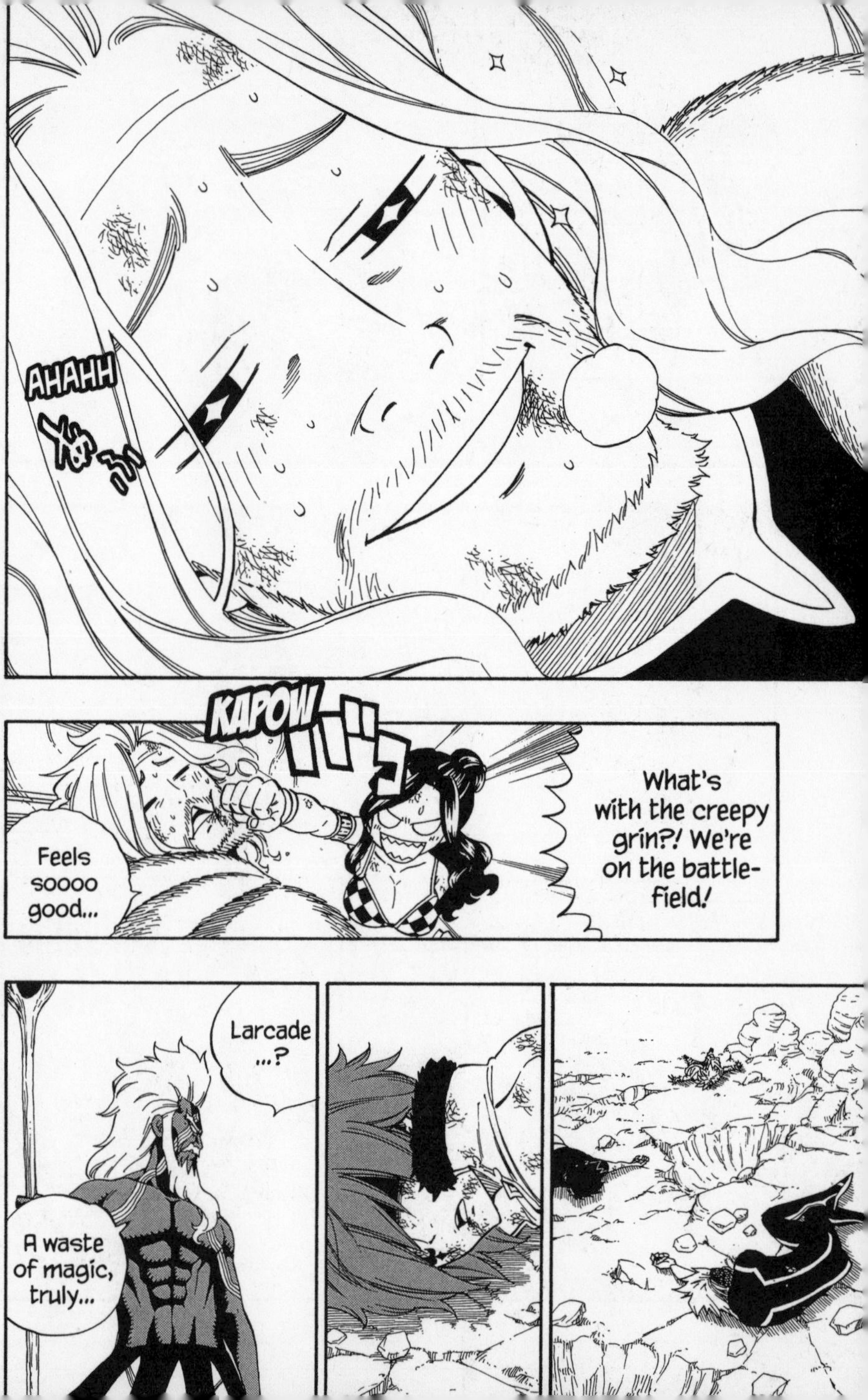
AHAHH
What's with the creepy grin?! We're on the battle-field!
KAPOW
Feels soooo good...
Larcade ...?
A waste of magic, truly...

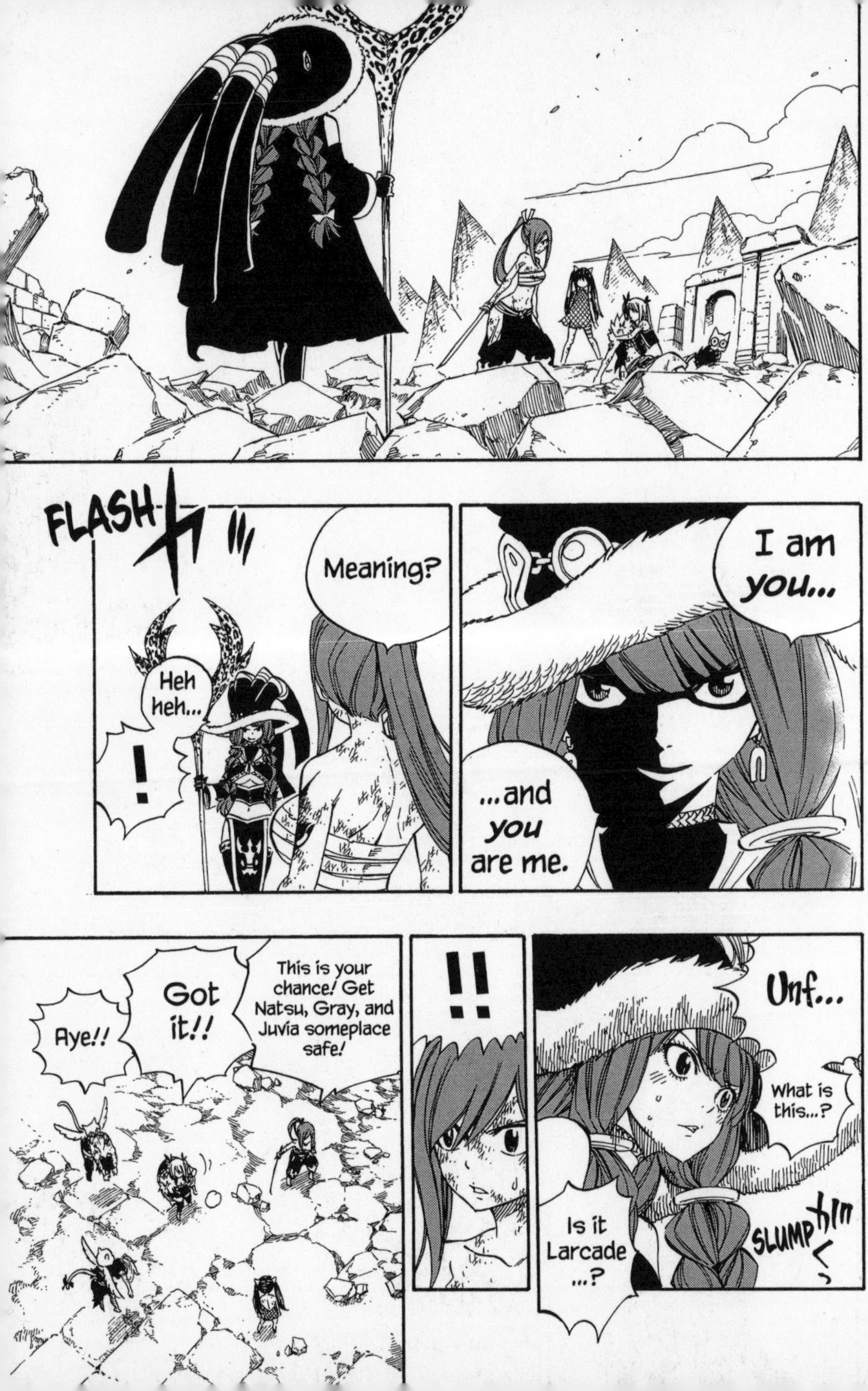
I am you...
...and you are me.
FLASH
Meaning?
Heh heh...
!
Unf...
What is this...?
Is it Larcade ...?
SLUMP
!!
This is your chance! Get Natsu, Gray, and Juvia someplace safe!
Got it!!
Aye!!

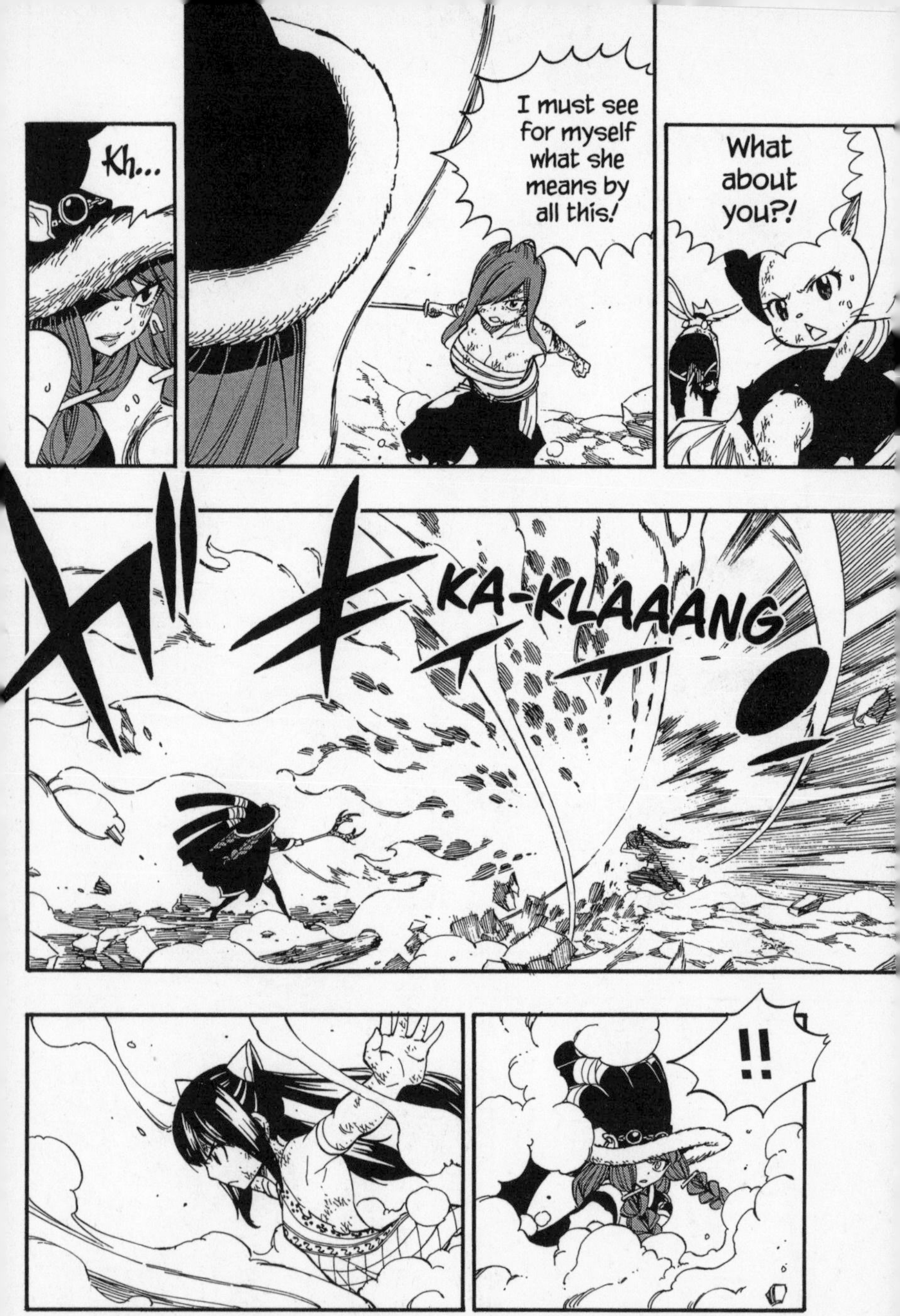

What about you?!
I must see for myself what she means by all this!
Kh...
KA-KLAAANG
!!

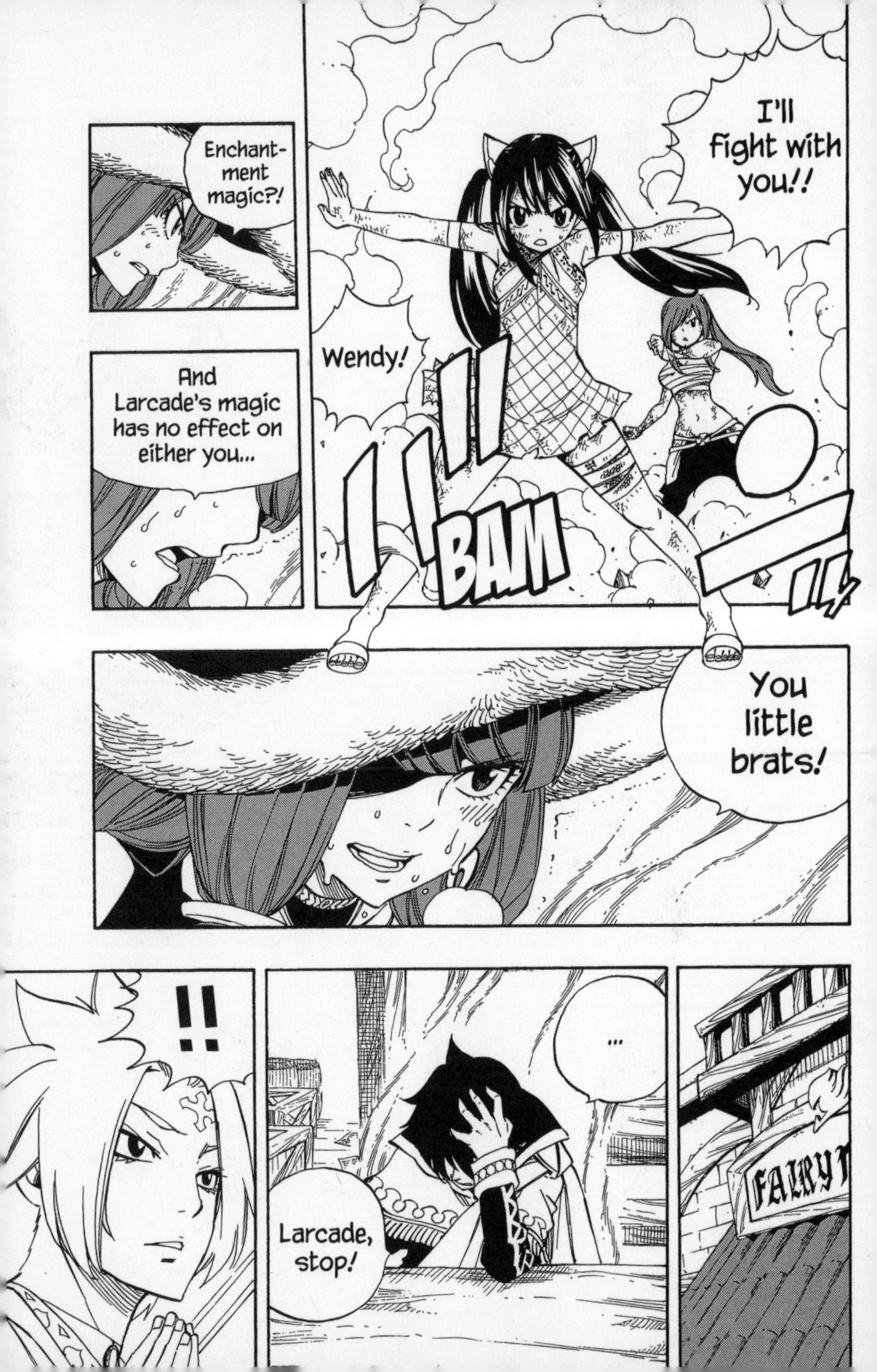
I'll fight with you!!
Wendy!
BAM
Enchant-ment magic?!
And Larcade's magic has no effect on either you...
You little brats!
FAIRY
...
Larcade, stop!
!!

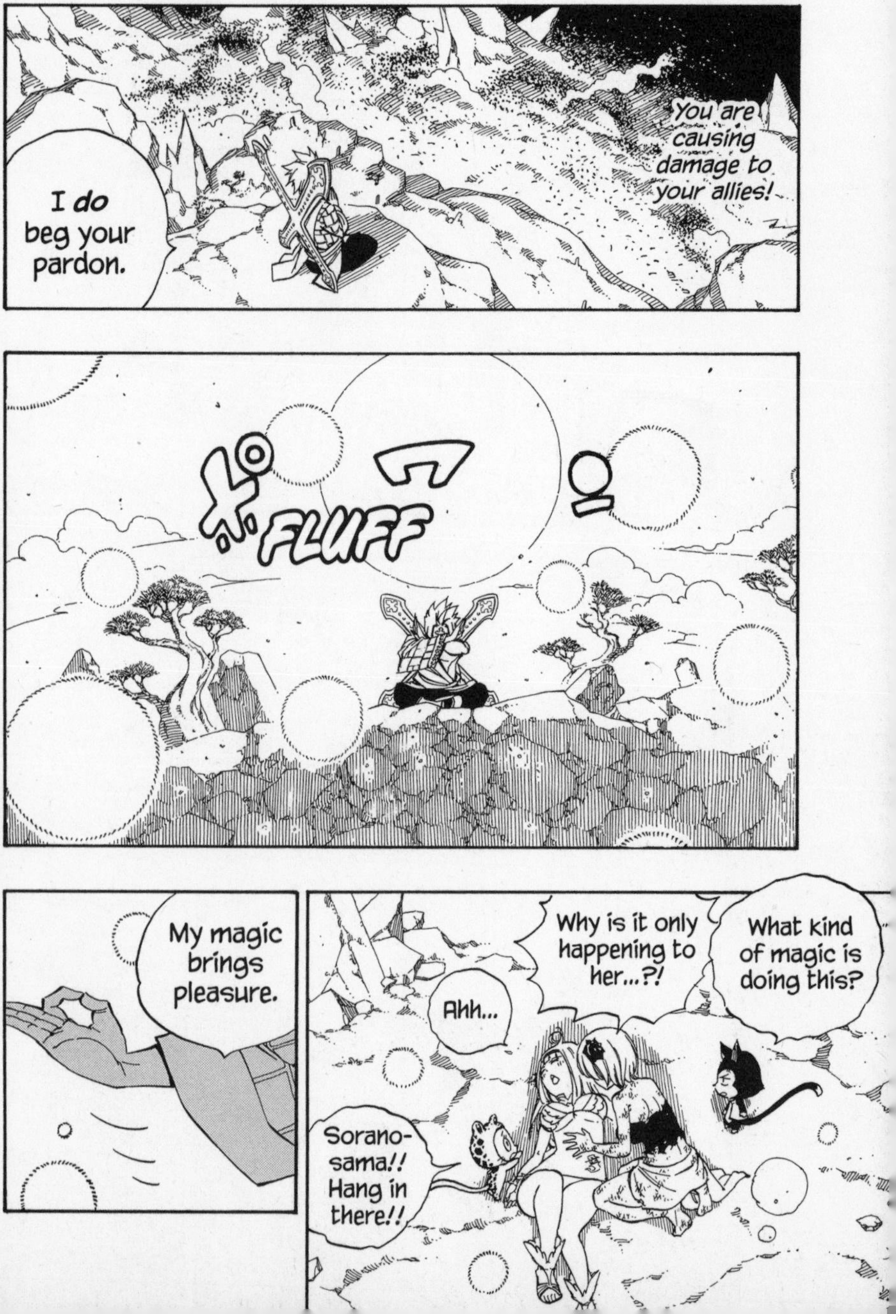
You are causing damage to your allies!
I *do* beg your pardon.
FLUFF
What kind of magic is doing this?
Why is it only happening to her...?!
Ahh...
Sorano-sama!! Hang in there!!
My magic brings pleasure.

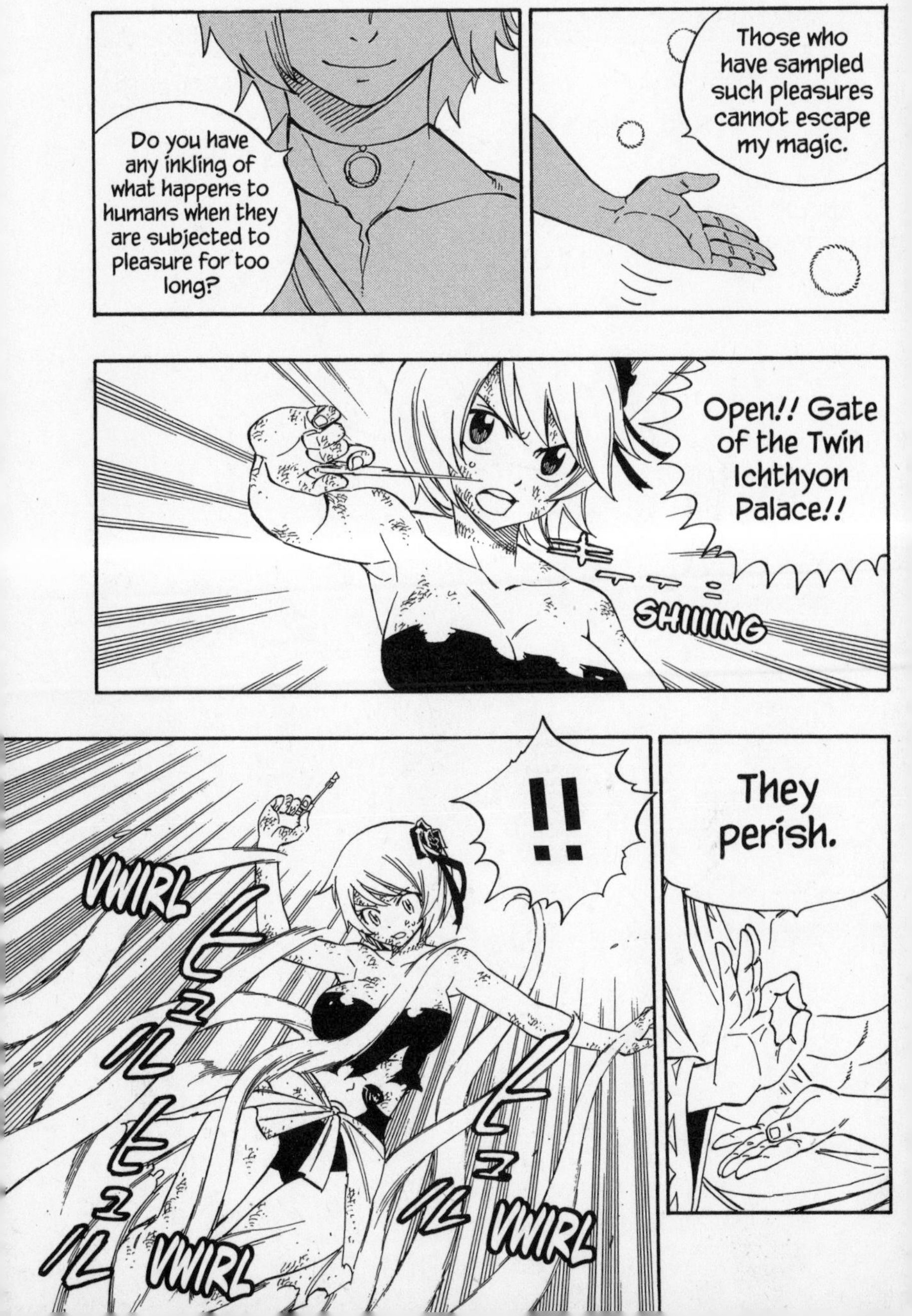
Those who have sampled such pleasures cannot escape my magic.
Do you have any inkling of what happens to humans when they are subjected to pleasure for too long?
Open!! Gate of the Twin Ichthyon Palace!!
SHIIIING
They perish.
!!
VWIRL
VWIRL
VWIRL

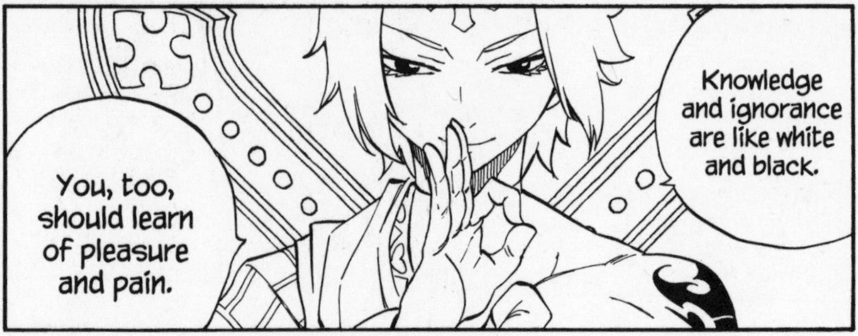
Knowledge and ignorance are like white and black.
You, too, should learn of pleasure and pain.

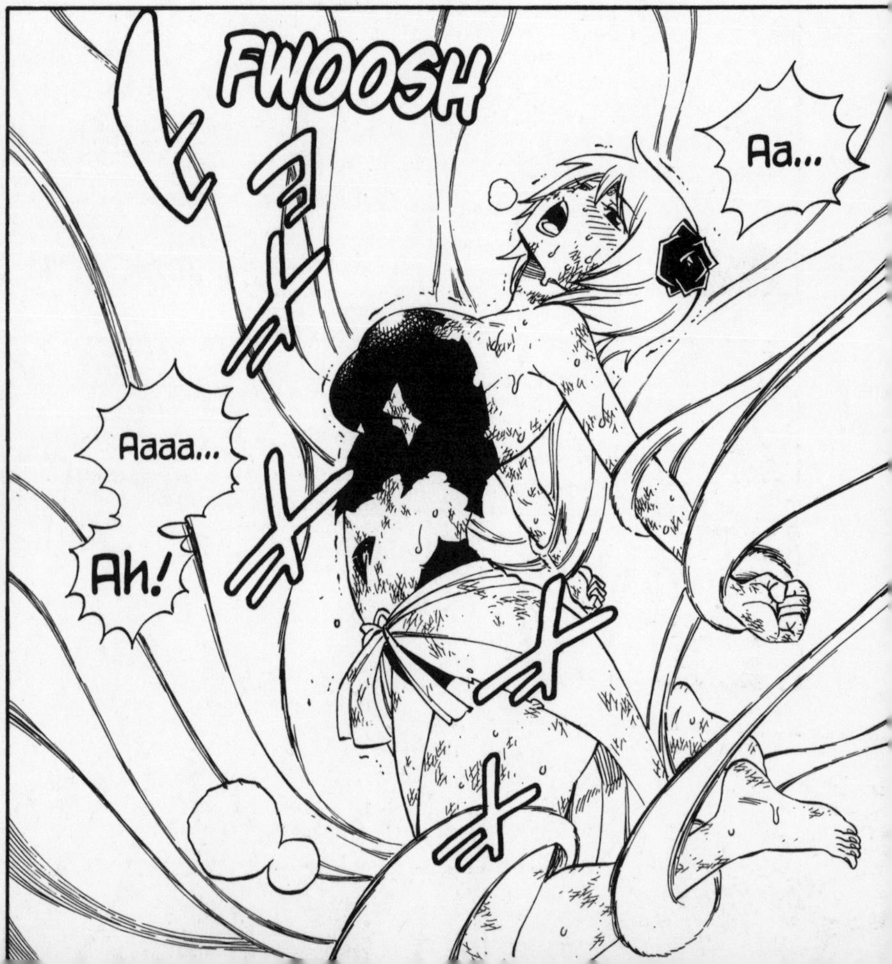
FWOOSH
Aa...
Aaaa...
Ah!

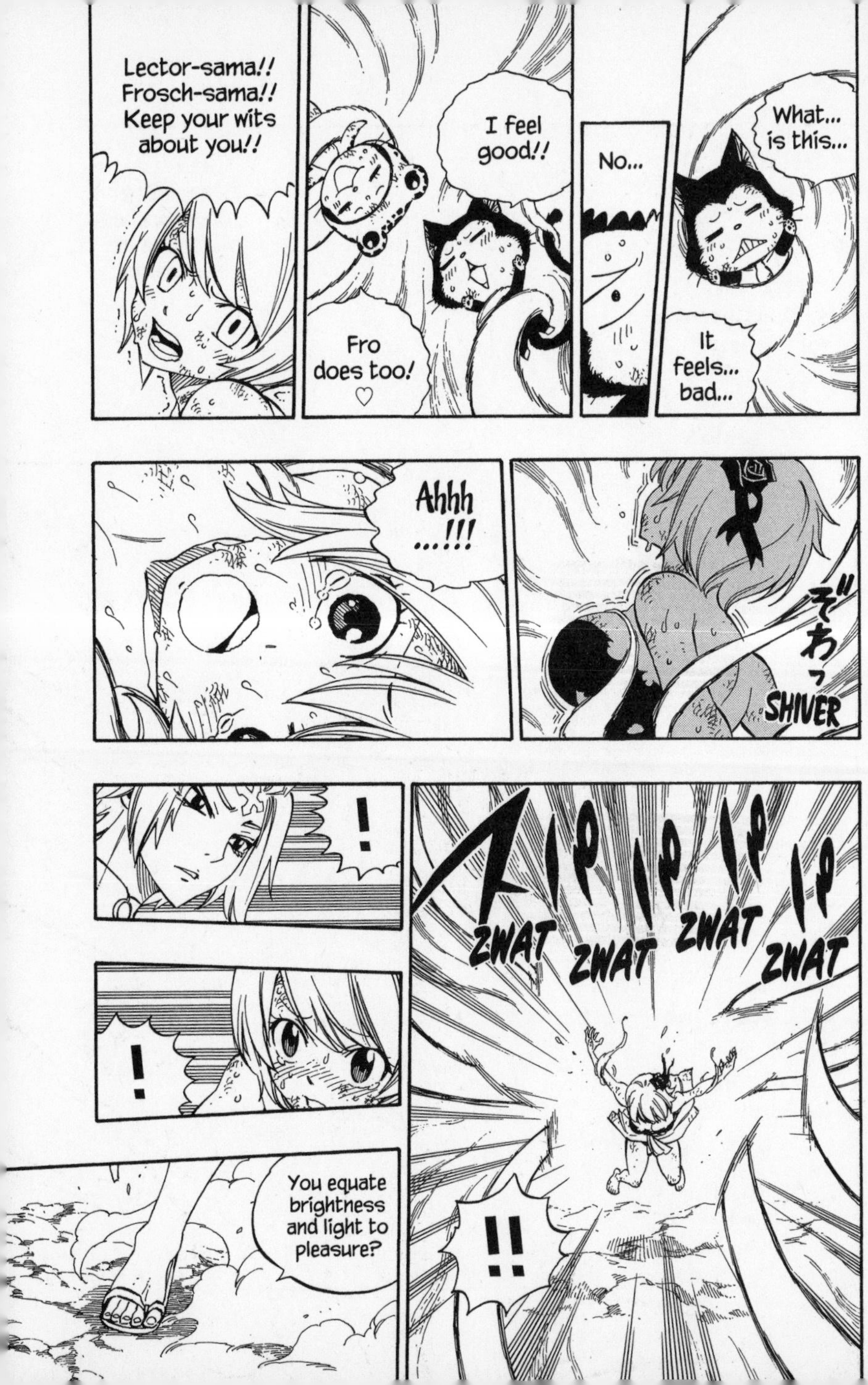
What... is this...
It feels... bad...
No...
I feel good!!
Fro does too! ♡
Lector-sama!! Frosch-sama!! Keep your wits about you!!
ざわっ
SHIVER
Ahhh ...!!!
ZWAT ZWAT ZWAT ZWAT
!!
!
!
You equate brightness and light to pleasure?

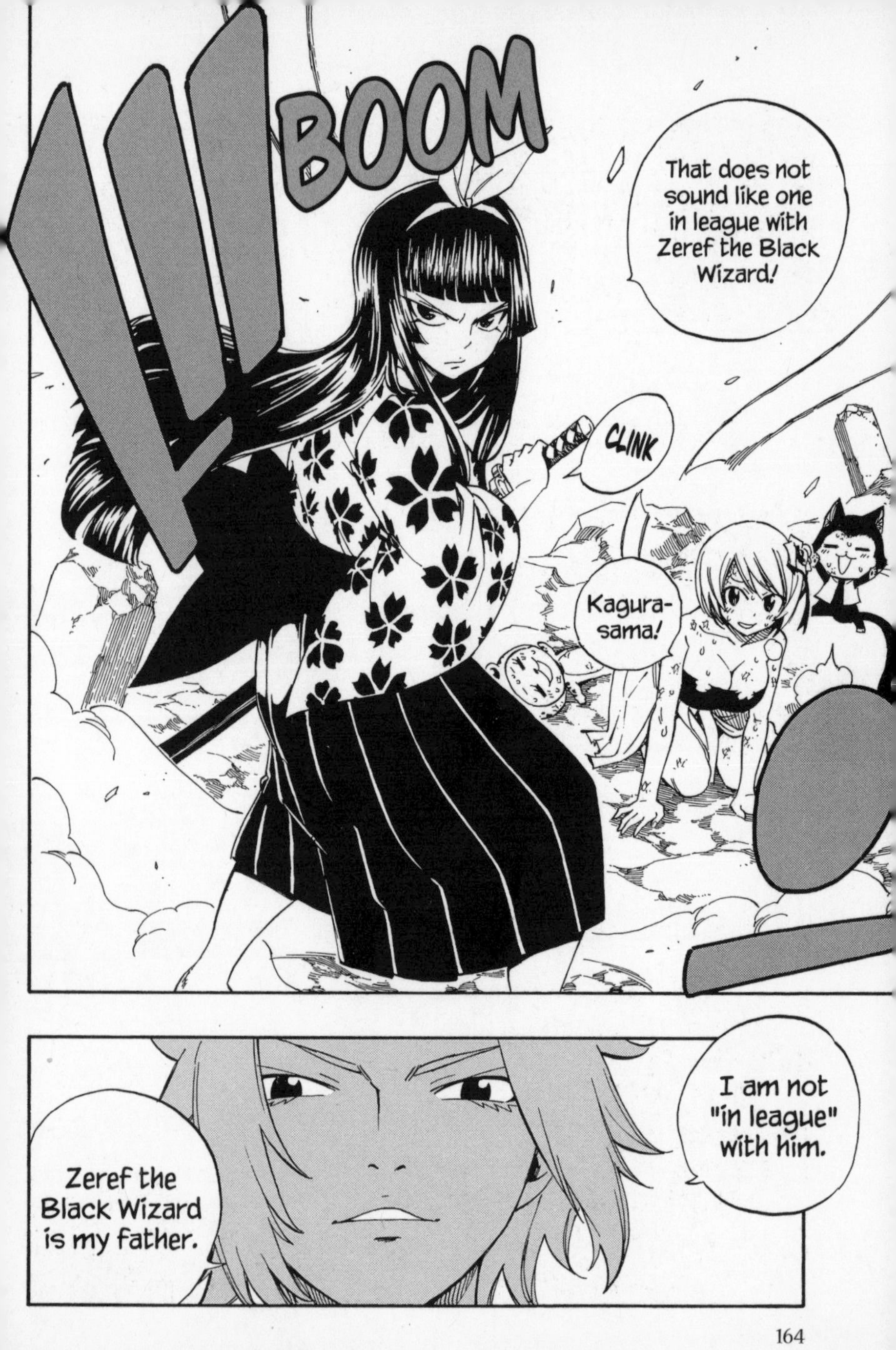
BOOM
That does not sound like one in league with Zeref the Black Wizard!
CLINK
Kagura-sama!
I am not "in league" with him.
Zeref the Black Wizard is my father.

FAIRY TAIL

フェアリーテイル

Chapter 509: Kagura vs. Larcade

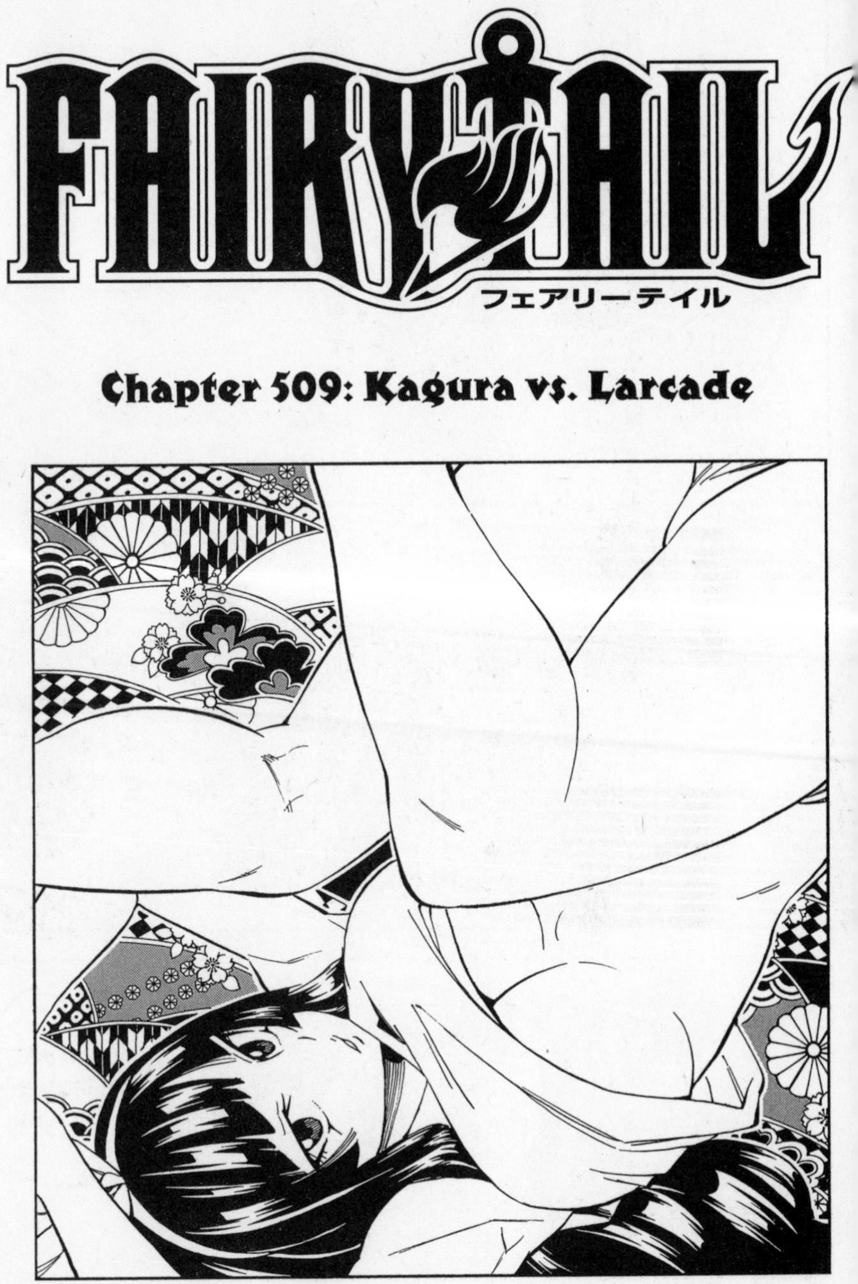

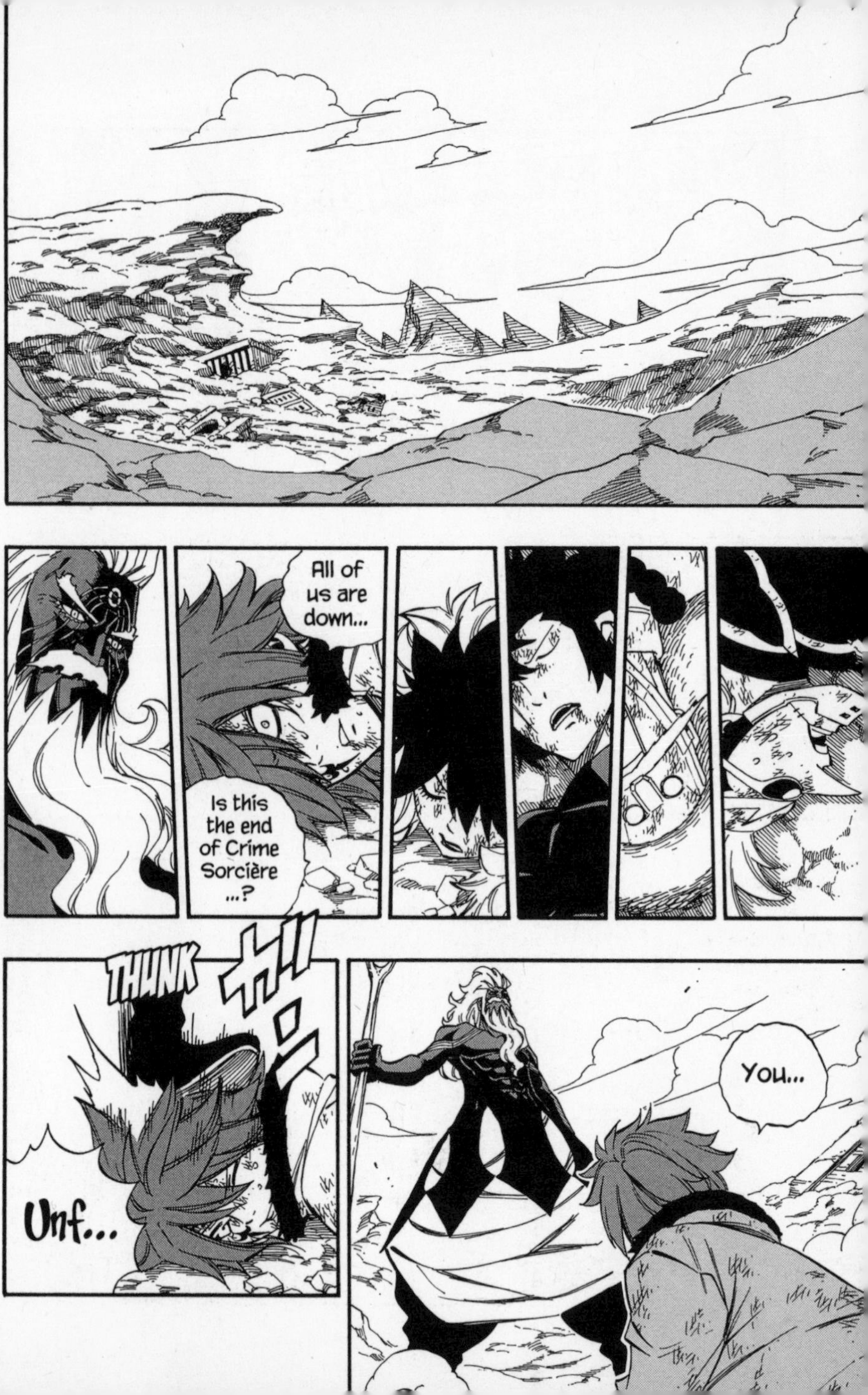
All of us are down...
Is this the end of Crime Sorcière ...?
You...
THUNK
Unf...

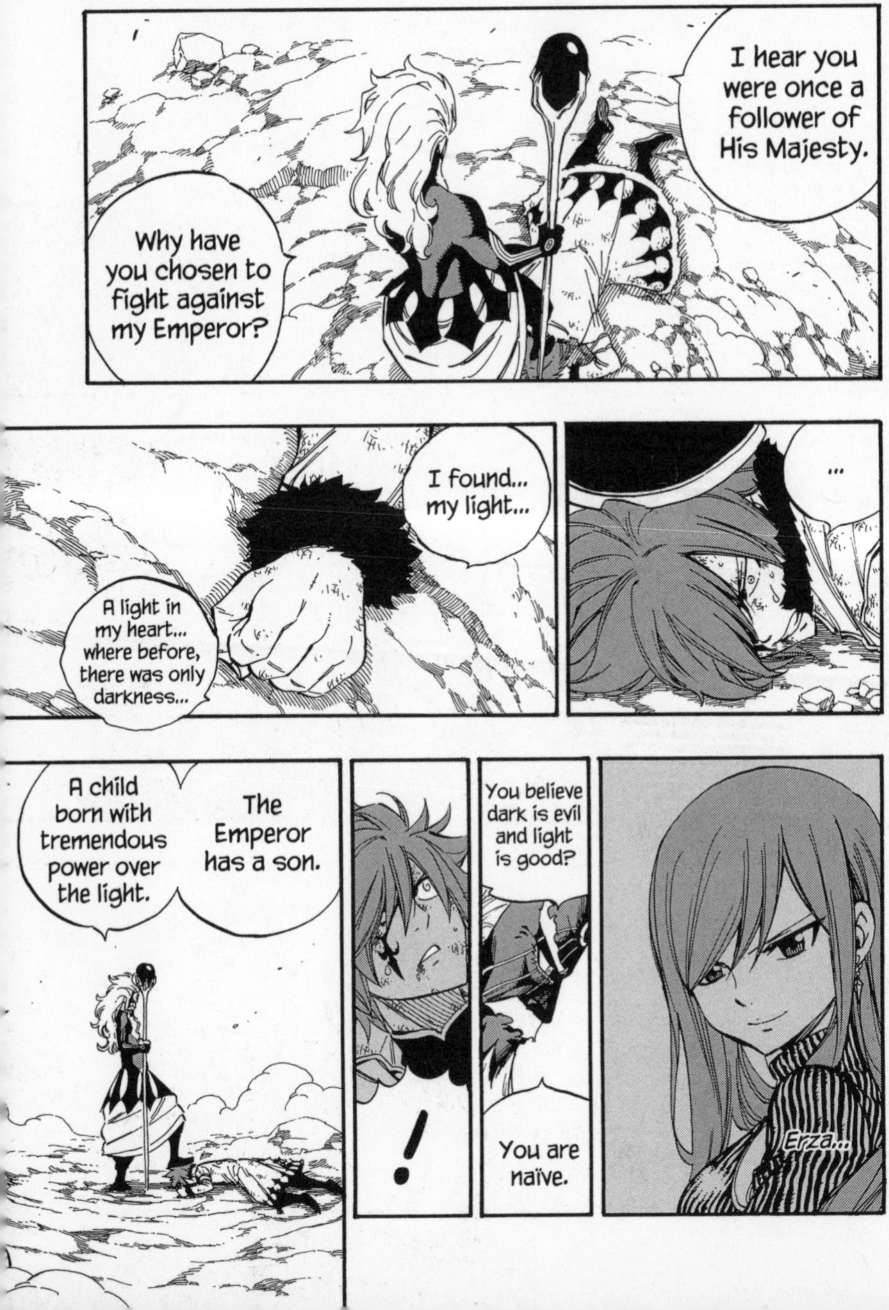
I hear you were once a follower of His Majesty.
Why have you chosen to fight against my Emperor?
...
I found... my light...
A light in my heart... where before, there was only darkness...
Erza...
You believe dark is evil and light is good?
You are naïve.
!
The Emperor has a son.
A child born with tremendous power over the light.

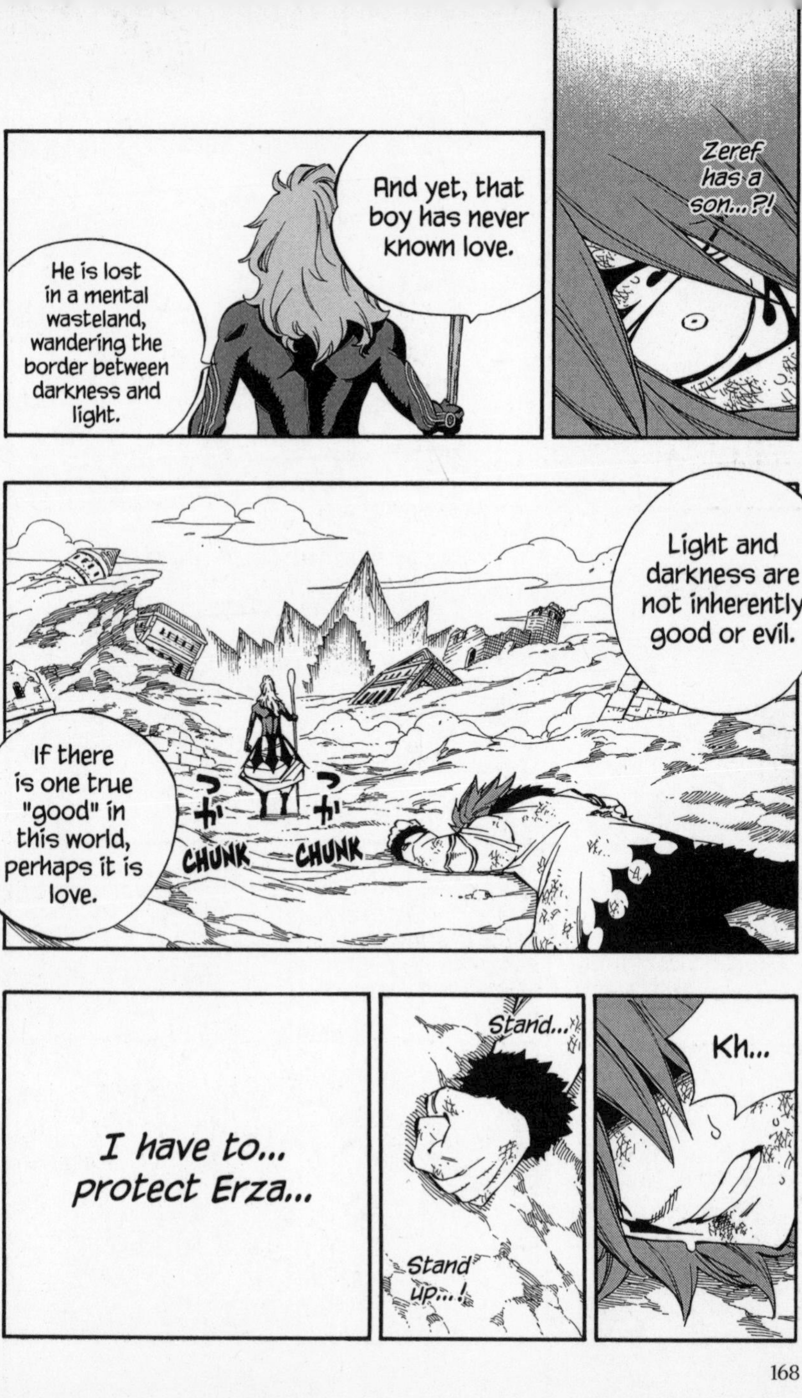

Zeref has a son...?!
And yet, that boy has never known love.
He is lost in a mental wasteland, wandering the border between darkness and light.
Light and darkness are not inherently good or evil.
CHUNK
CHUNK
If there is one true "good" in this world, perhaps it is love.
Kh...
Stand...
Stand up...!
I have to... protect Erza...

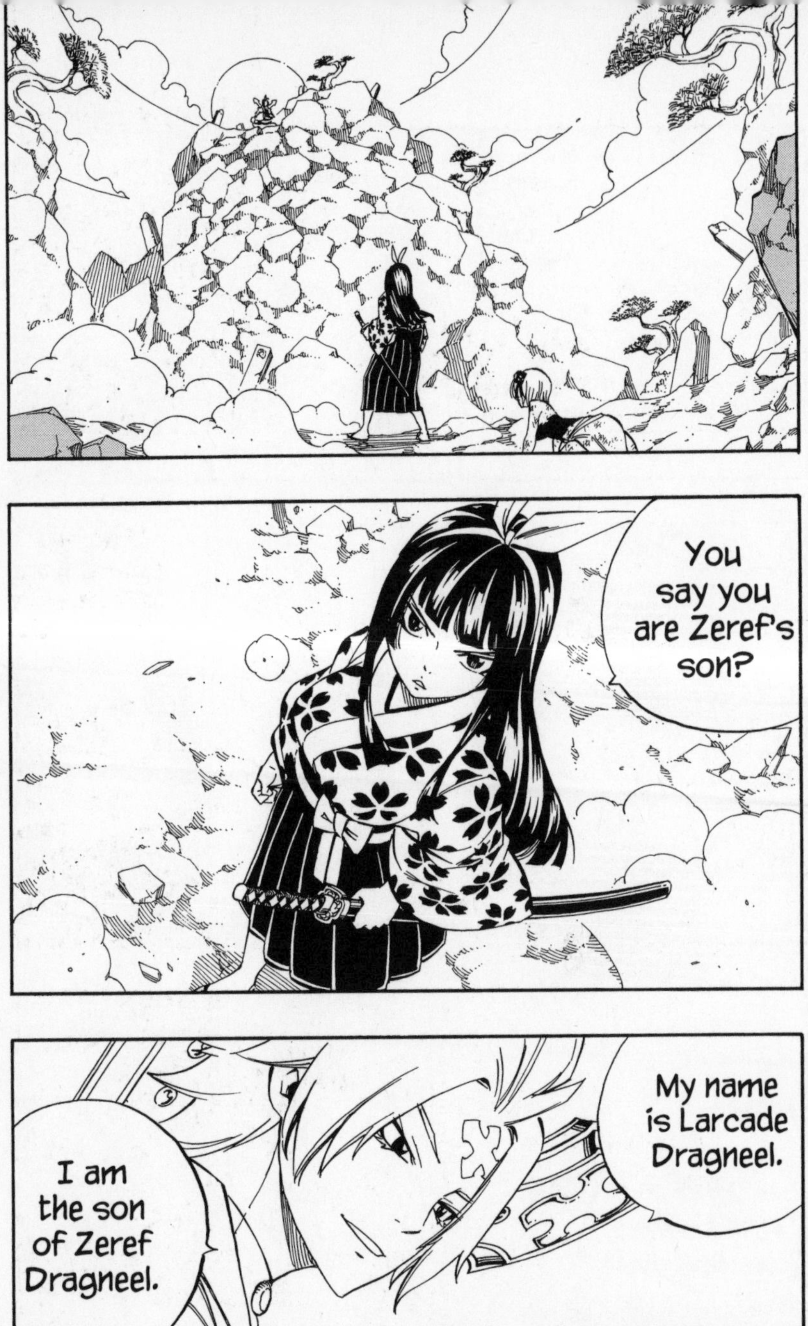
You say you are Zeref's son?
My name is Larcade Dragneel.
I am the son of Zeref Dragneel.

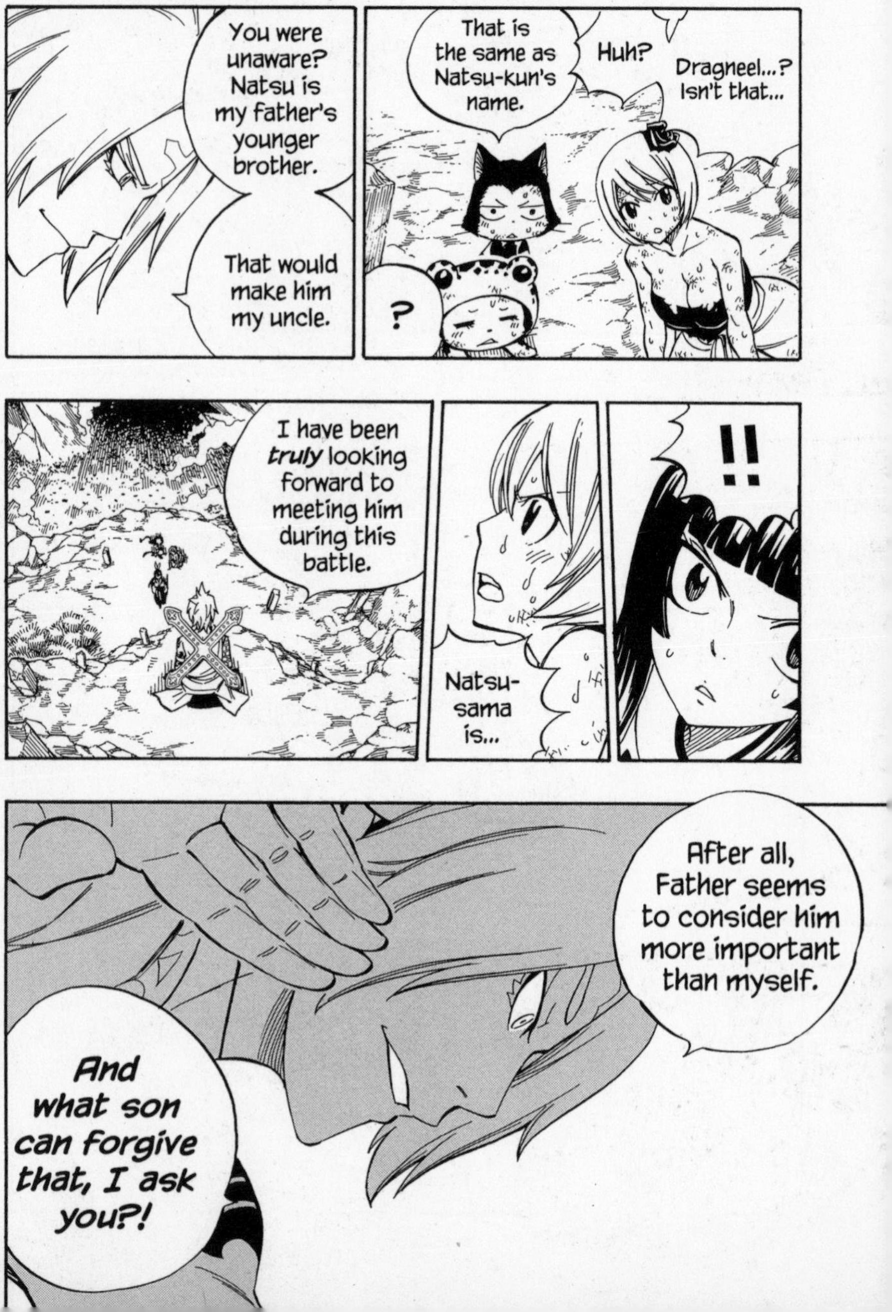
Dragneel...? Isn't that...
Huh?
That is the same as Natsu-kun's name.
?
You were unaware? Natsu is my father's younger brother.
That would make him my uncle.
!!
Natsu-sama is...
I have been *truly* looking forward to meeting him during this battle.
After all, Father seems to consider him more important than myself.
And what son can forgive that, I ask you?!

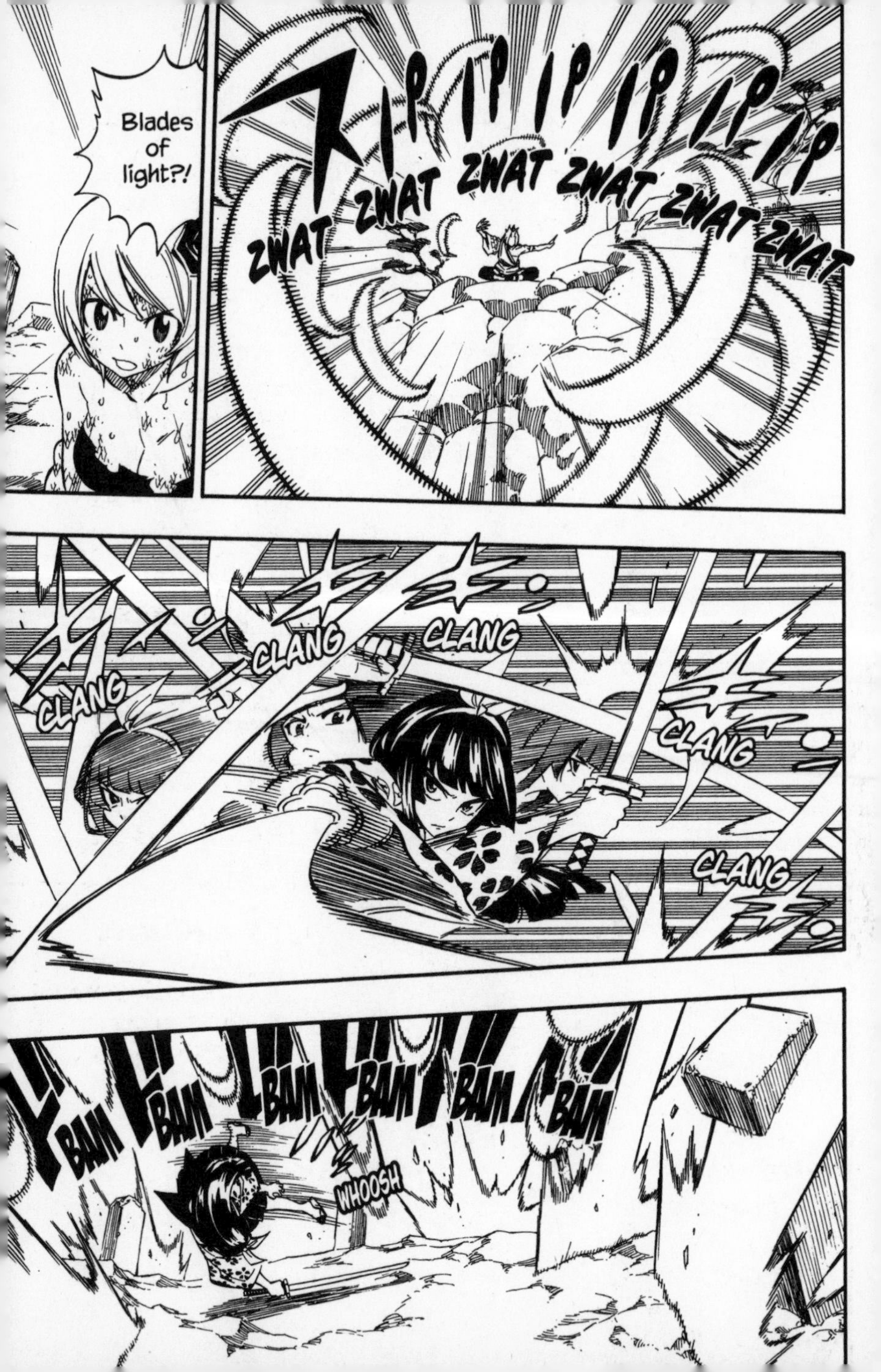
ZWAT ZWAT ZWAT ZWAT ZWAT ZWAT
Blades of light?!
CLANG
CLANG
CLANG
CLANG
CLANG
BAM BAM BAM BAM BAM BAM BAM
WHOOSH

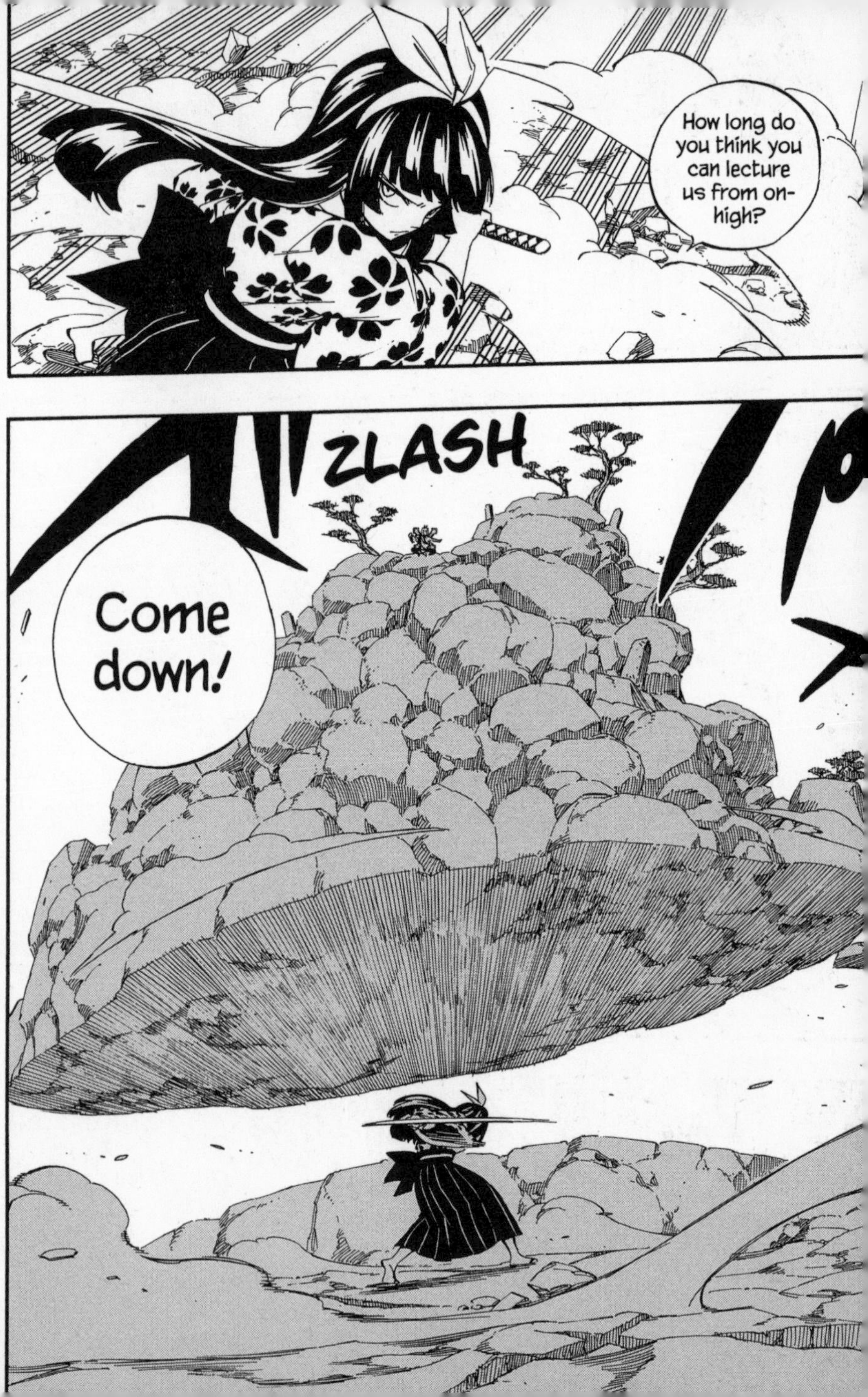
How long do you think you can lecture us from on-high?
ZLASH
Come down!

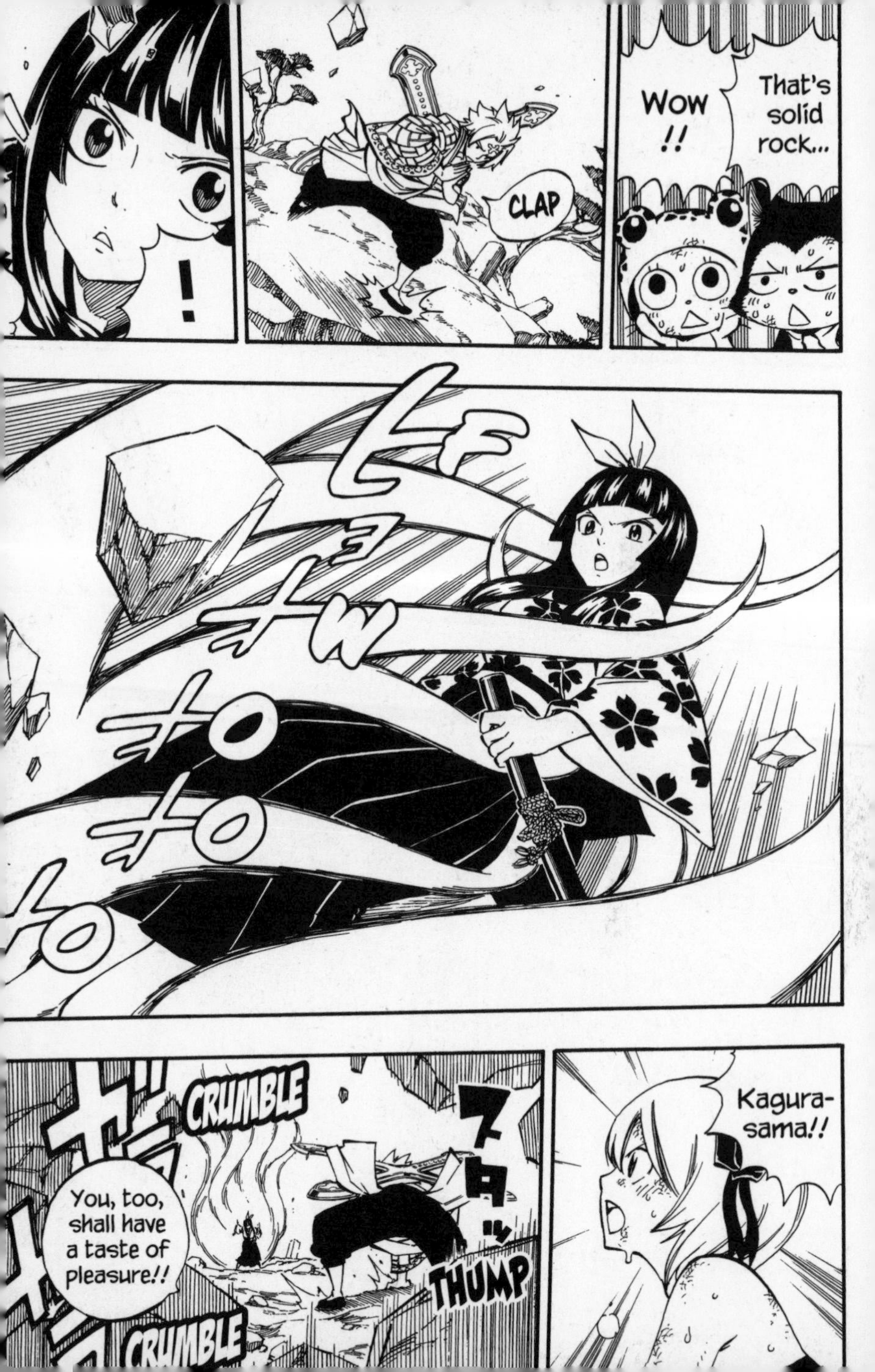
That's solid rock...
Wow!!
CLAP
!
Kagura-sama!!
CRUMBLE
You, too, shall have a taste of pleasure!!
THUMP
CRUMBLE

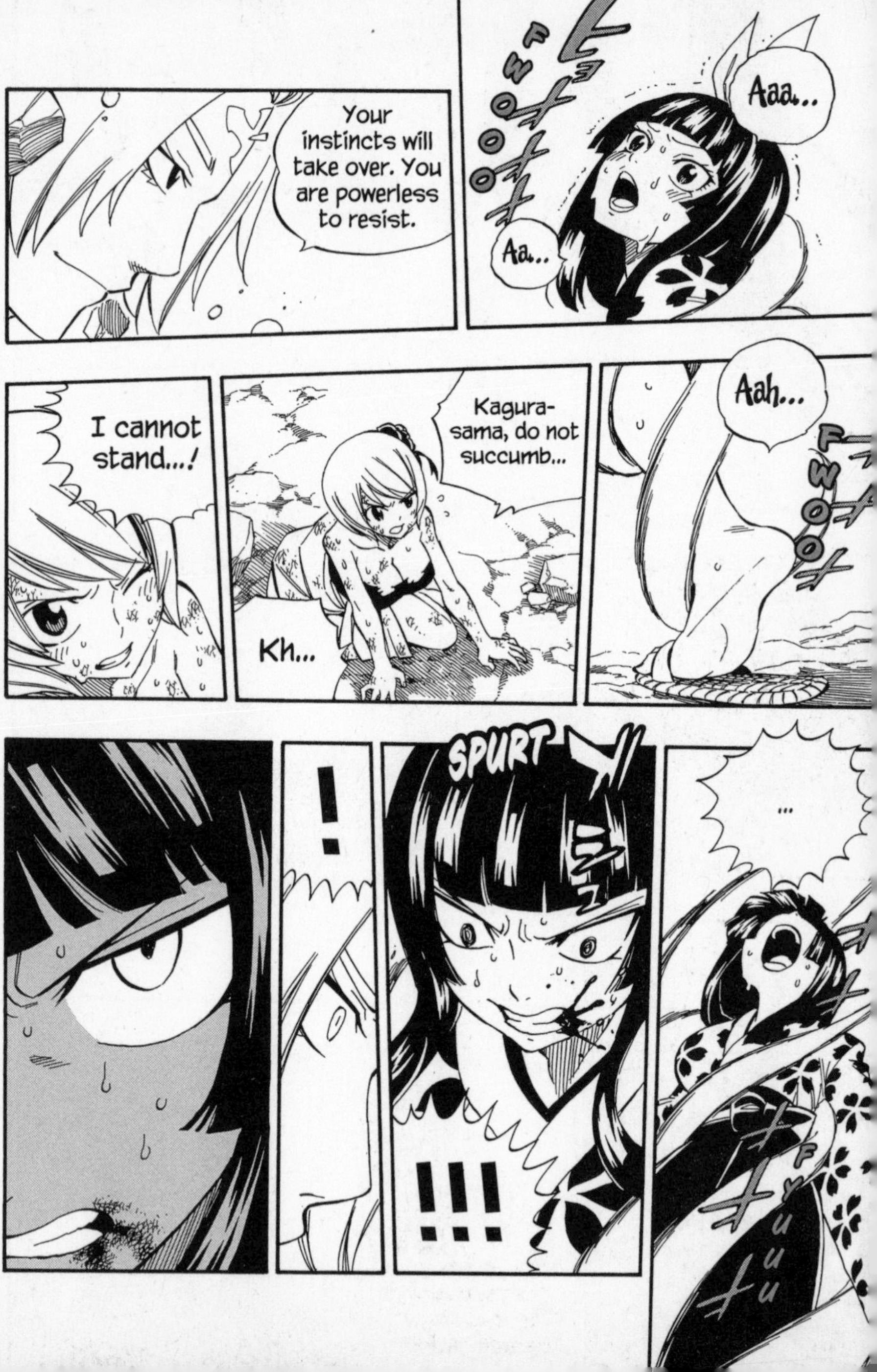
FWOOOO
Aaa...
Aa...
Your instincts will take over. You are powerless to resist.
Aah...
FWOO
Kagura-sama, do not succumb...
Kh...
I cannot stand...!
...
FYuuu
SPURT
!!!
!

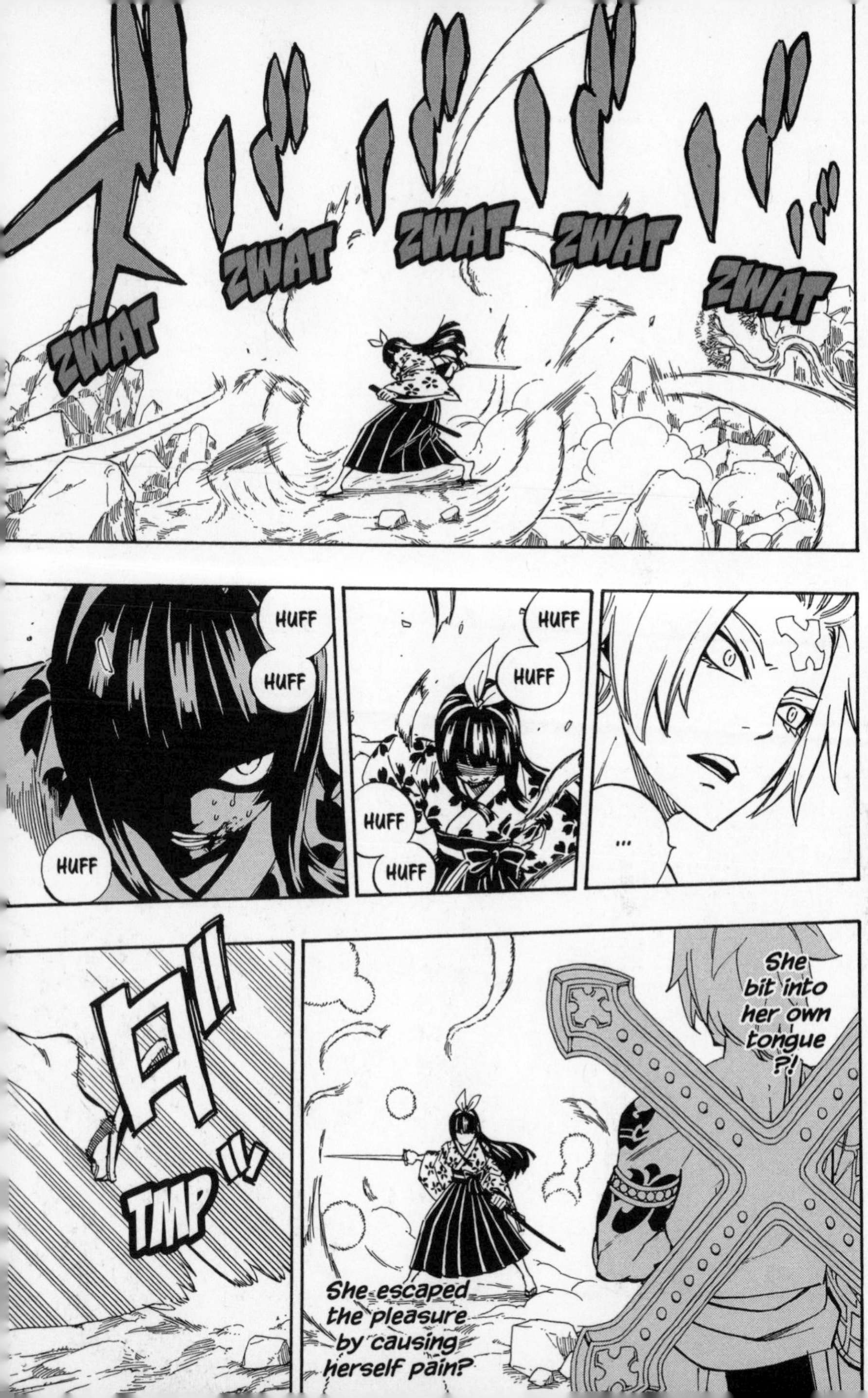
ZWAT
ZWAT
ZWAT
ZWAT
ZWAT
...
HUFF
HUFF
HUFF
HUFF
HUFF
HUFF
HUFF
She bit into her own tongue ?!
She escaped the pleasure by causing herself pain?
TMP

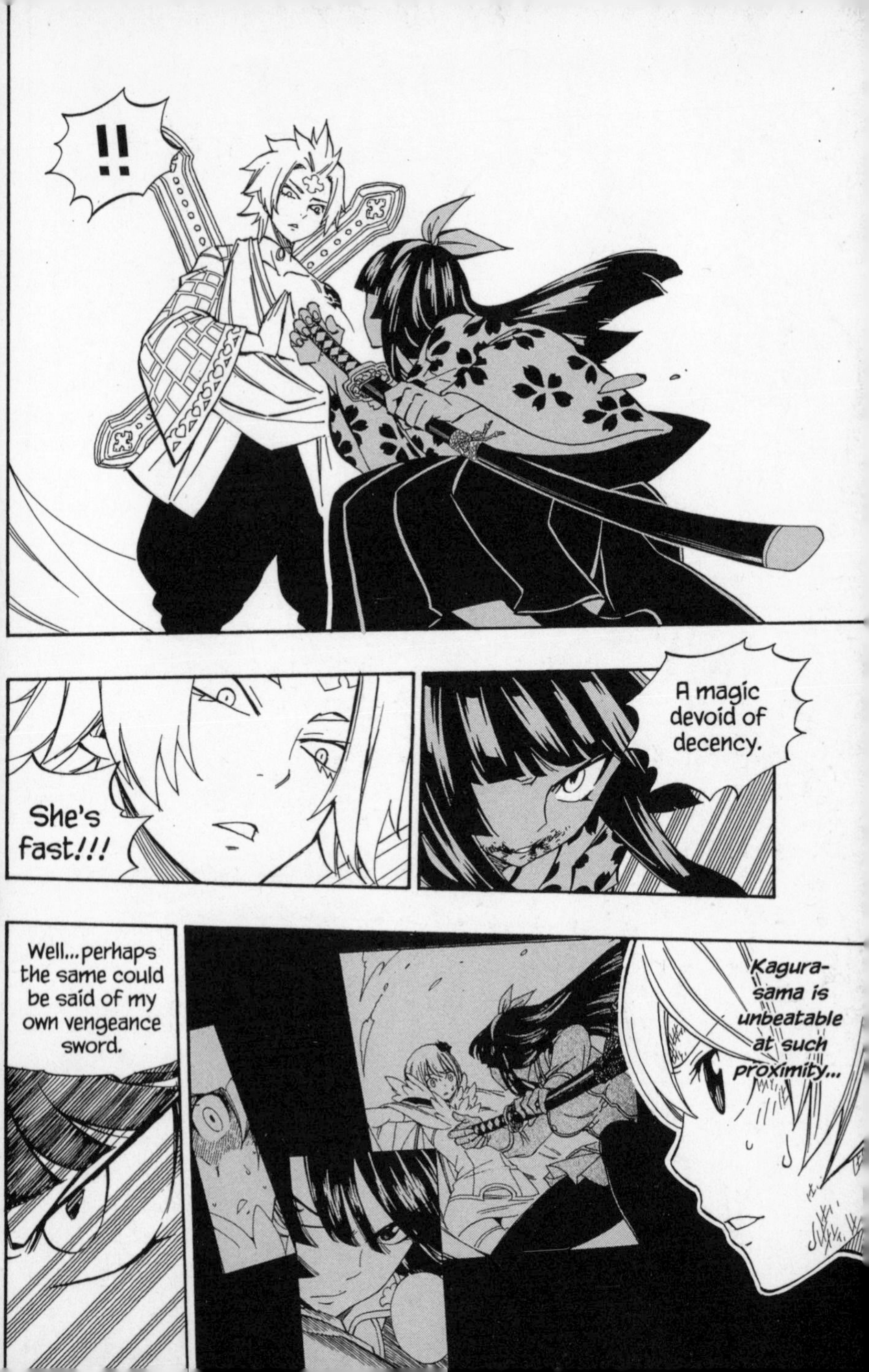
!!
A magic devoid of decency.
She's fast!!!
Kagura-sama is unbeatable at such proximity...
Well...perhaps the same could be said of my own vengeance sword.

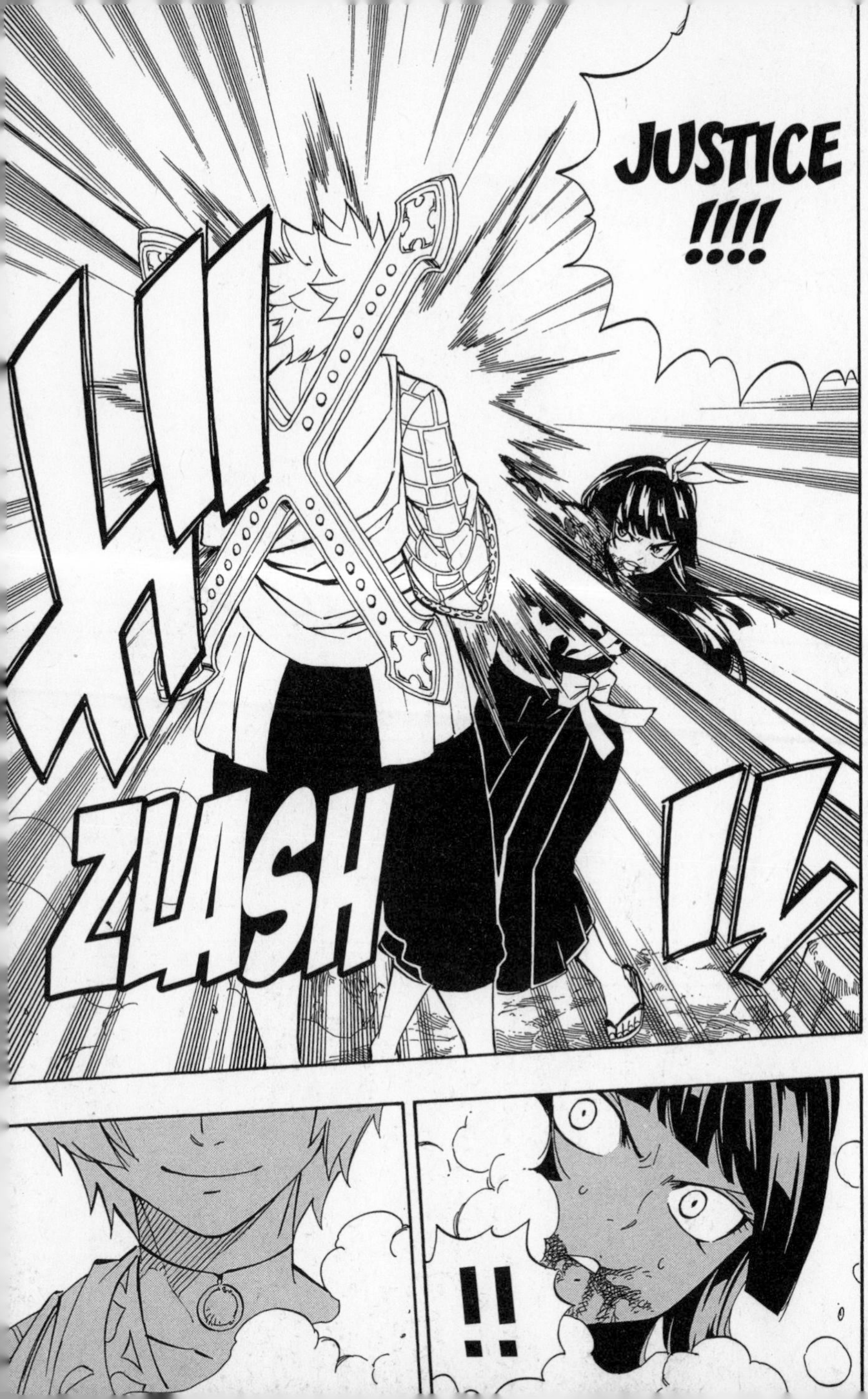
JUSTICE !!!!
ZWASH
!!

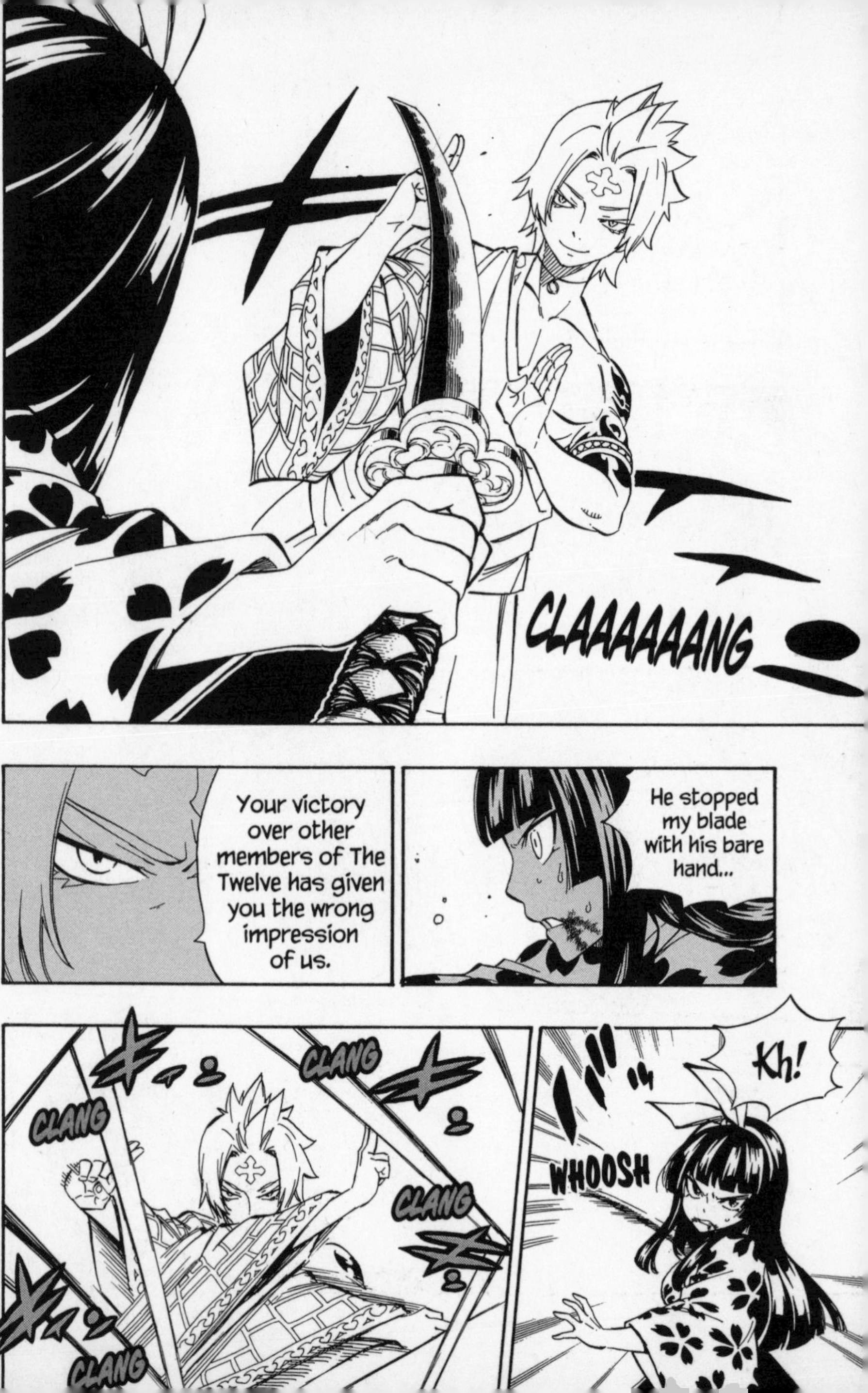
CLAAAAAANG
He stopped my blade with his bare hand...
Your victory over other members of The Twelve has given you the wrong impression of us.
Kh!
WHOOSH
CLANG
CLANG
CLANG
CLANG

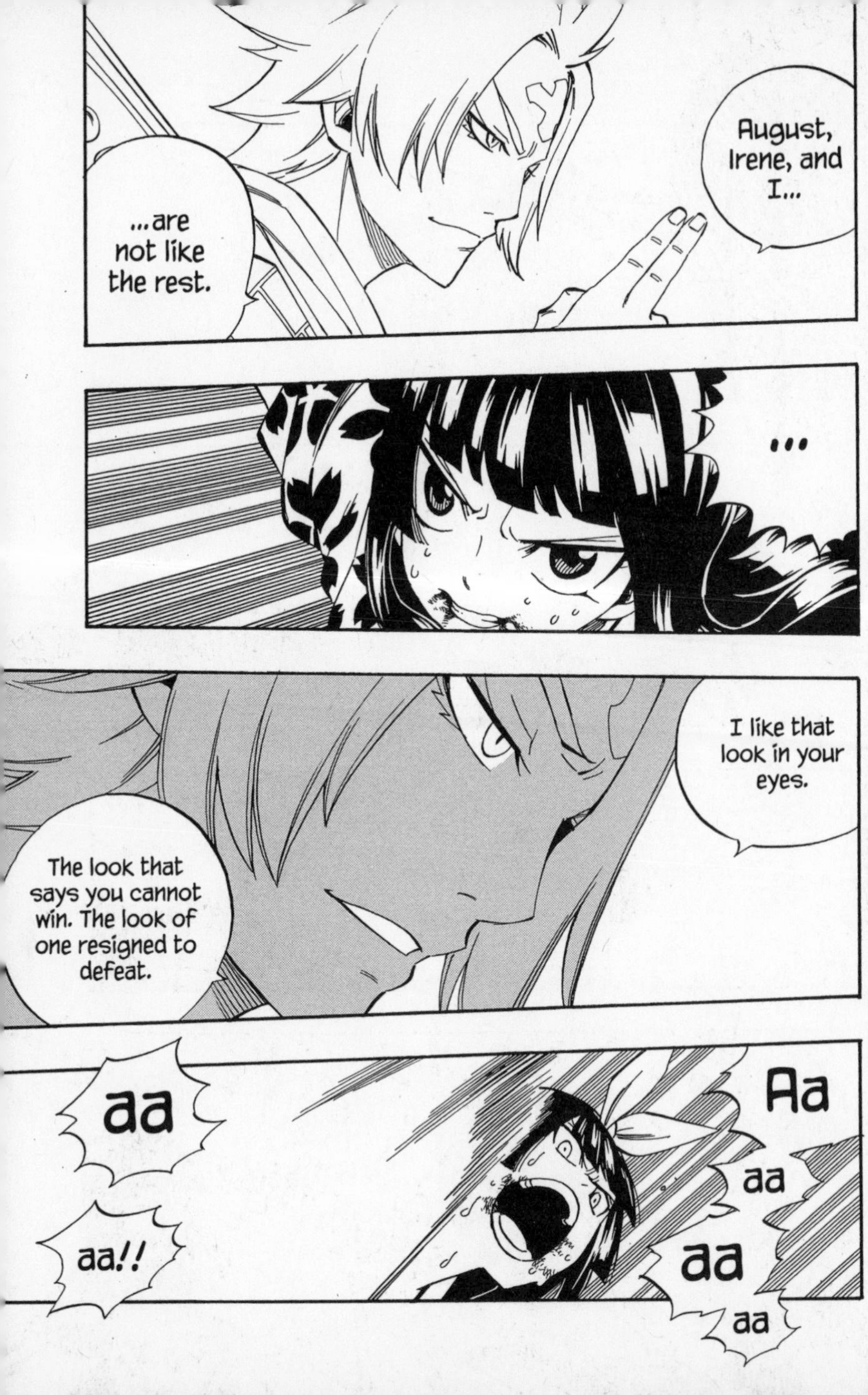
August, Irene, and I...
...are not like the rest.
...
I like that look in your eyes.
The look that says you cannot win. The look of one resigned to defeat.
Aa
aa
aa
aa
aa
aa!!

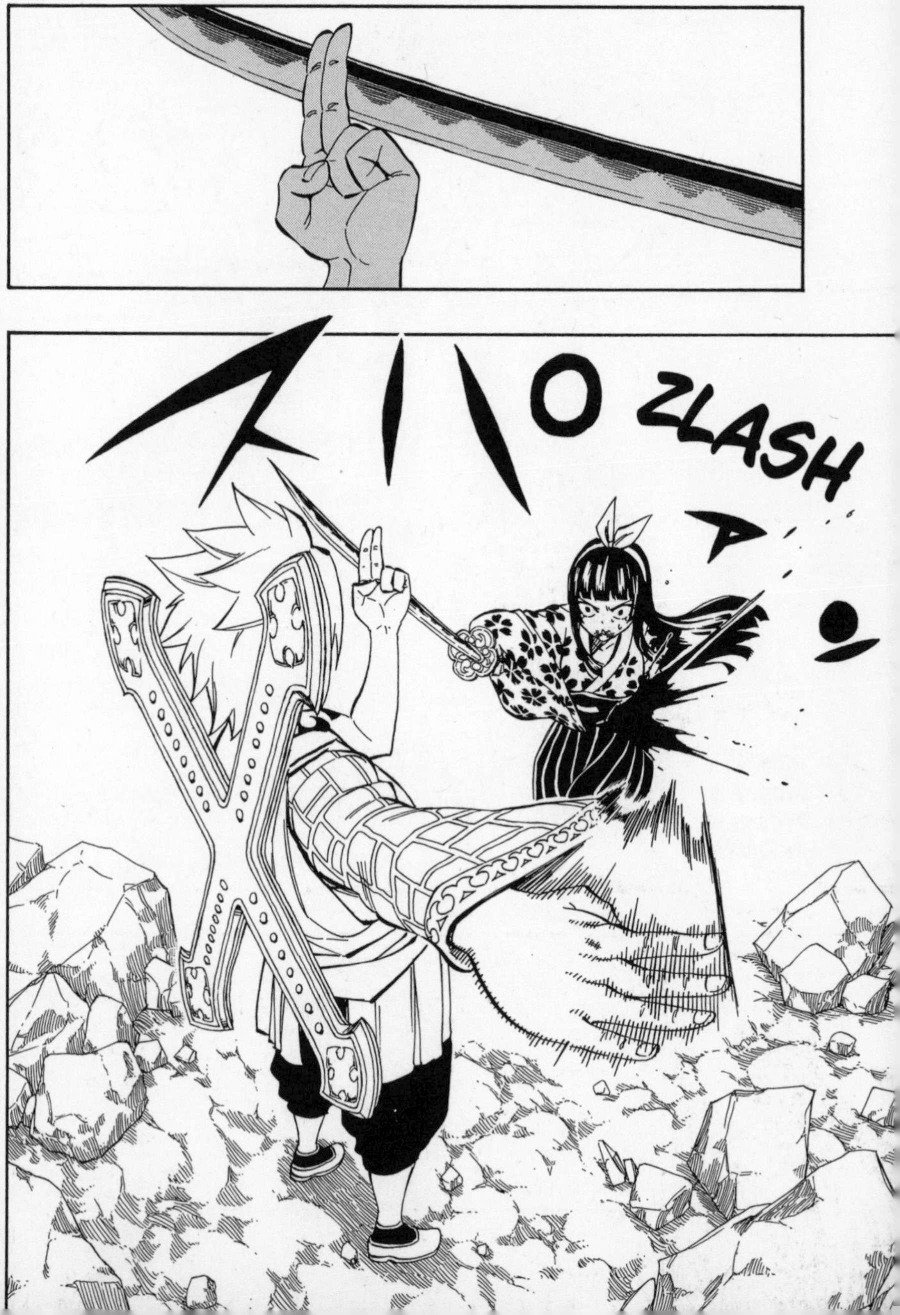
ZLASH

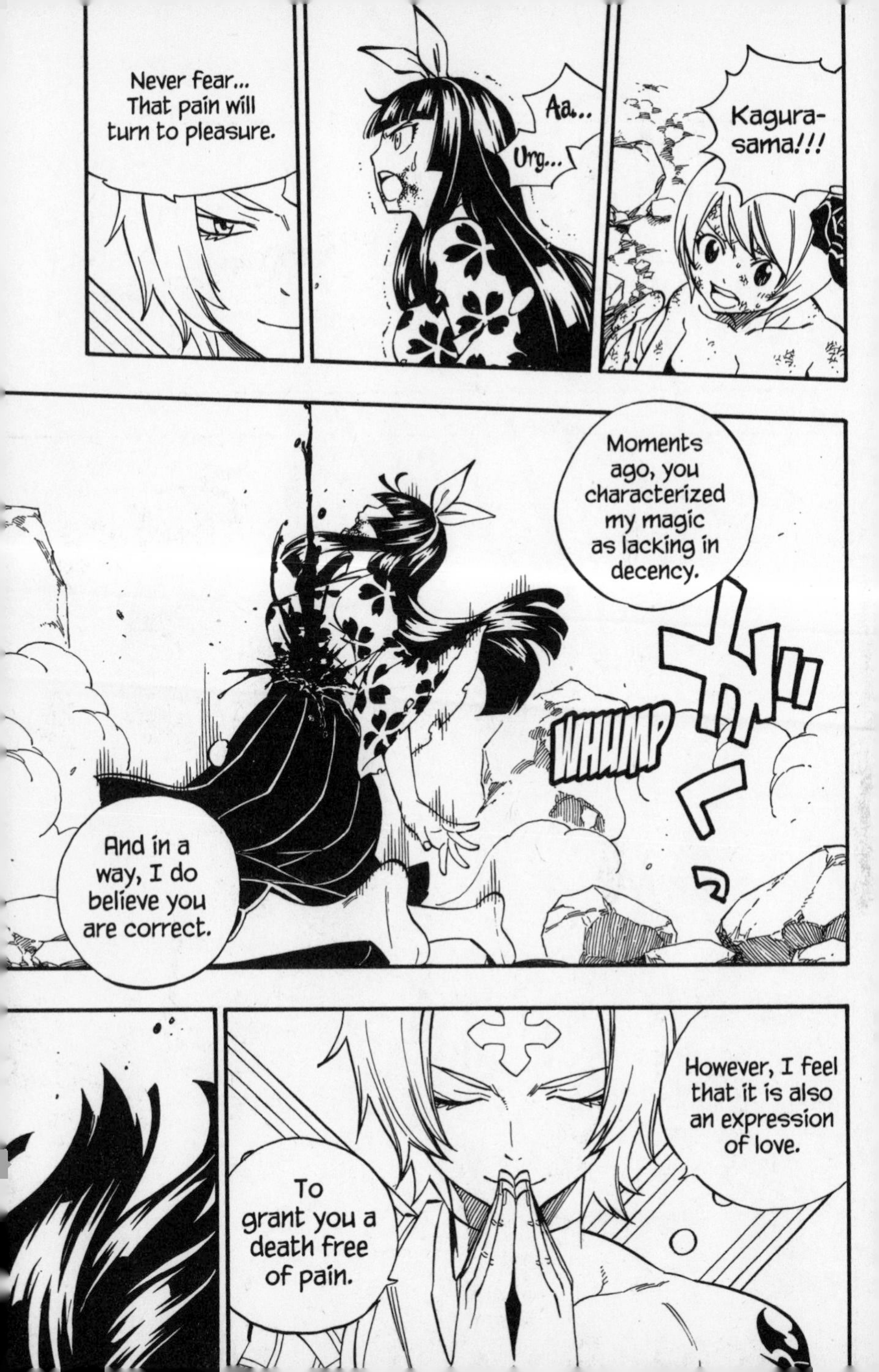
Kagura-sama!!!
Aa...
Urg...
Never fear... That pain will turn to pleasure.
Moments ago, you characterized my magic as lacking in decency.
WHUMP
And in a way, I do believe you are correct.
However, I feel that it is also an expression of love.
To grant you a death free of pain.

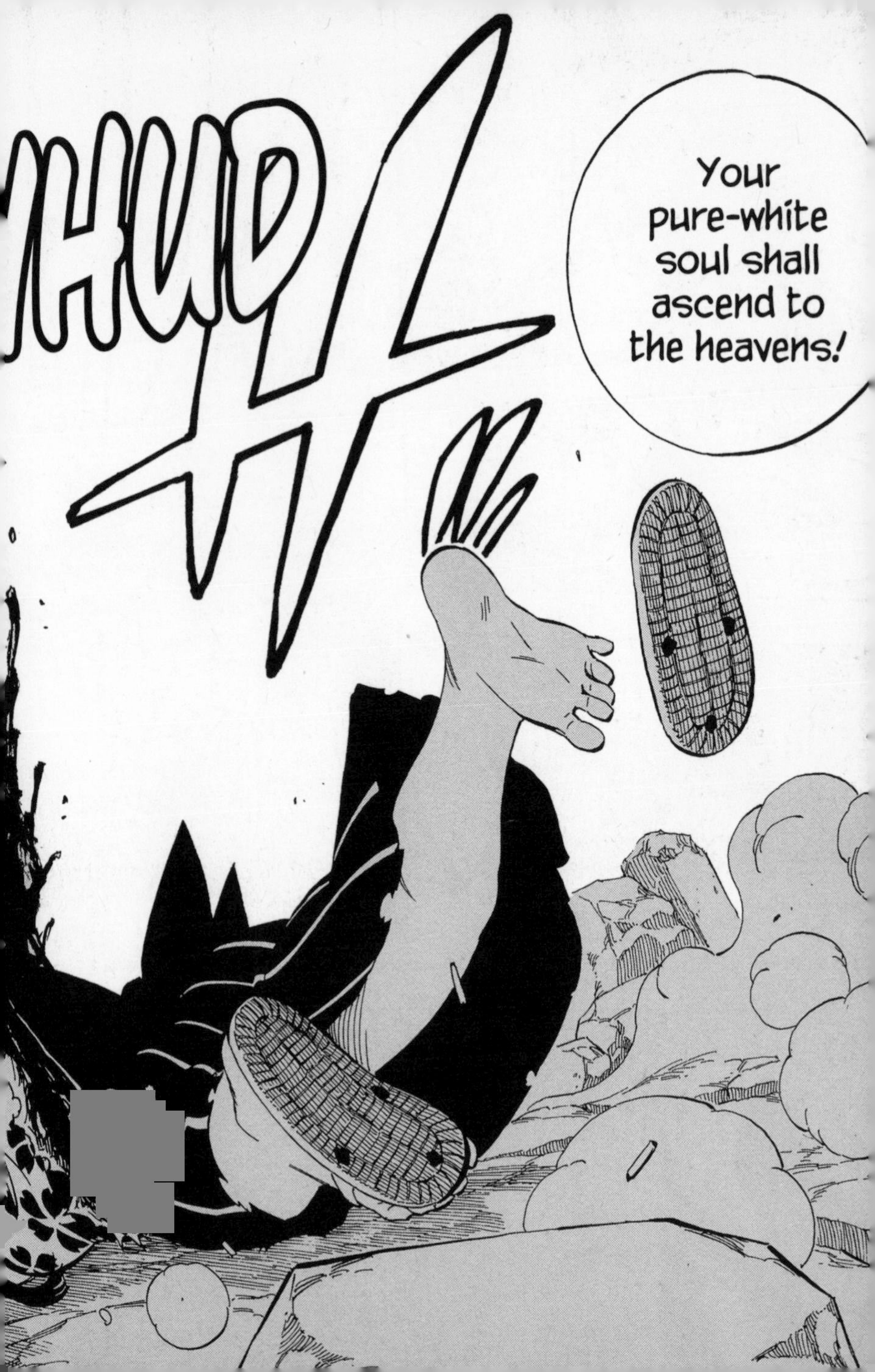
Your pure-white soul shall ascend to the heavens!
HUD

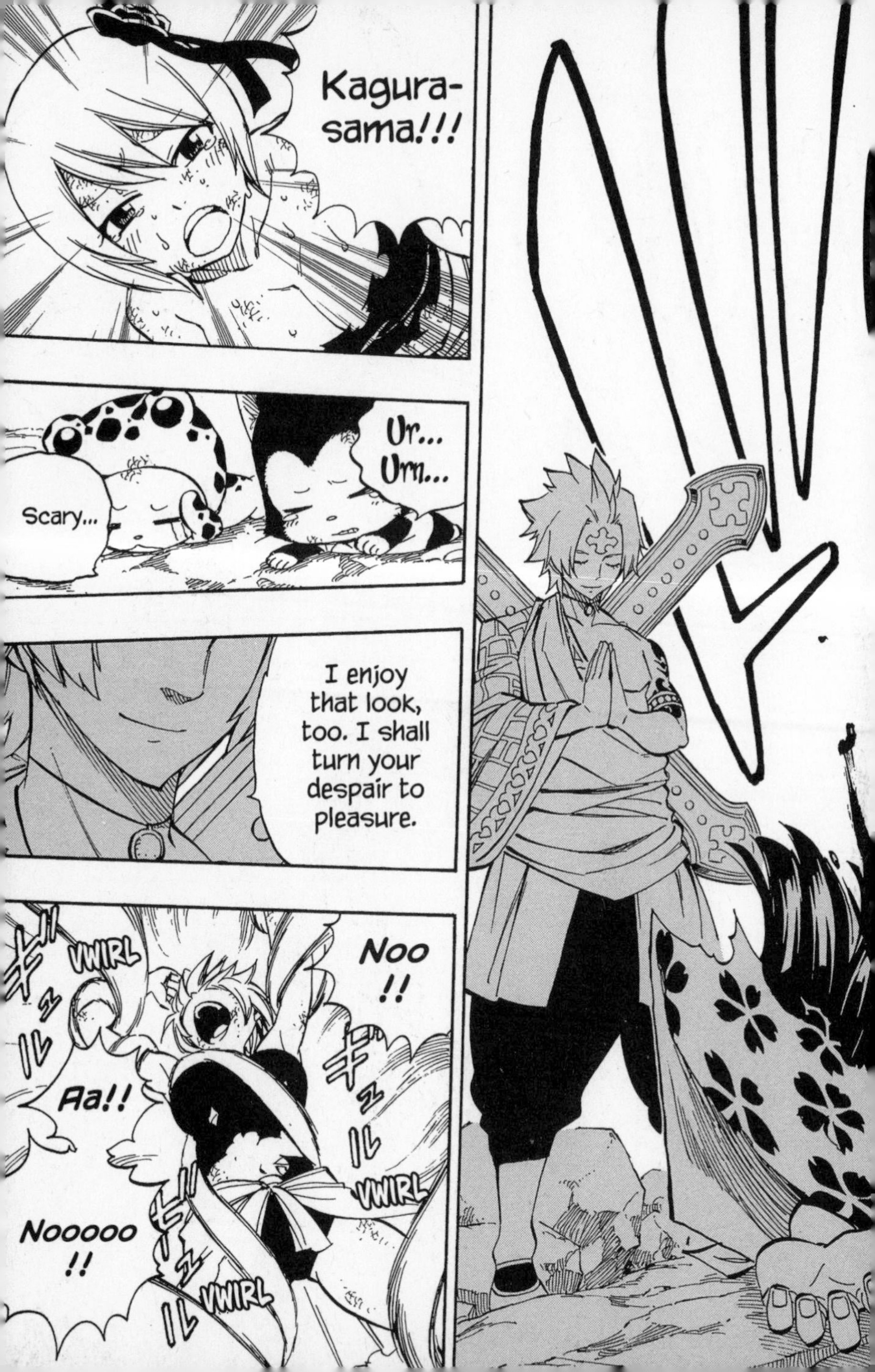
Kagura-sama!!!
Ur... Urn...
Scary...
I enjoy that look, too. I shall turn your despair to pleasure.
Noo !!
VWIRL
Aa!!
VWIRL
Nooooo !!
VWIRL

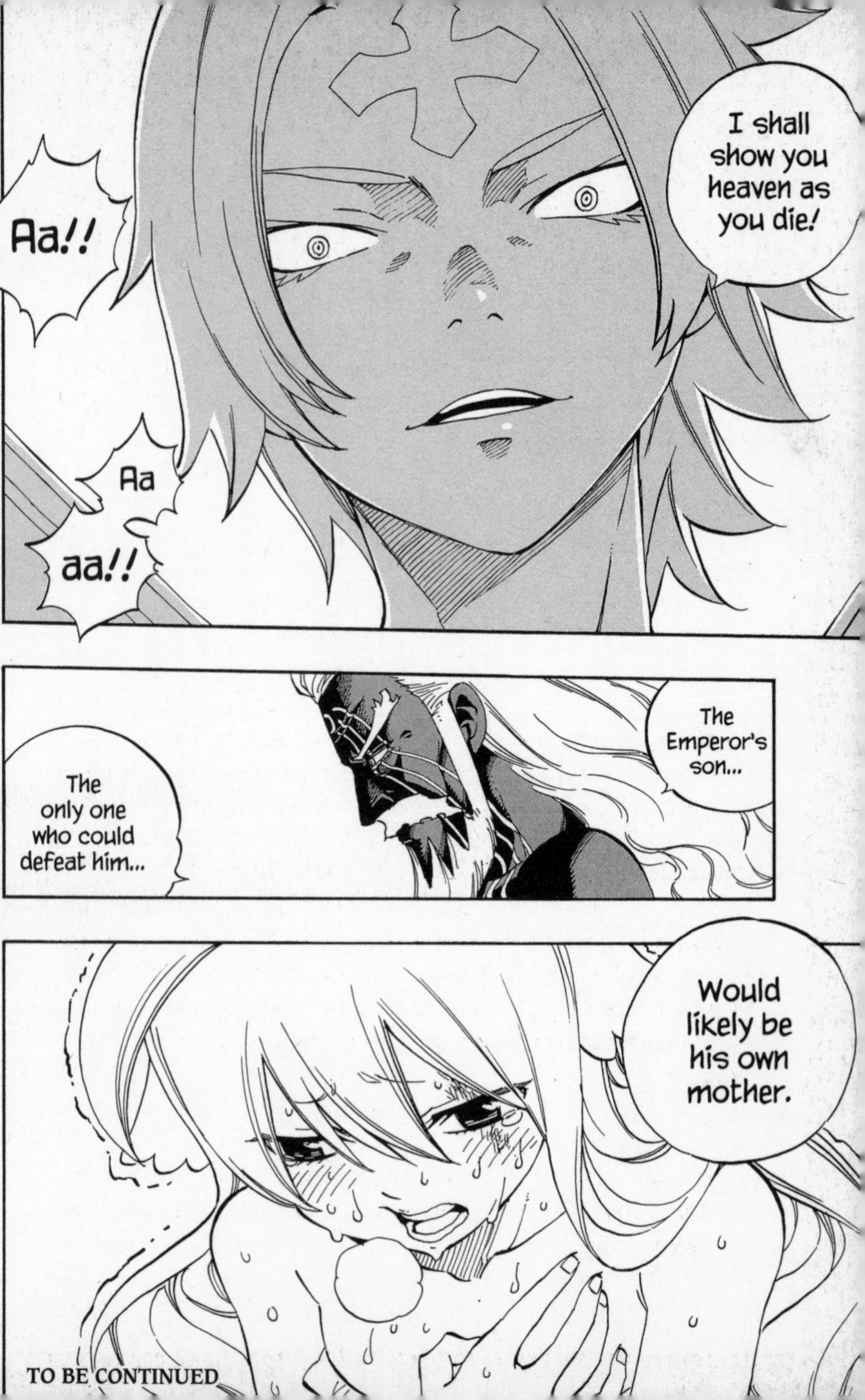
I shall show you heaven as you die!
Aa!!
Aa aa!!
The Emperor's son...
The only one who could defeat him...
Would likely be his own mother.
TO BE CONTINUED

あとがき
Afterword

Personally, I'm not the type who enjoys seeing some of my favorite characters in a manga facing off against each other. But now that the story brought us here, I can just picture the Natsu fans and the Gray fans getting a bit angry. While I'm drawing it, I do it with the knowledge that the twist and turns I have coming up will be really cool, but I imagine for a reader, this situation can be a bit frustrating. However, I don't want to betray my readers who have stuck with me this far, so I vow to keep working on continuing this story in a fun and interesting way. Stay tuned!

Now...for the first time in a long time, the Japanese release of two consecutive volumes, volume 58 & 59, came with a deluxe version that included an original anime DVD, and that version had a different cover. Sure, the pace of my work changes (and every time a new manga volume comes out, things get a little busier), but with two consecutive special releases, and with a bonus four-page manga that comes in the booklet included with the ninth OAD, we're getting near the, "Whoa, watch out!" zone. (Really, the schedule has been murderous!) The bonus manga may start out a little rough, but ends pretty nicely. It may be superfluous, but since it doesn't affect the main story, there's no need to pay it too much attention.

It seems like only yesterday, I was celebrating releasing 50 volumes, but now I notice that after only one more volume, we'll be at 60 (sweats). Hey, I'm surprised, too.

Continued from the left-hand page.

Mira: Um... Yes, in reality it is a little different.

Lucy: ***Very*** different! Erza's Requip magic allows her to make instantaneous changes of armor from a different dimension.

Mira: And ***your*** magic?

Lucy: My magic is about summoning Celestial Spirit power in the form of clothing!

Mira: ...

Lucy: Okay, maybe I was a little ***inspired*** by Erza's magic! (cries)

Mira: That's correct. They are the same.

Can Sherria's magic ever come back? Or rather, please give her magic back to her!

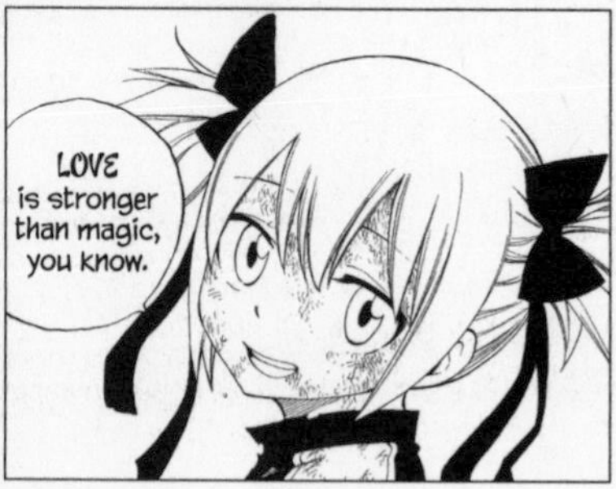
LOVE is stronger than magic, you know.

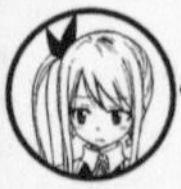
: That...was so sad.

Mira: Yeah...she abandoned her own future in order to save Wendy's life.

Lucy: But...!! She's definitely going to get back to normal! At least, that's what I'd like to believe.

Mira: Well, it's not like children who have just been born can use magic either. So if she can slowly recover her abilities...

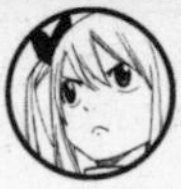
: She ***will*** get them back! Do it for Wendy! You got this, Sherria!

After Universe One, where did Ichiya-san get sent?

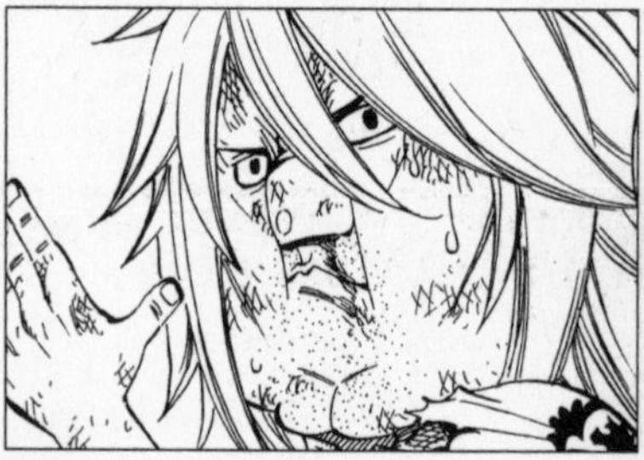

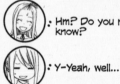

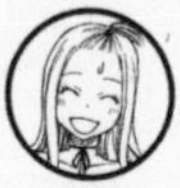
: Hm? Do you really want to know?

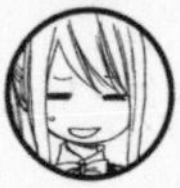
: Y-Yeah, well...

Mira: After that spell, Ichiya-san was sent to a certain mansion.

Lucy: Huh?!

Mira: It was there that he met a lovely young lady, and it was love at first sight. Even now, they are enjoying their tea parties together.

Lucy: He's doing that while we're all fighting a war?!

Mira: And he would comment, "My, how this tea gives off such a lovely ***perfume!***"

Lucy: Sounds like something he'd say.

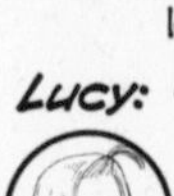
: Of course it is only in ***my imagination*** that this is true.

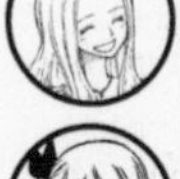
: Yeah, just forget this conversation ever happened.

EMERGENCY REQUEST! EXPLAIN THE MYSTERIES OF F.T.

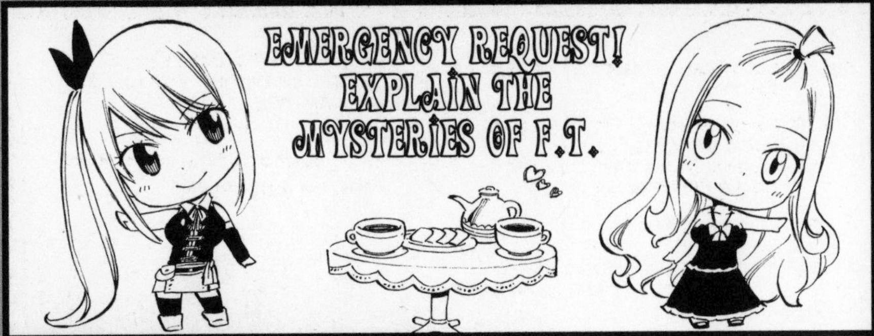

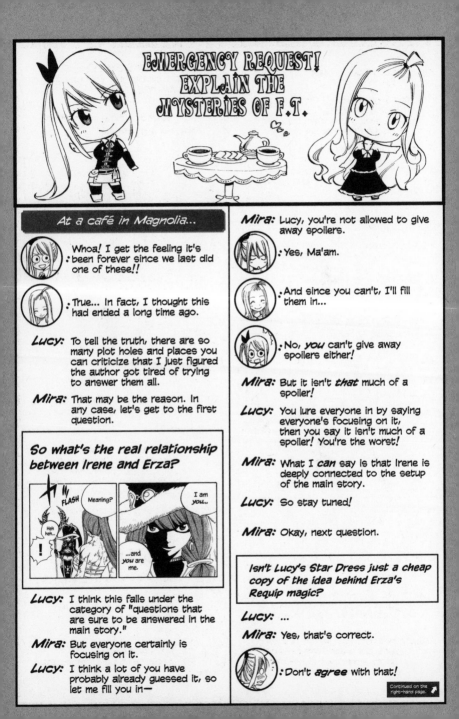

At a café in Magnolia...

: Whoa! I get the feeling it's been forever since we last did one of these!!

: True... In fact, I thought this had ended a long time ago.

Lucy: To tell the truth, there are so many plot holes and places you can criticize that I just figured the author got tired of trying to answer them all.

Mira: That may be the reason. In any case, let's get to the first question.

So what's the real relationship between Irene and Erza?

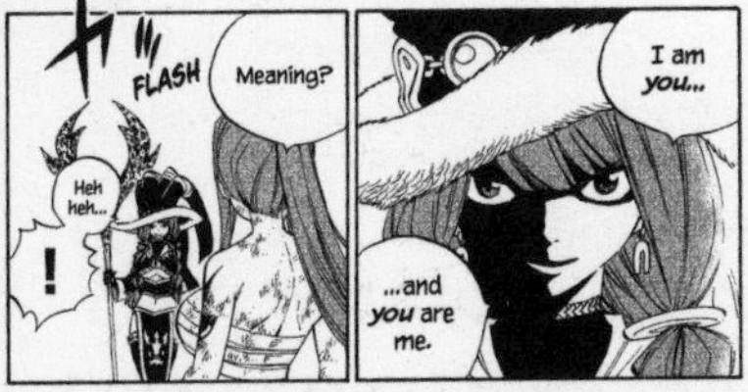

I am *you*...
...and *you* are me.
Meaning?
FLASH
Heh heh...
!

Lucy: I think this falls under the category of "questions that are sure to be answered in the main story."

Mira: But everyone certainly is focusing on it.

Lucy: I think a lot of you have probably already guessed it, so let me fill you in—

Mira: Lucy, you're not allowed to give away spoilers.

: Yes, Ma'am.

: And since you can't, I'll fill them in...

: No, *you* can't give away spoilers either!

Mira: But it isn't ***that*** much of a spoiler!

Lucy: You lure everyone in by saying everyone's focusing on it, then you say it isn't much of a spoiler! You're the worst!

Mira: What I ***can*** say is that Irene is deeply connected to the setup of the main story.

Lucy: So stay tuned!

Mira: Okay, next question.

Isn't Lucy's Star Dress just a cheap copy of the idea behind Erza's Requip magic?

Lucy: ...

Mira: Yes, that's correct.

: Don't ***agree*** with that!

Continued on the right-hand page.

TAIL de ART

The Fairy Tail Guild is looking for illustrations! Please send in your art on a post card or at post-card size, and do it in black pen, okay? Those chosen to be published will get a signed mini poster! ♪ Make sure you write your real name and address on the back of your illustration!

Ibaraki Prefecture, Kayutabashi

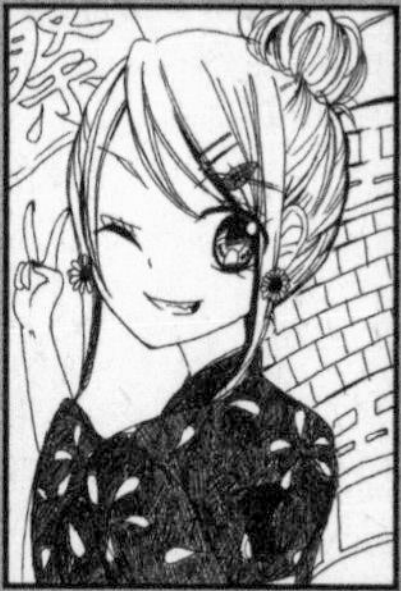

▲I never expected Lucy to look that good in a kimono! (Or a yukata?)

Gunma Prefecture, Kōki Ishizeki

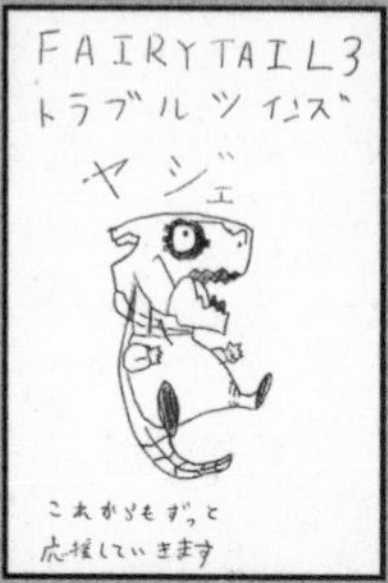
FAIRYTAIL3
トラブルツインズ
これからもずっと
応援していきます

▲This is from the novels. Those who feel a burning desire to know, go read "Trouble Twins!"

Iwate Prefecture, T.S.

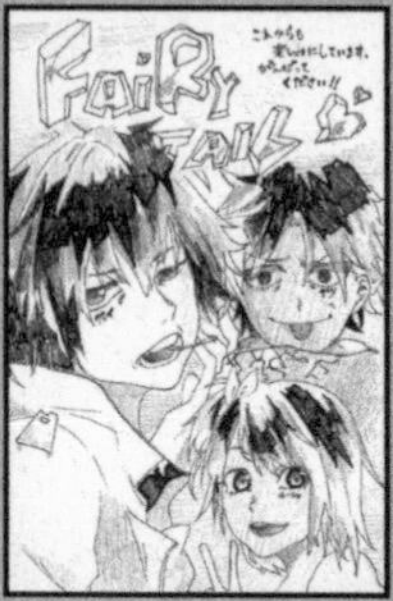

▲Whoa! Pretty stunning! I think the drawing of Gray is especially cool!

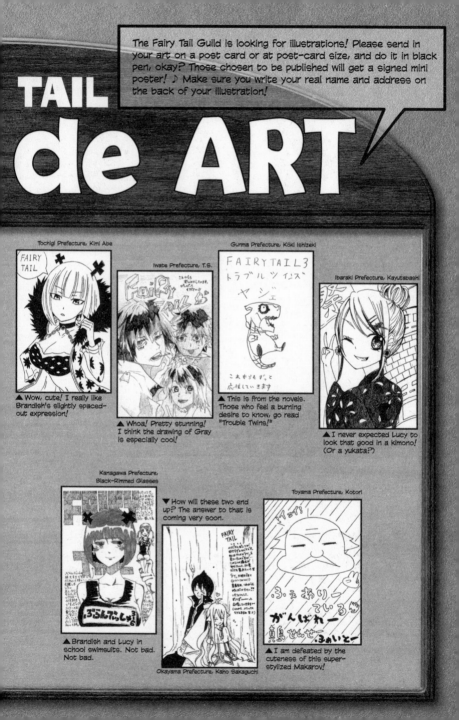

Tochigi Prefecture, Kimi Abe

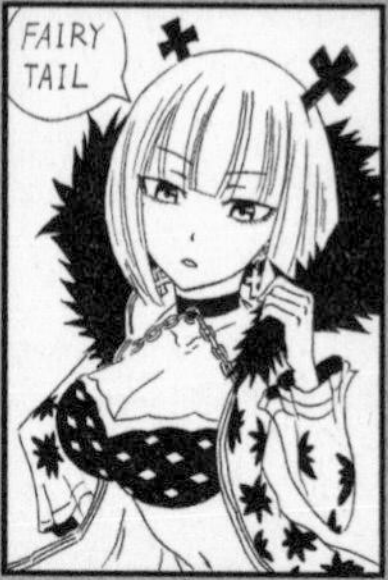
FAIRY TAIL

▲Wow, cute! I really like Brandish's slightly spaced-out expression!

Toyama Prefecture, Kotori

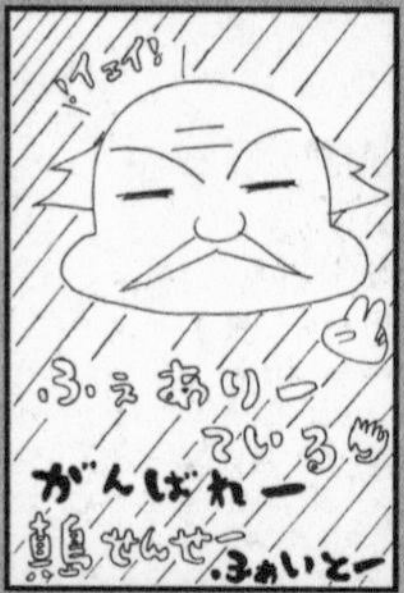
イェイ!
ふぇありーている
がんばれー
真島せんせー ふぁいとー

▲I am defeated by the cuteness of this super-stylized Makarov!

▼How will these two end up? The answer to that is coming very soon.

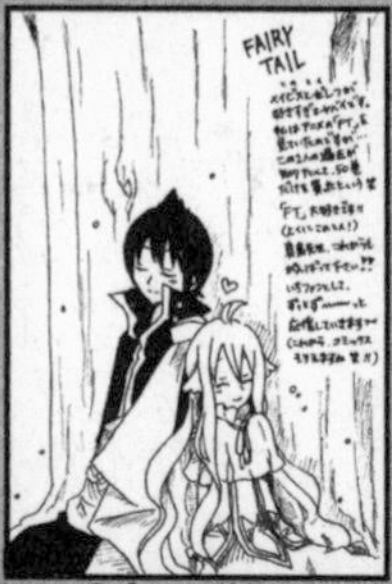
FAIRY TAIL

Okayama Prefecture, Kaho Sakaguchi

Kanagawa Prefecture, Black-Rimmed Glasses

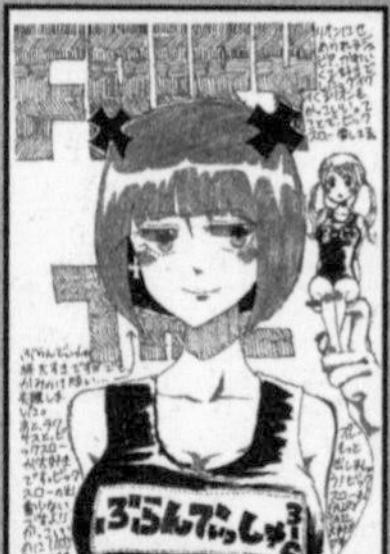

▲Brandish and Lucy in school swimsuits. Not bad. Not bad.

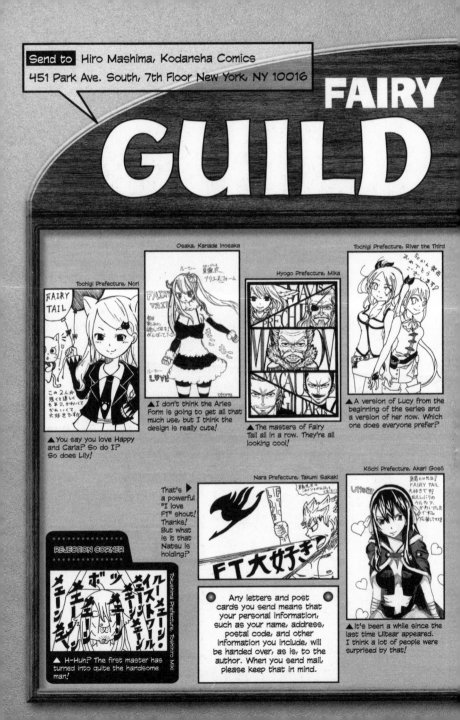

Send to Hiro Mashima, Kodansha Comics
451 Park Ave. South, 7th Floor New York, NY 10016

FAIRY GUILD

Tochigi Prefecture, River the Third

50巻発売おめでとうございます!

▲A version of Lucy from the beginning of the series and a version of her now. Which one does everyone prefer?

Hyogo Prefecture, Mika

▲The masters of Fairy Tail all in a row. They're all looking cool!

Osaka, Kanade Inosaka

ルーシー
星霊衣
アリエスフォーム
FAIRY TAIL
もこもこ
ルーシー
LOVE

▲I don't think the Aries Form is going to get all that much use, but I think the design is really cute!

Tochigi Prefecture, Nori

FAIRY TAIL

▲You say you love Happy and Carla? So do I? So does Lily!

Kōchi Prefecture, Akari Gosō

Ultear
真島ヒロ先生!
FAIRY TAIL
大好きです!
お久しぶりの
ウルティア、かわいかったです。
応援してマス!

▲It's been a while since the last time Ultear appeared. I think a lot of people were surprised by that!

Nara Prefecture, Takumi Sakaki

FT大好き

That's ▶ a powerful "I love FT" shout! Thanks! But what is it that Natsu is holding?

Any letters and post cards you send means that your personal information, such as your name, address, postal code, and other information you include, will be handed over, as is, to the author. When you send mail, please keep that in mind.

REJECTION CORNER

Tokushima Prefecture, Toshihiro Miki

▲ H-Huh? The first master has turned into quite the handsome man!

OAD 9 & VOLUME 59-01, SPECIAL
REJECTED IMAGE

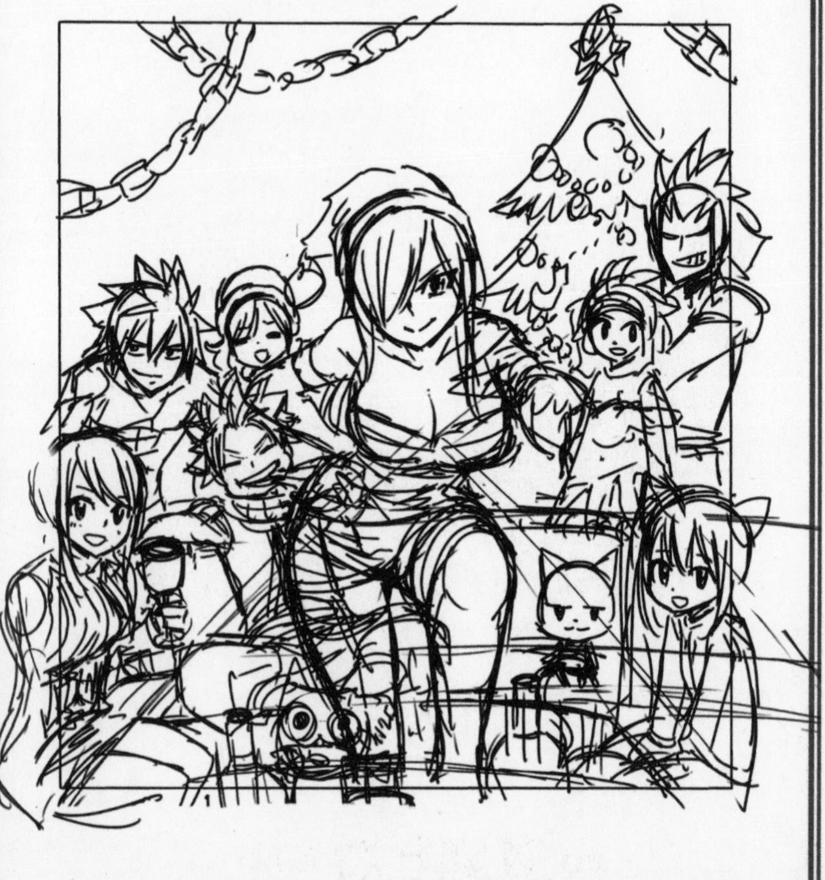

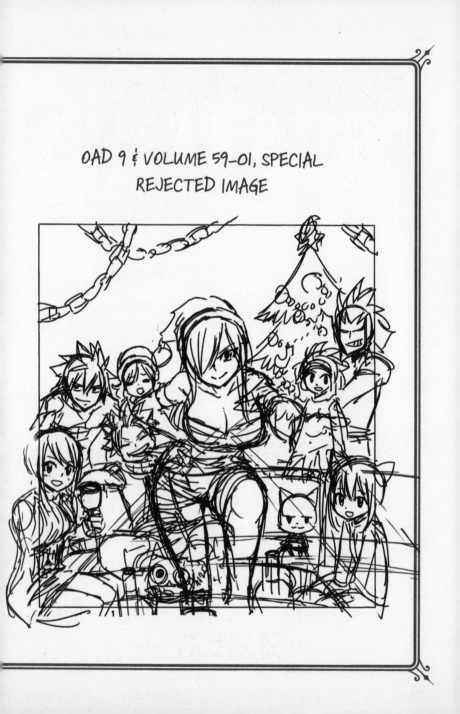

FAIRY TAIL

フェアリーテイル

59

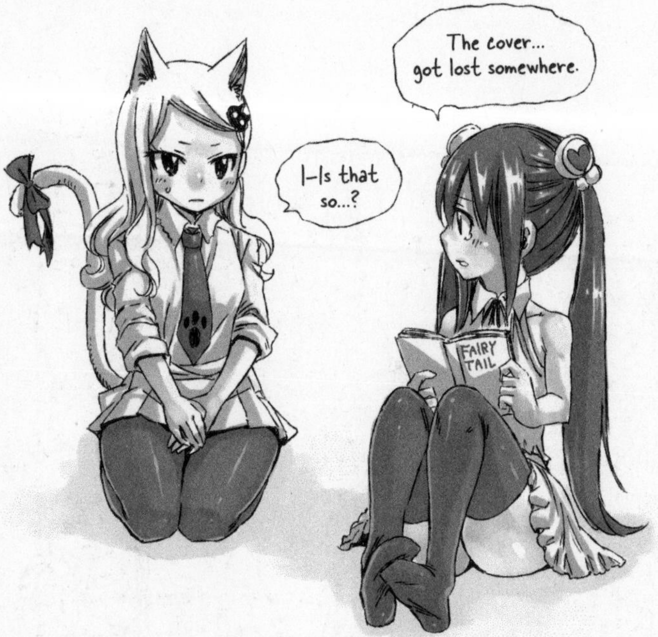
The cover... got lost somewhere.
I-Is that so...?
FAIRY TAIL

HIRO 真島ヒロ MASHIMA

FROM HIRO MASHIMA

Recently, I've been using lots of different tools to draw my pictures in various ways. I even drew this Natsu using methods I don't usually use. Digital technology is such a deep world. I really gotta practice more…

Original Jacket Design: Hisao Ogawa

Translation Notes:

Japanese is a difficult language and translation is often more art than science. For your edification and reading pleasure, here are notes on some of the places where we could have gone in a different direction with our translation of the work, or where a Japanese cultural reference is used.

Page 14, Aqua Metoria

This is a Japanese word for which there is no good direct English translation. The meaning refers to the composition and reading of poems that are about sights in the natural world. *Ginpû* is reading poems in gusty winds, and *rôgetsu* means a pleasant night out moon-watching.

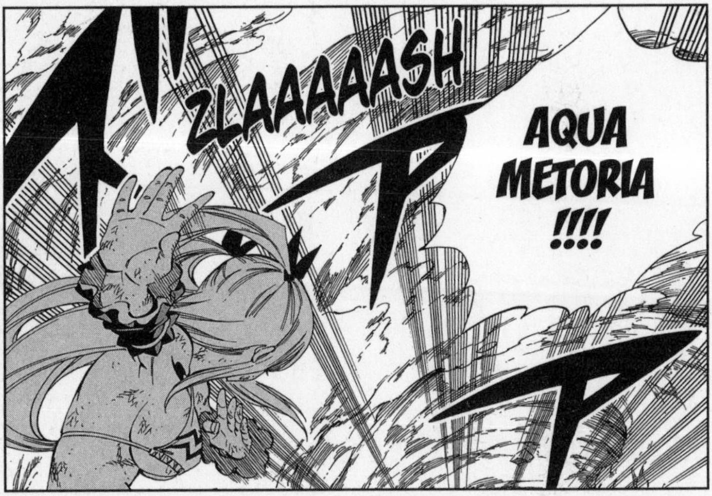
ZLAAAAASH
AQUA METORIA !!!!

Page 92, "This is my final crowning glory."

In Japanese, instead of "crowning glory," Makarov uses the term *hana-michi*, which refers to a final victorious path. These words in Japanese represent a Buddhist concept of breaking though false doctrines in order to find and protect the true path to enlightenment.

Page 161, Ichthyon

Ichthyon comes from the Greek word *ikhthus*, which means "fish."

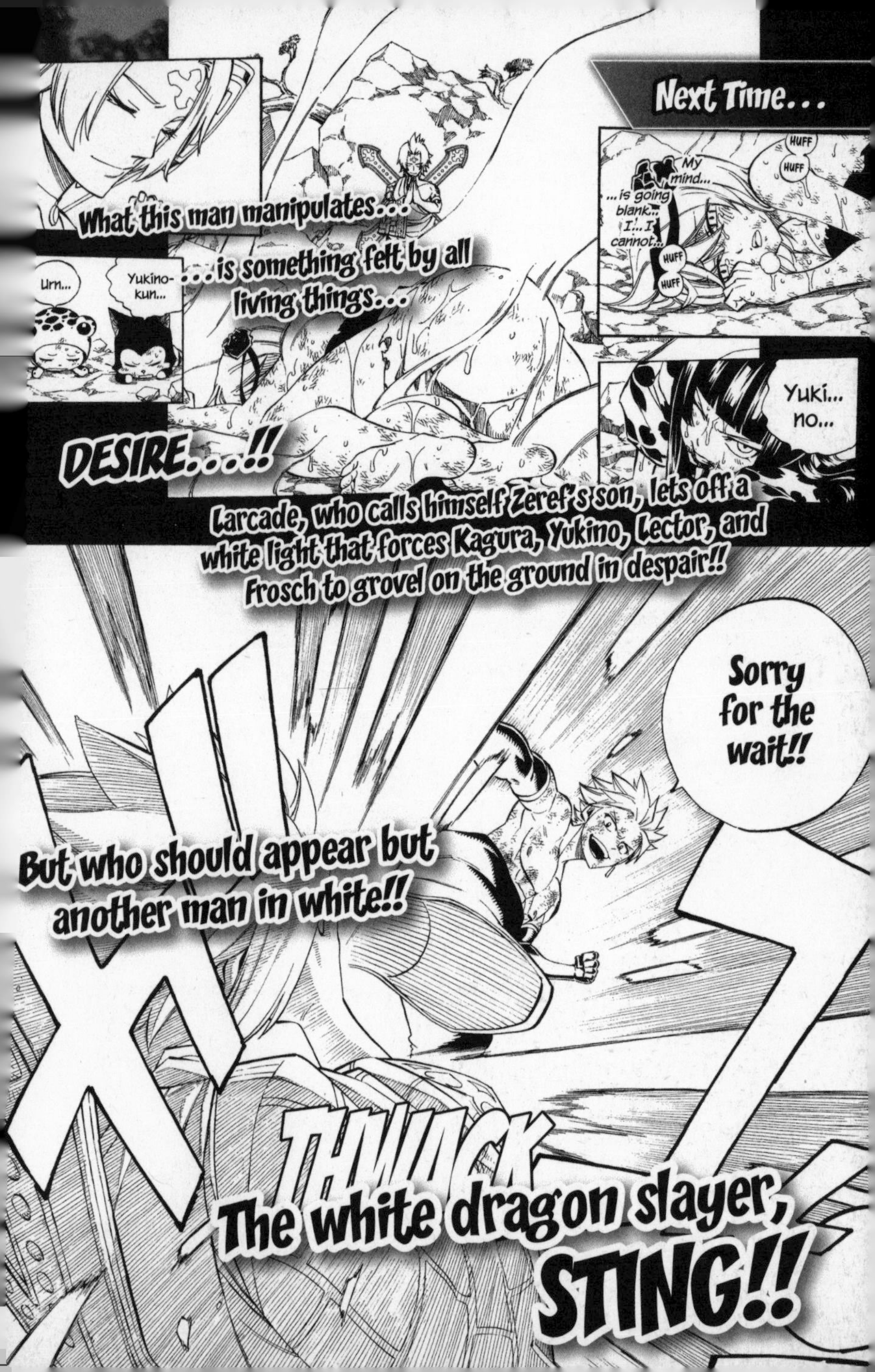
Next Time...
HUFF
HUFF
My mind...
...is going blank... I... I cannot...
HUFF
HUFF
Yuki... no...
What this man manipulates...
Yukino-kun...
Urn...
...is something felt by all living things...
DESIRE...!!
Larcade, who calls himself Zeref's son, lets off a
white light that forces Kagura, Yukino, Lector, and
Frosch to grovel on the ground in despair!!
Sorry for the wait!!
But who should appear but another man in white!!
THWACK
The white dragon slayer, STING!!

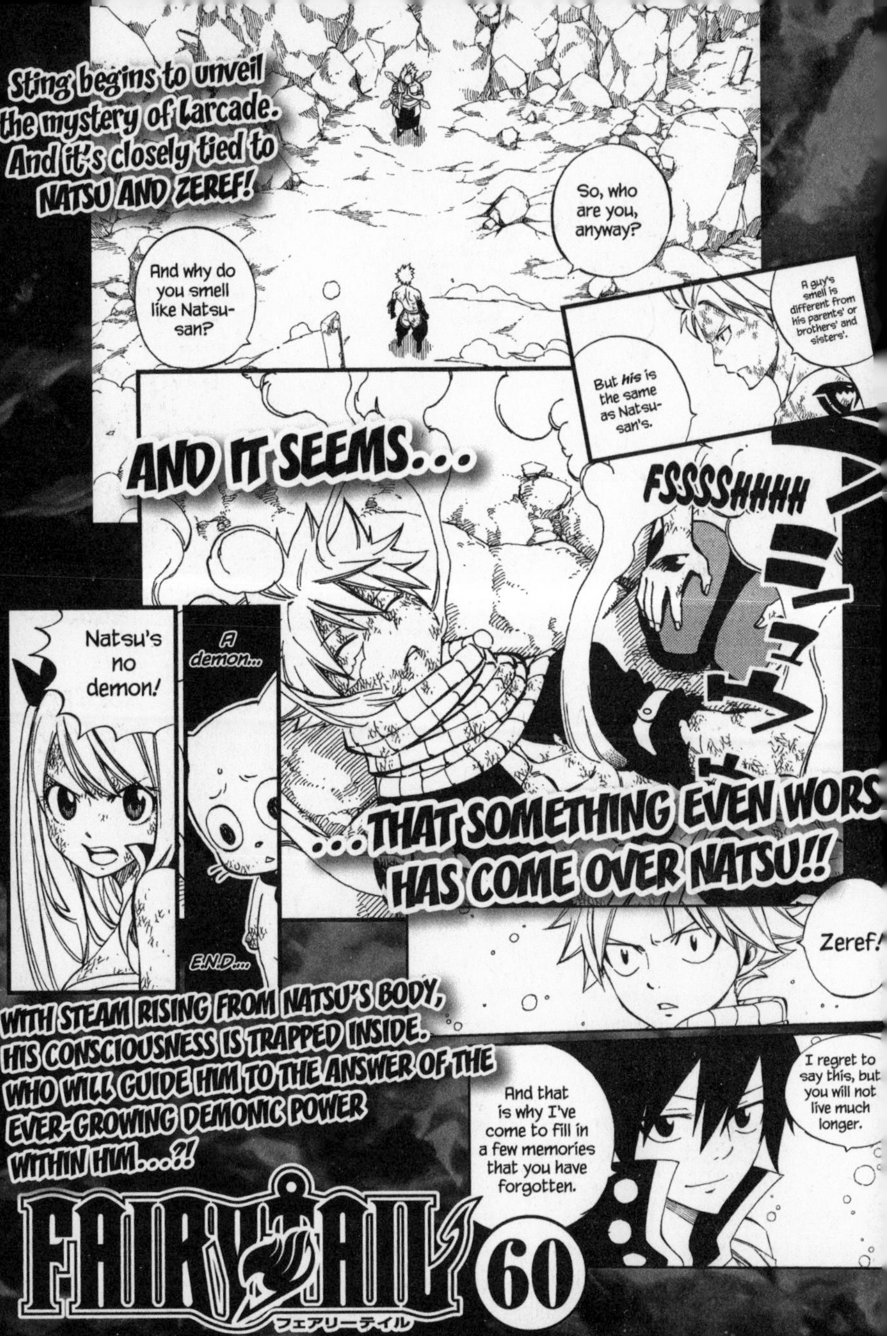

Sting begins to unveil the mystery of Larcade. And it's closely tied to NATSU AND ZEREF!
So, who are you, anyway?
And why do you smell like Natsu-san?
A guy's smell is different from his parents' or brothers' and sisters'.
But his is the same as Natsu-san's.
AND IT SEEMS...
FSSSSHHHH
...THAT SOMETHING EVEN WORS
HAS COME OVER NATSU!!
A demon...
E.N.D....
Natsu's no demon!
Zeref!
I regret to say this, but you will not live much longer.
And that is why I've come to fill in a few memories that you have forgotten.
WITH STEAM RISING FROM NATSU'S BODY, HIS CONSCIOUSNESS IS TRAPPED INSIDE. WHO WILL GUIDE HIM TO THE ANSWER OF THE EVER-GROWING DEMONIC POWER WITHIN HIM...?!
FAIRY TAIL
60
フェアリーテイル

ON SALE SOON!

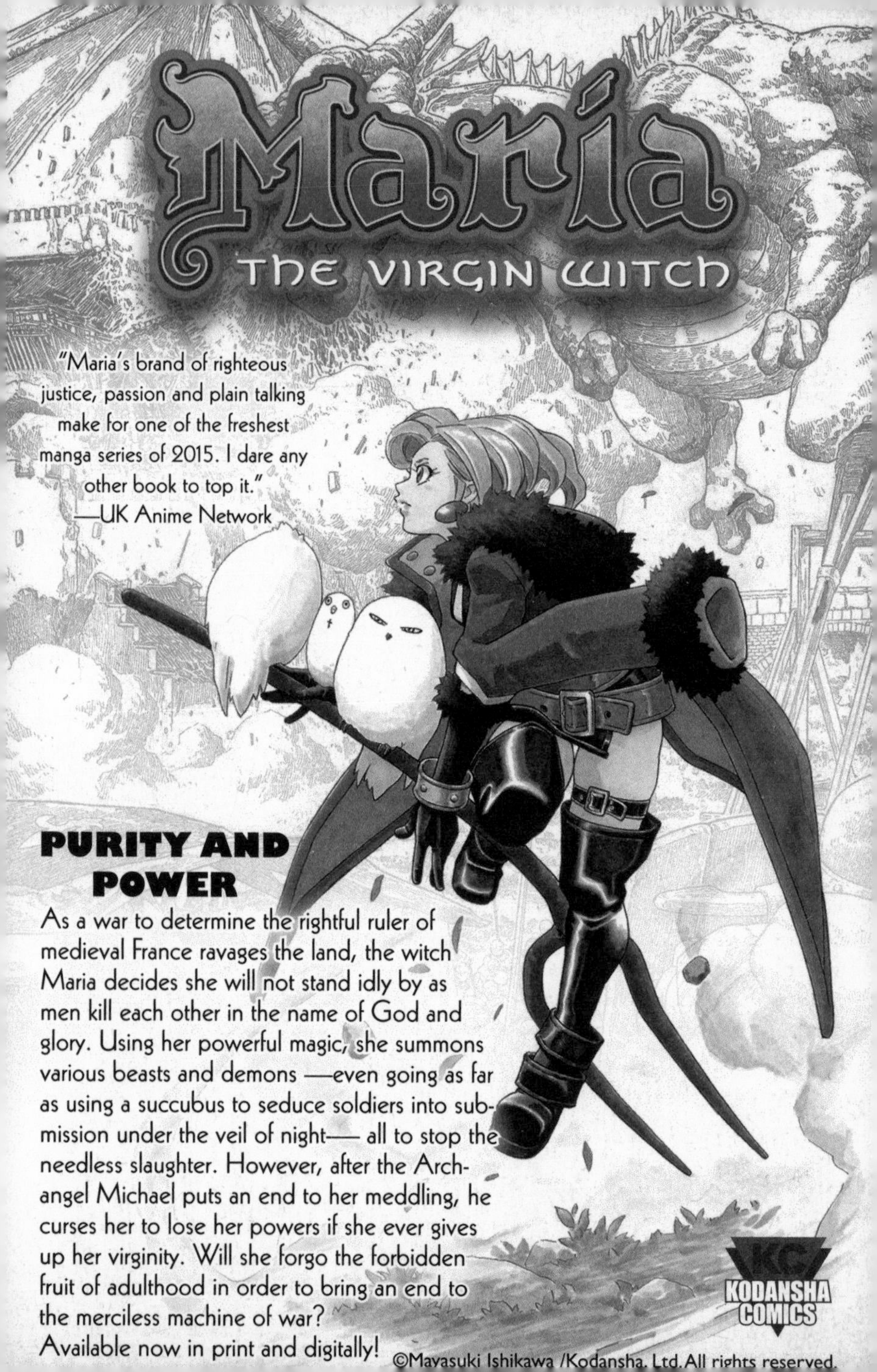
Maria
THE VIRGIN WITCH
"Maria's brand of righteous justice, passion and plain talking make for one of the freshest manga series of 2015. I dare any other book to top it."
—UK Anime Network
PURITY AND POWER
As a war to determine the rightful ruler of medieval France ravages the land, the witch Maria decides she will not stand idly by as men kill each other in the name of God and glory. Using her powerful magic, she summons various beasts and demons —even going as far as using a succubus to seduce soldiers into submission under the veil of night— all to stop the needless slaughter. However, after the Archangel Michael puts an end to her meddling, he curses her to lose her powers if she ever gives up her virginity. Will she forgo the forbidden fruit of adulthood in order to bring an end to the merciless machine of war?
Available now in print and digitally!
KC
KODANSHA COMICS
©Mayasuki Ishikawa /Kodansha. Ltd.All rights reserved.

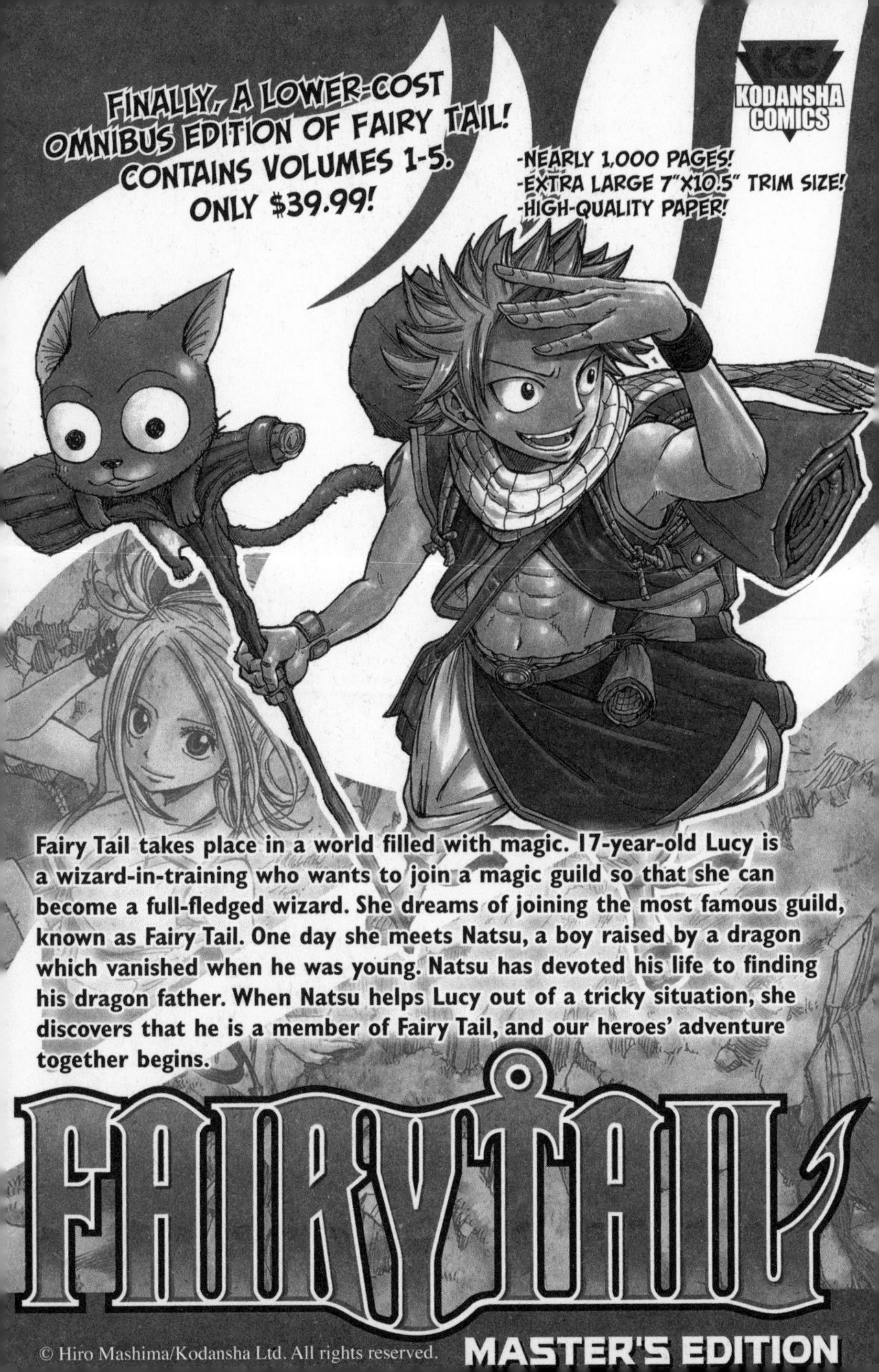
FINALLY, A LOWER-COST OMNIBUS EDITION OF FAIRY TAIL! CONTAINS VOLUMES 1-5. ONLY $39.99!
KODANSHA COMICS
-NEARLY 1,000 PAGES!
-EXTRA LARGE 7"X10.5" TRIM SIZE!
-HIGH-QUALITY PAPER!
Fairy Tail takes place in a world filled with magic. 17-year-old Lucy is a wizard-in-training who wants to join a magic guild so that she can become a full-fledged wizard. She dreams of joining the most famous guild, known as Fairy Tail. One day she meets Natsu, a boy raised by a dragon which vanished when he was young. Natsu has devoted his life to finding his dragon father. When Natsu helps Lucy out of a tricky situation, she discovers that he is a member of Fairy Tail, and our heroes' adventure together begins.
FAIRY TAIL
MASTER'S EDITION
© Hiro Mashima/Kodansha Ltd. All rights reserved.

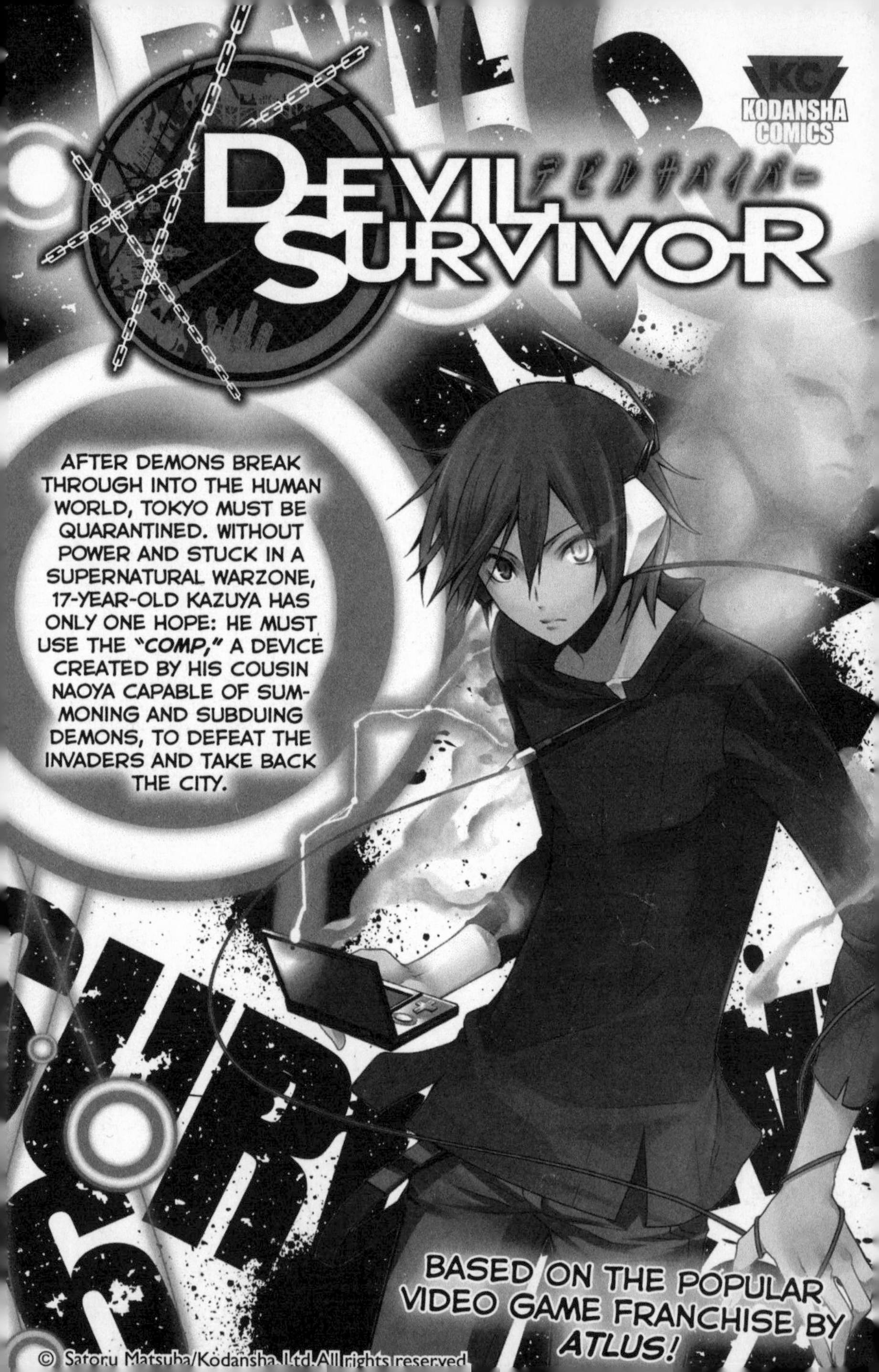
KC KODANSHA COMICS
DEVIL SURVIVOR
デビルサバイバー
AFTER DEMONS BREAK THROUGH INTO THE HUMAN WORLD, TOKYO MUST BE QUARANTINED. WITHOUT POWER AND STUCK IN A SUPERNATURAL WARZONE, 17-YEAR-OLD KAZUYA HAS ONLY ONE HOPE: HE MUST USE THE *"COMP,"* A DEVICE CREATED BY HIS COUSIN NAOYA CAPABLE OF SUMMONING AND SUBDUING DEMONS, TO DEFEAT THE INVADERS AND TAKE BACK THE CITY.
BASED ON THE POPULAR VIDEO GAME FRANCHISE BY *ATLUS!*
© Satoru Matsuba/Kodansha Ltd. All rights reserved.

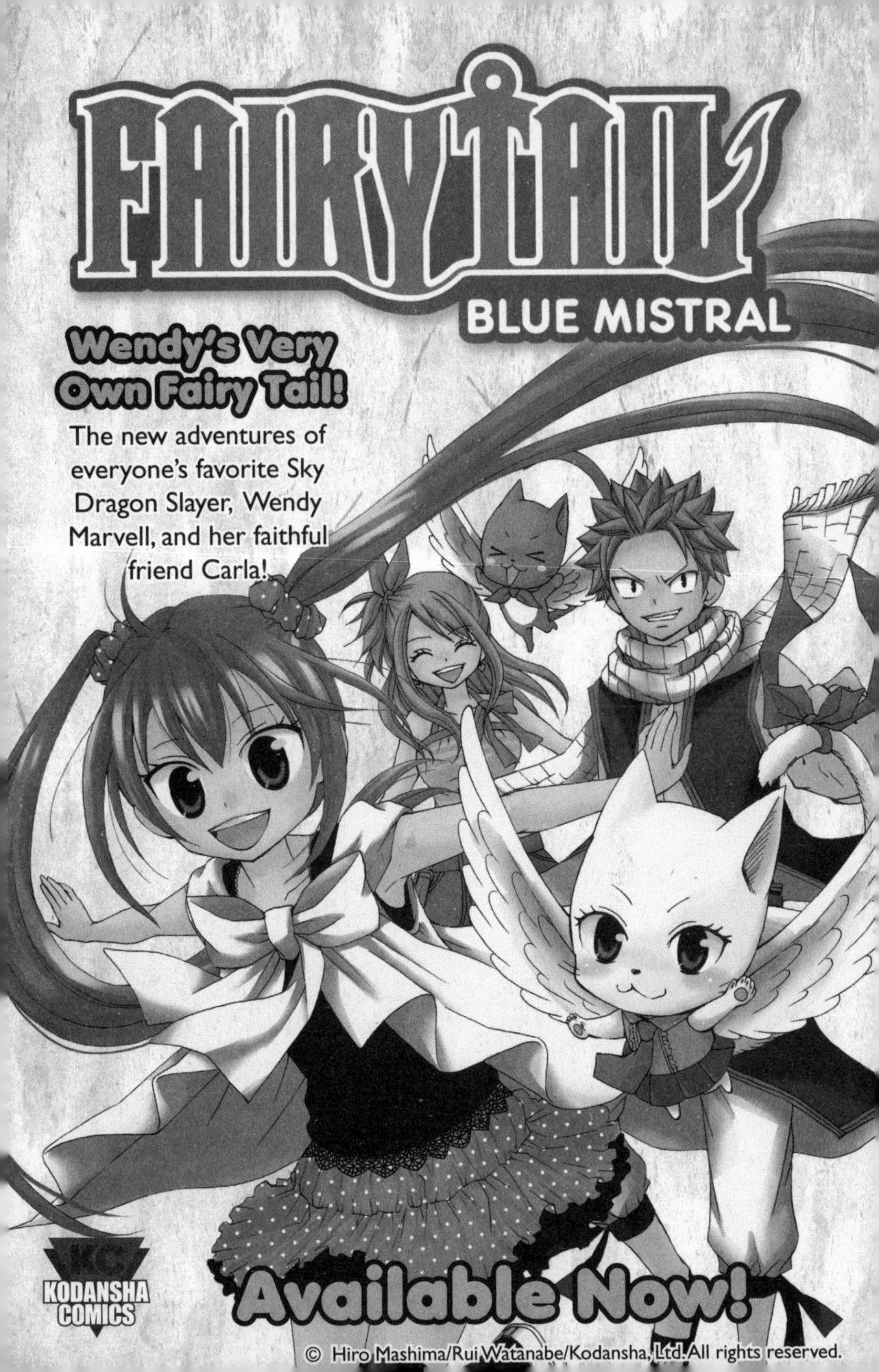
FAIRY TAIL
BLUE MISTRAL
Wendy's Very Own Fairy Tail!
The new adventures of everyone's favorite Sky Dragon Slayer, Wendy Marvell, and her faithful friend Carla!
KODANSHA COMICS
Available Now!
© Hiro Mashima/Rui Watanabe/Kodansha, Ltd. All rights reserved.

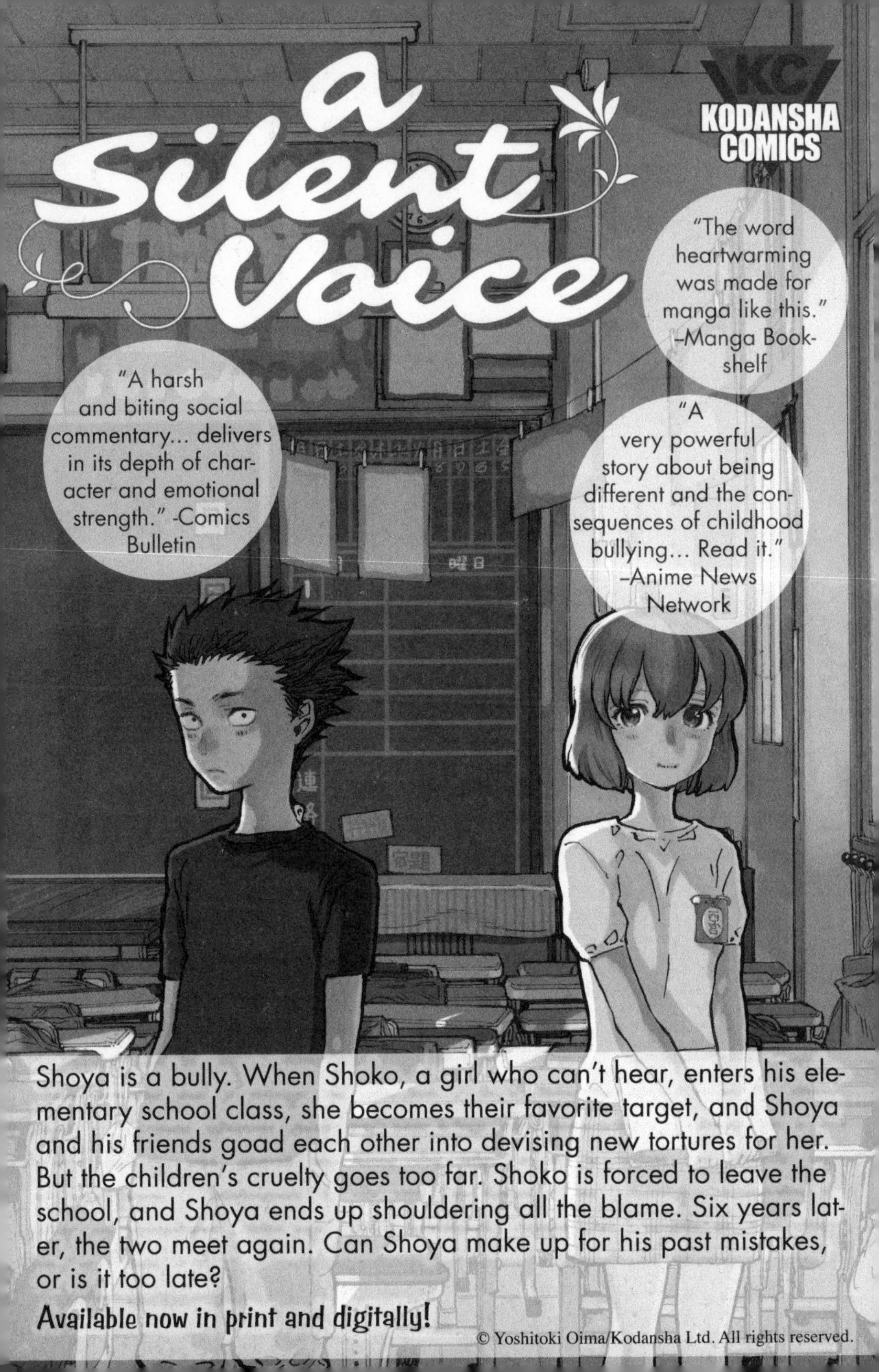
a Silent Voice
KODANSHA COMICS
"The word heartwarming was made for manga like this." –Manga Bookshelf
"A harsh and biting social commentary... delivers in its depth of character and emotional strength." -Comics Bulletin
"A very powerful story about being different and the consequences of childhood bullying... Read it." –Anime News Network
Shoya is a bully. When Shoko, a girl who can't hear, enters his elementary school class, she becomes their favorite target, and Shoya and his friends goad each other into devising new tortures for her. But the children's cruelty goes too far. Shoko is forced to leave the school, and Shoya ends up shouldering all the blame. Six years later, the two meet again. Can Shoya make up for his past mistakes, or is it too late?
Available now in print and digitally!
© Yoshitoki Oima/Kodansha Ltd. All rights reserved.

SHERLOCK BONES

KC
KODANSHA
COMICS

DEDUCTIVE DOG DETECTIVE

When Takeru adopts a new pet, he's in for a surprise—the dog is none other than the reincarnation of Sherlock Holmes. With no one else able to communicate with Holmes, Takeru is roped into becoming Sherdog's assistant, John Watson. Using his sleuthing skills, Holmes uncovers clues to solve the trickiest crimes. 🐾

Praise for the anime:

"The show provides a pleasant window on the highs and lows of young love with two young people who are first timers at the real thing."

-The Fandom Post

"Always it is smarter, more poetic, more touching, just plain better than you think it is going to be."

-Anime News Network

SAY I LOVE YOU.

Mei Tachibana has no friends — and says she doesn't need them!

But everything changes when she accidentally roundhouse kicks the most popular boy in school! However, Yamato Kurosawa isn't angry in the slightest— in fact, he thinks his ordinary life could use an unusual girl like Mei. But winning Mei's trust will be a tough task. How long will she refuse to say, "I love you"?

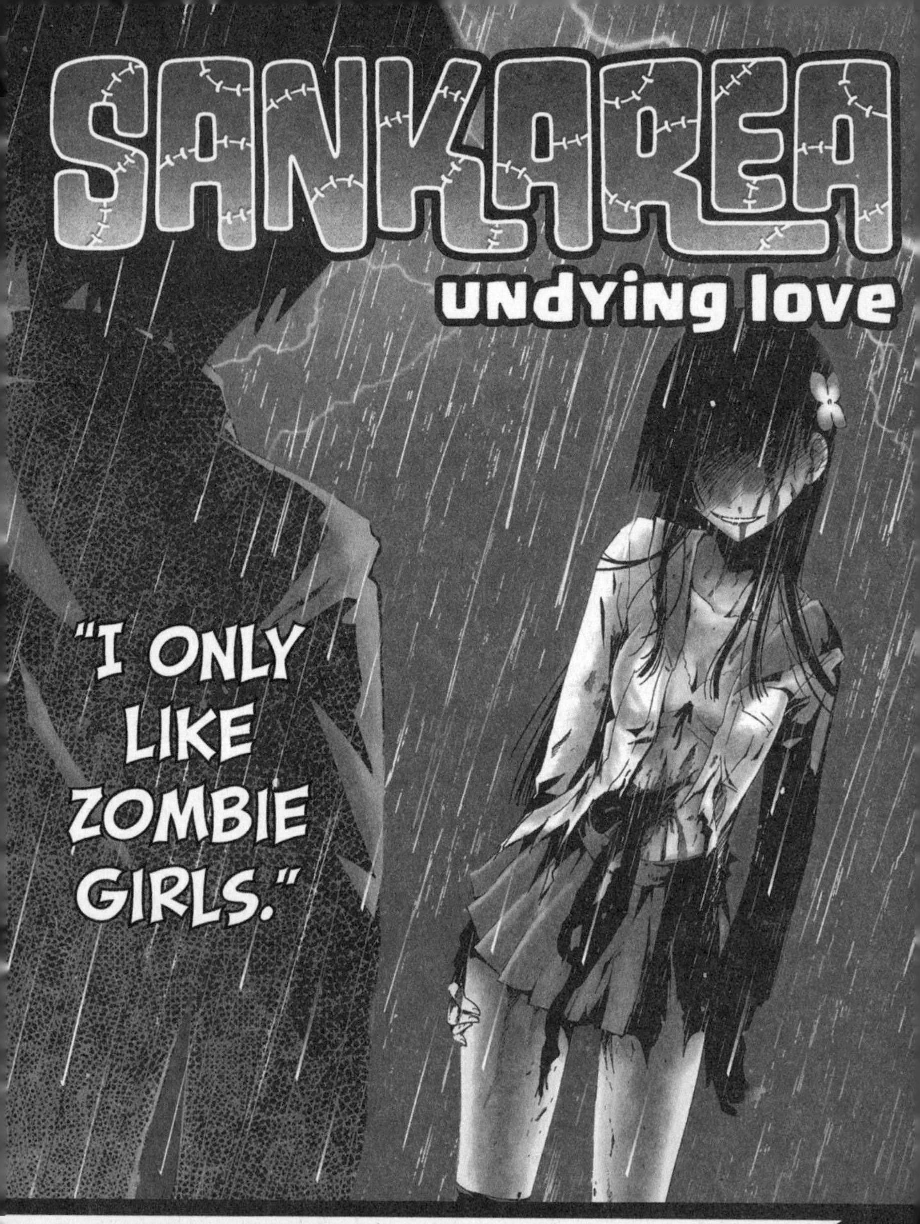

SANKAREA
undying love

"I ONLY LIKE ZOMBIE GIRLS."

Chihiro has an unusual connection to zombie movies. He doesn't feel bad for the survivors – he wants to comfort the undead girls they slaughter! When his pet passes away, he brews a resurrection potion. He's discovered by local heiress Sanka Rea, and she serves as his first test subject!

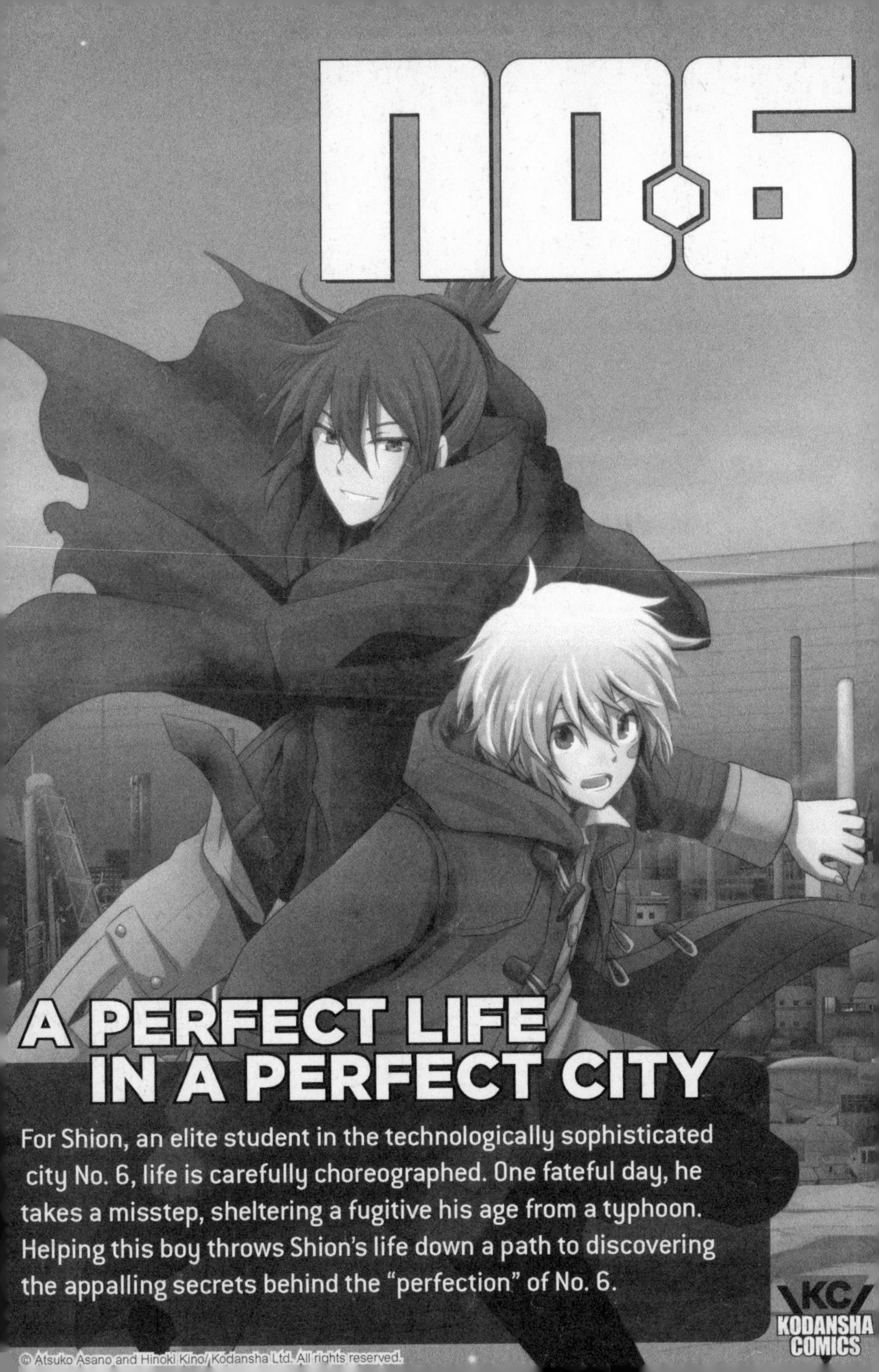
NO.6
A PERFECT LIFE
IN A PERFECT CITY
For Shion, an elite student in the technologically sophisticated city No. 6, life is carefully choreographed. One fateful day, he takes a misstep, sheltering a fugitive his age from a typhoon. Helping this boy throws Shion's life down a path to discovering the appalling secrets behind the "perfection" of No. 6.
KC
KODANSHA COMICS

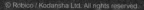

PRAISE FOR THE ANIME!

"This series never fails to put a smile on my face."
-Dramatic Reviews

"A very funny look at what happens when two strange and strangely well-suited people try to navigate the thorny path to true love together."
-Anime News Network

My Little Monster

OPPOSITES ATTRACT...MAYBE?

Haru Yoshida is feared as an unstable and violent "monster." Mizutani Shizuku is a grade-obsessed student with no friends. Fate brings these two together to form the most unlikely pair. Haru firmly believes he's in love with Mizutani and she firmly believes he's insane.

KC KODANSHA COMICS

A Kodansha Comics Trade Paperback Original.

Fairy Tail volume 59 copyright © 2016 Hiro Mashima
English translation copyright © 2017 Hiro Mashima

Published in the United States by Kodansha Comics, an imprint of Kodansha USA Publishing, LLC, New York.

Publication rights for this English edition arranged through Kodansha Ltd., Tokyo.

First published in Japan in 2016 by Kodansha Ltd., Tokyo
ISBN 978-1-63236-335-0

Printed in the United States of America.

www.kodanshacomics.com

9 8 7 6 5 4 3 2 1

Translation: William Flanagan
Lettering: AndWorld Design
Editing: Haruko Hashimoto
Kodansha Comics edition cover design by Phil Balsman

TOMARE!

[STOP!]

D0004139

You're going the wrong way!

Manga is a completely different type of reading experience.

To start at the beginning, go to the end!

That's right! Authentic manga is read the traditional Japanese way—from right to left, exactly the opposite of how American books are read. It's easy to follow: Just go to the other end of the book and read each page—and each panel—from right side to left side, starting at the top right. Now you're experiencing manga as it was meant to be!